D0215355

Popular Struggles
in South Africa

Popular Struggles in South Africa

EDITED BY

William Cobbett & Robin Cohen

Africa World Press, Inc.

P.O. Box 1892
Trenton, New Jersey 08607
(609) 695-3766

REVIEW OF
African
Political Economy

Regency House 75–77 St Mary's Road
Sheffield S2 4AN

in association with

James Currey Ltd
54b Thornhill Square, Islington, London N1 1BE

 Africa World Press, Inc.
P.O. Box 1892
Trenton, New Jersey 08607
(609) 695-3766

British Library Cataloguing in Publication Data
Popular Struggles in South Africa.
1. Anti-apartheid movements——South Africa
I. Cobbett, William II. Cohen, Robin
322.4'4   DT763
ISBN 0-85255-323-4
ISBN 0-85255-324-2 Pbk

Library of Congress Catalog Card Number: 88-71830

ISBN: 0-86543-112-4 Cloth
      0-86543-113-2 Paper

Typeset by Opus 43
Ganny House, Birker Moor, Eskdale, Cumbria CA19 1TJ
Printed in Great Britain by Villiers Publications London N6

This book is dedicated to
Phineas Sibiya · Simon Ngubane
Alphaeus Nkabinde · Florence Mnikathi
members of SAWCO
murdered in Mpophomeni
December 1986

Contents

Contributors

Debbie Bonnin is working on her Master's thesis in the Department of Sociology, University of Natal.

William Cobbett formerly tutored in sociology at the University of the Witwatersrand. While completing his doctorate on Botshabelo township, he is attached to the University of Warwick.

Robin Cohen is Professor of Sociology at the University of Warwick. His latest books are *Endgame in South Africa?* (1986) and *The New Helots: Migrants in the International Division of Labour* (1987).

Nkosinathi Gwala is the *nom de plume* of a lecturer at a black university in South Africa.

Jonathan Hyslop lectures in sociology at the University of the Witwatersrand. He studied at the Universities of the Witwatersrand, Oxford and Birmingham and is completing his doctorate on black education in South Africa.

Jeremy Keenan is Professor of Social Anthropology at the University of the Witwatersrand. He has previously conducted fieldwork in the Sahel and is currently undertaking research in the bantustans.

Rob Lambert, who lectures in sociology at the University of Natal, is also an editor of the *South African Labour Bulletin*. He is completing his doctorate on the South African Congress of Trade Unions.

Brian Nakedi was formerly a trade unionist with the South African Allied Workers' Union in Bloemfontein. Since completing a research project in Botshabelo township, he has joined the Centre for Policy Studies at the University of the Witwatersrand.

Eric Molobi is an executive member of the National Educational Crisis Committee.

John Saul, who works at the University of York, Toronto, is a well-known author on the political economy of Africa. He has written widely on Mozambique and Tanzania, while his latest book, with Stephen Gelb, is on *The Crisis in South Africa* (1987).

Jeremy Seekings has degrees from the Universities of Oxford and the Witwatersrand. He is currently at Nuffield College, Oxford, researching for a D. Phil. on the PWV townships in the 1980s.

Ari Sitas is Lecturer in Sociology at the University of Natal. He is a member of the editorial board of the *South African Labour Bulletin* and is a cultural activistwithin the labour movement.

Mark Swilling lectures in politics at the University of the Witwatersrand. He has published widely on the themes of state strategies, community politics and trade unions. He is currently studying community struggles in South Africa during the period 1979-86.

The Transvaal Rural Action Committee is a support organisation mobilising against forced removals in the Transvaal region.

Eddie Webster is Associate Professor of Sociology at the University of the Witwatersrand, and an editor of the *South African Labour Bulletin*. He has published extensively in the fields of labour history and industrial sociology. His latest book is *Cast in a Racial Mould* (1985).

Preface

In September 1986, the editors of the *Review of African Political Economy* convened their biennial conference in Liverpool on a current African theme. This time the theme was 'Popular Struggles in Africa' and although many parts of the continent were covered (the presentations being scheduled for separate publication in the *Review* and elsewhere) much attention was given to the South African contributions. The conference brought together academics, those involved in grassroots movements in South Africa and representatives of the movements for national liberation. The dialogue on the floor of the conference was sometimes tense, but most of the participants came away feeling they were privileged guests at a political and intellectual feast.

Our first thanks therefore go to the principal organiser of the conference, Pepe Roberts. She and our other fellow-editors at the *Review* commissioned us to act on their behalf but, as in all undertakings by the *Review*, the collective input in providing ideas and sustaining the spirit has been an important ingredient. Doris Burgess provided back-up; Gavin Williams and Barry Munslow offered useful advice; James Currey confirmed his standing as the publisher Africans and Africanists most like to work with.

As the rush of events gathered apace in South Africa, even excellent conference papers we thought central to our collection became dated. Revisions had to be sought and wholly new articles (some nine in all) had to be commissioned. Our contributors were asked to respond to almost impossibly short deadlines. They, like us, felt that the importance of popular struggles at the foot of the African continent demanded that many other obligations be put to one side. We would like to take this opportunity to thank them warmly for their efforts. Our sincere appreciation goes particularly to members of the Department of Sociology, University of the Witwatersrand, for their invaluable help.

W.C. & R.C.

Abbreviations
& Glossary

AALC	African American Labor Center (US)	CWIU	Chemical Workers' Industrial Union
AFL-CIO	American Federation of Labour — Council of Industrial Organisations	DET	Department of Education and Training (this title replaced the Bantu Education Department)
ANC	African National Congress	ERAB	East Rand Administration Board
ASRO	Atteridgeville-Saulsville Residents' Organisation	ERAPO	East Rand People's Organisation
		ERUCA	East Rand Urban Council Association
ASSA	Association for Sociology in Southern Africa	FAWU	Food and Allied Workers' Union
ATASA	African Teachers' Association of South Africa	FCWU	Food and Canning Workers' Union
AZACTU	Azanian Confederation of Trade Unions	FOSATU	Federation of South African Trade Unions
AZASM	Azanian Students' Movement	GWU	General Workers' Union
AZASO	Azanian Students' Organisation (now SANSCO)	GYO	Garankuwa Youth Organisation
		HSRC	Human Sciences Research Council
AZAPO	Azanian People's Organisation	IMF	International Monetary Fund
bakkie	open van	indaba	assembly
BC	black consciousness	induna	supervisor/headman
BED	Bantu Education Department	Inkatha	Zulu cultural/nationalist organisation
BTR	British Tyre and Rubber		
casspir	armoured vehicle	knobkierie/ kierie	hard wooden club
CAWU	Construction and Allied Workers' Union	kraal	protected enclosure/village
CCAWUSA	Commercial, Catering and Allied Workers' Union of South Africa	LIFO	last in, first out (trade union principle)
CDU	Christian Democrats (West Germany)	LMG	Labour Monitoring Group
		MACWUSA	Motor Assembly and Components Workers' Union of South Africa
CNETU	Council for Non-European Trade Unions	makgotlas	township courts
Congress Alliance	A loose association between the ANC, the Coloured People's Congress, the Indian Congress and the (white) Congress of Democrats	MAWU	Metal and Allied Workers' Union
		Mbokodo	armed vigilante group used by the regime in Kwandebele to suppress dissent (lit. millstone)
COSAS	Congress of South African Students	Medunsa	Medical and Dental University of South Africa
COSATU	Congress of South African Trade Unions	MP	Member of Parliament
		NAAWU	National Automobile and Allied Workers' Union
CP	Conservative Party		
CSU	Christian Social Union (West Germany)	NACTU	National Confederation of Trade Unions (CUSA/AZACTU merger)
CUSA	Council of Unions of South Africa		

NAFCOC   National African Federated
          Chamber of Commerce
NAMDA   National Medical and Dental
          Association
NECC   National Education Crisis
          Committee
NEUSA   National Education Union of
          South Africa
NFC   National Forum Convention
NIC   Natal Indian Congress
NP   National Party
NSMS   National Security Management
          System
NUM   National Union of Mineworkers
NUMSA   National Union of Metalworkers
          of South Africa
NUSAS   National Union of South African
          Students
NUTW   National Union of Textile Workers
OFS   Orange Free State
PAC   Pan Africanist Congress
panga   long knife/machette
PEBCO   Port Elizabeth Black Civic
          Association
PEYCO   Port Elizabeth Youth Congress
PTSA   Parent-Teacher-Students'
          Association
PWV region Pretoria-Witwatersrand-
          Vereeniging
R   Rand, the South African currency.
          Has fluctuated considerably in
          value (In September 1987,
          UK£1 $\frac{3}{8}$ R3.35)
RAWU   Retail and Allied Workers' Union
RDM   *Rand Daily Mail* (a now-defunct
          liberal newspaper)
RMC   Release Mandela Campaign
ROAPE   *Review of African Political
          Economy*
RSC   Regional Services Council
SAAWU   South African Allied Workers'
          Union
SACP   South African Communist Party
SACBC   South African Catholic Bishops
          Conference
SACTU   South African Congress of Trade
          Unions
SADF   South African Defence Force
SALB   *South African Labour Bulletin*
SANSCO   South African National Student
          Congress (formerly AZASO)
SAP   South African Police
SASM   South African Students'
          Movement
SASO   South African Students'
          Organisation
SASOL   Suid Afrikaanse Steenkool en Olie
          Maatskappy Beperk (South
          African Coal and Oil Company
          Limited)
SAWCO   Sarmcol Workers' Cooperative

SAYCO   South African Youth Congress
SAYO   Saulsville-Atteridgeville Youth
          Organisation
SFAWU   Sweet, Food and Allied Workers'
          Union
shebeen   private drinking place, normally
          illegal
sjambok(ed) rhino-hide whip (beaten with same)
SN   *Saspu-National* — newspaper of
          the South African Students' Press
          Union
SPCC   Soweto Parents' Crisis Committee
SRC   Students' Representative Council
SRR   *Survey of Race Relations*
          (published annually by the South
          African Institute of Race
          Relations)
SSC   State Security Council
SSRC   Soweto Students' Representative
          Council
TBVC   Transkei-Bophuthatswana-Venda
          -Ciskei (the four 'independent'
          homelands)
TGWU   Transport and General Workers'
          Union
TRAC   Transvaal Rural Action
          Committee
Tvl   Transvaal
UCASA   Urban Councils' Association of
          South Africa
UDF   United Democratic Front
UDW   University of Durban-Westville
umkhukhu shack (lit. chicken coop)
UMMAWSA   United Metal, Mining and Allied
          Workers' Union of
          South Africa
UNESCO   United Nations Educational
          Scientific and Cultural
          Organisation
UNIBO   University of Bophuthatswana
UNISA   University of South Africa
UNITRA   University of Transkei
UWC   University of the Western Cape
UWUSA   United Workers' Union of South
          Africa (Inkatha-linked union)
UYCO   Uitenhage Youth Congress
verligte 'enlightened', referring to less
          reactionary members of
          the National Party
VVPP   Vukani Vulahmelo People's Party
WECSAC   Western Cape Student Action
          Committee
WECTU   Western Cape Teachers' Union
wegkamp   transit (lit. wait) camp
WIP   *Work in Progress* (publication)
Wits   University of the Witwatersrand

INTRODUCTION
Popular Struggles or One Struggle: Dilemmas of Liberation

ROBIN COHEN AND WILLIAM COBBETT

INTRODUCTION

To the outside world, the course of change in South Africa has always presented a puzzle. One major source of misunderstanding is that commentators and politicians in metropolitan countries tend characteristically to work through an imagery that resonates with their own domestic experience or historic roles in the world.

Thus, for many in the UK, South Africa is an anomalous residue of the 'wind of change' that swept through the African continent, a process pointedly alluded to by Harold Macmillan in his speech to the Cape Town parliament in February 1960. In that year, the British empire in Africa was effectively dismantled. The French, Belgian and eventually the Portuguese continental empires were to follow. Even the settler countries like Kenya and Zimbabwe have now gained their independence, though twenty years later and after a gruelling guerrilla war in the case of Zimbabwe. But political freedom in South Africa for the black majority cannot be attained through a peaceful or violent process of decolonisation. There will be no green baize tables set out by the Foreign and Commonwealth Office in London. The tenuous hold on the subcontinent by the Dutch, the Batavians and later the British, the origins and patterns of white occupation, the political settlement after the Boer War, the importance of gold to the world economy — these factors and others dictate that South Africa cannot be considered as a colony, except in the most convoluted understanding of that term.

The new western metropolis, the US, is equally crippled by its recent history in coming to terms with what is seen as the stubbornness, even the insolence, of South Africa's rulers. For many in the US, South Africa's black majority can and should attain its rights through a civil rights campaign — Bishop Tutu simply needs to learn a few lessons from the late Martin Luther King. The difficulty with this perception is that it takes no account of crucial differences in the two situations. In the US, political rights were denied *illegally* to blacks, particularly Southern blacks. Once political mobilisation had occurred, the Constitution, a powerful liberal lobby and the force of arms of the Federal agencies could be evoked to start closing the gap between formal and actual rights. In South Africa, the limited rights granted to the black majority are enshrined and defined by national laws, a situation upheld by state force and historically hardly challenged by the occasional twinges of liberal conscience found amongst the white voters at election time.

1

The images of a decolonisation exercise or a civil rights campaign, though slowly shifting as the complexities of South African political change attain some recognition, are nonetheless powerful lenses which distort western perceptions of the pace, nature and fulcrums of change in the country. How then do we characterise the sources of change and induce some greater sense of verisimilitude to popular beliefs and western debates?

THE LIMITS TO EXTERNAL PRESSURES

Such a task must start with a brief assessment of the effectiveness and relevance of external measures. Pressure against the South African regime has become a moral crusade in western, Comecon and third world countries in a manner unparalleled since the rise of Fascism and German National Socialism in the 1930s. Danish housewives spurn Cape apples; West Indian fans berate their talented but poor countrymen for playing cricket in South Africa; in New Zealand helmeted policemen club down citizens protesting against the South Africans playing rugby against the national team (ironically called the 'All Blacks'); in Britain and the US a pop musician, Paul Simon, is reviled for recording music with black artists, despite helping to provide a world platform for black South African music. Cultural, academic and sports boycotts proliferate in response to pressures to 'do something' in demonstration of official condemnation of the policy of apartheid. Potentially more powerful external pressures include trade embargoes and policies for non-investment and divestment.

The connection between some of these measures and their intended results is not always clear. Clearly, they do provide a focus for campaigning and for building an anti-apartheid movement in a country far from the scene of action. They may also provide an element of uplift to black South Africans who can sense that many sections of world opinion consider their cause just and the South African authorities' actions illegitimate. But whereas rallies and campaigns are constructed in certainties, social scientists have also to deal in unintended consequences.

Witness, for example, the sale of local assets over the period 1985-7 by ninety US corporations operating in South Africa.[1] Were these sales motivated by a desire to do something effective against apartheid, or by other considerations such as the so-called 'hassle factor' — the amount of time taken in the boardroom to discuss the issue compared to the share of world-wide profits the South African company represented? It would not perhaps be unduly cynical to believe that the moral factor did not weigh heavily in corporate calculations. Behind the company declarations the results on the ground are there for all but the blind to see. A fledgling South African capitalist class, facing economic uncertainties brought on by a political crisis, was given a welcome boost. Valuable assets, licensing and franchise arrangements were sold off cheaply while nearly all the companies concerned minimised their losses by guaranteeing continuing supplies to their now locally-owned subsidiaries. The phenomenon is redolent of the post-Sharpeville period in the early 1960s, when international capital fled the perceived impending catastrophe and domestic capital rapidly bought up many of the assets at bargain prices, emerging greatly strengthened from the period of crisis.

Take as a specific instance the case of Barclays Bank — a major international clearing bank heavily involved in South Africa. After many years, a British-based campaign, including a student boycott and account withdrawals by a number of local authorities, propelled the bank to sell its assets in South Africa in 1986. The buyer? None other than Anglo American, the powerful South African multinational, which now added to its prime share of the gold mines and its vast property and industrial holdings, the second largest bank in South Africa. In mid-1987, Anglo added Citycorp's interests to its banking portfolio. Some sixty-three percent of all shares quoted on the Johannesburg stock exchange are currently owned by Anglo. Is the consolidation of the power of this vast conglomerate in the ultimate interests of black liberation? Though Anglo American has always propounded a more progressive position than the government, it is at least a moot point as to whether a black majority government of the future will be in any position to tame such an awesome multinational economic giant.

Finally, it must be a somewhat doubtful proposition that the cause of freedom in South Africa is well served by discouraging actors, musicians, dramatists, academics, trade unionists or writers with politically progressive ideas from visiting the country or allowing their works to be published or performed there. Such individuals could both demonstrate their solidarity with the forces working for change on the ground and press the repressive tolerance of the South African regime to its upper limit, a tactic with potentially useful ideological pay-offs to the liberation movement.[2]

We should make clear immediately that we do not believe that *all* contacts are necessarily a good thing. The political challenge is to devise methods of ensuring that such visits and contacts that do occur are of tangible value to the progressive forces within South Africa. Such a challenge presents a more difficult option than simply calling for a blanket boycott of all things South African or vetoing any idea of contact. Totalising and negative strategies such as those described above ('what we can agree we are against') have several effects, which do not always seem to be consonant with the declared aims of those who advocate them. Five such effects can be noticed.

1) Self-righteous postures are struck over minor issues, with the (often conscious) effect of deflecting attention from more important measures. For example, the German, French and British governments are able to make various disapproving but ineffectual anti-apartheid gestures in deference to European and Commonwealth opinion, thereby helping to conceal a substantive continuation of ordinary trade, including a flourishing arms trade.

2) Certain multinational companies can take the pressure off themselves in their home bases, while continuing covertly to do business as usual in respect of supplies, licensing, franchising and exports. Local capital, or capital from other, pariah, countries (Israel, Taiwan), often with worse labour records and practices, are given the opportunity to take over local production facilities.[3]

3) The black majority in South Africa become 'disabled', the inbuilt assumption of foreign boycotts, etc. being that the local forces are unable to free themselves without help from outside. As will be seen in the contributions to this book, this assumption may be wholly wrong.

4) The possibilities and limitations of the current level of struggle are misjudged. This leads to the rapid 'mood swings' amongst external observers and supporters of the movements for liberation. One moment a naive sense

of exhilaration predominates: the bottle-throwers in Soweto today will be storming the gates of the Government Buildings in Pretoria tomorrow.[4] The next moment, a sense of utter despair overwhelms: 'the Revolution' (often wrongly imagined as a single event) will have to be postponed indefinitely.

5) The totalising strategy also creates an artificial unity in the way the forces of opposition to apartheid are depicted. Struggles at different levels, at different sites and with different scope and political motivation coexist and overlap. It suits the external opponents of apartheid to elide these differences. They are thereby better able to claim the sole privilege for defining the tactics and strategy of a supposedly single path to liberation.

Let us probe the implications of this last effect. While few would wish to challenge the major historic role of the ANC or question the regard in which it is held by black South Africans, numerous contemporary struggles inside the country cannot be reduced to a simple extension of ANC aims. Independent, or 'relatively autonomous' actors have articulated local priorities under the impact of local pressures. Their perceptions demand, at the very least, a sympathetic hearing by those from outside the country.

Again, it is important not to be misunderstood. A vigorous and comprehensive sanctions campaign must play a vital role in liberating South Africa. We are not advocating an undisciplined free-for-all for all foreign well-wishers to relate to the struggles in South Africa in any way they choose. Rather we are suggesting that the complex dynamics of the struggles in South Africa and the unexpectedly negative or ambiguous results of some external acts in support of the black majority require that we conceive of the interplay between internal forces and external levers in a more guarded and prob-lematised manner than hitherto.

It is the analysis of the internal dynamic of the struggle against the apartheid state that provides the main thrust of this book. Through more than a decade of intensifying struggle, of failures and victories, of innovation and mistakes, bloody violence and gratifying displays of humanity, hundreds of organisations committed to the destruction of apartheid and to building an alternative South Africa have emerged.

These organisations have had to learn rapidly from their mistakes. They have had to identify new tactical spaces and devise new strategies — sometimes to advance the common struggle, at other times merely to survive. In so doing, these organisations have adopted relevant examples and theories from all over the world. Where none existed they have displayed a remarkable degree of innovation in adapting themselves to the particular demands of the moment. It is these realities which demand recognition, and the sacrifices of those inside the country which entitle them to have a primary say in what support is necessary and how it best can be applied.

NEITHER BLACK NOR WHITE:
SHIFTING ALLIANCES AND COALITIONS

To many anti-apartheid campaigners overseas, mobilising against the apartheid state has been a relatively straightforward matter both because the situation inside South Africa was so demonstrably immoral, violent and unjust and also because the issue could be seen, literally and figuratively, in black and white terms. Sloganeering was supplemented by a simple political analysis, which ran something like this: *the situation in South Africa can be accurately characterised as a unified white minority subjugating and denying to an undifferentiated black majority any meaningful rights by means of a combination of overtly racist legislation, a powerful administrative machine and the use of military force.*

Such a limited analysis may have sufficed until 1973, but after that date significant challenges from below began to shake the structures of white hegemony. The strikes of that year, the 1976-7 uprising and, finally, the more recent phase of dramatically intensified struggle all occasioned significant shifts of political alignment. In particular, it became no longer possible to assume that race was the sole determining feature of ideology and political stance. As struggles have intensified, new organisations and new alliances have emerged which defy analysis along the old and predictable faultlines of race.

When the community organisations, often spearheaded by youth displaying what Lambert and Webster call 'militaristic voluntarism', began to challenge the ability of local government structures to administer the townships, the state played a crucial role in introducing a chilling new variable into township politics — the right-wing vigilante forces. The activities of one of these groups, *Mbokodo*, are graphically described in the article by TRAC on Kwandebele. *Mbokodo* was just one of many such vigilante groups to emerge — Thabong had its *A-Team* (imitating a US television programme), Crossroads spawned the *Witdoeke* (openly supported by the police), Leandra was terrorised by the *Inkatha*.[5] Other vigilante groups included the *Pakhatis*, the *Mabangalala*, the *Amadoda*, the *Amabutho* and the *Green Berets*.[6] Though it would be comforting to believe that these groups were simply bribed thugs of the government, there is every indication that they had at least some organic roots in the communities. In addition to these informal allies of reaction, by 1984 there were 21,009 black policemen in a total force of 45,660.[7] It is also worth remembering that the leadership of the largest of the independent black churches, the Zionist Christian Church, with a following of anything between 2.5 and 4 million, has a political position explicitly in support of white minority rule.[8]

Allies in the central repressive state apparatus are supplemented by the satraps in charge of the ten 'homelands', whose regimes are subsidised to the tune of about R2.5 billion a year. Such a sum buys a considerable degree of loyalty. Not that the ruling classes in the bantustans seem too inhibited from assaulting, detaining, torturing or banishing political opponents on their own account.[9] When the repression reaches embarrassing levels, Pretoria can hide behind the convenient legal fiction that these are 'independent' states.

Within the towns and cities of South Africa, the United Democratic Front (UDF) and the Congress of South African Trade Unions (COSATU) have become particular targets for right-wing violence. Buthelezi's Natal-based Inkatha movement, which is often thought to be a moderate organisation by many white South Africans and by the Reagan administration, is also implicated in violent acts. Gwala's contribution to the book points to Buthelezi's own inflammatory statements and the activities of the Inkatha Youth Brigade on a black campus, while Lambert and Webster refer to the murder of two union activists, an act widely believed to be the work of Inkatha. The possibility of state connivance is indicated by the electricity supply to the township mysteriously failing as the death squads set about their grisly work.

'Black-on-black' violence is often welcomed by the state as a useful distraction, and portrayed either as genetically programmed or the inevitable outcome of endemic tribal enmities. Such violence can also be used as 'evidence' to demonstrate the continued virtues of white 'civilisation'. While such a depiction of black violence would be rejected by liberals within and outside South Africa, the positive stereotype of blacks held by such groups often proclaims a mirror image, showing them as all-suffering, saintly and virtuous. Both stereotypes fallaciously turn the black population into a homogeneous mass with a clear set of behavioural characteristics, thereby failing to analyse the various forms of internal stratification and divisions of interest.

If the racial analysis of South Africa fails to demonstrate the salience of conservative and right-wing black opinion, it equally misrepresents white politics as monolithic. In recent years, this picture has been more fully drawn, but most of the attention has been focused on the ultra-right and neo-Fascist groups, which have occupied the obsessive attention of both media and political pundits. The recent whites-only election in South Africa did indeed confirm some gains for the ultra-right at the expense of the parliamentary liberals, but much more saliently it reaffirmed the hegemony of the National Party within the limited arena of white parliamentary politics.[10]

How limited this arena has become was demonstrated by the post-election attempt by fifty representatives of liberal and progressive white opinion to start a dialogue with the exiled ANC at a meeting in Senegal in July 1987. For their pains, those who talked to the ANC were dubbed traitors and greeted by right-wing demonstrations on their return. Other sections of the extra-parliamentary white left in South Africa, whose existence is much less visible internationally, may, however, act as more significant *trägers* of a non-racial politics. Of course there has always been a small group of whites involved in radical or left politics, but the current oppositional movements, particularly amongst students, have some distinctive attributes that require contextualisation.

The positions of the left student movement derive principally from the struggles on the campuses in the 1970s when black students, under the influence of Black Consciousness (BC), split away from the white liberal-dominated National Union of South African Students (NUSAS) to form their own South African Students' Organisation (SASO). The split provided an equal challenge to both groups — for SASO the task being to overcome a black inferiority complex and to assert the right to determine black priorities in the goal for liberation, whereas the white students were required to rid themselves of their paternalism, to examine the contradictions in their own position and to discover a new political role. The most tangible results of this shake-up in student attitudes were increased activity on the black campuses (see Gwala) and, within the white camp, the creation of the NUSAS Wages Commission in 1973.

The nascent trade unions also became a natural arena for white intellectuals to play a facilitating, informing and, to some extent, an organising role. Another ideological current feeding into the campus left was the return of academics from a Europe shaken by the events of 1968 and after. This led to a sometimes slavish adherence to the latest western European debates, including those of a structuralist marxist variety, but within a decade a more critical and a more indigenous marxism began to develop.

The emergence of the UDF in August 1983 with its commitment to non-racial politics, provided another avenue into which white anti-apartheid activists were able to move. Through the UDF and the trade unions the white left has transcended the limitations of campus politics. An even more powerful stimulus to the growth of anti-apartheid forces was the invasion of the townships by the South African Defence Force (SADF) in the Spring of 1984. White males, all subject to military conscription, were now faced not with some vaguely-defined 'communist threat' on the borders of South Africa, but were placed in the situation of having to defend the state against school children armed only with stones in a nearby township. The effect of the township invasion was twofold. It spurred the growth of community organisations, civic associations, street committees and the super-militant 'comrades' in the townships, while within the leafy suburbs of white South Africa, a quieter, but nonetheless profound crisis of conscience began to emerge.

This led to the formation of the End Conscription Campaign (ECC), a movement roughly analogous to the anti-war movement in the US during the Vietnam war. In both cases, the question of the political legitimacy of the hegemonic state was called into question by people who had been relied upon to support it. Consequently, the state took the formation of the ECC in very bad part, attempted to demonstrate that it was led by tools of 'international communism' and enforced a censorship of any political debate about the desirability of national service. ECC members have been detained, attacked and had their houses petrol-bombed, precisely because they dared to organise within the sensitive area of the so-called 'defence' of the state.

The dominant theme in this book centres around the issue of black liberation. Implicit in this liberation, however, is white liberation. Even defenders of the *status quo* are constrained to refer to restrictions on their freedom — talking of 'necessary sacrifices in the defence of Western civilisation'(by which they mean white rule). But few whites are actively concerned at the paucity of their own freedoms. Where they differ from the majority is that they have been happy to trade real freedom for material well-being, bought at the expense of black advancement and often black lives. It is one of the current ironies that blacks are also struggling to emancipate white South Africa. This has been recognised only by small sections of the white community, who have aligned themselves with the forces for liberation. For the rest, they are enslaved by fear, ignorance and avarice. So deeply have these irrationalities penetrated, that it is likely that the minds of most white South Africans will be the last product of apartheid to be liberated.

UNCOVERING PEOPLE'S STRUGGLES

Having shown how the fissures dividing South African political life have opened out across race lines, the major justification for this book can now be identified more explicitly. This is not a grand interpretation of events by an earnest foreign correspondent, or a crude political tract on behalf of any of the main protagonists in the conflict. The cavortings and posturings of white electoral politics are equally eschewed, for underneath that level of reality is another — the construction of a set of peoples' initiatives, at the level of their workplace, their places of residence, in the 'homelands' and other rural areas and in the places where black South Africans are consigned to a second-class education.

The book contains a wide ranging and up-to-date *tableau* of such initiatives and experiences. We wanted our authors to achieve the sense of relevance and urgency characteristic of a journalist, then combine this with a measure of detachment and evaluation characteristic of an academic. The stance we sought, in short, was one of 'critical engagement'. This is a recalcitrant rabbit to pull out of most academics' hats, and we shall have to leave it to the final judgement of reviewers and readers as to how well our contributors have succeeded. For our part, as editors, we were delighted at the gusto and enthusiasm shown by contributors. Nearly all are close to the sites of encounter and resistance they are describing; consequently their work reflects both a close attention to detail and a recognition of the place 'their' struggle finds in a wider picture. We will comment on the question of the link between different struggles below.

Labour Struggles

The book begins with two chapters on the place of labour struggles. It is, of course, an orthodoxy of marxist discourse to find in the working class the seedbed of revolution and the harbinger of the new order. However, as Burawoy[11] points out, even in Marx there is a paradox in this description, as the factory is at one and the same time the place where class organisation, consciousness and action are immanent, but also the site where capital disorganises, dehumanises and degrades the proletariat.

The opening chapter, by Lambert and Webster, surveys the national labour scene in the wake of the most significant attempt to federate the industrial, ideological and regional sections of the emergent labour movement, namely the formation of the Congress of South African Trade Unions (COSATU). Their thesis is that a form of 'political' or 'social movement' unionism has re-emerged in South Africa. They use the word 're-emerged' because an earlier federation, the South African Congress of Trade Unions (SACTU), formed in 1955, had complemented its relative industrial weakness by a close political alliance with the Congress movement. The authors maintain that this link with the national struggle was not incompatible with factory organisation — and indeed may have facilitated it. Whatever the final judgement on this issue, there is no dispute that SACTU was subsequently seriously enfeebled by state repression, and by the 1960s, with the economy booming, effective labour organisation languished.

One decade on, beginning in the 1970s, the long industrial peace was shattered and employers had to become attuned to the frequent occurrence of, often wildcat, strike action. The year 1987 commenced with shop workers, members of the Commercial, Catering and Allied Workers Union (CCAWUSA) at a major departmental store, the OK Bazaars, coming out for higher wages. By May and June 1987, a major transport strike took place. The South African Railways and Harbours Workers' Union (SARHWU) claimed there were 22,000 strikers out for six weeks. The strike was accompanied by a good deal of sabotage, the authorities avowing that 50 railway coaches had been burnt out.[12] These successful strikes were, however, wholly overshadowed by a strike called by the National Union of Mineworkers (NUM) in August for a 30 per cent increase in wages. Even accepting the figure of 250,000 strikers issued by the Chamber of Mines (the independent Labour Monitoring Group supports the NUM's estimate that 330,000 men obeyed the strike call), this is the most extensive strike in South African history.

The current strike wave was ushered in by industrial workers in Natal in 1972-3, and has continued with some interruptions ever since. The strikes reflect the increased bargaining and organisational strength of the black working class. Starting with virtually a zero base, some 20 per cent of the black work force is now unionised. The trade unions that emerged in the late seventies, and particularly the industrial unions, placed much emphasis on strong shop floor structures, accountability and workers' control. Confident of their own base, they have lately moved their strength beyond the workplace. One distinguishing feature of the labour movement is a strong propensity to relate its growing industrial strength to the township battles and the wider struggle for black emancipation. The trade unions cannot easily insulate themselves from these wider issues. In the first place, the issues afflicting township residents (unemployment, rents, transport costs, schooling) equally affect workers. Secondly, the harshest aspects of the apartheid regime (influx control, residential segregation) are directed at segmenting the labour market and preventing the emergence of the conditions permitting free collective bargaining. As Lambert and Webster show, the attempt by the unions to construct a strategy compatible with these various pressures has hinged around the notions of 'workerism' or 'populism'. As we will want ourselves to comment on the artificiality of this distinction later, we simply here draw the attention of the readers to Lambert and Webster's useful discussion of these supposed ideological alternatives.

In South Africa, the question of working class organisation historically has also been overlaid by the racial division of the work force. As a result of the settlement of the 1922 Rand Revolt when white miners, with some black support, turned in fury on their employers, the state concluded a deal to grant the white workers a relatively privileged and secure status.[13] Since that time, and despite many good intentions and the formation of multi-racial union federations, it has always been impossible permanently to link the interests of black workers with those of whites sharing a similar relationship to the means of production. Many black workers were migrants (particularly on the mines) or seasonal or squatter labourers (on the farms). In addition, legal restrictions and the bureaucratic segmentation of the labour force compounded and extended divisions by skill, gender, region or ethnic origin.

Faced with such an unpropitious context it is remarkable that workers have organised at all, let alone with such evident success. The work sites and the townships have become crucibles in which a common identity and spirit has emerged, despite constant official attempts to disaggregate and decompose the working class. To see how this process occurs and to complement Lambert and Webster's national picture, we have included Bonnin and Sitas's fascinating ethnography of organisation of a work force at one factory. Their site for investigation is Sarmcol, a subsidiary of the multinational, British

Tyre and Rubber. Our authors open their account with the assassination of four young organisers, to whom this volume is dedicated. An emotional funeral was tightly policed by the state, the company dug its heels in over a recognition agreement and the union, the Metal and Allied Workers Union (MAWU), was forced into constructing a wider movement drawing in women, youth and unemployed people from the surrounding township. This drift towards the community as a lifeline again illustrates the inevitable inter-twining of political and social issues. To give form to this unity of purpose, workers and residents created a cooperative that has become a model for the form of 'social movement unionism', tied into local community grievances as well as national political issues, now observable in South Africa. The Bonnin-Sitas contribution is also notable in that the authors have had extensive discussions with the members of the cooperative about the content of the chapter and the resultant feedback has been incorporated into the argument.

Urban Struggles

The next pair of chapters furthers a discussion of community struggles in the urban areas of South Africa. While Marx focused on struggles at the point of production, recent theorists (notably Castells; Lebas and Harloe[14]), have pointed to the salience of urban social movements as sites for political struggle. In South Africa, the place of residence has always been a locus of resistance against the state. This has very basic origins. As is well known, the black majority has been confined to thirteen percent of the country's land area, and much of that is barren. The implementation of the Group Areas Act (defining racially-exclusive residential, and to a degree business, areas) has involved the displacement of millions of people off productive land or rented and freehold urban property. Artificial 'homeland' states have been constructed for these expelled persons, often involving the loss of South African citizenship, residential and working rights. Finally, vast dormitory towns (like the South Western Townships of Johannesburg, Soweto, with its endless lines of standardised housing or the newer sprawl, Botshabelo, outside Bloemfontein, with its vast collection of rude shanties), have been constructed for the urban labour force.

Given the nature of governmental intervention, community-based struggles have taken a number of forms: (a) an attempt to construct viable areas of residence and recreation, to turn the heartless blocks of public housing or hastily-erected shanties into a decent environment; (b) an attempt to secure a space free from arbitrary searches and pass-law arrests; (c) an attempt to stop the consignment of long-standing urban residents to rural states, largely fabricated as 'imagined communities' by government bureaucrats and ideologues; and (d) an often unrecorded struggle by rural people to prevent their land from being seized and to protest at being cavalierly assigned to a phoney 'independent' bantustan.

Seekings's study of the politics of the Pretoria-Witwatersrand-Vereeniging (PWV) townships illustrates some of the dynamics of the specifically urban con-flicts. The only way the government could secure any degree of public acceptance for the councils they put in place as organs of limited urban self-government was to accord these bodies a massive increase in resources. Instead, the councillors found themselves asked to implement large rent rises in a situation where transport costs were subject to rapid inflation, schools were being shut by protest actions, unemployment was rising and services deteriorating. The exercise of arbitrary power by the councillors only inflamed township residents who could also observe the emptiness of these cardboard Napoleons' claims to authority when the troops, sent in by the government, swept them aside to contain periodic displays of disorder.

The confluence of many of the streams of encounter and resistance by numerous rural and urban communities came together in the UDF which Swilling describes as 'a national political and ideological centre'. Approximately 600 organisations were affiliated to the UDF, predominantly youth organisations, civic associations, women's groups, student unions, and religious and political bodies. Trade unions have not joined in great numbers, but there have been a number of national protests in which the principal unions and union federations have worked closely with the UDF. Swilling's chapter is a well-informed account of the nature, origins, regional and sectoral strengths and political thrust of what is now the most important internal anti-apartheid organisation. Neither pressure group nor political party (for such bodies need a representative legislative chamber to survive), the UDF has evolved a unique structure to fuse popular demands, the lessons of the black consciousness period and the 'Charterist' tradition of the Congress movement. This yeast has catalysed a potent brew: a powerful and popular body, operating mainly though not exclusively in the cities, and one which will not easily be flattened even in the wake of the *carte blanche* given to the National Party in the 1987 white election.

Rural Struggles

Our next group of chapters, centring on rural struggles, stand as an important corrective to the common assumption (fed by the proximity of the international media) that opposition to apartheid is overwhelmingly an urban phenomenon. Cobbett and Nakedi examine the 'hidden' struggle of a group of Sotho from Herschel who formed part of a district suddenly switched to the Transkei in 1975 in a cynical swap for another parcel of land. Four years later, the Chief Minister of QwaQwa, Mopeli, offered to buy Herschel from the Transkei. The voices of the victims of these deals are presented largely in their own words in this chapter. Though they were at first prepared to negotiate with Mopeli, and even adroitly attempt to use the governmental doctrine of separate development to their advantage, the Herschelites eventually denounced him as a 'liar' who would be unable to deliver either security or land. The level of their demands escalated as their political consciousness increased, to the point where, as the authors state, their politics 'echo[ed] the language of the township' and their wish for justice for their own ethnic group gained expression in a wider demand for a democratic and united South Africa. In short, they came to realise that even their limited demands could not be met under apartheid, but required a fundamental restructuring of the entire social formation.

The chapter by the Transvaal Rural Action Committee (TRAC) shows how powerfully rural people will react to the manipulation by apartheid bureaucrats and the installation of a state-sponsored leadership. From 12 May 1986, a three-month 'war' against the independence of Kwandebele commenced. Chief Minister Skosana's pro-independence group was supported by a violent right-wing force, the *Mbokodo*, whose methods alienated large sections of the Ndebele people. TRAC vividly describes how the royal family, the young comrades, the civil service and the white farmers linked forces in a popular alliance to oppose, so far successfully, Pretoria's customary offer of 'independence'. Of course, the groups in opposition to this status had different interests. For many of the youths, the programme of a united South Africa under the leadership of the liberation movement was the goal; for the white farmers, their continued association with the republic was perceived as the best guarantee for an untroubled supply of cheap labour; for many adult Ndebele, the attractions of a limited and unrecognised citizenship were far outweighed by the need to seek work in industrial South Africa, a prospect that 'independence' would have made far more difficult. But whatever the motives, the campaign was an object lesson in alliance politics. Disparate elements were welded together with tactical mobility and considerable political sophistication to achieve what the Speaker of the Kwandebele Legislative Assembly himself described as 'the eradication' of the roots of independence and its casting away 'into the deep ocean'. However, the deep ocean regurgitated a familiar monster in the wake of the reassertion of power in the May 1987 election by the National Party — another unwelcome re-introduction of the independence issue.

The attempt to resist the siren of 'self-determination' partly reflects the bitter harvest that the peoples of the four currently 'independent' bantustans are reaping. As Keenan shows, the nature of the internal struggles within the bantustans is not widely considered, despite its direct or indirect effect on most black South Africans. He argues that bantustan residents are facing growing poverty and unemployment, the increased use of security legislation and violence and the manipulation of their rights to mobility and citizenship on the part of a corrupt central and local ruling group. Despite the evidence of illegitimacy and failure, it is necessary for political and ideological purposes for the central government to show some evidence of political viability and economic success in the bantustans. The attempt to sustain the 'development' of the bantustans in the face of mass opposition results, so Keenan argues, in the transmutation of 'reform' into 'counter-revolution'. In this sense, the bantustans have become self-created Trojan horses, exposing the limitations and contradictions of government policy as it moves off the terrain of politicians' fantasies and administrators' drawing boards into the world of flesh and blood.

Education Struggles

Like the bantustan scheme, the question of an appropriate education for blacks has been at the core of the apartheid system ever since the master architect of the theory, Verwoerd, argued that 'Education must train and teach people in accordance with their opportunities in life according to the sphere in which they live.'[15] The inequitable and ideologically-insulting educational provision for blacks in fact triggered the modern period of opposition to apartheid. This was marked by the Soweto riots of 1976, when unarmed school children and unemployed youths confronted armoured cars and machine guns in the streets of the townships.

Hyslop provides a retrospective review of how South African 'youth' (that elusive to define, but nonetheless potent, revolutionary force), after two decades of 'Bantu education', turned its fury on this odious attempt at social control. The increased number of students, their limited job opportunities but also their generational consciousness (urbanised, influenced by BC, politically tuned-in to the independence struggles in Mozambique and Angola), led to the direct challenge to state control that the Soweto uprising signified. Hyslop also convincingly analyses the second (1980-1) and third (post-1984) cycles of the student movement, the slogans and theories they have generated, as well as the counter-response of the state and its tame ideologues in the Human Sciences Research Council.

While Hyslop's chapter is particularly powerful in showing the rapid-fire dialectic between educational demands and state reaction, the remaining two chapters on education illustrate a similar dynamic. The contribution by Molobi, a key member of the National Education Crisis Committee (NECC), is an authoritative statement of how a representative body of the victims of apartheid education perceives the alternatives to the government's plans. Molobi lays particular emphasis on the theme of 'people's education'. As he suggests, this goes far beyond the alternatives posed to Bantu education by sections of local capital and external donors. It includes democratisation, accountability to and involvement by local communities, as well as a critical and relevant curriculum, highlighting worker education and the closing of the gap between mental and manual labour.

No doubt some of these educational objectives will require much further specification as the contours of a post-apartheid educational system begin to evolve. One crucial segment of that system is the university sector — currently trisected between right-wing Afrikaner universities, liberal English-speaking universities and the black so-called 'bush colleges', largely brought into being by apartheid planners. Gwala, who writes from inside a black university, warns against them being written off. He shows how, despite the tight grip held on these institutions by Afrikaner or Afrikaner-trained academics and the bantustan 'petty bourgeoisie', the students have nonetheless mounted an effective challenge to their second-class status. However, he points also to the paradox of student success at the level of national politics and their relative failure to throw off the shackles of the narrow neo-positivistic training being force-fed to them. Clearly the ideological tangles of apartheid ideology have a grip even amongst dissenting students; and these remain to be uncoiled by the development of progressive thought and free traditions of enquiry.

THEORIES OF LIBERATION

Our final chapter, by John Saul, seeks to link the current phase of social and political unrest in South Africa with the course of change undertaken and predicted by the theories of the key liberation movements, in particular the

ANC. Some reservations to this exercise must be recorded here. In no sense should Saul's chapter be read as a conclusion to the book or a set of propositions that the individual authors or the editors would, necessarily, subscribe to. Nonetheless, as editors, we considered it important to publish the views of an author who was close to, but at the same time critical of, the ANC. He shows how the organisation came to develop a 'two-stage' theory of revolution, the socialist component post-dating an initial struggle for national liberation. We would hold that the theory essentially was derived from the Comintern debates in the 1920s and depends on continuing to see South Africa as a colony, though 'of a special type'. Provided one can accept such a depiction (in our view a difficult task), the theory can reconcile the multi-class interests of the Congress movement,[16] whose fight would be against 'colonialism', with the special class interests of the proletariat, whose fight would be against capitalism. The two-stage theory could also reconcile the countervailing tugs of race and class and help to square the not entirely rounded circles of the Freedom Charter, the key document of the movement, which promised the fulfilment of both liberal and communist demands.

Saul weaves his way intriguingly through the morass of prescient insights, *ex post facto* reasoning, rationalisation, the rewritings of history and the gropings toward new logics that characterise a predominantly exile-led movement trying to catch up with realities on the ground. In his role as a friendly critic, he does not conceal his points of disagreement, nor withhold his praise of the ANC where he feels it has correctly discerned the mood of the subordinate peoples of South Africa. He also argues strongly that the ANC is much less able to 'make a deal' with capital than some outside observers and some sections of South African capital would appear to believe (or want to believe).

Like Lambert and Webster, Saul also makes a number of useful comments concerning the notions of 'workerism' and 'populism' around which the internal political debate (amongst the anti-apartheid forces) has come largely to be polarised. While we do not take issue with our contributors' observations and conclusions on this debate, it would perhaps be useful for us to set the discussion in a wider context.

In origin, the terms 'workerism' and 'populism' have a rather different provenance from, but are nonetheless subtly linked to, their current South African usage. This applies particularly to the word 'populism'. It has echoes, of course, of the 'popular fronts' of the 1930s which were promoted by communists to enable their own followers to ally with liberal and socialist parties and unions to create a common front against Fascism. The Fascist/Nazi analogy is sometimes (though again we feel misleadingly) used by members of the SACP[17] and others to describe South Africa. Though the exact comparison is in error, the idea that all anti-apartheid forces (from progressive white businessmen to poor black peasants) may need to be mobilised in order to defeat apartheid is a perfectly plausible proposition. Seen in this sense populism is simply about coalition or alliance politics. However, 'populism' has also been used in a totally different sense to refer to non-class-based mass movements, principally in Latin America, led by demagogic figures like Peron or Vargas, seeking to reconcile the interests of labour and capital through appealing to the lowest common denominator of nationalist rhetoric.[18]

The pejorative implication of the South African use has been inherited from Latin America, though with none of the context of the seizure of state power by a Bonapartist figure. 'Populist' has come to mean without class principles and in particular without loyalties to, and a full acceptance of, the primacy of the working class struggle. Deployed in this way, the cry of 'populist' has been used against those in the Charterist or Congress tradition by two quite separate groupings (thereby inducing a source of great confusion and acrimony). On the one hand, the accusation that the Charterists have betrayed class principles has become a familiar cry of the non-Congress South African left (for example, those like the Unity Movement influenced by Trotskyism). On the other hand, sections in the emergent labour movement who have no organic connections with Trotskyism also use the description 'populist' to emphasise that they see the struggle against capitalism to be a more important objective than the seizure of state power by a broad coalition of anti-apartheid forces. Only workers, or worker-led movements, so this argument runs, would be able to effect a complete revolution on behalf of the most oppressed sections of the South African population, the black working class and peasantry.

From the foregoing comments, it becomes apparent why spokespersons for the mainstream ANC/SACP tradition, particularly those whose bitter exile has reduced thought to epithet, can conflate the wishes of ordinary trade unionists not wishing to see the fruits of their struggles lost to a group of parasites riding on their backs, with the posturings of the Trotskyist left. Such spokespersons are often indiscriminate in denouncing those pushing solely for a worker-led and worker-based revolution as 'ultra-leftists' or 'workerists'. Advocates of 'workerism' are held to be deploying a misguided notion of revolutionary orthodoxy which will only serve to alienate potential allies in the struggle to rid South Africa of apartheid, perhaps with wholly deleterious effects. Again, the debate echoes the turn-of-the-century communist attacks on the 'ouvrièristes', influenced by syndicalists and anarchists. Probably the boldest variation on that discussion was Sorel's argument that whatever the class composition of a revolutionary movement, it needed the 'myth' of the exclusive revolutionary authenticity of the working class to galvanise and energise itself. In this sense, the myth of the general strike became more potent than the reality.[19] In the most rigid of the non-Congress left's statements, something of the Sorellian myth survives, 'working class revolution' being evoked as a slogan with little attention given to the mechanics either of how workers can seize state power, or how they could hold it if ever they attained it.

As our contributors have noted, the workerist/populist dichotomy contains an element of caricature and unreality. The leading theorists of the ANC/SACP (as quoted for example in Saul's chapter) would not accept any definition of themselves as 'populist'; nor do they discount the importance of the proletariat. Indeed what is striking in ANC/SACP theory is an almost pristine clinging to the orthodoxies about the working class as a 'vanguard', a 'leading class', etc., long after these simplicities have been abandoned by other left parties in other countries. On the other hand, those involved in the organisation of the working class in trade unions have not hesitated to seek the support of the surrounding community, women's groups or student organisations as allies in their struggles, as a number of contributions to this book have demonstrated.

The debate between 'workerists' and 'populists' takes on a further air of unreality precisely because political organisation and dialogue within South Africa is artificially constrained by state repression. Where a representative political organisation of the black populace, like the ANC, is illegal, other organisations, like the trade unions, have to assume a wider political and social role and act as general representatives of the subordinate sections of the population. Equally, the fact that the ANC (or for that matter, the Pan Africanist Congress) cannot openly seek support or contest elections means that they appear exclusively as anti-state movements rather than as representatives of particular classes or coalitions of classes.

CONCLUSION: ONE STRUGGLE OR MANY?

Perhaps enough has been said to suggest that the slanging match between 'workerists' and 'populists' can now usefully be superseded. The experiences described in this book suggest a number of salient questions that remain unanswered by debates that allow too little for local initiatives, innovatory ideas and novel structures. Let us try to specify a few of these questions by way of conclusion.

Given that a politically and socially conscious trade union movement by force of circumstance has already evolved in South Africa, will it seek to maintain some organisational autonomy from the wider liberation movement? The lessons from other societies where a national liberation campaign has successfully been fought[20] suggest that unions would be foolish to surrender their role as class representatives. 'Independence' or 'majority rule' or 'revolutionary state power' brings its own constraints. Foreign exchange has to be earned, production maintained, international competitiveness assured. The independent trade unions in South Africa are unlikely to be satisfied with the politically inert and productionist role they assume in the Soviet Union and other centrally-planned economies. This does not mean, of course, that trade unionists cannot be allies, or indeed members of a post-apartheid government. The fact that the unions have taken a vital role in the wider movement for emancipation both guarantees their place at the top table and ensures a measure of functional autonomy.[21] It also demonstrates the extent to which the debate itself is being overtaken by events on the ground.

What exactly is the optimal organisational form that will permit the multifarious women's, labour, community, educational, etc. struggles to feed off each other, learn from each other's mistakes and provide mutual support? The worker/populist debate, precisely because it is located in earlier debates in other contexts, provides little clue. *Satyagraha*, the mass strike, *foco* guerrilla tactics, sabotage and plain old-fashioned insurrection have all been advanced at one time or another as preferential theories and have all been deployed with partial effect. But consider for a moment the sturdy home-grown varieties of action and organisation — the Defiance Campaign of the 1950s, 'commoners' movements in the countryside, the civic associations, the loose UDF coalition, the powerful National Union of Mineworkers led by a lawyer coming, like so many other leaders in the unions and the UDF, from a BC background. All these examples demonstrate that one cannot pre-programme the organic development of a movement with pre-set formulae determining the organisational form it should take.

Do struggles like those described and analysed in this book signify 'incremental' change which may or may not lead to a revolutionary outcome? Are such struggles inherently 'reformist', that is, capable ultimately of being transmuted into more sophisticated channels of social control? Are such struggles, finally, the muted trumpetings of a fundamental social transformation, a revolutionary event of the scope, say, of the Chinese, Russian, French or Nicaraguan revolutions? A possible analogy with the Russian revolution is one made both by the government, in its propaganda war against communism and by ANC/SACP theorists who apparently draw some inspiration from that event. Yet, as Johnson[22] pointed out a decade ago, such is the sophistication of the repressive instruments of government that the most one can say is that the oppositional movements presently only have the capacity to disrupt and destabilise the social and political order, but not yet to replace it. Under this scenario, the Russian analogy will yield many 1905s, but no 1917.

One of the difficulties in using such historical parallels is that they virtually pre-determine the conception of how the appropriate means of furthering a radical transformation might occur. When Lenin stepped out of a sealed train at the Finland station, he confronted an inchoate swirl of revolutionary demands in a context where central authority had all but broken down. Only three months earlier, he had said that 'We of the older generation may not live to see the decisive battles of this coming revolution'.[23] In fact, the combination of demagogy, conspiracy, discipline and monosyllabic demands (land, peace, bread, work) were adequate to the situation. In South Africa, the regime is far from demoralised and the opponents to the regime are likely to be far less amenable to a Bolshevik-style appeal.

The various struggles described in this book already show a high level of internal organisation and coherence — whether they be for better wages, fairer educational access, civic representation, cultural self-expression, workers' participation or access to land. It would be an anachronism to believe that the levels of self-expression and autonomy displayed in our case studies can simply be sublimated to the demands of a single insurrectionary party. The existence of distinct sectoral demands should not necessarily be seen in a negative light. The centralisation of all struggles can promote effectiveness, but it can also provide the opportunity for a ruthless government to leave a central body headless and rudderless.

Even in the context of seemingly overwhelming state power and brutality, the dominant message from these diverse struggles remains one of hope. It is within the organisation and nature of these struggles that the future South Africa is being created. Popular struggles, insofar as they represent authentic rank-and-file expression, are a claim to future involvement, and incubators for the practice of democracy in the workplace, home and school. As such they provide small-scale models of what a future South Africa might look like.

NOTES

1. The list reads like a Who's Who of US industry and includes such names as Citycorp, IBM, Exxon, General Electric, General Motors, Ford, Kodak and American

Airlines. Announcing its own withdrawal, ITT commented that its South African sales only amounted to one tenth of one per cent of global sales. In addition to the question of a disproportionate amount of time being taken to discuss such small profit centres, US corporations are also influenced by the threat of city and state governments in the US to restrict investment of public funds or prevent the award of contracts to firms doing business in South Africa.

2. The 'cultural' boycott was first called for by Father Trevor Huddleston in an article in the *Observer* on 10 October 1954. Recently, the Anti-Apartheid Movement in the UK has sought to reassert the totality of the boycott in the face of some of its apparent absurdities. The movement argues for non-selectivity as being 'consistent' and in line with the views of a 'wide range of organisations', including the ANC. Selectivity is said to be difficult for the public to understand and tending to a weakening of the campaign for total isolation (*Anti-Apartheid News*, April 1987). The claim to be acting in conformity with the ANC's views is, however, now somewhat dubious in the light of a major shift of direction announced by its President, Oliver Tambo, in the Canon Collins Lecture in May 1987. According to Tambo, 'The moment is upon us when we shall have to deal with the alternative structures that our people have created through struggle and sacrifice, as the genuine representatives of these masses in all fields of human endeavour. . . . Not only should these not be boycotted, but more they should be supported, encouraged and treated as the democratic counterparts within South Africa of similar institutions and organisations internationally.' (*Guardian*, 29 May 1987)

3. W. Cobbett, 'Industrial decentralisation and exploitation: the case of Botshabelo', *South African Labour Bulletin*, Vol.12, No.3, 1987.

4. As an example of such rhetoric we can cite the case of one of the four black candidates elected in the June 1987 British general election for a Brent (London) constituency who proclaimed in his euphoric victory speech, 'Brent today, Soweto tomorrow!'

5. Not the same organisation headed by Chief Buthelezi, but the choice of name is instructive.

6. Again the name is instructive and a conscious indication that the black right perceives the US Marine Corps in fraternal terms.

7. R. Omond, *The Apartheid Handbook: a Guide to South Africa's Everyday Racial Policies* (Harmondsworth: Penguin, 1985) p.136.

8. Because of its publicity-shunning ethos, the activities of this church, often known simply as the 'black Zionists', were not well-known in South Africa or outside, until the church invited President Botha to address their Easter service in 1986. In fact, millions assemble for this annual event — reputed to be the biggest regular gathering in Christendom, if not the world (see *Guardian*, 21 April 1987).

9. See Keenan in this volume for the Bophuthatswanan case. For Transkei examples, see B. Streek and R. Wicksteed, *Render unto Kaiser* (Johannesburg: Ravan Press, 1981) pp.74-99.

10. The whites-only election of May 1987 returned a score of seats for the ultra-right Conservative Party, thus narrowly displacing the liberal Progressive Federal Party as the official opposition.

11. M. Burawoy, *The Politics of Production* (London: Verso, 1983).

12. *Guardian*, 21 April 1987.

13. R. Davies, 'The 1922 strike on the Rand: white labor and the political economy of South Africa' in P.C.W. Gutkind *et al, African Labor History* (Beverly Hills: Sage Publications, 1978) pp.80-108.

14. M. Castells, *The Urban Question* (London: Edward Arnold, 1977); M. Harloe and E. Lebas (eds), *City, Class and Capital* (London: Edward Arnold, 1981).

15. Cited L.E. Neame, *The History of Apartheid* (London: Pall Mall Press) p.95.

16. Historically, the Congress movement comprised a multi-class, multi-racial, alliance of the ANC, the Coloured People's Congress, the Indian Congress and the

(white) Congress of Democrats. Over the last 25 years, the ANC, in practice, has become the dominant force and the component units have largely lost their identity.

17. See B. Bunting, *The Rise of the South African Reich* (Harmondsworth: Penguin, 1964). A brief critique of the Nazi analogy is developed in R. Cohen, *Endgame in South Africa?* (London: James Currey, 1986) pp.3-6.

18. This usage, amongst others, is found in G. Ionescu and J. Gellner (eds), *Populism* (London: Weidenfeld and Nicolson, 1970) Chs. 2, 9 & 10.

19. G. Sorel, *Reflections on Violence* (Glencoe, Ill.: The Free Press, 1950) (first published in 1906). J. Plamenatz in *Ideology* (London: Macmillan, 1970) summarises the Sorellian view like this: 'The myth [of the revolutionary working class] justifies the act and proceeds from the impulse. The myth is accepted, not because it has been critically examined and found to be true, nor because it justifies the pursuit of common interests, but because it justifies what those who accept it are impelled to do.' (p.126)

20. For Algeria see I. Clegg, 'Workers and managers in Algeria'; for a comparison with Vietnam see K.W.J. Post, 'The alliance of peasants and workers: some problems concerning the articulation of classes', both in R. Cohen *et al*, *Peasants and Proletarians: the Struggles of Third World Workers* (London: Hutchinson, 1979) pp.223-47, 265-85.

21. The contrast with Zimbabwe should be noted. Because Mugabe came to power primarily as a result of a rural guerrilla struggle, the claims of urban workers were largely ignored in the post-independence period.

22. R.W. Johnson, *How Long will South Africa Survive?* (London: Hutchinson, 1977).

23. E. Wilson, *To the Finland Station: a Study in the Writing and Acting of History* (London: Fontana, 1960) p.459.

1. The Re-emergence of Political Unionism in Contemporary South Africa?

ROB LAMBERT AND EDDIE WEBSTER

During the past three years South Africa has experienced unprecedented levels of social conflict. The structures of racial oppression have been severely challenged by a powerful national liberation movement. Like most Third World national liberation struggles, the South African struggle has mobilised the oppressed classes around the common goal of a non-racial democratic state. However, unlike most national liberation movements, the working class has begun to play a central and, at times, leading role in these struggles.

The racially-based South African state has always served to buttress severe forms of labour exploitation. It has been, historically and in contemporary struggles, a cardinal force shaping the form, character and goals of the progressive, non-racial, trade union movement. This is not to imply that the state was, and is, a *determining* force in this regard. Such theorisation would de-emphasise the dimension of leadership and the potential choices that emerge within tactical and strategic debates.[1] Our own approach in attempting to assess the direction and potential of contemporary trade unions in South Africa would be to assert the critical importance of these tactical and strategic debates.

We would argue that fundamental differences in the perceptions of the trade union role exist, differences that have divided the trade union movement since unions first emerged in nineteenth-century Europe. The division lies between those who discern significant potential in trade union activity, and those who argue that such activity does not in itself facilitate (indeed some hold that it may even inhibit) the transformation of capitalist society. Hyman refers to the former as the optimistic tradition and the latter as the pessimistic tradition.[2]

These differences need to be thoroughly debated, for they do have consequences for the choices trade unions make in the face of the unfolding of the state's reform strategy. Furthermore the outcome of these debates affects the class content of any national political struggle and ultimately will influence the character of political and social change in South Africa.

Our central argument holds that two approaches exist in the non-racial trade union movement at present: orthodox, or collective bargaining unionism, and political, or, social movement unionism.[3] By orthodox unionism we mean a form of trade unionism which concentrates almost exclusively on workplace issues; fails to link production issues to wider political issues; and finally encourages its members to become politically involved without necessarily engaging itself in the wider political arena, believing that this is best left to other organisations more suited to the task. The political content of such unionism

20

varies widely, but in each instance what is common to this orientation is an accommodation and absorption into industrial relations systems, which not only institutionalises conflict, but also serves to reinforce the division between economic and political forms of struggle so essential to the maintenance of capitalist relations in production, in the community, and in the state.

The alternative tendency — political, or social movement unionism — attempts to link production to wider political issues. It is a form of union organisation that facilitates an active engagement in factory-based, production politics *and* in community and state power issues. It engages in alliances in order to establish relationships with political organisations on a systematic basis. We would contrast this form of trade unionism with what we call populist unionism in which trade unionism and struggles in the factory are downplayed. The latter is a tendency that neglects struggles over wages, supervision, managerial controls at the workplace and job evaluation. It places in its stead a political engagement that only serves to dissipate shop floor struggles.[4] Political unionism, on the other hand, attempts to link the above struggles with community and state power issues. Unlike syndicalism, it does not negate the role of a political party, but rather asserts the need for a co-ordinating political body that is democratic in its practices and therefore able to relate to political unionism in a non-instrumental manner.

Political unionism emerged within the South African Congress of Trade Unions (SACTU) in the 1950s, indicating an orientation that held real promise not only for challenging the apartheid state, but also for generating a worker consciousness. SACTU was formed in 1955 as a predominantly African trade union federation drawing on the defunct Council of Non-European Trade Unions (CNETU) — a federation which had concentrated exclusively on collective bargaining — but included amongst its affiliates the 'left' non-racial strand of the registered trade union movement formerly organised in the Trades and Labour Council (TLC). SACTU's alliance with the ANC and the Congress movement resulted in a novel redefinition of its trade union role along the lines of 'political unionism'. Faced by a weak power base in the factories, a hostile state and intransigent employers, SACTU chose to engage politically with nationalism as a means of transforming its small factory base.

Extensive research into SACTU's development during the late 1950s reveals that it grew most rapidly in those regions where political unionism was consciously pursued.[5] Political unionism co-existed with orthodox unionism within SACTU, despite the general commitment of the federation to political struggle through the alliance. Some have argued that this engagement in the alliance led to the subordination of the trade unions and working class demands to nationalism, or populism.[6] We would argue to the contrary: engagement in the alliance facilitated the rapid development of trade union organisation, where attention was paid to the importance of factory structures and production politics. This is not to deny that in certain unions and in certain regions populist unionism existed. However, the most systematic organising work within SACTU was along the lines of social movement, or political, unionism.

The 1950s' experiment in political unionism hardly had time to consolidate before it was pre-empted by the state repression of the early and mid 1960s. South Africa was to experience a decade of industrial peace. However, it was a decade in which the economy experienced a structural transformation financed by a massive influx of foreign capital, accelerated expansion of industry, a restructuring of capital and the growing concentration and centralisation of ownership. The extent of cartelisation by the late 1970s may be gauged by the information supplied by the Mouton Commission on Monopolies in 1977. According to the commission a mere 5 percent of the total number of firms in the manufacturing sector between them accounted for 63 percent of the sector's turnover; only 5 percent of those in wholesale accounted for 69 percent of turnover; 5 percent of those in construction accounted for 63 percent of turnover; and 5 percent in transport for 73 percent of turnover.[7]

Coupled with these changes went a corresponding growth in the black working class which brought black workers firmly to the centre of the industrial stage. In particular, we see the growth in the number of semi-skilled black workers, the organisational base for industrial unionism. As Hemson writes:

> With the growth of monopoly capitalism and the concentration of production in large-scale, highly mechanised factories, went a black proletariat neither differentiated by traditional skills, nor having experienced the benefits of reform. These are the conditions for a rapid advance in class consciousness as the political resistance to apartheid gains momentum.[8]

Through the concentration of large numbers of workers in production, the material conditions for a strengthened shopfloor-based trade unionism had been created by the early 1970s. It was the mass strikes in January and February 1973 in Durban that were to highlight these changes dramatically: an estimated 100,000 workers broke the decade-old 'industrial peace' and took to the streets to demand wage increases. As a result of these strikes trade unions were formed in Durban and Pietermaritzburg.

Managerial consultants and state strategists were forced to place 'the worker' on the agenda as militancy destroyed comforting myths and exposed the weaknesses of the 50-year-old dualistic system of industrial relations that conceded certain rights to non-Africans, while at the same time excluding African workers. The exclusion from these rights under the 1924 Industrial Conciliation Act was reinforced by a unilateral system of control over black workers that rested on the despotic power of the supervisor.

This despotic regime inside the factory was backed up by a tight system of control exercised by the state through influx control over black workers outside the firm. This dualistic system of control entrenched a dualism in the labour market — between a predominantly skilled and privileged white labour aristocracy, and a non-unionised and vulnerable black and generally unskilled labour force.

This system was to trigger off a crisis of control in the 1970s. The crisis was a result of a multiplicity of forces, both economic and political, that led to challenges on the shop floor to the managerially-controlled liaison system. The shopfloor-based unions that emerged in the early 1970s eschewed political action outside of production. They believed that it was important to avoid the path taken by SACTU in the 1950s, arguing that its close identification with the Congress Alliance and its campaigns was the cause of its demise in the 1960s.

The emerging unions chose to devote their attention to building democratic shopfloor structures around the principle of worker control, accountability and mandating of worker representatives, as a basis for developing a working class leadership in the factories. This strategy was justified in two ways. First, strong shop-floor organisation had a better chance of surviving state repression which would be directed in the first instance at 'leaders'. Second, they argued, at least until 1980-81, that its political impact would have been insignificant, whilst at the same time these fledgling unions had everything to lose by adopting a confrontationist stance.

These challenges were to culminate in the establishment, in 1977, of the Wiehahn Commission to investigate industrial relations. Arising out of this investigation, the Industrial Conciliation Act was amended to allow for the recognition of black unions for the first time in South African labour history. It would be better, Wiehahn concluded, to allow African trade unions to register at an early stage in order to control the pace of union development.

The Wiehahn solution was clearly contradictory. The intention was to control the emerging unions by drawing them into the established industrial relations structures, in particular the Industrial Councils, thus pre-empting attempts by these unions to establish a shop-floor presence and to widen the scope of their activities into 'non-industrial relations' arenas. This required giving unregistered unions state recognition, enabling them to win space in their attempt to move beyond the struggle for recognition to direct negotiation at shop-floor level. Recognition at plant level was not won without struggle but, in the years immediately after Wiehahn, a new frontier of control was being defined as recognition agreements at plant level became increasingly common in different sectors of the economy.

In the immediate post-Wiehahn period, South Africa's industrial relations practitioners embarked on the difficult task of attempting to integrate black workers' demands into the new collective bargaining system. Their aim was to institutionalise industrial conflict along classical pluralist lines. The oft-stated intention was the patterning of union development on the West European model, where unions tend to confine themselves to workplace issues only.

Political engagement is left to political parties, which individual unions may attempt to influence. State strategists saw the concession of collective bargaining rights as the first step in a gradual reform process that would culminate in certain, yet-to-be determined, political rights for blacks. The unacceptable alternative for the apartheid state was a radical politicisation of labour with an overtly political trade union movement engaged with the national liberation movement.

It is now seven years since the state introduced these reforms — enough time for a tentative evaluation of just how successful the strategists have been in attaining their goals. Nearly two million workers — black and white — now belong to trade unions affiliated to two major federations — the National Council of Trade Unions (NACTU) combining the Council of Unions of South Africa (CUSA) and the Azanian Confederation of Trade Unions (AZACTU), and the Congress of South African Trade Unions (COSATU). How effective has the state been in patterning union development along 'pure' collective bargaining lines? To what extent have the new unions been absorbed into the industrial relations system in a way that institutionalises the separation between economic and wider political struggles? Or has the dynamic of the struggle begun to give shape to a creative strategy in response to these questions?

The underlying theme of this chapter is that a creative response has emerged among black workers that has begun to transcend the over-polarised workerist/populist debate. The new unions that emerged in the 1970s were never narrowly economistic. They were social movements from their conception, challenging South Africa's system of racial capitalism. The majority joined unions out of a desire to defend worker rights from what they saw as arbitrary and unfair treatment by the state.

They recall the early working class movement in nineteenth-century England, 'first and foremost a "human rights" movement in a very comprehensive manner concerned with the recovery of the dignity of "freeborn Englishmen" . . . in terms of an effort to retrieve dignified living and working conditions from the onslaught of the Industrial Revolution'.[9] These 'political movements' were absorbed into the emerging British industrial relations system in a way that successfully institutionalised the separation between 'economic' and 'political' struggles.

This chapter is concerned to show how the South African state began to embark on a similar project in the late 1970s through the Wiehahn report. The paper is divided into three parts. The first section deals with the gains made in collective bargaining in the post-Wiehahn period. The second part traces the re-emergence of alliance politics in the trade union movement, while the final section examines some of the obstacles to this alliance. In this paper we concentrate on developments in COSATU and one of its predecessors, the Federation of South African Trade Unions (FOSATU).[10]

COLLECTIVE BARGAINING UNIONISM

In our view, the results of the reform strategy are contradictory. On the one hand, it would *appear* that significant gains are being made in the immediate post-Wiehahn period in developing a system of collective bargaining along traditional industrial relations lines. They can be summarised as follows:

1. An estimated 20% of the labour force now belong to trade unions. A major contributing factor to this growth has been the dramatic rise of the National Union of Mineworkers (NUM). The foundations for nationally based industrial trade unions have now been laid in all major sectors of the economy.
2. Perhaps more significant was the organisational depth of these emerging unions. By the end of 1985, these unions were organised in 43,500 workplaces, had signed 450 plant agreements, had an estimated 1,500 shop steward committees/councils and over 12,500 shop stewards.[11]
3. Management's unilateral power to dismiss has been curtailed by the emergence of a system of industrial legality in the workplace, laying down a set of procedures to be followed in the event of dismissal or retrenchment. These procedures have been strengthened by the dramatic increase in the use of the Industrial Court by trade unionists from 20 instances in 1981 to over 2,000 in 1986.
4. Strikes are beginning, with the exception of the public service sector, to become a normal part of the collective bargaining process, losing many of the sinister implications attached to them in the past. This is possibly best illustrated by the growth in the number of mediations by the Independent Mediation Service of South Africa, from 39 in 1984 to 131 in 1986. Most

strikes continued to be over wages. However, dismissals, retrenchment, recognition and detention were a major cause of strike action. Of particular interest is the growing sophistication in the range of tactics used by workers, from go-slows and overtime bans, to factory occupations and sit-ins.

5. The post-Wiehahn period has seen the beginning of serious collective bargaining in South Africa.[12] Many of the emerging unions have now joined the Industrial Councils and have begun to draw on the skills of professional economists in their negotiations. In addition to wage bargaining, a number of other issues that have previously been the prerogative of management, such as health and safety, have become industrial relations issues.

6. In the post-Wiehahn period, the state has begun to withdraw from two key areas of the labour market — from all forms of statutory job reservation except the mines and, more ambiguously, from the pass laws in June 1986. The latter retreat establishes freedom of movement as a nominal right only — residence in urban areas still depends on 'approved accommodation.' The state now controls movement through such 'racially neutral' legislation as the Slums Act, Trespass Act and Prevention of Illegal Squatting Act. Rather than controlling the movement of people into the urban areas through the pass laws, Cobbett argues, the state now controls the space by, for example, bulldozing 'illegal' squatter camps such as Crossroads or Kabah.[13]

From a trade union perspective, the significance of these gains lies in the rights established on the shopfloor rather than the benefits won by organised workers. A survey by Levy and Associates found that wage increases in unionised plants in 1985-6 exceeded the average increase in black wages but did not reach the inflation rate.[14] In the metal industry, for instance, average actual wage increases in 1986 were 11 percent whereas the inflation rate was 19 percent. No union has yet attained the goal of a living wage. Managements now have to be more circumspect with dismissals, although they still call the tune on the question of retrenchments.

The substance of these marginal, but not insignificant, wage and job security gains rests in their implications politically. They have empowered ordinary workers: organised workers have experienced a new sense of collective power, born in everyday struggle on the factory floor over abusive supervision, the dismissal of workers now regarded as comrades, and a multitude of contested working conditions. This new sense of power has developed out of the democratic character of these shop floor struggles, and the union's commitment to the longer-term goal of worker control of the production process.

While these gains contain a wide range of political possibilities, they are also contradictory in a less apparent sense. In fighting and advancing in this way, the new unions are increasingly drawn into an industrial relations web that is not without cost. Collective bargaining, *per se*, comes to dominate. The struggle becomes defined in terms of the factory only; immediate economic and production politics issues absorb all energy, and the wider political questions begin to fade into a more distant realm that seems beyond the capacity of a union to engage; political engagement is reduced to purely rhetorical flourishes.

We would argue that there are objective social pressures from the state and from capital, pulling the democratic unions in this direction so that the impact of these gains is *both* transformative and conservative. On the one hand militant industrial unions have made real, albeit limited gains for their members, while on the other they have channelled conflict in ways that can be contained and institutionalised by the industrial relations system. The state has made gains in establishing a collective bargaining system that, as with all such systems, can seal off reasonably effectively economic from political struggles. This is not a startling conclusion. Capitalist states have been relatively effective in containing trade union pressures and actions within acceptable boundaries.

While the state has attained a degree of success in this regard, it has also seriously undermined its own reform programme. Historically, capitalist reforms have gained a reasonable degree of success only when collective bargaining concessions were backed by political rights, as happened in 19th century Britain.[15] The institutionalisation of industrial conflict presupposes the early (and relatively peaceful) attainment of formal social and political rights by significant sectors of the working population. Production as a consequence, Wood argues, ceases to be an immediate political issue.[16]

The roots of 'economism' lie in this necessary shift of conflict to the point of production. The struggle over appropriation appears not as a political contest but as a battle over the terms and conditions of work. In South Africa, the state's intervention in production makes its racial form clear for all to see, linking directly the politics of production with global politics. Although Wiehahn foresaw the necessity for political rights, the South African state has been unable to move in a direction that is acceptable to the black majority. The contradiction in the Wiehahn reforms is now clear — it created the legal space for the rapid growth of industrial unions while failing to provide the conditions for their political incorporation.

Instead of accepting the universal franchise which has always served as a useful integrating mechanism, the state has moved hesitantly towards a racially-based restructuring that still excludes Africans, while maintaining white control. This has led to an intensification of the demand for national liberation. At the same time, the recession has deepened, producing high levels of youth unemployment. It is above all this social category — along with students — that has led township resistance since 1976.

Trade unions have therefore been more sharply confronted with a dual challenge since 1984: they have been forced to confront the question of national liberation, and they have been forced to relate to the youth-led civil war in the townships. These pressures have forced union leaderships to think through the relationship between trade union, factory-based struggles, and broader political struggle. The resolution of this central question has been twofold: firstly, certain unions have thrown their resources into broader-based resistance; secondly, a vigorous debate has opened up within the unions, which still leaves a more strategically thought out response to the question of the trade union role and the precise form and content of national liberation unresolved for the present.

THE RE-EMERGENCE OF ALLIANCE POLITICS

The economy has been in recession since 1982, resulting in closures, retrenchments and mass unemployment. The falling rand has fuelled internal inflation and threatened the balance of payments. For the state, the effect has been to provoke a major fiscal crisis which in turn restricts its ability to finance 'reform'.[17]

The crisis has been met by unprecedented levels of mobilisation and resistance in the factories and communities over economic and political issues: the highest strike levels in South African history; rent strikes; bus boycotts; consumer boycotts; school boycotts; anti-constitutional campaigns and stay-aways; all these forms of resistance became permanent features of the political terrain between 1984 and 1986. Moreover, this phase of resistance has been marked by new organisational, ideological and political alignments. This was most clearly evident in November 1984 when unions, community and student organisations joined together in the massive Transvaal stay-away.

This is not to say that a struggle within the union movement to define its political role began only after 1984. This would ignore earlier attempts to engage politically and the interesting debates that accompanied these struggles. Thus in 1979 the Food and Canning Workers Union (FCWU) called on the community to support their union in a dispute with management in the Fattis and Monis plant in the Cape. Later that year the formation of the Port Elizabeth Black Civic Organisation (PEBCO) was to force community issues onto the shop floor when African workers in the Ford Cortina plant went out on strike in support of their community leader, Thozamile Botha. This was to lead, in 1980, to the establishment of the Motor Assembly and Component Workers' Union of South Africa (MACWUSA) which, along with the formation of South African Allied Workers' Union (SAAWU) in East London a year earlier, forced the unions to confront national politics.

The Food and Canning Workers Union argued in an article written in 1982 that while there was a need to become involved in community issues, a separate form of organisation was required:

> We do believe that separate forms of organisation are needed for these struggles. A trade union is not a community or political organisation. A union which tries to be a community or political organisation at the same time cannot survive.[18]

At the same time FOSATU entered the debate with a keynote speech by their General Secretary, Joe Foster. Foster's speech called for the building of a workers' movement, much more broadly defined than simple collective bargaining trade unionism. It made provision for alliances and joint campaigning with other progressive organisations and called on union members to become involved in community and political organisations. However, Foster went on to warn against unions being drawn into political action which was not worker-controlled but was 'populist ' in character. Anti-populism was to remain an important political perspective of many of the FOSATU unions.

Foster's speech reaffirmed the principles of worker control but now applied these to political action beyond production. However, the guidelines set down were of a general nature, allowing for very different interpretations: the criticism of populism reinforced a narrow 'workerism' in some quarters; the provision for alliances and community involvement was welcomed by those with national democratic leanings; whilst references to 'workers' control' were interpreted by the South African Communist Party (SACP) as a form of syndicalism.

The debate came to focus on whether or not trade unions should affiliate to the United Democratic Front (UDF), newly formed in 1983. Unions such as MACWUSA and SAAWU articulated a position which favoured affiliation on the grounds that workers were also members of the community, and that unions must also fight for their members' interests outside of production. They also argued that trade unions encompassed only a part of the working class, and further that a successful political challenge to the state demanded alliances with other social groups, and the widest possible unity of those who are oppressed under apartheid.

The General Workers' Union (GWU) on the other hand, asserted the need to ensure democratic and worker control. The argument was that the UDF was made up of activist-based organisations, with no structures for mandating and acountability. The trade unions would be swamped by a host of organisations with equal voting power, but often little real membership. Furthermore, the UDF represented a multi-class alliance. Its very style and language were at variance with the traditions established in the unions, and did not contribute towards working class leadership. These arguments became the rallying cry of the anti-populist tendency.

While these issues were being debated, new forms of organisation began to emerge on the ground. On the East Rand, the shop steward councils spear-headed agitation against the destruction of shacks by the authorities. These councils readily concerned themselves with non-factory issues, pushing unions beyond 'pure-and-simple' trade unionism. At the centre of this social movement in the East Rand hostels was the migrant worker. Faced by rural collapse and growing retrenchment, these migrant workers found in the new unions a movement that was able to express their discontent and give direction to their energies.[19]

This widening of the scope of union action beyond production to the sphere of reproduction — including demands for adequate pensions, maternity rights, housing and unemployment benefits — reflects the deepening crisis in the social formation as a whole. In the Eastern Cape — and to a lesser extent in the Western Cape and Natal — trade unions played a major role in the anti-tricameral election campaign in 1984. In the same year FOSATU locals led by certain FOSATU unions began to meet with student and youth organisations to exchange views. Simultaneously, community-based subsistence struggles led by unionised workers — as in the case of the one-and-a-half year long East London bus boycott — pointed to the possiblity of a more direct role for unions in politics.[20]

However, these efforts remained localised and partial. In the main, trade unions did not develop a unified national approach to the question of political action. The movement remained divided in its approach: the community unions, particularly SAAWU, engaged in direct confrontation with the authorities (the Ciskei 'government' especially). Some FOSATU unions such as the Sweet, Food and Allied Workers' Union (SFAWU) and the Metal and Allied Workers' Union (MAWU) moved cautiously onto this terrain on the local level. Others, such as the National Union of Textile Workers (NUTW), maintained an anti-populist stance, concentrating on collective bargaining issues in the factory. Foster's speech was not concretised, leaving a political vacuum and intensifying divisions inside the labour movement.

The development of shop steward councils during this period illustrates the contradictions and political hesitancy at this stage. Shop steward councils in East Rand townships such as Katlehong, grouped shop stewards who lived in the same area, but who worked in different factories and in different industries. They took up township problems as well as organising solidarity for particular factory struggles. There was a strong tinge of syndicalism in their politics: unions could extend their structures into the community and embrace all issues. However, while FOSATU generally took a positive attitude to this development, these councils failed to develop a *structured* response to the township and wider political problems.[21] Significantly when the United Mining and Metal Workers of South Africa (UMMAWSA) split from MAWU in June 1984, the break was justified in terms of MAWU's and FOSATU's alleged lack of political involvement and leadership.[22]

By August 1984, when the South African defence force (SADF) invaded the townships, the industrial unions were facing numerous pressures that forced them to reconsider their organisational and political strategies. On the one hand, there was increasing militancy on the shop-floor as strike levels escalated, while on the other hand there was a need to consolidate their organisational capacity in the face of a deepening recession. In addition, the crisis in the townships and the general level of nation-wide political mobilisation had forced the unions to take an appropriate stand.

Organised workers demanded a direct involvement in the struggle for political rights and urban change. However, in the absence of one united national trade union federation, there was no unified strategy in response to these pressures. Consequently, strategies were shaped at a local level. This can best be illustrated through the first-hand accounts of activists in a particular area — we will focus on the East Rand after the invasion of the townships in August 1984 but similar processes were at work in other townships in the Transvaal such as Alexandra.

The SADF invasion of the townships had a dramatic impact on the lives of workers, as the journey between township and factory became extremely hazardous. A SFAWU shop steward from Tembisa township spoke of the new set of questions this posed for the unions:

> The streets of the township are (normally) more or less flat with lots of people moving up and down all the time. Then the soldiers came carrying guns and raiding the houses. They would just come in without permission. When they tried to put the rents up from the First of August, pamphlets were distributed calling for a rent boycott. At night the SADF raided the houses of those not paying rent and took whole families to the police station. They would release one and tell him to go and get the rent.
>
> It was a terrible experience. We had no voice. All the community organizations had been banned. We had no platform to raise issues and we realised that the trade union was our only platform. We had to learn to use our power at the workplace on these issues.[23]

In the ensuing months, workers *did* use their workplace power. This took the form of stay-aways. In this the student organisation, the Congress of South African Students (COSAS), was a catalyst. When student demands were not met, COSAS took the initiative and called for support from community and trade union organisations. A positive relationship existed between youth and sections of the organised workforce as a result of the Simba Chips boycott that served to establish a working relationship between youth and employed workers. As a shop steward commented,

> This was an eye opener to many of the workers who had not taken youth seriously. For instance, I discussed with some of the youth in the townships and I was surprised to hear them talking in terms of class struggle and being clearer than many of the workers themselves.[24]

Unions and community organisations responded to the COSAS call. They set up parent-student committees in a number of townships. In the Transvaal between August and November 1984 a working relationship between community/ student organisations and trade unions began to emerge. This led to the November 1984 stay-away. It was the beginning of united mass action between organised labour, students and community organisations, with unions sometimes taking a leading role. For key sectors of the democratic union movement, it marked a decisive break with abstentionism. The sheer scale of the stay-away must be understood in terms of the build-up of conflict and struggle in three key areas — the townships, the schools and the factories.

The significance of this joint action is that alliance politics were being forged in the process of intensified struggle, where workers confronted the township crisis daily, rather than in refined political debate as to the problems of populism. Organised workers, students, unemployed youth, and other township activists gained experience in working together as they faced issues daily: township rents and the need for an organised response to this crisis; police and army action, arrests, deaths of 'comrades' and the need to organise funerals and local stay-aways in protest.

This was to begin a process of redefinition of the trade union role and prioritised the question of national liberation. These pressures were moving sections of the trade union movement towards political unionism. It was, however, only the beginning of a process that would require systematic debate and a more permanent structured response, rather than *ad hoc* relationships in response to particular problems. Also, other areas that did not experience township occupations as in the Transvaal, particularly in Natal, did not move in the same way.

The emergence of political unionism was therefore partial, uneven and embryonic at this stage. It was still as if the union movement was being pulled in opposite directions: a primary focus on the factory and the need to bargain more effectively, win higher wages, pre-empt dismissals, resist retrenchments; and an increasing focus on township issues that could no longer be ignored. The problem at this point was that the union leadership was divided on how to respond. One union General Secretary commented, 'The situation is getting out of hand. Township issues are distracting us from our real work as trade unionists'.[25]

In contrast to this negative response that saw in every township involvement another example of 'nationalism dragging the trade union movement along by its shirt tails', others were far more positive in their assessment. For them, the township demands had led to a creative response on the part of organised labour, a response that opened the way for the union movement to engage with national liberation. The issue of the trade union role remained in the melting pot — its direction undecided. Much depended upon whether, and on what basis, a new unity could be created.

While November 1984 was an historically important moment in which united mass action took place, during the following months a number of obstacles and problems emerged which inhibited the realisation of this potential unity. Many of these problems came to the fore when the non-UDF unions opposed the PEBCO call for a Black Weekend consumer boycott on March 16-17 and a stay-away on the 18th as a response to the political and economic crisis in the Eastern Cape. PEBCO identified the following issues: mass retrenchments, the AMCA-Ford merger and increased petrol prices, with the latter becoming the final focus of the stay-away.[26]

The non-UDF unions gave a number of reasons for opposing the stay-away at that time. In particular, their public statements were concerned that a call made by PEBCO — an African community organisation — would exclude 'coloured' workers; a local response to what was a national problem was likely to be ineffective; there was inadequate consultation with the workers who would be vulnerable in the smaller and the unorganised establishments.

In the event, the stay-away was successful among African workers but had limited success among 'coloureds'. These differences reflect the reality of a divided working class — divisions that find organisational expression in the previous division between PEBCO and the FOSATU trade unions. In addition, the recession — particularly severe in the auto industry which has historically been concentrated in the Eastern Cape — affected workers in different ways. While unions such as the National Automobile and Allied Workers' Union (NAAWU) were concerned to consolidate their position, seeking to preserve jobs and the gains already made through collective bargaining, unemployed workers — many of whom were members of the Port Elizabeth Youth Congress (PEYCO) — played an important role in the mass protests in the townships.

This again illustrates that the process whereby unions have begun reaching out to those sectors outside the formal proletariat and developing forms of social movement unionism is not necessarily a smooth progression from one form to another. During this phase, instances of a tense and conflictual relationship between trade union leaders committed to collective bargaining gains, and community organisations striving to assert a wider political engagement, were not uncommon. Transcending this divide would be a central challenge that the newly formed federation, COSATU, would have to face.

The launch of COSATU in December 1985 represented a broad shift of key trade unions towards a more direct concern with non-factory issues. COSATU identified publicly with the national liberation struggle early in 1986 after a visit by a COSATU delegation to Lusaka, where the ANC has its headquarters. The joint ANC-SACTU-COSATU statement acknowledged the independent existence of COSATU, while at the same time viewing trade unions as an essential component of the national struggle.

> As a representative of our working class, COSATU is seized with the task of engaging the workers in the general democratic struggle, both as an independent organization and as an essential component of the democratic forces in our country.[27]

This statement of intent by the COSATU leadership, based on the November 1985 Congress resolutions, was an attempt to come to terms with the crisis in the townships. Essentially, this meant thinking through the relationship with the national liberation movement and the relationship between students, unemployed youth and the organised workforce.

The SFAWU National Executive Committee had, in an earlier discussion paper influenced by the events on the East Rand in 1984-5, attempted to come to grips with this issue. The document argued that in the context of a deepening economic and political crisis, the country had entered a

> phase of uninterrupted struggle. It is the youth who are at the vanguard of that struggle. It is the youth that are demanding through their struggles fundamental change and a restructuring of society. In this flow of struggle the organised power of workers is crucial.

The document continued:

> Township struggles are being waged and determined by youth...who also constitute a major part of the masses of the unemployed.[28]

There was therefore a need to work for a convergence of workplace and township forms of struggle, rather than the existing situation where such struggles were being waged in parallel.[29]

The document argued further that such alliances should only be formed on a principled, or disciplined basis, that is, the union movement should spell out the terms upon which it is prepared to enter such an alliance. These terms should include a recognition of the right of workers to control society, since they produced the wealth; consequently other groups in an alliance would have to recognise that the interests of workers could not be subordinated to the interests of other social classes.

During 1986 the COSATU leadership began to spell out what such control could mean in practice. It would emerge, they believed, out of the organising style that the unions had developed.[30] This was based on the 'absolute control' that workers exercised over all 'decision-making in the organisation'. This could be achieved through constitutions that entrenched such a principle; through shop steward elections in each department of a shop, factory or mine; through such leaders only acting on the basis of mandates from the membership and regular report-backs; and by structures of the unions that would incorporate a worker majority at all levels.

This, COSATU believed, would lay the basis for developing an 'alliance between students, youth and worker parents' that would point the way forward to 'people's power', that is, the power of an alliance of classes, rather than the working class striving on its own. This required the development of forms of organisation appropriate to the different terrains of struggle. These included Students' Representative Councils (SRCs) in the schools, civics in the townships, unions in the factories and the organisation of an unemployed workers committee, so that the various spheres of struggle could be linked and not 'fought on isolated and individual fronts'. Thus the alliance that had been called for in 1983 by unions such as SAAWU was now taking place. It was, however, taking place on union terms and without necessarily affiliating to the UDF.

CHALLENGES AND PROBLEMS WITHIN THE ALLIANCE

How did this strategy unfold during 1986? COSATU has encountered a number of challenges in attempting to put into practice alliance politics: strong opposition to alliance politics on the part of a section of COSATU; further debate amongst the larger COSATU affiliates as to the precise content of the general principles outlined by the leadership; the failure to meet the unrealistic deadline of 'one union one industry within six months'; an ongoing search for appropriate forms of organisation for the unemployed; and, finally, meeting the challenge of the State of Emergency and the debate over forms of self-defence that could be effective under the new conditions.

Opposition to alliance politics was to emerge openly in the months following the COSATU launch among a section of the leadership that were critical of COSATU's new political direction. They charged that this new political direction was 'misdirected', and that this 'rush' to espouse 'alliance politics' might result in a situation where years of painstaking work might be swept aside and the working class again be without democratic trade unions.[31] The essence of the argument is that populism and nationalism, which have gained increasing support during the current crisis, stand in absolute contradiction to working class politics.

The organisational styles and political content of each are such, it is argued, that any involvement of the working class in such politics can mean only one thing: the abandonment of trade union independence and with it the abandonment of working class politics. Alliance politics which stresses 'the people' and not the working class is a non-class based politics that fails to prepare the workers for socialism. Unions that become embroiled in populist campaigns will lose their organisational independence, because they will find themselves unable to control such campaigns. Populist organisations, it is argued, are anti-democratic in character because the actions of the 'leaders' are not accountable, as no recognisable membership exists.

The anti-populists are also concerned with what they see as the inability of the unions to control the 'confrontationist' strategy of the populists. The personal attacks by some COSATU leaders on KwaZulu's Buthelezi is cited as an example of the consequences of such a strategy as it has caused problems for unionists in Natal. These practices, it is argued, will 'exhaust' the unions rather than their opponents, as unionists get 'dragged into each and every adventurous action that is initiated'. Critics of alliance politics have seen evidence of such 'adventurous action' in the poor response to COSATU's call for a 'day of action' on 14 July 1986 to protest against the State of Emergency.

Increasingly, the larger unions have been far more interested in giving specific content to the rather general and abstract principles outlined by the COSATU leadership in its early phase, rather than debating whether or not alliances are in the interests of the working class. Such debate now centres on the form such alliances should take, the definition of socialism, and its relationship to national struggle. The Metal and Allied Workers' Union, for example, at its National Congress in July 1986 committed itself to building socialism in South Africa in a struggle spearheaded by the working class. The resolution argued that:

> Worker leaders are increasingly playing a leading role in the community. The lack of initiatives, and the confusion that exists within the community itself on political issues arises from the lack of a working class programme.

The union went on to set itself the task in the coming period, 'of beginning to define what we mean by socialism'.[32]

Similarly, the leadership of NUM at their congress in March 1987 began to give content to their notion of alliance politics by inviting Winnie Mandela, wife of the jailed ANC leader and Honorary President of NUM, Nelson Mandela, and Murphy Morobe, acting Publicity Secretary of the UDF, to speak at the opening of the congress. James Motlatsi, NUM President, spelt out his understanding of the political direction of the union:

> Attempts by the government to impose the tricameral parliament system and community councils have failed totally. Its reform plans have been met with large scale opposition from every part of the country — urban and rural. Today the state's plans lie in ruins. . . . Only a democratic socialist order, which uses the country's resources for the benefit of its people will solve the crisis. . . . We must build firm, disciplined and effective alliances with the democratic organisations.[33]

It is significant that these debates are taking place amongst the larger, industrially-based affiliates of COSATU, for it is here that real power lies. This power consolidated during 1986, when mergers took place in the transport sector (the merger of the Transport and General Workers' Union (TGWU) with GWU to form the new TGWU), the food sector (the FCWU, SFAWU and the Retail and Allied Workers' Union (RAWU) into the Food and Allied Workers' Union (FAWU)), and the absorption of a plastic union in the Western Cape into the Chemical Workers' Industrial Union (CWIU). Although COSATU failed to meet its ambitious deadline, the principle of mergers has now taken hold. A major merger in the metal industry has resulted in the formation of the National Union of Metal Workers of South Africa (NUMSA); the South African Railway and Harbour Workers' Union (SARHWU), which will merge into TGWU, has now been launched (and was recently victorious in its bitter dispute with the South African Transport Services (SATS)), as has the new construction union, the Construction and Allied Workers' Union (CAWU); plans to establish a nation-wide agricultural union are proceeding.

Apart from consolidating power industrially, the crucial issue of the relationship of organised workers with the unemployed remains. While difficult to avoid, it remains a challenge that union movements, in other societies with substantial welfare state provisions, have not had to confront in any concrete organisational sense. At present, the potential for real tension exists between organised and politicised unemployed youth, and unionised workers.

Political oppression has compounded the generational tensions in township households. The attitude of the youth is complex and contradictory: they recognise that their parents are victims of racial oppression and economic exploitation, and therefore empathise with them; but they blame their parents for not fighting against this with sufficient vigour, and therefore feel anger and frustration at what they perceive to be their parents' failings.

> Our parents still have that old image they grew up under. They tell us that the white man, is a white man, and what he says is final. When we try to argue with our parents they will just say, 'What do you know, you were only born yesterday. You have got to listen to what we are telling you.' We are caught in a trap. What our parents don't seem to have is a desire for us to be better peoples. . . . If you bring your parents in and sit them there, and discuss with them, they just fold their arms and say nothing. So now we do everything for ourselves without consulting our parents because it is useless to speak to a stone.

A potentially antagonistic attitude towards the unions exists among some of the youth:

Many unions just ask for wage demands and the reduction of working hours. I know factories where workers just ask for boots and overalls . . . but don't find there's an importance in the struggle. But we are the highly politicized ones. . . . We embrace one cause, we understand what the cause is, and we sacrifice, even our lives, because we understand what is actually happening. But workers, ha! If you only receive those boots and those boots are being torn up again, then you will start boycotting the factory and demanding new boots, because this one is a bit old!

That is why when we call for actions like stayaways they often don't understand the importance of the stayaway. . . . They are often narrow, and just look at the disadvantages of stayaways. They just say, 'If we don't work for a week, we won't get money for that week'. So what they normally do is to take another route and walk through fences and jump those bridges to go to work. . . . If individuals were highly organised and politicised their response would be positive enough. They would be able to sacrifice even for the whole month by staying away from the factories. Liberation would be bought easily. It just depends on how the unions will operate.[34]

The establishment of an *organised* relationship with the unemployed will undoubtedly ease these tensions as the youth come to understand trade unionism at a deeper level. Much will depend on the way that the trade union movement unfolds in the coming years. An alliance has the potential to ease these tensions. Orthodox unionism will reinforce them. From their vantage point of the streets, youth have no stake in any gradual struggle. The longer the struggle, the longer their misery. Tomorrow, they say, the struggle must be won. It is, some have suggested, a form of 'immediatism'. These are the pressures of the township that many trade union leaders have had to contend with.

After the army occupied the townships, protest became increasingly militaristic as large numbers of youth began engaging the security forces in running street battles that claimed hundreds of lives. The militaristic voluntarism of this section of the youth has sometimes eclipsed the organisational concerns of union activists as the townships have become ungovernable. In these cases trade unionists and community activists have found themselves sandwiched between the militarism of the youth and the terror tactics of the security forces. Whereas sections of the youth were criticising them for being too moderate, the security forces were hunting them down and detaining or killing them.

However, COSAS youth who have had organisational experience do recognise the organisational concerns of unions. They recognise the tensions between organisation and mobilisation, as they themselves are confronted with problems arising from what they regard as the undisciplined actions of unorganised, often anti-social elements in the townships. Once an organised relationship is established, the concerns and the perspectives of trade union leadership could be articulated in a constructive manner. Tensions and potential conflicts could be transformed into interlacing and unified struggle. That is why they believe an alliance is necessary.

COSATU has resolved to establish an unemployed workers' union, and the leadership is presently exploring the form that this should take. Unemployed youth are themselves involved in this initiative, which will have a significant bearing on the type of labour movement to emerge in South Africa. Furthermore, COSATU has launched a Living Wage Campaign in which they call for a ban on overtime, a 40 hour week, a sharing of work on full pay and a massive public works programme.

These challenges are being met in the context of the State of Emergency and the onslaught of Inkatha in Natal, and right-wing vigilante terror in other provinces. The second State of Emergency affected COSATU leadership particularly badly. The Labour Monitoring Group's (LMG) December report showed that 614 union leaders, about 80 percent of them with COSATU links, had been arrested in terms of the emergency regulations.[35] More than half were still in detention. Over 2,000 rank-and-file union members suffered the same fate in mass detentions during disputes in the second half of last year.

More disturbing was the murder of two MAWU shop stewards as well as some of their relatives at Mpophomeni near Howick on 5 and 6 of December 1986 by vigilantes reported to be carrying Inkatha flags. The launch of the Inkatha-backed United Workers Union of South Africa (UWUSA) in May 1986, in direct organisational and ideological opposition to COSATU, has further sharpened divisions in factories in certain parts of Natal.

The most effective response to this onslaught is still being debated. Some are reflecting on whether it would not be wiser to return to collective bargaining unionism.

> Workers want real gains. They want to be able to see concrete improvements, in wages, in working conditions and in transport. Before the emergency many were caught up in the idea of liberation. It seemed as though we were on the move at last. Now all of that has changed. We must return to tangible gains. Workers can't be kept going on ideas.[36]

A tactical retreat could be one important effect of the Emergency. In some senses such an option would be prudent — real gains, we argued earlier, have been made by unions in the post-Wiehahn period. Furthermore powerful forces both locally and internationally are encouraging such a direction. One example internationally is the African American Labor Center (AALC) in Washington. In a May 1986 report, recommending the criteria that should be used in selecting which unions to give financial support to, the author makes clear that the AFL-CIO should only support 'business trade unionism and not ideological trade unionism', and that they should be 'careful to avoid any affiliation with the active partisans in the political trade union arena'.[37]

In sharp contrast to this attempt to assert the apolitical tradition of American 'business unionism' is the more creative response of some far-sighted managers who have realised the disruptive effect of political conflict on the delicate industrial relations structures and have tried to mediate in these conflicts in order to absorb them into the collective bargaining structures. This approach takes as its point of departure the inevitability of the 'politicisation' of industrial relations because of the lack of political rights in South Africa. Traditional industrial relations theory, it is argued, needs to be adapted to the peculiar conditions of South Africa where management and employees have sufficient common interest to enter into agreements on certain political issues.[38]

Some companies have already begun to put this approach into practice. The 1986 Anglo American Annual Report notes that:

> Several companies have taken the initiative in mediating directly between the police and local authorities on the one hand, and company employees, on the other hand, in endeavouring to resolve conflicts which have spilled over into the workplace.[39]

The benefits of this kind of institutionalisation are clear, as emerged in a Federated Chamber of Industries (FCI) discussion document:

> . . . by accepting an involvement in problem-solving outside the factory gate, management gains greater certainty in its employee relationships and simultaneously opens up avenues

of common interest in which management and its employees can pursue common goals.[40]

Other managers have embarked on the more conventional path of attempting to pressurise the government into a clearer 'reform' direction. Increasingly alarmed at the spread of radical, even socialist, ideas among workers, the business community has stepped up its pressure on the government to remove some key features of apartheid such as the Group Areas Act. The meeting of prominent businessmen with the African National Congress in late 1985 is an index of both the degree of impatience with the 'pace of reform', and the seriousness with which the business community is now exploring and campaigning for their version of a post-apartheid society.

The most ambitious attempt to date is the Federated Chamber of Industries Business Charter. Conceived of as an alternative to the Freedom Charter, the Business Charter spells out the principles of a free enterprise economy and society. Importantly, this includes a firm commitment to less involvement of the state in welfare, coupled with the extension of privatisation and deregulation. For some, such as Douwes-Dekker of the Wits Business School, the conditions now exist for an open alliance between management and labour in the form of bilateral agreements involving organised labour and organised capital. This, he believes, will provide the base for moving towards a more effective industrial relations system and ultimately a form of corporatism or social democracy.[41]

Not surprisingly, deep scepticism exists among black workers towards any notion of an employer-employee alliance against the apartheid state. The recession has led to a decline in wages in real terms and retrenchment has swelled the ranks of the unemployed, putting the trade union movement onto the defensive. Employers have intensified work through work study programmes. This intensification of struggle on the shop floor makes an alliance between unions and employers unlikely.

A more significant reason why such an alliance is unlikely is that employers are seen by black workers as the chief beneficiaries of the apartheid system as well as its driving force. They are sceptical of employers' attempts to distance themselves from apartheid. They point to the fact that this is not the first time that employers have called for the end of apartheid — in the immediate post-Sharpeville period and after Soweto in 1976, employers called for the removal of certain racial laws, only to adapt to the dominant norms once the unrest had subsided. They do not believe that employers have the will or the capacity to remove the apartheid state.[42]

It is significant that NUM has chosen not to retreat from alliance politics, but rather to begin to spell out what they mean by an alliance. 'Our organisation has taken a political stance because in the five years of its existence it found politics were responsible for our problems', NUM president, James Motlatsi, said at their 1987 congress.[43] This stand is important not only because of NUM's size but also because the mining industry rests on the political foundations of the apartheid system.

CONCLUSION

We have attempted to trace some of the social forces that have come to play a part in shaping the trade union role. In our view, the alliance is still embryonic. Powerful forces are determined to break any attempt to link production politics and state politics in the union's strategic programme. The entire state security apparatus is in a state of mobilisation to try and contain the vigorous movement of resistance that has emerged in the post 1984 period. Managements strive to integrate demands into the industrial relations system. What all these forces have on their side is an objective set of conditions that make orthodox unionism appear to be a more prudent option for union leadership.

But the lack of political rights and the economic recession make such an option difficult to follow in practice unless certain key demands can be met within the foreseeable future. Many of these demands can only be met once a non-racial democracy has been established in South Africa. This is a conclusion that at least some of the businessmen who travelled to Lusaka in 1985 must have come to.

Under the specific conditions of South Africa, a new form of unionism has begun to emerge that is quite different in many respects from the mode of professional and bureaucratic union leadership that characterises industrial relations in industrialised countries. It differs from conventional trade unionism in that it is concerned with labour as a social and political force, not simply as a commodity to be bargained over. As a result its concerns go beyond the workplace to include the sphere of reproduction.

Under these conditions the trade unions, in alliance with students, the youth, the unemployed and community groups, have begun to play a leading role in the struggle for democracy and political rights in society at large. This new form of unionism has the potential to forge an alliance with the popular movement on the basis of equality, and a commitment to defend a working class, socialist programme in a liberated South Africa. By combining links at community level with an engagement in national liberation, these unions have begun to take on the characteristics of social movement unionism.

Structural transformations in the South African economy have created this potential.[44] In summary these are:

1. The establishment of effective structures of collective bargaining through the growth and consolidation of nation-wide mass based industrial trade unions in most sectors of the economy.
2. Accompanying this has been the growth of fully proletarianised working class communities, including large numbers of militant students and unemployed youth without adequate social infrastructure.
3. The intervention of the state — particularly since 1984 and intensified since the State of Emergency — into a range of areas of social life, combined with the lack of political incorporation of the black population, has ensured that localised grievances are soon translated into confrontation with the state. This also, of course, ensures the persistence of the national tradition.

As in Poland with the Solidarity union movement, these unions are now taking up the concerns of working people as a whole, and posing new horizons for trade union work. In this they are responding to the needs of working people as a whole. Unlike Solidarity, the South African union movement has a greater chance of success because of the relative strength and durability of the shop floor structures that have been established in the workplaces.

When faced, for example, by a direct state attack on its leadership, as happened during the State of Emergency, some of these unions were able to win significant concessions, such as time off for shop-stewards to run the union offices when certain leaders were detained. This innovative use of collective bargaining structures in the face of political repression has the potential to succeed in the long term, *if* it is able to retain the gains made on the shop-floor in the post-Wiehahn period, and *if* present debates and initiatives towards other social groups shift into the realm of structured relationships.

This is the promise of the new union movement in South Africa — and the challenge it poses to managers trained in traditional industrial relations theory and practice, as well as to those in the national movement who see trade unions simply as the transmission belt in a future centrally planned economy.

NOTES

1. The extent to which rank-and-file members share the perception of politics that is being developed by the leadership is a question that can only be answered by further research. In spite of this limitation in our paper, we believe that a focus on leadership is important. As Hobsbawm has suggested, the less developed the country and its labour movement, the more likely that 'charismatic' leaders and intellectuals will play a leading role. E. Hobsbawm, 'Intellectuals and the labour movement', *Marxism Today*, July 1979.
2. R.Hyman, *Marxism and the Sociology of Trade Unionism* (London: Pluto Press, 1971).
3. The idea of a new form of unionism — social movement unionism — has been developed in the context of semi-industrialised authoritarian countries such as Brazil, the Philippines, Poland and South Africa. A recent book has attempted to define the concept: 'To speak of a "labour movement" implies a certain level of economic, political and social cohesion, conditions which are increasingly rare in the metropolitan countries. However, trade unions in the Third World are increasingly reaching out to those sectors outside the formal proletariat and developing forms of social movement unionism. The new social movements include church rank and file organisations, neighbourhood committees, women's movements, and others traditionally seen as outside the labour movement. Under the rubric of social movement unionism we should also include those trade unions who turn to political answers for their members' problems. This need not entail a subordination of labour organisations to the nationalist movement but does entail the adoption of national-level political responses.' R. Munck, *Third World Workers and the New International Labour Studies* (London: Zed Press, 1987) pp232-3. The term 'political unionism' captures the SACTU period better than it does the contemporary period, where changes in the social structure have created a different alliance. Furthermore the term does not capture the complexity of political debate in the 1980s. We have used the concepts interchangeably in this paper, as we do not feel either term adequately captures the combination of community linkages and engagement in nation liberation.
4. The question of accountability is a complex one. Populist unions often act as if they have a clear mandate, since they assume their members agree on a political programme. This is seldom the case in a trade union.
5. Political unionism is the central focus of Lambert's Ph.D thesis on SACTU, 'Political unionism in South Africa: an analysis of the South African Congress of Trade Unions'.
6. See, for example, E.Feit, *Workers Without Weapons — SACTU and the Organisation*

of African Workers (New York: Anchor Books, 1978) and Steve Friedman, *Building Tomorrow Today* (Johannesburg: Ravan Press, 1987).

7. *Report of the Commission of Inquiry into the Regulation of Monopolistic Conditions Act,* 1955. RP 64/1977.

8. D. Hemson, 'Trade unions and the struggle for liberation', *Capital and Class,* No.6, 1976.

9. Michaela von Freyhold, 'Labour movements or popular struggles in Africa', paper presented to the *Review of African Political Economy* conference on Popular Struggles in Africa, University of Liverpool, September 1986.

10. See separate paper by E. Webster at the conference mentioned above.

11. J. Lewis and E. Randall, 'Trade union survey', *South African Labour Bulletin (SALB)*, Vol.11, No.2, 1985.

12. These collective bargaining gains are discussed in detail in the Labour section, *South African Review IV* (Johannesburg: Ravan Press, 1987).

13. W. Cobbett, ' "Orderly urbanisation": continuity and change in influx control', *SALB,* Vol.11, No.8, 1986.

14. Quoted in J Maller, 'Wage bargaining in South Africa', *South African Review IV* (Johannesburg: Ravan Press, 1987).

15. This point has been developed in a recent book by Fox: 'The nineteenth century had therefore seen a pattern developing whereby a capacity for strong horizontal, though only sectional, cohesion among organised labour on industrial issues at the workplace coexisted with the possibility of strong vertical cohesion with sections of the higher classes on political issues. Only a small and politically uninfluential minority were ever to want to see economic class conflict at the workplace translated into revolutionary political class conflict beyond it.' A. Fox, *History and Heritage. The Social Origins of the British Industrial Relations System* (London: Allen and Unwin, 1985) p.435.

16. E.M. Wood, 'The separation of the economic and the political in capitalism', *New Left Review,* No.127.

17. This section is based on joint work done during 1985 and 1986 by members of the Labour Monitoring Group at the University of the Witwatersrand, in particular Stephen Gelb, Jon Lewis and Mark Swilling.

18. Food and Canning Workers' Union, 'Search for a workable relationship', *SALB,* Vol.7 No.8, 1982.

19. A. Sitas, 'Moral formations and struggles amongst African metal workers on the East Rand', *Labour, Capital and Society,* Vol.18, No. 2, 1985.

20. M. Swilling, 'The East London bus boycott, 1983', *SALB,* Vol.9, No.6, 1984.

21. The growth of shop steward councils led to two further innovations; the establishment of shop steward committees uniting representatives from different companies and the establishment of shop steward councils for a particular sub-sector such as foundries. The intention behind these innovations was to steer shop steward organisation into collective bargaining structures. For a discussion of these issues see M. Swilling, 'The politics of working class struggles in Germiston, 1979-1983', paper presented to the History Workshop Conference, University of the Witwatersrand, 1984.

22. M. Swilling, 'Workers divided: a critical assessment of the split in MAWU on the East Rand', *SALB,* Vol.10, No.1, 1984.

23. Interview, SFAWU shop steward, and NEC member, October 1985.

24. *Ibid.*

25. Informal discussion, May 1985.

26. Labour Monitoring Group, 'The March stay-aways in Port Elizabeth and Uitenhage', *SALB,* Vol.11, No.1, 1985.

27. Joint ANC-SACTU-COSATU statement. *SALB,* Vol.11, No.5, 1986.

28. Sweet, Food and Allied Workers' Union Discussion Paper, August 1985. We would like to thank those involved in writing this paper for allowing us to quote from it. The quotations that follow are all taken from this document.

29. An example of the convergence of workplace and community struggles is the April 1987 railway strike over recognition and dismissals, and the Soweto stay-away called over rent evictions.

30. COSATU General Secretary, Jay Naidoo, 'Building people's power: a working class perspective', paper delivered at the Grass Roots Conference, 5th May 1986. The quotations that follow are from this speech.

31. We have constructed this critique from a number of different sources inside COSATU. The authors prefer to remain anonymous.

32. *South African Metal Worker*, Vol.1, No.4, 1986.

33. M.Siluma, 'The birth of a new force for change', *Sunday Star*, 1 March 1987.

34. These extracts are from a national workshop on youth unemployment organised by the Community and Labour Research Group, University of Natal, Durban. Moses Ngoasheng, Rob Lambert and Ari Sitas were involved in organising the workshop from 2—6 June 1986.

35. *Labour Monitoring Group Report on the Effect of the State of Emergency on Industrial Relations*, 29 December 1986.

36. Discussion with the National Organiser of a large COSATU affiliate, 27 February 1987.

37. Evaluation of the African American Labor Center Project in the Republic of South Africa, 12 May 1986.

38. This construction of the argument has been drawn from a number of discussions with a group of managers who would prefer to remain anonymous.

39. *Anglo American Corporation Annual Report*, 1986.

40. 'Managing Political Uncertainty', unpublished seminar given at an Institute of Industrial Relations Seminar, Johannesburg, July 1986.

41. L. Douwes-Dekker, 'Industrial relations in South Africa', unpublished paper delivered at the International Industrial Relations Association 7th World Congress, September 1986, Hamburg, West Germany.

42. See D. Lewis, 'Capital, trade unions and the national liberation struggle', *SALB* Vol.11, No.4, 1986.

43. M. Siluma, *op cit.*

44. These points emerged in discussion with three of our colleagues in the Labour Monitoring Group, Stephen Gelb, Jon Lewis and Mark Swilling. Of course we are responsible for the interpretation given in this paper.

2. Lessons from the Sarmcol Strike

DEBBIE BONNIN AND ARI SITAS

INTRODUCTION

On 13 December 1986 the people of Mpophomeni, together with the striking Sarmcol workers, the Natal Midlands' youth organisations and metalworkers from further afield, were denied the right to freely bury their dead. Phineas Sibiya — chairperson of the Sarmcol shop stewards, regional MAWU worker leader and leader of the local cooperative movement; Simon Ngubane — shop steward and soul of the cooperatives' cultural workers, himself a leading performer in the Sarmcol play; Alpheus Nkabinde, youth activist; and Florence Mnikathi — young Health Committee activist and the daughter of a Sarmcol worker, were assassinated on the evening of the 5th by Inkatha-led vigilantes. They were abducted, taken to a deserted place by a river, and executed. In the early hours of the following morning, during another attack on the township, a youth was also killed.[1]

The state effectively took control of the funeral, enforcing strict rules and regulations on the thousands of mourners in Natal. The second State of Emergency's draconian measures were used to their full: only 600 out of the 15,000 local people were allowed into the hall. Twenty-two buses, transporting workers and youth from Pietermaritzburg, Durban and Newcastle were turned back; private cars were chased away from the entrance to the township. Armed vehicles surrounded the graves and the hall, while no political comment was permitted. Finally, there were to be separate funerals for the four dead. The people of Mpophomeni mourned their dead inside a ring of steel and potential fire.

By 1984, political funerals in South Africa had become explosive demonstrations of the majority's will to continue its struggle against apartheid, and had assumed the function of powerful rituals and spectacles of symbolic resistance to white domination.[2]

Within this general insurrectionary climate black workers had also had more than their share of deaths and militant retorts: 'Comrade', incanted Nise Malange, the union poet, over the death of another worker leader,

I did not come here to open up a wound/ or mourn . . . I am here to challenge the minister of law and order/ and, I am here to say: '*qinani basebenzi lomthwalo umzima*'.[3]

And in another poem she added:

those who died in the struggle of the people/are here . . . holding our hands/ just that touch/ moving through our bodies/ like a bloodstream.[4]

Death, and its transcendence through struggle, has animated the sinews of

42

popular and class protest. Nevertheless, the state's tight control of the Sarmcol funeral contained the overt political outbursts though it could barely conceal the anger, the grief and the tears: Maxwell Xulu, MAWU's President, rose up to speak in front of Sibiya's coffin and choked over his anger and frustration and burst into uncontrollable tears; Malange rose up to translate and choked likewise . . . the entire leadership of MAWU Natal was grieving inside the ring of steel constructed by the state.

Sarmcol's leadership, and especially Lawrence Zondi, the leader who traversed at least two generations of resistance — the area's *imbongi* — was quietly grieving. For him and the other Sarmcol workers the dead were not abstract leaders, but people with whom they had shared both the daily struggle of the strike, and the worries and triumphs over starvation in the area.

In a clean sweep the assassins had eliminated some of the central activists of the present two-year-old struggle at Howick. They had selected people directly involved in the cooperatives, Ngubane from the Cultural Project, Minikathi from the Health Project, and, in Sibiya, the grassroots brain of the Sarmcol workers' struggle. But most distressing for the majority was the fact that the attack on Mpophomeni was a regional affront: Sarmcol workers had come to represent, and their leaders to embody, a unique model of worker resistance in Natal.

Our task in this chapter is to unravel a few of the features of this model tradition of resistance. For two years (at the time of writing) the Sarmcol workers have been involved in one of the most important struggles in the South African labour situation. This struggle by close to a thousand workers, assisted by their communities, the unions and the political organisations in the Natal Midlands, is already the lengthiest dispute in South African labour history.

However, over and above that we would like to argue that this struggle throws new light on the following three areas: the politics of the working class in South Africa; the novel way in which alliances were created for and around the Sarmcol workers' struggles; and the birth of new democratic institutions out of the crisis in the area.

In order to grasp the full significance of these struggles it is necessary to outline both the historical and contemporary features that characterise this labour force. By etching out this background it will become evident how tradition, experience and organisation combine in these people's lives to create the tremors that have been felt in the region since 30 April 1985, when they decided to down tools for the recognition of their trade union.

THE WORKFORCE

On any visit to Howick and its environs it could be that you would stumble into a black man and stop to inquire about his life. This would have been a typical reply:

> I am somewhere between 51 and 60 years of age. At present I live at Mpophomeni, the black township 15 kms outside Howick.
>
> However I was not born in that township. My ancestors were born on the land, in a place where they could plough and keep cattle. . . . And I was born on the land which had always belonged to my ancestors and their chiefs. But by the time I was born, our land had been taken over by the white farmers and our chief was pushed to Impendle. Look around at this countryside: Howick, Cedara, Merrivale — all green and fertile. It all belonged to Nxamalala

and his people. But now our chief is in Impendle — a place of hills, rocks and the great wind — Inkanyamba. . . .

. . . After that, the white farmers kicked us off the land and we came to live near Howick, just next to the dam at a place called Zenzele. I went to the factory where my father, my brothers and my neighbours had worked. But we were not to stay at Zenzele.

Soon we were moved again by the government to Mpophomeni. . . . In Mpophomeni, I live here with my wife and my four children. My family attends the Roman Catholic Church, and my children go to school here. I have six other people dependent on my wage. I am fortunate because all seven of us stay in a four-room house, because most of my neighbours are up to ten people per house.

. . . My first job was at Sarmcol. I started there sometime after sixteen years old but definitely under twenty. All my life I have worked for only this firm. I have been working for Sarmcol for more than thirty years. . . . Working at Sarmcol has not been easy. The conditions were hard, the wages were low. . . . And recently there has been the fear of retrenchment. But now we are fighting for our dignity — we are strikers. . . .[5]

This story is typical of most strikers — it is, after all, a computer construct from 172 interviews with Sarmcol workers, and thus represents the 'average worker' there. However let us examine this 'construct' in more detail.

The workforce is relatively old, with sixty percent of the strikers being older than 40. As such they are predominantly married men — 78.5 percent, with large families — 81.6 percent of the strikers support between three and nine people. If this is broken down further, 70 percent of them support families of between six and fifteen people. 84.3 percent are the sole breadwinners. In the remaining 15.7 percent of the cases, it is in 42 percent of the cases the daughter, and in 26 percent the wife, who is in employment. These women find employment in domestic service at Howick. Most of the young men, in short, are unemployed. Finally, 67 percent of the strikers have an educational level of up to Standard 4, with 23 percent having no education at all. The single most important residential area is Mpophomeni (39.5 percent) with the rest living in surrounding peri-urban areas.[6]

Sarmcol's labour market was drawn from the surrounding magisterial district of Lions River, as well as some of the reserve areas such as Impendle and Bergville. Seventy-three percent of present-day Sarmcol workers were born into the families of labour tenants — a system whereby in return for access to land (both for ploughing and grazing) and a place to stay, the household head would provide labour to the farmer for six months — the other six months was worked at Sarmcol. Due to the increasing demand from industrial capital and the agricultural sector for a permanent labour force, the state tightened control over labour tenancy until it was eventually abolished in the late 1960s. Consequently, the former labour tenants became full-time industrial wage labourers at Sarmcol.[7]

The 'white' town of Howick and Mpophomeni — the township that was erected in 1969 to minister to its needs — form a little industrial island in the Midlands surrounded by an enormous agrarian sea. Before the construction of Mpophomeni, Sarmcol workers lived in Howick's developing shack areas — Hohabe, George and Zenzele. These were vibrant areas, common to many of South Africa's cities during the 1950s — places of mud, politics, beer, music, police raids and crime.[8]

During the 1960s the state, displeased with such urban concentrations of black people, attempted to impose stricter controls over them. From then on destruction flowed out of a series of state decrees, each remarkable in its sinister nature — group areas, homelands, removal of black spots and removals due to new plans for agrarian expansion.[9] Howick did not escape the legislators' pen. In 1966 the town was proclaimed a white group area, leading to the removal of the African residents of George and placing the Indians and coloureds under threat, until a group area was proclaimed for them in 1979.

Zenzele was affected by 'urban relocation' legislation (1967) which provided for the deproclamation of African townships which fell within urban areas, and for the removal of residents to townships which were to be built in the bantustans. The residents of these areas were moved to Mpophomeni, some 15 kilometres from Howick, located within the KwaZulu bantustan and specifically built for the purpose.[10] Many of the workers experienced up to three physical relocations in their lifetimes, and all of them at least one. Yet, over and above such histories they shared another experience: working for Sarmcol.

WORKING FOR SARMCOL

Industrial demand and apartheid policy begat Mpophomeni; before long it became Sarmcol's labour pool, and in a short span of time its labour dumping ground. Sarmcol was essentially a jobbing factory, and its labour force consequently fluctuated in size depending on the demand for its goods. Workers were hired for a few months, fired once the order had been completed, only to be re-hired when production increased.[11]

Yet it is possible over the last decade to notice the rationalisation of its labour processes, which has led to a substantial overall reduction in the labour force from an average of 4,500 in the early 1970s to a mere 1,300 by the time of the strike, to fewer than 1,000 after the employment of scab labour.[12] Given the general state of recession in the economy, as well as the lack of employment opportunities in the Howick region, this has resulted in an increasing level of unemployment in Mpophomeni.[13] Sarmcol can effect the demise of the community with the same bravado it employed in its creation.

The owner of Sarmcol, British Tyre and Rubber (BTR), is one of the largest multinational corporations in the UK, and among the 10 largest multinationals in Europe. Its holdings include firms like Cornhill Insurance, Pretty Polly Tights, Dunlop Holdings, Pan Books and Heinemann (the latter until 1986). It has therefore ironically been the publisher of some of the most progressive authors of this century, e.g. Gabriel Garcia Marquez, Vargas Llosa, Canetti, Ngugi wa Thiong'o, Wole Soyinka, Sembene Ousmane, Salman Rushdie and so on. It has investments in most Commonwealth countries, the USA and South Africa.[14]

The Sarmcol factory started up at Howick in 1919. After an initial attempt to establish themselves on the Witwatersrand, its founders made contact with Spencer Moulton & Co, who agreed to invest money in Sarmcol. Soon after the influx of British money, Sarmcol decided to move to Howick, due to its 'natural' attractions:

> . . . the prospect of generating current from the waterfall, combined with the availability of cheap land and plentiful labour, black and Asian, had turned the attention of Sarmcol to Howick.[15]

Sarmcol initially manufactured hoses, belts, rubber and asbestos, packing and trimming. Later there was a brief incursion into tyre manufacturing. It was essentially a jobbing factory: manufacturing mainly rubber products according to orders received, with little specialisation or standardisation occurring for some time. However, the first changes to affect the labour process began in the early 1930s when Sarmcol started to investigate time and motion studies, which resulted in the reorganisation of the factory. By 1936 Sarmcol employed some 450 people, starting a gradual process towards greater mechanisation and, by the 1980s, semi-automation.[16]

This forward march, through fifty years of development, left a distinctive trail of hardship in the memory of its workers.[17] Given that most of them have been long-service employees, it is possible to turn to some of their memories for its reconstruction. We can trace this experience back to 1932 when work was both physical and crude in nature:

> It was very difficult work. At that time all the heavy jobs, like carrying heavy pipes, wrapping them with canvas, and all of it was done by hand. It was very heavy at that time. If the pipes come out of the pots, you strip it off and it was so hot we used to burn our fingers because when the pipe gets cold you couldn't take the canvas off.

Sarmcol began to introduce new machinery and, after a period of dramatic expansion during and after the Second World War, its workforce exceeded 1,000 by 1951. For many this meant new jobs and thus employment; yet, for workers entering the industry for the first time, satisfaction at getting employment was sooner or later harshly tempered:

> At first when I was employed at Sarmcol I thought, hey, I was just a lucky man, now I'll earn a lot of money. Only to find out. I was given a certain machine to operate, that machine was cutting small rings in different sizes and there were drums that I was compelled to fill. At that time the foreman of the department was Mr Masisang and we used to sweat like hell getting those drums full. Again we were told if we don't fill those drums we are out.

Sarmcol's expansion stabilised for only a brief period in the 1950s. By the late 1950s a new phase of expansion was under way. A number of new departments were initiated owing to new demands, while others were amalgamated and reorganised. Despite the company's expansion and growth in employment, its labour processes did not change much:

> At the time the job was still very hard/difficult because most of the job was held by hand unlike today when there are chains. Some of the jobs are pulled by chains.

As Sarmcol stood at its peak in employment in the early 1970s, a new wave of growth and rationalisation was introduced. Workers found that while the pace of work did not change, the work was becoming easier through sophisticated mechanisation. They started to experience the reality of semi-automation and the beginnings of mass lay-offs. Workers were daily discovering the sting in the tail of automation. The work process had become progressively easier, but fewer workers were needed. Lay-offs started. Management claimed that retrenchment was the result of the economic recession.

While the recession most probably did play a role, the implications of automation cannot be underplayed:

> [They] say no work. In new mixing a new machine was introduced, a lot of people were retrenched. In moulding 5 people were retrenched and those people who were left there were

given more jobs of those who were retrenched. You were doing 4 or 5 peoples' job but you were alone.

The retrenchment of workers, so radical in numbers in such a short period of time, achieved two things: firstly, it halved the labour force and, secondly, it angered, alienated and frustrated worker feelings about the working environment. Their frustrations were compounded by the arbitrary nature of these lay-offs. They felt that managements 'selection' of people to be retrenched was based on middle management's personal likes and dislikes. In the process of halving Sarmcol's workforce nobody knew who would be next.

One worker described the process:

> [It was] the time before the union come in, just come with a list, the manager, and just point 10 or 20 people. All out. Everyone was afraid of that, doesn't know what will happen to him. Some of the workers, scabs now, we were fighting for them because they not supposed to be retrenched — they got 30, 35 years service.

Workers with long service records were put on early retirement. But even this turned sour with Sarmcol claiming that they were not due for their pension; rather, they were supposed to be grateful for the monthly payments the company was prepared to make (in some cases as low as R4.60 but never higher then R35). Finally, it was the issue of retrenchment which enabled the union to sign up the majority of Sarmcol workers and it was also the issue of retrenchment which was one of the major contributing triggers of the strike. This will be examined below.

To understand the full extent of bitterness, harboured by Sarmcol workers until they dared a major confrontation, it is important to note the harshness of managerial authority on the shop floor. Workers' grievances exceeded the statements of heavy manual work, but focussed on the arbitrary powers of management and the lack of correct grievance and discipline procedures.

> . . . [if you have a complaint] you don't worry because they say you are talking too much, out.

> . . . so the foreman who's running that department he's got the full power to do what he wants providing he tells the labour department, 'That certain member we giving him notice', or, 'We transferring him because of these reasons'. As long as the foreman says that, there is no other person who can say anything.

> . . . like punishment. Say you are late from tea, they say now you are going to change from the machine you are on and put to a hard place, that place is just known when you have to punish people you just put them there. That place is a low grade and so on. So those things were abolished [when the union came]. It was confinement. Just like confinement where you punish people. So we remember an incident of how punishment was done. There were just boots — gumboots put aside. When you have done something wrong. You don't know who last wore those. You are told, take these boots put them on, you are given a wheel-barrow and load the rubber on it and now you deliver the rubber from where it has been manufactured to dispatch or where it has been kept, with a wheelbarrow.

Workers' grievances abound in all the interviews conducted so far: arbitrary discipline and punishment, lack of health and safety measures, lay-offs, bad canteen facilities, low wages, no time to shower after work, callous treatment and racism. And as their historical experience had shown, the only way to overcome these was through union organisation. It is to this experience, which management saw as the work of small bands of 'agitators', that we shall now turn.

THE WORKERS ORGANISE

The Sarmcol strikers have two experiences of worker organisation: one is the present MAWU, and the other is in the past, 'Gwala's union'.[18] However for many workers these two experiences are conflated. Dates are meaningless as the past and the present merge into one experience of unionisation and struggle. Nevertheless, their organising style was different: Gwala organised the factory relying less on the shop steward structures but more on his charismatic leadership qualities.

Of course, there are overlaps between the two as well. According to older workers, Gwala returned to organise in 1972 after a sojourn on Robben Island, which in popular memory signifies the beginnings of MAWU organisation. Organisation began around the General Factory Workers Benefit Fund, with the Natal University-based Wages Commission offering workers assistance. The massive strike wave in 1973 was the turning point in the re-emergence of progressive trade unions in South Africa, with MAWU being the first to emerge.

According to older workers Gwala's presence at Howick goes back to the 1940s, unionisation only takes off on a sound basis in the 1950s. According to a retired old worker in the area, in those days,

> the union and Harry Gwala used to call the meeting openly in front of the police. He couldn't care a damn about the police.

Membership increased and with the formation of SACTU the Sarmcol workers were linked with broader national demands and struggles. Yet they did not lose sight of issues which affected them directly. On the one hand they participated in the national stay-aways of the late 1950s, boycotted potatoes and burnt their passes. On the other, they continued to build their organisation and win demands inside the factory. Old workers interviewed insist that they won the SACTU demand for one pound a day during the late 1950s.

By the end of the 1950s all workers in the factory were supplied with overalls by the company; prior to this they were working in their own clothes. Better facilities for the hostel dwellers were also on the agenda. In many cases the workers linked the broader demands of SACTU to their own workplace issues: for example, not only did they stay away from work to demand one pound a day but they also demanded that the company provide firewood for the hostel inmates. The Natal Midlands therefore witnessed the merging of broader political campaigns with local worker issues.

However, with the banning of the ANC and the subsequent arrest of Gwala, organisation in the factory could not survive:

> At that time things became difficult again after Gwala was arrested. There came another organiser after Gwala was arrested, by the surname of Gumede. He tried to organise and he was also arrested. Came another third chap who tried to organise by the surname of Bengu he was also arrested. Came a fourth chap by the surname of Ndlovu, he was also arrested. People started to drop again. . . .

> So the organisation continued for a few months and then we find that it was dropping, there was no leader. People are not clear as we are today, or else we would have put in another leader to instruct.

With the state clampdown, the organisation of the 1950s faded into the distance of time. It was something the workers remembered during the hard times of the 1960s when Sarmcol pushed back the frontier of struggle, and the work process inside the factory became harsher and more regimented. But the stories of Gwala's union were not forgotten — new workers learnt about those times from their fathers and brothers, but also from the *imbongi* of Sarmcol, Lawrence Zondi.[19] Gwala left behind one important message to the workers he had organised — unity. Only by uniting and standing together could workers achieve their demands — this was also the message that the new workers had learnt.

Organisation of the workers began again in the 1970s. As some remarked later, it was none too soon: 'it was a long time that things are upside down'. The birthplace of the Metal and Allied Workers' Union was Pietermaritzburg, 1973. Howick is 20 kilometres away; one of their first tasks was to organise the Sarmcol workers. A worker described the first years of organisation:

> During MAWU days I used to see University girls there around the gate during 1972. . . . I used to see the university girls coming giving pamphlets to us. And police coming, looking at the pamphlets. They just used to give pamphlets to us, that's all.
>
> . . . Those pamphlets used to say we must unite and be one. So once we are united, all our meetings will be organised by MAWU. We must join MAWU. And the bosses will take hearing if we are united and have a meeting. . . . From them I joined MAWU, right up till now. . . . I remembered Harry Gwala's words, that's why I joined MAWU. Harry Gwala used to tell us 'there will be people coming to talk for us, to the management', so I decided to join MAWU.

The task of organising the union in the factory was not an easy one. Union organisers and members faced continual police harassment and the threat of arrest. Management had set up a liaison committee and were only prepared to communicate with workers through their liaison committee representative. Union organiser Moses Ndlovu was banned. Again the Sarmcol workers were left leaderless, only hearing the rumours that once more their organiser was jailed. Workers found the liaison committee ineffective; it did not represent them, neither could it force the management to accept the workers' demands:

> . . . the liaison committee didn't do anything for the workers . . . the workers have good hope because there were some members of the union on the liaison committee but nothing came of that.

The workers noticed that conditions inside the factory had improved since the union had begun organising. They were not prepared to go back to the times of the 1960s. They would not give up on their union. Key individuals continued to organise the workers. A shop steward explained that in the task of organising, management became the union's hidden ally.

> Mostly what makes the people join the union is bad management inside the factory. See the people who've got 30 years, 35 years, sick people, injured people coming from hospital when he comes back he's gone. He's join the union.

After a short spurt of success following its formation in 1973, MAWU faced a static period as they were dogged by state intervention — the bannings of many activists in 1974 and 1976 — and employer intransigence — works and liaison committees were set up in an attempt to stunt the growth of the embryonic union movement. MAWU experienced renewed and sustained growth from the late 1970s, and the Sarmcol plant became the focus of serious union attention from early 1979. By that time retrenchments had taken their toll, and the campaigns over bus fares and township rents were under way. In 1981, a mass relocation of people occurred from Zenzele. Consequently the Mpophomeni population trebled in size to 15,000.

Despite this rapid state-engineered growth, the township remained desperately neglected: homes were not fenced, roads untarred, no street drainage was introduced; there was to be only one tap for every four houses and an inefficient bucket system for sewage disposal. On top of this was the fact that the rents demanded were higher than the residents had being paying in Zenzele.

Workers responded by arguing that they did not choose their accommodation, they were dumped there by the government. Not only were the rents higher but they were also continuing to rise; in response to this and the failure of the authorities to meet with the residents to discuss the issue, a rent boycott was initiated, which continues to date. The reality is, with the mass unemployment in the area and then the strike, people could quite simply not afford to pay the rent. Simultaneously, a bus boycott was under way resisting fare hikes.[20]

Furthermore, MAWU was at the same time experiencing a vibrant renewal and phenomenal growth nationwide.[21] Committed as it was to strong grassroots shop-steward organisation, to workers' control of the union and a militant approach to the gaining of workers' rights, it was able to infuse the simmering discontent with both structure and direction. In short, after a decade of unionisation drives MAWU began to get a serious foothold in the factory.

When Sarmcol refused to acknowledge this, the union proceeded against them in the Industrial Court, alleging that the company had committed an unfair labour practice in laying off workers without negotiation, notice or compensation. In an out of court settlement in 1983, Sarmcol granted the union stop-order facilities and limited access. Within a month, 90 percent of the workers were MAWU members.

> When they came to know that it was going to be given the right to come in, the guy who is in personnel said, 'Men, the union has a right to come in, the government has allowed it, I will make an election'. He said we make boxes. Those who elect the union make a cross here. Those who don't want the union, here. Many elect the union and little that don't want it. Many crosses elected the union. The factory allowed and Makatini came.

But, two years later, no union recognition agreement satisfactory to the workers was forthcoming. Then came the strike.[22]

BACKGROUND TO THE STRIKE

The primary cause of the strike was the failure of MAWU and BTR Sarmcol to conclude a full recognition agreement. After two years and more than twenty discussions between MAWU and BTR management, no accord was reached and no recognition agreement was forthcoming — too many issues remained unresolved. Central to the dispute and discord was, predictably, the issue of retrenchments. Management refused to accept the union's proposals over the 'Last In — First Out' (LIFO) principle, severance pay and an adequate period of notice. Furthermore, the union and management were at loggerheads over another two areas: the company would not accept restrictions on the summary dismissal of workers involved in legal strikes, neither would it accept compulsory arbitration in disputes over individual workers' rights. The retrenchment issue was very important given the extent of reorganisation taking place at that and at the previous stages.

The workers were adamant that they would not accept any recognition agreement that did not allow their union a right to protect them against management's arbitrary authority:

> I wanted my rights at work. So I was fighting also to get my service pay when retrenched or out of Sarmcol so as to show my children this is all my power, this is where I got so much, from where I work. Because it's somehow an insult to me. Other factories they do come, where we live, they do come with some money after being retrenched. My wife will say to me that I have misused money while I was in town, it means I was involved with other wives. So it makes division now in the family. I don't want to come to the point where my children will insult me or kick me out, saying, 'You have been working at Sarmcol and what have you gained at that time having three legs?' That's why I have to fight while I'm still alive for my power.

Finally, in February 1985, the union held a strike ballot. With the exception of four ballot papers all voted in favour of the strike. The strike started on April 30 and by May 3 all the workers were dismissed. One of the workers described what happened:

> They say they will sign the next day, then that day won't come, then they will sign the next day and then on and on and on until today. It came the time when we decided to strike. We stayed there not working from Tuesday morning, Wednesday, Thursday, Friday. Friday morning came letters here saying from now work is finished. Must come and fetch your money. I do not know the exact date. May 1st was Wednesday. They said we that stay in compound must from the 10th be out of this compound. We didn't go to grab our money. Going out to write if you want to be re-employed. We gave those letters to shop stewards. They went to see the lawyer of the union. They said we must go fetch it, if it is more than what we are earning we mustn't take it. We must take our weekly wage only. We did go Wednesday they give us our weekly wage and say it's finished with us as far as wages are concerned. But in the compound we just stay as we were till now.

The union and the worker leadership were faced with an immediate crisis: what were they to do now that they had lost their traditional power base? How were they to carry the struggle forward and demand reinstatement? A major problem was the refusal of the company to reinstate the workers *en masse* — in this they were following the advice given to them by industrial relations consultants, Andrew Levy and Associates.

Six weeks before the strike, Sarmcol executives met a member of the consultancy who advised the company to sack the entire workforce for striking, then selectively rehire the workers they wanted, being careful to exclude the shop stewards. According to the consultancy, Sarmcol was warned to expect some international reaction to the dismissals, although little leverage on the company was to be expected.[23]

Given the importance of Sarmcol in the life of Mpophomeni, it was only natural that the Sarmcol strikers would turn to their community for support. With the already high rates of unemployment from prior lay-offs in the area, the firing of the Sarmcol workers could not help but become a volatile community issue. Before long, community meetings were being held in Mpophomeni and Howick West. After the strikers explained their plight, the community agreed to support them. It was decided upon a boycott of white shops in the Howick area, in order to force the shopkeepers to put pressure on Sarmcol to negotiate with the strikers. This boycott was also a result of rising discontent over the complicity white shopkeepers showed in Sarmcol's plans to resist a prior canteen boycott.[24]

Furthermore, realising that this was to be a protracted conflict which would stretch both the workers and their communities far beyond their means of survival, support groups in Pietermaritzburg and Durban were soon formed. They were comprised of sympathetic individuals and groups answerable to the union and the shop stewards. These groups were to function as fund-raisers and also as helpers to convene meetings with community organisations; in Pietermaritzburg the support group undertook the bulk buying of food; in Mpophomeni a clinic, assisted by a doctor, was set up on a weekly basis. These support groups were thus supplementary to union organisation, an attempt to bolster the limited union resources already strained by the magnitude of the strike, its unknown duration and its distance from union offices.

As a trade unionist asserted:

> meetings with organisations of the people started in early June. There were many organisations in Durban like the Indian Congress and their community organisation, like the church people from the centre (Ecumenical Centre) in town, like the doctors (NAMDA) and the university students black and white, like COSAS and the Sash and also the people who look after detainees and so on. This was a very representative grouping for Durban and it helped in support and publicity. Before long Sarmcol shop stewards were addressing people far and wide on their plight to get back their jobs.

Furthermore, a slide and tape show was prepared which was used extensively to educate people on the Sarmcol workers' struggles.[25]

The workers themselves continued with their drives towards publicising their predicament. For example, 60 workers from Sarmcol went to Johannesburg to picket BTR's head office and to hold a press conference. The police got to hear of the planned action and trailed the workers, making the picket impossible. However, the press conference was held. The frustration of the workers at what happened in Johannesburg contributed to the escalation of tension during the weekend.

The workers arrived back from Johannesburg, accompanied by Natal branch members who had attended MAWU's AGM in Johannesburg, in the early hours of Sunday 23 June. As one of the participants remembered:

> We came back hot and ready to support our brothers. We sung and marched getting the community together and waking them up to the real issues. Many people gathered to discuss the events and the feeling of it all was great.

Shop stewards estimated a crowd of 2,500 in the general assembly outside the community hall. Once again, the community pledged its solidarity to the strikers' cause; social pressure on scabs was agreed upon, and a decision was taken to continue with the boycott of white shops. As the people were returning home, clashes ensued with the police who had been present in the township since daybreak. Police claimed that they were stoned by rampaging crowds and only teargassed the crowd after warnings to disperse were not heeded. Witnesses said that the crowd became angry when police attempted to arrest a youth. Trade unionists and local clergy accused the police of provoking the conflict, which resulted in injury to four policemen.

As the Labour Monitoring Group (LMG) noted, the next evening, Monday

24 June, a crowd stopped a bus, belonging to the Impendle service which was carrying workers, stoned it and killed two workers, one of them employed by Sarmcol. Several homes belonging to scab workers were set alight over the weekend. Police began to patrol the streets of Mpophomeni heavily to escort buses into the township. A 21 day ban on meetings was imposed in the area.[26]

Late in June we hired buses and on that Saturday morning we all rode into Pietermaritzburg; I think it was a dozen buses. People from Durban also joined us like from Dunlop. We were taking our our news across to the capital.[27]

They were trying to reach a wider audience for their plight. On 29 June their convoy stopped in the heart of the commercial district of the Natal capital. The ensuing chaos gave workers a golden opportunity to blitz passers-by and assembling crowds with stickers, pamphlets and information. As the Sarmcol play satirically portrays, the police were caught completely unawares, and stood by in disbelief. The workers, escorted by traffic police, made their way to the Edendale Lay Ecumenical Centre, where a large meeting was held in which student and community organisations participated.

The LMG report tells how from Edendale the convoy moved to Imbali, the largest black township in the Pietermaritzburg area. The police stayed out of the township but kept happenings under surveillance. The workers' convoy went around Imbali street by street, with youths marching and chanting in front of the buses. Union banners and those of political and student organisations were carried. A COSAS member remarked that this was the first time that students had been able to march in the township in solidarity with their parents without being dispersed by the police. At intervals the procession stopped and the workers addressed people who had gathered about the strike, asking for their support. The workers 'held' the township for two hours and most inhabitants began understanding the issues and discussing the strike.

Discussions around the theme of the stayaway started on 30 June when the FOSATU regional congress met. Sarmcol was the main issue under discussion. The idea of a work stoppage in support of the striking workers was referred back to the locals. Eventually the decision taken by FOSATU was to confine the stay-away to Pietermaritzburg and build up support activities in the rest of Natal. After this decision MAWU and FOSATU representatives started discussions with community and youth organisations in order to effect its implementation.

The stay-away observed by 92 percent of the black working class in Pietermaritzburg succeeded: it shut the town down, and demonstrated the capacity of labour and youth to forge a militant alliance in the townships. The day of the stay-away was also a day of pitched confrontations between youth and police in Mpophomeni. The support of the community organisations, although fraught with difficulties, was significant and decisive. But furthermore, the close cooperation of all progressive forces in the Midlands under the direction of MAWU and the Sarmcol shop stewards was a new development in South Africa's taut struggles against a repressive state. As a newspaper observed:

When a normally bustling Pietermaritzburg central business district and its industrial suburbs can be brought to a halt for a whole day by black workers demonstrating their solidarity with the employees of a factory in another town, it is clearly a matter of significance. . . .

And yet, even this dramatic action had little repercussion on the fate of the Sarmcol workers' reinstatement.[28]

THE BIRTH OF SAWCO

Union officials and shop stewards began discussing the idea of a Sarmcol Workers Cooperative towards the end of 1985. Initial responses were largely sceptical, but the shop stewards, especially Sibiya, were not prepared to give up their vision, 'of teaching our children about democracy'.[29]

After many meetings and much discussion SAWCO became a reality. Its uniqueness (in terms of union organisation) was as much a result of the specific circumstances of the Sarmcol strike as of the aspirations of the strikers themselves.[30]

SAWCO consists of five cooperatives — T-shirt, bulk buying, agriculture, health and culture. Some of these existed as a part of strike organisation in the community. Bulk buying was one of the first, having been set up in the early weeks of the strike in order to coordinate the distribution of weekly food parcels to the strikers and their families. Today it still continues the task, consulting with strikers over what food should be purchased. The weekly delivery of food to Mpophomeni has become a social event. With the appearance of the truck on the dusty road leading to the township, strikers begin to make their way to the church hall, where their help will be needed in the off-loading of the food. No one needs to be asked and there is never a shortage of volunteers. The intention is that other members of the community, through membership of SAWCO, will also be able to buy their food through the bulk-buying scheme.

The culture project also existed prior to the formation of SAWCO. Originally six strikers came together to workshop and create a play which would tell the story of their struggle. The play, entitled *The Long March*, was to be used to gain support — financial and moral — for the strikers. Today the cultural project includes a gumboot dance group and a choir.

The health wing was also present, in a somewhat embryonic state, before the formation of SAWCO. Doctors were almost immediately involved in providing health care for the dismissed strikers and their families. The formation of SAWCO formalised and expanded this relationship. The health committee members have been sent on short training courses and now run health screening clinics for the strikers' children and provide supplementary food parcels for the malnourished. Screenings for the strikers are also important. Plans include the training of the community in first aid, the aim being a trained person in every street.

The remaining two cooperatives are more directly linked to the establishment of SAWCO. There was much discussion and many pilot projects before it was decided initially to limit SAWCO to the making and printing of T-shirts, and to agriculture. The T-shirt cooperative is the most visible of SAWCO's ventures. Strikers have been trained in silk-screening and printing and are able to produce about 300 emblazoned shirts per day, mainly for other unions in the COSATU federation. Furthermore, eight hectares of arable land and 40 hectares of grazing land have been leased from the Catholic Church, for the agricultural cooperative. Crops harvested so far are cabbage, spinach and carrots, which are being sold to workers at a very low price. Sarmcol workers, once evicted from the land as labour tenants, once more have access.

How does this all work? What is the relationship between the union, the shop stewards, the community and SAWCO? SAWCO is run by a controlling committee. The areas from which the strikers come have been divided into fifteen residential areas and each area elects a representative to the SAWCO committee. Additionally, each project has proportional representation on SAWCO. Finally, SAWCO is represented on MAWU's regional structures, thereby ensuring that the dismissed workers are still integrated within the union. Strikers may join SAWCO individually and associate membership is also open to all members of the community.

The formation of SAWCO caused much debate within strikers' meetings. Many did not see the need for a separate constitution and organisation. They had their shop stewards and union, why something else? Others argued that it was the only way forward, and that organisation had to change from a shopfloor representation basis to an area/community basis. There is also the worry, voiced by the leadership, that although most workers support and are proud of SAWCO and its achievements, not all have actively joined it. Many see it as a stop-gap measure until the strike is settled. No one, however, has denied that it is an appropriate democratic forum for decision making and consultation.[31]

CONCLUSION

The Sarmcol experience has been one of innovation and hardship; or rather, innovation in hardship. The workers' common history, their common pasts as a dispossessed population, their memories of prior forms of resistance and their lengthy lives as workers in the factory have all served to harness them together to overcome the grind of the strike experience for months on end. But their mental and emotional resources were stretched beyond the ordinary: the strike was not the outcome of an overall plan of action by the union, but rather a series of responses in order to sustain the struggle for reinstatement and winning demands.

In this process, this 'long march', there were important landmarks. They initiated a new labour politics in the area, where workers could exercise leadership in mass campaigns. The mobilisation, leadership and discipline of a mass campaign saw a climax in the Pietermaritzburg stay-away — the largest in the city's history. There were of course tensions between MAWU and the UDF over this: the UDF leadership felt that it was not adequately consulted and disagreed on the campaign's narrow focus. Still, youth organisations affiliated to the UDF were central to the mobilisation and implementation of the stay-away alongside workers and FOSATU unions.[32]

Such leadership was, importantly, exercised on a single-issue basis, after which the shop steward leadership channelled their energies into creating SAWCO. This does not answer the question whether such leadership can be sustained over time. The entry of worker leaders into the political arena was tactical, swift and effective. It has left behind a legacy of cooperation and a demonstration that meaningful alliances can be implemented.

Furthermore, once the workers decided to set off on their 'long march' and MAWU decided to put all its meagre resources into the fray, an impossible situation had to be overcome through sacrifices and creative protest: the state had declared its first State of Emergency (the strike continues through the second) and it was hostile to any manifestations of opposition; the media, including the so-called 'liberal' press, kept a cynical muzzle on labour issues. This meant that the plight of a dying black community has been poorly publicised.

In such a climate, the Sarmcol workers had to become innovative: the jamming of Pietermaritzburg traffic at peak shopping hours to publicise their cause, the marches through Imbali to discuss their plight with the community, the solidarity actions of other workers in other areas, the single-file protest marches over Christmas, the national tour of their play and so on, kept mobilising more and more support.

Finally, the building of SAWCO as a cooperative, as an area committee and as a community organisation, has extended people's understanding of grassroots democracy: it is one of the few examples where workers have taken their democratic principles of shop floor organisation and translated them into a viable community structure. The dominance of Sarmcol as an employer of people in Mpophomeni has made this translation of structures easier. It would be difficult, for example, to do something similar in the larger townships of Durban, yet — as SAWCO shows — difficult does not mean impossible.

Democratic representation on an area basis is possible. A working cooperation with women and youth in the community is achievable; finally, the relationship of an unemployed striking workforce through union structures with other workers can be very effective. The test of this project is whether the majority of workers are committed to it as a permanent structure or whether it is seen as a temporary stop-gap institution to facilitate decision-making during the strike days.

To COSATU workers further afield SAWCO is a symbol of organisation and resistance; for some it is becoming a model of democracy; for the enemies of the labour movement it is a cancerous growth which ought to be eradicated. On 5 December 1986, Inkatha-led vigilantes attempted to break it, and failed. But they took away some of its best militants. Sarmcol itself has now concluded a recognition agreement with the Inkatha-backed United Workers Union of South Africa (UWUSA). UWUSA has made significant concessions in terms of job security, a central issue in Sarmcol's dispute with MAWU. The state has also intervened by banning public meetings in Mpophomeni.[33]

It is fitting to conclude with the words of COSATU oral poet Hlatshwayo's funeral lament with its promise of transcendence:

we shall remember
your smiling and simple faces

there
    stark against
    our sorry faces
    of regret and hopelessness

your smiling and simple faces
that drove other men

to
   rape our unity
to
   raid our camps
and kill our pride

you-you . . .
your smiling and simple faces
meant sleepless nights
to bosses, rulers and their puppets

your smiling and simple faces
gave hope to Sarmcol workers' struggle
to our liberation struggle
your death now
comrades
proclaims our earthly triumph.[34]

NOTES

1. See S. Marie, 'Sarmcol killings', *SALB*, Vol.12, No.2, 1987, p.3; and *Sunday Times*, 6 December 1986.
2. On the contexts and symbolic power of political funerals see M. Swilling and T. Lodge, 'From protest to people's power: the UDF and the revolt in the townships' (unpublished paper, 1987).
3. A. Qabula and Mi S'dumo Hlatshwayo, *Black Mamba Rising: South African Worker Poets in Struggle* (Durban: Worker Resistance and Culture Publications, 1986).
4. *Ibid.*, pp.64-5.
5. Based on a survey carried out by Debbie Bonnin involving 172 structured interviews with Sarmcol workers. For methodology see her 'From labour tenant to industrial worker: the case of the Sarmcol strikers', paper presented as expert evidence for the Industrial Court case of the Sarmcol dispute in Pietermaritzburg, 1986 (pp.1-8).
6. *Ibid.*, p.9.
7. *Ibid.*; also see J. Woodhouse, 'The life of a labour tenant in Natal's Midlands', Industrial Sociology research project, 1985. On the abolition of labour tenancy, see G. Maré, *African Population Relocation in South Africa* (Johannesburg: SAIRR, 1980) for a brief but useful discussion.
8. Over and above the 172 structured interviews (*op. cit.*) another 22 in-depth interviews have been conducted thus far in order to recreate the oral history of the area (hereafter, Oral Interviews, 1986).
9. On the implications of apartheid policy on urban and rural black concentrations of people, see D. Hindson, *Pass Controls and the Urban African Proletariat* (Johannesburg: Ravan Press, 1987). Also A. Stadler, *The Political Economy of Modern South Africa* (Cape Town: David Philip, 1987), Chapters 7 and 8.
10. C. Walker and L. Platzky, *The Surplus People* (Johannesburg: Ravan Press, 1985). See also G. Maré, *op.cit*, for a useful typology of relocation.
11. From Oral Interviews, 1986.
12. Labour Monitoring Group, Natal, 'Monitoring the Sarmcol struggle', *SALB*, Vol.11, No.2, 1985, p.92.
13. From Oral Interviews, 1986.
14. From *BTR UK Company Records*, 1979-1986, London. Also press clippings from the Trade Union Research Project, University of Natal, Durban.
15. E. Rosenthal, *The Sarmcol Story* (Howick: E. Rosenthal, 1981), p.27.

16. *Ibid.*, p.20.

17. This and the following quotations from Sarmcol workers' experiences, both historical and contemporary, have been reconstructed from the Oral History Interviews, 1986. The unevenness in language is due to the fact that some workers insisted on being interviewed in English whereas others were interviewed in Zulu. Our attempt here is to build an 'experiential mosaic' — see Sitas, 'Black worker responses on the East Rand to changes in the metal industry', Ph.D. thesis, University of the Witwatersrand, 1984 — out of the accounts of these workers. For more biographical details of the interviewees see D. Bonnin's forthcoming Master's dissertation (1987).

18. On SACTU, see K. Luckhardt and B. Wall, *Organise or Starve!* (London: Lawrence and Wishart, 1980). On the role of Gwala see the more detailed account in D. Bonnin,'Two generations of worker leadership', History Workshop paper, University of the Witwatersrand, 1987. On popular traditions in Natal, see A. Sitas, 'The flight of the Gwala-Gwala bird: ethnicity, populism and workers' culture in the Natal labour movement' (unpublished paper, 1986).

19. On Zondi see Bonnin, *op. cit.* The poetry and orations of this worker creator are being collected for SAWCO by the Culture and Working Life Project, University of Natal, Durban.

20. Oral Interviews, 1986.

21. On MAWU see *Our History and Principles* (Durban: MAWU, 1986), also E. Webster, *Cast in a Racial Mould* (Johannesburg: Ravan Press, 1985), p.231, and A. Sitas, *op. cit.*, 1984.

22. For the reconstruction of the strike and subsequent events we have relied on Oral Interviews, 1986; on trade union correspondence with the company; on interviews with union officials and the affidavits and evidence by both parties in the Industrial Court case over the Sarmcol dispute. We would like to thank MAWU for making all this and their time available to us.

23. *Weekly Mail,* 3 July, 1987.

24. From Oral Interviews, 1986, and the LMG Report, *op. cit.*, p.96.

25. LMG, *op. cit.*, pp.98-99.

26. LMG, *op. cit.*, pp.99-100.

27. Interview with Phineas Sibiya, September 1985.

28. LMG, *op. cit.*, p.99.

29. Interview with Phineas Sibiya, *op. cit.*

30. Interviews with SAWCO representatives by Debbie Bonnin and Pippa Green. Also *SAWCO Update,* the cooperative's newsletter, 1986.

31. Oral Interviews, 1986, and SAWCO interviews, *ibid.*

32. Mi S'dumo Hlatshwayo, 'To you comrades', *SALB*, Vol.12, No.2, 1987, p.2.

33. *Work in Progress (WIP)*, No 48, July 1987.

34. Mi S'dumo Hlatshwayo, *op. cit.*

3. The Origins of Political Moblisation in PWV Townships, 1980-84

JEREMY SEEKINGS

Since mid-1984 South Africa's townships have been the site of chronic violent confrontation; at the same time, they have witnessed an unprecedented proliferation of extra-state organisations. Whilst it is unclear as to whether the South African state can reimpose its authority and suppress resistance (if only transiently), it is reasonable to state that the protests of 1984-86 have constituted the most severe challenge yet to the apartheid state. Curiously, there has been an unfortunate failure to examine contemporary township politics. This failure has been the most pronounced for the townships in the Pretoria-Witwatersrand-Vereeniging (PWV) region, which is by far the largest of South Africa's metropolitan areas.

The heightened confrontations of 1984-86 can, however, only be understood in terms of processes of political mobilisation and radicalisation that *predate* mid-1984. This chapter is a preliminary account of these processes up to late 1984 in the PWV. It first considers how the changing structural context has shaped the transformation of township politics, focussing specifically on the interaction between the financial and political contradictions facing the local state. It then examines some of the responses to these changes inside the townships, leading up to the confrontations in the Vaal Triangle and elsewhere in 1984.[1]

THE CHANGING STRUCTURAL CONTEXT

From the mid-1970s, the state and capital in South Africa responded to a chronic political and deepening economic crisis by reconstituting the political and economic constraints and opportunities relating to black South Africans. In the townships this involved the reform of influx control, rising state investment in (and the deregulation of) housing and township development, the opening up of opportunities for greater intra-township accumulation and, finally, the restructuring of local government.

This reconstitution of many of the basic state policies governing the townships has proved insufficient to resolve the fundamental political and economic problems. However, it has effected a transformation of financial and political relations within the townships. It is these changes which underlay political mobilisation and protest in the early 1980s, distinguishing contemporary conflict from that of previous periods.

Whilst there were significant changes in many of the state's urban policies, the central state remained committed to the principle that local government in the townships should be financially self-sufficient, i.e. that township administration and development should continue to be funded through revenue raised locally. However, from the late 1970s, the local state was required to provide more extensive public housing and public services if (re-)differentiated labour power [2] was to be reproduced according to state policy, but within the broad constraints imposed by struggles from below. As has been pointed out: 'This is the nub of the contradiction in the state's policy towards urban Africans: the urgency of providing shelter and services . . . yet a totally inadequate form of revenue to do this.'[3]

Most administration boards had generated financial surpluses in the early 1970s, but by the early 1980s they were accumulating colossal deficits. The boards' aggregate deficit for 1982-83 was estimated at R32m.[4] Expenditure was rising, as both the volume and the unit cost of house construction and particularly the provision of township services increased, amid rising administration costs. At the same time, several sources of income were falling, especially the profits from beer and liquor sales, which were used to subsidise the provision of housing and services.

The state increased rents and service charges rather than introduce either further taxation of businesses or central state subsidisation.[5] Large increases were required to raise rents to 'economic' levels — rates which would completely pay for the provision of housing and services. In the East Rand, for example, the administration board stated in 1977 that rents would need to be increased at least fourfold.[6]

These attempts to achieve economic rentals coincided with continuing urban poverty. It is difficult to gauge the precise scale of changes in the extent of poverty, as available statistics (both official and unofficial) are inadequate, and often inconsistent. Some patterns and trends are nonetheless clear.

Firstly, township residents have suffered less, on average, during the post-1974 recession, than have their counterparts in the rural areas, including those resident in the bantustans. Indeed, in most parts of the country, the average *per capita* income has risen in real terms in the period 1975−1985. Secondly, this average growth comprises very uneven experiences between different townships. For example, average real *per capita* incomes fell in Soweto between 1975 and 1985, and in the Vaal Triangle between 1980 and 1985.

Thirdly, economic differentiation within townships increased rapidly throughout the PWV over this period. The falling real incomes of a significant proportion of the township population were not always reflected in statistics for average real *per capita* incomes, as the latter were being pushed upwards by the very rapid enrichment of a minority of township residents. Fourthly, incomes were rising or falling from a very low starting point.

In short, poverty remained extensive, and the incidence of severe poverty actually increased. Appendix 1 provides data taken from household income and expenditure surveys conducted by the Bureau of Market Research (BMR), which have been criticised for overestimating both income levels and growth rates. Even this data, however, illustrates the above trends. The proportion of households with incomes below a Minimum Living Level (MLL) had, by 1985, risen to between 22 per cent and 30 per cent in different parts of the PWV. The proportion with incomes below a marginally more generous Supplementary

Living Level (SLL) had risen to between 30 percent and 43 percent. The BMR data, conservatively interpreted, suggest that at least 25 percent of households in the PWV (and a much higher proportion in the Vaal Triangle) had falling real incomes between 1980 and 1985.

Appendix 2 presents data from other sources. Keenan estimates that the proportion of households with incomes below a Household Effective Level (HEL) in three parts of Soweto in 1985 was between 48 percent and 62 per cent. Data for income distribution provided by an independent research agency (Markinor) suggest that, as early as April 1980, about 80 percent of the households had incomes below the HEL.[7]

Rent increases were therefore a very important material burden on a significant proportion of households. Besides those whose real incomes were actually falling, there were even more whose incomes were still too low (even if slowly rising) to be able to accommodate easily major increases in a non-discretionary item of expenditure such as rent. This was particularly the case in the Vaal Triangle, where rapidly rising rents coincided with the highest incidence of poverty and the most widely falling real incomes.

THE COUNCILS AND INTRA-TOWNSHIP POLITICAL RELATIONS

Resolving the local state's financial dilemma through increasing rents was, however, politically problematic. Residents could effectively and passively resist increases, either through a proliferation of shacks, increasing overcrowding, or through growing rent arrears. Revenue could therefore only be increased if informal housing was controlled and/or taxed; rents were increased; and rent defaulters were evicted (and replaced by tenants who would pay the rent). Each of these actions could precipitate active resistance.

The state's restructuring of local government in the townships was, at least in part, designed to resolve this political problem. But this restructuring generated unanticipated changes in political relations within the townships. These changing political relations, interacting with the intensifying financial contradictions, provoked and shaped the range of conflicts which led to the Vaal Uprising and other major confrontations since mid-1984.

Local government restructuring began with the establishment of community councils under the 1977 Community Councils Act. Elections were held in the PWV townships between November 1977 and November 1980. Administration board officials hoped that black councillors would be able to absorb and defuse discontent. As the boards made clear:

> It is not the Minister's problem to solve the communities' shortage of money. This is something that must be done by the community itself. . . . The community must therefore elect leaders to act on their behalf to collect the money needed and to provide these services.[8]

In 1978 the West Rand Administration Board delayed a sizeable rent increase until the three community councils in Greater Soweto had taken office. The new Soweto Council announced an 88 percent rent increase in August 1979.

In 1980 the Local Government Bill was first published, providing for the upgrading of community councils to town or village councils, with increased powers and responsibilities. Elections due in 1980-81 to councils that were to be upgraded, and all elections after July 1982, were postponed, in the hope that this further reorganisation of local government would generate greater support. P. J. Riekert (then chief director of the Western Transvaal Administration Board) unambiguously recognised this, saying: 'These local authorities will serve to defuse pent-up frustrations and grievances against administration from Pretoria.'[9] The redrafted bill was finally passed as the Black Local Authorities Act in 1982, and 16 community councils in the PWV were upgraded. Elections were held in November and December 1983.[10]

The ability of the councils to absorb the political costs of resolving the fiscal contradictions was undermined, however, by the changing political relations within the township that resulted from the changing local government system. In many townships the old Urban Bantu Councils, and for varying periods the new Community Councils, enjoyed some legitimacy. This was based on the councillors' roles as arbiters of justice and dispensers of certain forms of patronage. According to one Tumahole resident:

> If you fought with your wife, you could be taken [to the councillors], and they will sort out the problems . . . most of the cases were not handed over to the police, but were being solved by them. Or if you have a relative living in the rural areas, and you want that relative to live in the township, this can be done through the councillors. . . . Whenever you have a problem, they can solve it quickly.

According to another resident:

> The councillors were people who were just going to help with family disputes. Our people didn't think of them playing any active political role whatsoever, they were just like social workers, or marriage councillors. They will just say, 'we'll make sure the woman next door doesn't commit adultery with your husband'.[11]

Councillors were locked into a popular form of patronage network. Such networks were a mechanism for coming to terms with oppression and exploitation, and a way of circumventing white authority through preserving autonomous space in the township.

Under the Community Councils Act, and even more so under the Black Local Authorities Act, the councillors' roles changed. Instead of making life easier, the councillors were now seen to be making life more difficult. Councillors' powers now included control over the allocation of housing, business sites, students' bursaries, and other council funds. This led to an important change in the nature of township patronage relations, as the councillors commanded greater resources, playing a directly allocative rather than just a mediating role. Patronage became a more commercial and less moral relationship. Increasingly, the patrons (i.e. the councillors) demanded more of their 'clients', in the form of escalating bribes.

The reorganisation of local government coincided with increasing differentiation within the townships. Rapidly rising real incomes for some residents resulted from their involvement in the expansion of skilled and white collar employment outside the township. But others' real incomes were also increasing because of the expansion of opportunities for accumulation within the township, in retailing (including supermarkets, semi-clandestine shebeens and official liquor stores), transport services (taxis and buses), and, in a very few cases, small manufacturing enterprises.

'Net profit from own businesses' rose as a proportion of average household income over 1980–1985 (according to the BMR data) from 4 percent to 7.5

percent (Vaal), 7.4 percent to 12.3 percent (Soweto), and 3.6 percent to 12.7 percent (Mamelodi and Atteridgeville). Thus economic as well as political relations within townships were changing.

Many of the councillors were aspiring businessmen; many used the councils to become such. Increasing economic differentiation shifted the relative bargaining position within patronage relations still further in favour of the councillors. It also increased the social distance between them and residents, thereby reducing any residual moral content in their patronage. Finally, whilst there seems to have been a widespread endorsement of the individualism which led to limited enrichment, the rapidity with which wealth was acquired often suggested ill-gotten gains, made at the expense of other township residents.

As residents grew increasingly discontented with councillors throughout the region, allegations of council corruption and mismanagement became rife. The opportunities for corruption were certainly growing, but corruption was also accorded a symbolic importance (beyond its very material content). What had previously been seen as the appeal of limited patronage was transformed into the crime of uncontrolled corruption, as councillors crudely manipulated their powers to favour themselves or their supporters. As one middle-aged man from Tumahole put it: 'After someone is elected a councillor, all avenues are open to him' — literally true in Tumahole, as the first road in the township to be tarred linked a leading councillor's house to his supermarket![12]

Two separate motions of no confidence brought by disaffected members of the Lekoa Town Council, detailing examples of corruption by leading councillors, were both ruled out of order by the mayor on spurious grounds. One motion had spelt 'Lekoa' incorrectly, and the other referred to the 'Lekoa Town Council' as opposed to the 'Town Council of Lekoa', its official title. Tjaert van der Walt, in his official report on the Vaal Uprising, recorded that: 'No resident I spoke to had a good word for the Lekoa Municipality', and recommended that there should be an independent judicial investigation into allegations of corruption and maladministration.

The former community council chairman and deputy-chairman were convicted in July 1985 of receiving extensive bribes; other councillors have admitted that knowledge of such corruption was very widespread, and was a key factor in the Vaal Uprising when so much hostility was directed specifically at leading councillors — 'Because this is happening to the community and is a pinch to the community, therefore the community knows about it even before it goes to court.'[13]

Council corruption prompted resistance not only because it destroyed the image of responsible leadership on which the council system depended, but because corruption and extravagance coincided with rent increases and evictions. The Katlehong Council began demolishing shacks soon after it received R2m for new offices, but was failing to address the huge housing shortage. Lekoa councillors went on trips to Europe whilst rents spiralled and defaulters were locked out of their homes.

Councillors throughout the PWV repeatedly violated prevailing popular notions of justice. Besides their apparent corruption and self-service, and their disregard for patrons' historic responsibilities, they failed to address themselves to residents' grievances or hold meetings to discuss council actions.

The Populist Response in the Councils

Many councillors recognised the contradiction they faced and sought to achieve a balance between the financial costs of township administration and development, and the political costs of increasing rents and ordering evictions. A few of the leading councillors condemned the financial constraints imposed by the central state, and demanded external funding. Steve Kgame, the mayor of Diepmeadow and president of the umbrella Urban Councils Association (UCASA), boldly stated that: 'Without finance, the councillors may as well fold up their gowns and go home' — which of course he never did.[14]

In a few townships, critical opposition to incumbent councillors emerged within the local government framework, allowing councils as institutions to retain legitimacy and support. This was reflected in some of the 1983 council elections. In the 16 town and village council elections in the PWV, a total of 119,000 people voted, representing 8 percent of the resident adult population, and less than 12 percent of the registered voters. The overall percentage poll was lower than in the 1978-80 elections. The lowest poll (for contested seats) was 5 percent, in Evaton. In general, therefore, the results reflected considerable lack of interest and opposition.[15]

In several townships, however, there was considerable competition. In Mamelodi, for example, the incumbent councillors were successfully challenged by the radical-populist Vukani Vulahmelo People's Party, which had opposed high rents and slum-clearance, denounced financial irregularities, demanded low-cost housing, and had even taken the Central Transvaal Administration Board to court. Despite a campaign against the elections by the UDF-affiliated Mamelodi Action Committee, there was a 28 percent turnout.[16]

In Soweto, the official turnout of 10.7 percent was the second lowest in the PWV, but was actually higher than in 1978, probably due to the populist stand taken by the opposition Sofasonke party. Sofasonke candidates promised rent cuts, leniency towards defaulters, permanent house ownership, and even the abolition of influx control for people born after 1945! Sofasonke had been formed to represent squatters in the late 1940s, and the council's action against squatters in 1982-83 boosted its old populist appeal. Seventeen Sofasonke candidates were elected, unseating both the former council chairman (i.e. mayor) and his deputy. Only 11 of the 30 new councillors had served on the old community council, a much smaller proportion than the 59 percent average throughout the PWV.[17]

In most townships there were individual councillors who opposed rent increases and evictions, and voiced strong criticism of the governing group on the council. For example, in Daveyton the populist councillor Shadrack Sinaba was even detained in 1979 for assisting squatters.[18] In Katlehong, the whole council opposed evictions for several years.

CONFLICT AND PROTEST 1980-83

Councillors, however much populist rhetoric they employed, were unable to absorb the tension arising from interacting political and financial contradictions within the council structures.[19] These contradictions became more acute during the 1980s. Councils became increasingly critical of the financial and administrative constraints of the administration boards and government departments, but to little effect. They therefore presided over rising rents and resorted to coercive measures against squatters with ever-increasing frequency. In short, they attempted to resolve the financial contradiction at the expense of their political credibility. The result was a rising occurrence of protests outside the council structure.

The housing shortage was particularly acute in the East Rand townships and in Soweto. Expanding township populations led to a proliferation of squatter shacks. The East Rand housing shortage in 1981 was estimated to be some 24,000 units, with an estimated cost over ten times what the administration board had actually budgeted for 1981-82.[20] In Katlehong, the number of shacks (or '*umkhukhu*', meaning chicken coops) rose from an estimated 3,000 in 1979 to 44,000 by mid-1983, with almost twice as many shacks as 'legal' houses. The council in effect authorised this illegal accommodation — and so avoided losing support — when its chairman announced that no shacks would be demolished until alternative housing became available.

Tolerating, and even encouraging, squatting enabled councillors to maintain a balance between financial and political demands in the short term only. The very success of squatters in creating a space that was relatively free from the authority, as well as from the financial demands of the local state, made necessary an escalating use of force if the state was to either reimpose its authority or preserve a 'balancing' revenue which would enable some infra-structural development in the townships under existing legislation.

The Katlehong Council soon responded to the proliferation of shacks. The council desperately needed revenue in 1980-82, to offset the deterioration of services that was in part due to the rapid pace of urbanisation. A strict enforcement of influx control was not possible during this period due to local capital's pressing need for labour. The council therefore first sought control, and finance, by imposing a R3 levy which was then raised to R5. This was not a long-term solution, however, and in November 1982 the council began bulldozing shacks.

Shack residents were partially able to circumvent the council's measures: 'As the Administration Board knocks down homes like a wave, workers jump ahead and around the wave and reconstruct their *umkhukhu* behind it', and confrontations therefore continued through 1983.[21]

Similar events took place in Daveyton and Thokoza. In Daveyton, women had picketed a council meeting in 1980 to protest against the imposition of lodgers' permits (effectively taxing many shack residents). In February 1981, 100 women, all members of Sinaba's party, protested against shack demolition and the housing shortage. By 1982, 3,588 families lived in shacks. Sinaba himself 'arranged for his supporters in the area to build shacks, but when it came to the crunch, agreed with the East Rand Administration Board that illegal shacks be demolished'.[22]

By the end of 1982 there was an estimated shortage of 35,000 houses in Soweto, and an estimated 23,000 families were living in 'zozos' — easy to assemble instant accommodation. In May 1982, shack demolition began in Jabavu. Two thousand alleged illegal residents were arrested in massive pass raids in September. In February 1983, the council began demolishing shacks in Orlando East. Despite resistance, including demonstrations and court action, the Soweto Community Council and West Rand Administration Board proceeded with shack demolition.[23]

Rent increases were a more general cause of discontent than evictions, and often provoked more organised responses. Soweto was the first township where there was significant protest against rents. In 1979 opposition to proposed increases, led by the new Soweto Civic Association, prompted the government to write off the council's R11.5m deficit, and the council backed down. The following year, further proposed increases provoked legal action and massive demonstrations.[24]

Rent increases elsewhere in the PWV soon led to similar responses. A surprise rent increase in April 1981 in Tembisa prompted residents to demonstrate outside the East Rand Administration Board offices. When police violently dispersed the protesters, and prevented public meetings to discuss the issue, residents rioted, causing an estimated R80,000 damage to administration board and council property.[25] In Wattville residents protested against rent increases introduced in May 1981. When rents were further increased in October, 48 women marched to the ERAB offices, where they were arrested and charged with holding an illegal procession.[26]

The announcement of rent increases in West Rand townships similarly provoked opposition to the councils and administration board. At a mass meeting in Mohlakeng, which the mayor refused to attend, 3,000 residents decided not to pay until they had been given satisfactory reasons. One speaker told the meeting: 'You should not allow these people to dig holes in your pockets. They should first clean the streets, tar them, and electrify the township.' In Kagiso, on the West Rand, residents called for all councillors' resignations, and decided to boycott their businesses.[27]

Some councils refused to authorise the rent increases that had been mooted by the administration board. The Daveyton Community Council decided to reduce rents by almost 50 percent from March 1981, but ERAB said that the council had no power to increase or reduce rents. The chairmen of the Ikageng and Orkney community councils were sacked by the administration board for refusing to agree to a 105 percent increase in 1982. But where councils held out one year, they caved in to board pressure the next. The Daveyton Council actually raised rents in March 1981 after its abortive attempt to lower them. Both the Mamelodi and Atteridgeville community councils refused to increase rents in 1981, but in 1982 backed down and allowed huge rises.[28]

In a number of PWV townships in the early 1980s the state proposed costly development plans focussing on electrification and sewerage systems, with the cost, unsurprisingly, being passed on to residents. In Duduza, the East Rand Administration Board proposed a so-called 'master plan' for the installation of a sewerage system to replace night buckets in 1982. The cost would be recouped over twenty years, with rents/service charges being increased by more than 100 per cent over the first three years. Residents, dissatisfied with their council, formed a civic association in October.

Discontent was not simply due to the cost of the development; rather, it arose from the state's violation of popular notions of justice. Duduza residents had been moved from the old Nigel location in 1964, and given the impression that their removal would facilitate prompt development. Until 1982, however, nothing had been provided, whilst the old location, now designated a 'coloured' township, had been developed.[29]

In some townships, short-lived organisations emerged in the early 1980s. The April 1981 protests in Tembisa led to the formation of a Tembisa Residents Action Committee. Intermittent and unsustained organisation gave way to more permanent organisation with the recognition that councils did not have the power to change living conditions in the townships, and that they could and should be effectively opposed. The nature of protest organisations also changed with increasingly widespread and sustained mobilisation. Early organisations, such as the narrowly based Soweto Committee of Ten, had tended towards conservatism and elitism. Many of the organisations formed in the early 1980s drew on broader support, and were thus more responsive to residents' grievances.

A growing belief in the viability of challenge was in part the result of the revitalisation of nationalist politics in the early 1980s. The United Democratic Front's campaigns concerned national political issues (primarily the 1983 constitutional proposals and the 'Koornhof Bills') and not local and immediate issues such as rents and evictions, but nonetheless were important because they linked local with national political developments, thereby contributing to the reshaping of local political consciousness and organisation. Township politics was also increasingly influenced by the growth of the independent trade union movement. On the East Rand, especially, workplace organisation and the strike waves of 1981 and 1982 informed protests in the townships.

A noticeable feature of political mobilisation in the early 1980s was the frequent prominence of women, reflecting their particular interest in the underlying grievances of rents and housing. Their involvement in protests in Wattville and Daveyton has been mentioned above. In Duduza, women played a central role in the sewerage issue, because, as they complained, they were the people who had to empty the buckets. It was a woman who suggested direct action, taking the buckets to the administration offices, so that the township manager 'would feel the smell'. However, the inital impetus of women and their specific concerns have rarely been translated into a sustained organisational role.

THE TRANSFORMATION OF RESISTANCE IN 1984

Councils throughout the PWV announced considerable rent increases between April and July 1984. Opposition to the councils increased markedly from previous years. Previous rent increases had been justified in terms of providing services in the townships. Little progress was visible to residents — admittedly in part due to the delayed visibility of the results of capital expenditure — whilst the wealth (and corruption) of many councillors was very apparent. Popular suspicion of the councillors had consequently increased.

Furthermore, the economic recession was deepening. General Sales Tax (GST) was increased, from 6 percent to 10 percent, in the 1984 budget. Bus fares had been widely increased in January, provoking bus boycotts in Alexandra, KwaThema and Daveyton.[30]

Finally, disputes in many township schools during early 1984 further contributed to councils' unpopularity, and in some areas constituted an example and precedent for further protests.[31] The growing crisis in many township high schools became increasingly important as grievances and participants interacted and together shaped emerging patterns of mobilisation. Whilst the confrontations of late 1984 were rooted outside the classrooms, and in the period before school students initiated major protests, students and ex-students did play a central role and influenced the nature of the unfolding revolt.[32]

During 1983 there had been limited and isolated protests in many schools, but the Transvaal's first sustained class boycott (in Atteridgeville) did not start until January 1984. The initial protests were restrained and concerned purely educational grievances. Nonetheless, the move to widespread and active protest cannot be attributed to educational grievances in the same manner as in 1976, when there was a single key issue. In 1984, the increasing political opposition in many townships provided a context conducive to student militancy.

In Atteridgeville complementary strands of opposition had come together in late 1984. National opposition to the introduction of the Black Local Authorities, and specifically local opposition to the existing council, came together with the formation of the Saulsville-Atteridgeville Youth Organisation (SAYO) and the Atteridgeville-Saulsville Residents Organisation (ASRO), to oppose elections for a town council.

Students were very soon made aware that the schools could not be isolated from wider issues. In Atteridgeville, school protests were transformed by the unprovoked killing of a student, on school premises, by police in February. Conflict escalated still further with the suspension of student leaders, and the closure of schools. The council failed to make any significant attempt to solve the educational crisis — in contrast to ASRO — or to restrain the police.[33]

This pattern of events in Atteridgeville was repeated elsewhere. Rising levels of student activism could not be divorced from the context of broader township conflicts. Indeed, the Van der Walt Commission, which was originally established to consider the crisis in black education in the Vaal, recognised that 'the crux of the problem was not to be found in the school system *per se*' and 'the investigation inevitably had to be extended to the local community and even to some facets of wider national interest'.[34] The state's reaction to student protests, in the form of repression rather than meaningful negotiation, propelled educational protests onto the streets — literally, when the Department of Training (DET) closed schools. By August, schools were closed or classes suspended in Alexandra, Daveyton and Tembisa, besides Atteridgeville.[35]

When rent increases were announced, unprecedented opposition coalesced. In Atteridgeville, residents called on the councillors to resign, and ASRO successfully opposed the increases with legal assistance. In August, increased service charges were proposed. These were also soon abandoned in the face of local opposition, including the petrol-bombing of the mayor's house, and escalating conflict elsewhere in the PWV. Despite the abandonment of the proposed increases, many residents were unable to pay their rent. In early November, the town council stated that rent arrears stood at R300,000, and its budget deficit was now R2.9m.

The Daveyton Town Council announced rent increases of R14 to meet its R4m deficit. The East Rand People's Organisation (ERAPO) opposed the increases, and 2,000 residents refused to pay rents. The increase was finally cut by R5.[36] In Ratanda, the mayor called public meetings over the rent issue, but either didn't turn up, or arrived drunk when he did. Residents finally persuaded two councillors to address them at a meeting in August, where it was resolved not to pay the increase.[37]

The first township where protests against the rent increases led to violent conflict during 1984 was Tumahole. In May the council announced a 42 per cent increase. This would mean that rents had risen a cumulative 155 per cent in three years. Even two councillors opposed the increase. The other councillors, however, adopted a dismissive and uncompromising position in meetings with residents, and failed to explain why their earlier promises of township development did not seem to have been fulfilled. In July, a march was held against the rent increase. Residents felt that a mass demonstration was the only way of making their outrage known. When the police dispersed the marchers with teargas and sjamboks, residents retaliated by burning and looting councillors' property. One resident who was arrested by the police died in their custody.[38]

The events in Tumahole in July were soon overshadowed by the 'Vaal Uprising' in September in the townships of Sebokeng, Sharpeville, Evaton, Bophelong and Boipatong. Whilst the Vaal had been the fastest growing industrial region in South Africa during the 1970s, it was devastated by the recession of the early 1980s. The growing disparity between incomes and rents made housing a potentially explosive issue. As early as 1978, one study estimated that income in over three-quarters of Sebokeng households fell below a conservatively defined Household Subsistence Level (HSL).[39]

Between 1978 and the beginning of 1984, rents in the Vaal rose by over 400 percent, making them over 20 percent higher than in any other metropolitan area, as the Orange Vaal Development Board (OVDB) sought to raise rents and maintain them at 'economic' levels. By April 1984 the Lekoa Town Council admitted that 35,000 households, representing over half the total in the townships concerned, were in arrears on rent and service charges, with the council's deficit for the first quarter of the year at over R1.5m. The announcement that rents were to increase yet again provoked widespread protests, led by the Vaal Civic Association. On 3 September, rioting broke out, extensive property was destroyed, and four councillors were killed.[40]

Ministers blamed the protests on agitators. According to Law and Order Minister Louis Le Grange:

I am not convinced that the rent increase was the real reason. . . . There are individuals and organisations clearly behind what has happenned in the Vaal Triangle.

Gerrit Viljoen blamed 'external elements', and Piet Koornhof was moved 'to express my strongest displeasure to those who are behind these events and who are misusing innocent people and inciting them to chaos'.[41]

Others were more perceptive. The Van der Walt Report described the rent increase as having been handled 'overhastily, unwisely, clumsily and insensitively' by the council, and decided it was 'the final straw, the spark that caused the powder keg to blow up'.[42]

Many councillors also recognised the root causes of conflict. Alexandra's mayor, Sam Buti, accepted that increasing rents

. . . would throttle our people. It would be absurd if the development of Alexandra were to become a threat to our own people. The uprisings in black townships are tied to this same issue.

And Katlehong mayor Khumalo recognised that: 'Our people have turned against us because they have lost confidence in us. . .' A memorandum prepared by the East Rand Urban Council Association (ERUCA) acknowledged that 'residents are saying we are doing nothing for them except increasing tariffs'.[43]

At least 38 PWV councillors resigned by the end of November. Many of those who remained voiced increasingly strident criticisms of the government. Members of the 14 councils in ERUCA put pressure on the government by threatening to resign.[44]

THE CHANGING CHARACTER OF RESISTANCE

The violent confrontations of September 1984 and thereafter followed a period of increasingly widespread political mobilisation and protest in the PWV townships. During the early 1980s, a wide range of grievances became increasingly acute. During 1984, these disparate grievances and demands converged, leading to the further intensification of mobilisation and radicalisation of political cultures. In the words of a historian of a very different period of history:

> Anomic and associational movements, social protest and political demands, well-organised and clear-sighted interest groups and 'direct-action' crowds, leaders and followers came together in a chorus of united opposition.[45]

Political mobilisation and protest cannot be reduced to the work of a small group of clear-sighted 'agitators' or 'radicals', as the government generally claims, nor to an automatic response to the denial of national political rights, as is often suggested from outside the country.

The grievances that provoked mobilisation — education, rents, housing, township development, evictions, corrupt or unaccountable councillors and repression — were both local and diverse. But they were increasingly seen to be inter-connected, bound together through the interweaving of moral, political and material relations. And, as residents responded to grievances by organising themselves, and the state responded to protest with overtly political repression, the initially localised grievances were seen to be bound up with the fundamental issue of access to formal political power, both locally and nationally.

The issue of rents was particularly central to mass mobilisation in the early 1980s. In 1976-77 school students had, for the most part, protested alone. In the 1980s, discontent with rent prompted older residents, often including hitherto remarkably conservative people, to organise, to support or endorse the protests of others, and even to protest themselves. What made the issue of rents particularly important, however, was the way in which it combined with other grievances, in particular through growing opposition to incumbent councillors, and, to a lesser extent, the whole system of community and town councils.

Councillors were widely condemned as 'collaborators' and as 'sell-outs'. There is an interesting and significant difference in emphasis between these two terms. 'Collaborator' focusses on the relations between the councillors and, it is inferred, the apartheid state. 'Sell-out', on the other hand, focusses on the relationship between the councillors and other township residents, and expresses the perception that seems to have been the primary motivation for large numbers of residents to participate in, or support, new township organisations as an alternative to the councils, and demonstrations as a protest against them, generally over the issue of rising rents.

In most townships there were activists who publicly condemned the councillors as collaborators, identifying the councils as institutions established by the government as a substitute for African representation at a national level in the new tricameral parliament. However, while this view may have been widespread in the townships, it does not seem to have been the primary motivation for protest. This appears to have remained the case in most townships, even during mid-1984 when school students, who (unsurprisingly) seem to have been more responsive to national political discrimination,[46] widely boycotted classes. The opposition to councillors as collaborators intersected with the more widespread discontent with them as sell-outs, thereby strengthening and increasing the political coherence of this perception.

The centrality of the issue of rents, and the perception of councillors as sell-outs, helps to explain why the first major violent confrontation occurred in the Vaal Triangle, in townships which had been almost totally unaffected by the events of 1976-77; where there had been wcak campaigns against the Black Local Authority elections in 1983; where there seems to have been little agitation over the elections to the tricameral parliament on the eve of the Vaal Uprising; and where there were only weak links between local extra-state organisations and the United Democratic Front.

The state responded to the protests with repression. Of the almost 1,000 people killed in 'unrest' between September 1984 and January 1986, almost two-thirds were officially listed as killed by the security forces. In October 1984, 7,000 troops and police occupied and searched the Vaal townships during Operation Palmiet, the first of a series of massive displays of force.

Repression only served to politicise popular grievances. Explicitly, it led to demands for the resignation of councillors (who were now increasingly tainted with collaboration) and to the withdrawal of troops from the townships; implicitly, it concerned the underlying issue of the control and accountability of township administration and the instruments of state repression. Protests in the townships increasingly addressed explicitly political issues, not because the origins of political mobilisation had primarily involved a concern for national political rights, but rather because the state refused to tolerate township residents' struggles to define the townships in terms of their needs and demands, rather than the local state's fiscal or political requirements.

Since late 1984, and especially during the intensification of conflict during early 1986, the middle ground between residents and the local state has been further eroded. Many more councillors have resigned. In July 1986 the Mayor of Tembisa, Lucas Mothiba, resigned. His stated reasons capture the interaction between the financial and political contradictions facing councillors:

I joined the Tembisa Council in good faith and with the hope that I would succeed in helping my people. But I am convinced that unless the government is prepared to subsidise 90 percent of the black local authorities, they will never succeed.[47]

The fundamental contradictions were also manifested in the proliferation of rent boycotts — from the Vaal in September 1984 to the northern Orange Free State and Eastern Transvaal in early 1985, to Pretoria in late 1985, and to the Rand in 1986.[48]

Regardless of the success of the state in repressing active protest in the townships, it seems very improbable that the resistance that developed during the early 1980s can be defused without, at the very least, major transfers of resources into township housing and development. It is unclear whether the state will be able to restore its authority on any basis other than coercion. But if a non-coercive solution is achieved, the transformation of intra-township political relations in the early 1980s (and since) must surely ensure that such a solution will be markedly different from the bankrupt system of community councils or Black Local Authorities.

NOTES

I am very grateful to Matthew Chaskalson for his many suggestions, and for sharing his knowledge of the recent history of the Vaal Triangle. My thanks also to Janet Hersch, Karen Jochelson, and Laura Menachemson — who did much of the original interviewing — and Mark Swilling.

1. This chapter is a revised version of part of a much longer paper, 'Political mobilisation in black townships in the PWV region of South Africa', presented at the *Review of African Political Economy* conference on Popular Struggles in Africa, University of Liverpool, September 1986. The longer paper considered not only the interaction of political and economic relations and the origins of political mobilisation up to September 1984, but also the transformation of township politics during late 1984 and early 1985. The whole period is the subject of continuing research.
2. The concept of 'differentiated' labour power was originally applied to apartheid labour policy in D. Hindson, *Pass Controls and the Urban African Proletariat* (Johannesburg: Ravan Press, 1987); the re-differentiation of labour power is examined in W. Cobbett, D. Glaser, D. Hindson and M. Swilling, 'South Africa's regional political economy: a critical analysis of reform strategy in the 1980s', in *South African Review 3* (Johannesburg: Ravan Press, 1986), and W. Cobbett,'"Orderly urbanisation": continuity and change in influx control', *South African Labour Bulletin* (*SALB*) Vol. 11, No.8 (September/October 1986).
3. Quoted in Heather Hughes and Jeremy Grest, 'The local state', in *South African Review 1* (Johannesburg: Ravan Press, 1983), p.127.
4. Simon Bekker and Richard Humphries, *From Control to Confusion: The Changing Role of the Administration Boards in South Africa, 1971-1983* (Pietermaritzburg: Shuter and Shooter, 1984), p.132.
5. Rents and service charges are indistinguishable to township residents. Rents in principle comprise site rent, and house rent for state-built houses, whilst service charges cover the cost of capital development and service provision. Below I refer simply to rents, but include in this service charges. Service charges actually constituted most of the 'rent' in many townships, and its share markedly increased in the early 1980s. On the issue of finances, the state sought to phase out the few remaining extra-township sources of revenue. The Riekert Commission called for employers' contributions to be progressively reduced and eventually abolished.

6. Bekker and Humphries, *op. cit.*, p.148.
7. See appendices 1 and 2.
8. Quoted in Hughes and Grest, *op. cit.*, p.127. On community councils, see Robin Bloch, 'All little sisters got to try on big sister's clothes: the community council system in South Africa', *Africa Perspective*, 21 (1982).
9. Quoted in Bekker and Humphries, *op. cit.*, p.111.
10. Cf. J. Grest and H. Hughes, 'State strategy and popular response at the local level', in *South African Review 2* (Johannesburg: Ravan Press, 1984).
11. Quoted in J. Seekings, 'The anvil: politics in Tumahole, 1984-85', *Africa Perspective* (1987).
12. *Idem.*
13. *Report on the Investigation into Education for Blacks in the Vaal Triangle Following upon the Occurrences of 3 September 1984 and Thereafter*, by Professor Tjaert Van der Walt (Pretoria: Government Printer, 1985) (henceforth the Van der Walt Report), pp.29, 33; Councillor Mokoena, evidence in *The State v Baleka and 21 Others* (i.e. the 'Delmas Treason Trial'), p.2222; *The Sowetan* 3 Dec. 1985; the Lekoa Town Council's jurisdiction covers the townships of Sebokeng, Bophelong, Boipatong and Sharpeville (north of the Vaal), and Zamdela (south of the Vaal); for alleged incidents of corruption elsewhere, cf. 'The black town councils — a study of their performance and reception in the urban black communities', unpublished Urban Foundation report (1985) pp.7-9.
14. Quoted in *City Press*, 11 March 1984.
15. Election statistics from 'An analysis of the first 29 elections held under the 1982 Black Local Authorities Act', unpublished Urban Foundation report (March 1984).
16. Interviews with Mamelodi residents, conducted by Janet Hersch, Karen Jochelson, and Jeremy Seekings, April-May 1986; Georgina Jaffee, 'Beyond the cannons of Mamelodi', *Work in Progress (WIP)*, 41 (April 1986), pp.9-10.
17. *Saspu National*, 5, 1 (March 1984); Nigel Mandy, *A City Divided: Johannesburg and Soweto* (Johannesburg: Macmillan, 1984), pp.240-4; 'An analysis of the first 29 elections', *op. cit.*
18. South African Institute of Race Relations (SAIRR), *Race Relations Survey 1979* (Johannesburg: SAIRR, 1980), p.420.
19. Populist rhetoric unmatched by concrete results probably increased opposition to the councils. The Van der Walt Report (p.31) noted that 'some of the candidates apparently made election promises too glibly without necessarily realising their implications. . .'; needless to say, Sofasonke could not abolish influx control in Soweto, nor did they prevent rent rises.
20. SAIRR, *Race Relations Survey 1981* (Johannesburg: SAIRR, 1982) pp.260-1, and *Survey 1982*, p.317.
21. 'Katlehong removals', *SALB*, Vol.8, No.6, 1983; Mark Swilling,'The politics of working-class struggles in Germiston, 1979-83', unpublished History Workshop paper, University of the Witwatersrand, February 1984; *Saspu National*, 4, 1 (March 1983). The quote is by Baznaar Moloi, former secretary of the Katlehong FOSATU Shop Stewards Council, quoted in 'Katlehong removals'; Alf Stadler has detailed similar responses to demolitions in Soweto in the 1940s, in 'Birds in the cornfield: squatter movements in Johannesburg, 1944-1947', *Journal of Southern African Studies*, Vol.6, No.1 (1979); later reports of conflict include *City Press*, 9 Oct. 1983. As Mark Swilling has pointed out to me, this response is a sign of relative weakness — in particular of the shop stewards' councils — rather than strength.
22. SAIRR, *Race Relations Survey 1980*, *op. cit.*, p.329; *Survey 1981*, p.261, and *Survey 1982*, pp.317-19; *Saspu National*, 4, 4 (October 1983).
23. *SASPU Focus*, 1, 3 (December 1982); *Saspu National*, 4, 1 (March 1983); Mandy, *op. cit.*, p.235.
24. SAIRR, *Race Relations Survey 1979*, *op. cit.*, p.418, and *Survey 1980*, p.324.
25. *Saspu National*, 2, 3 (May 1981).

26. SAIRR, *Race Relations Survey 1981*, p.262.

27. *Saspu National*, 1, 3 (December 1982); *City Press*, 20 April 1983.

28. SAIRR, *Race Relations Survey 1981*, p.262; *The Star*, 14 Feb. 1985.

29. Interviews conducted in Duduza by Laura Menachemson and Jeremy Seekings, April-May 1986.

30. Cf. John Perlman, 'Bus boycotts, monopolies and the state', *WIP*, 31 (1984); Stuart Essig, *Transportation Boycotts in South Africa, 1940-1984* (SAIRR/Cape Western Region, June 1985).

31. On the 1984 school boycotts, cf. M. Bot, *Schools Boycotts 1984: The Crisis in African Education* (Durban: Centre for Applied Social Studies, University of Natal, 1985).

32. The inter-relations between different age-groups in most townships defy any simple dichotomisation between either 'workers' or older residents, and 'youth'. In some cases there is an organisational gulf and even ill-will between members of different age-groups, but generational differences seem to be the characteristics and not the causes of such divisions. Indeed, it is often unclear whether the term 'youth', so frequently used, refers to people in a particular age group or people engaged in 'unrest' (i.e. particular forms of protest). For example, Lawrence Schlemmer's article 'Township unrest as seen by township residents' is based on surveyed responses to the following question: 'Why do you think that young people in the townships are behaving the way they do?', *Indicator SA*, 2, 4 (January 1985).

33. Interviews with Atteridgeville residents, conducted by J. Hersch and K. Jochelson, April-May 1986.

34. Van der Walt report, *op. cit.*, p.1.

35. Bot, *op. cit.*; many more schools were periodically boycotted.

36. *Saspu National*, 5, 4 (August 1984), and 5, 5 (September 1984).

37. Interviews with Ratanda residents, by A. Creecey and others; *Saspu National* (September 1984), and 5, 7 (December 1984).

38. Seekings, 'The anvil', *op. cit.*

39. S. Bekker, 'The local government and community of Sebokeng', unpublished mimeo (1978).

40. See *Saspu National*, 5, 5 (September 1984); Johannes Rantete, *The Third Day of September* (Johannesburg: Ravan Press, 1984); Southern African Catholic Bishops Conference, *Report on Police Conduct during Township Protests August-November 1984* (1985).

41. *Rand Daily Mail*, 5 Sept. 1984; 7 Sept. 1984; 25 Sept. 1984.

42. Van der Walt Report, *op. cit.*, pp.28-9.

43. *Sunday Express*, 9 Dec. 1984; *The Star*, 4 Oct. 1984; *The Sowetan*, 11 Oct. 1984, quoted in 'The black town councils', *op. cit.*, p.3.

44. *The Star*, 4 Oct. 1984. But many of these councillors were soon praising the police for containing 'unrest', and launching very hostile tirades against protesters and organisations such as the UDF — see Tom Boya in *The Sowetan*, 9 Nov. 1984; and Khumalo in *The Sowetan*, 19 Nov. 1984.

45. George Rudé, *Paris and London in the Eighteenth Century* (London, 1970), p.319.

46. See Bekker, *op. cit.*, Van der Walt Report, *op. cit.*, and Bot, *op. cit.*

47. *The Weekly Mail*, 1 Aug. 1986.

48. See M. Chaskalson, K. Jochelson and J. Seekings, 'Rent boycotts and the urban political economy, 1984-87', paper presented at the History Workshop, University of the Witwatersrand (February 1987).

Appendix 1: Selected Economic Indicators, Black Households in the PWV (Data from Bureau of Market Research)

	PTA	WR/ER	JHBG	VAAL
Average income:				
per household (rand) — 1985	9359	8628	9624	7401
per person (rand) — 1985	1505	1615	1756	1335
Growth of real income per person (%)				
1975-1980	7.2	6.8	−10.7	na
1980-1985	17.3	12.2	28.2	−5.0
Percentage of households with income:				
(1) below Minimum Living Level (%):				
1980	23.3	17.7	28.8	28.4
1985	26.4	22.3	25.1	30.3
(2) below Supplemented Living Level (%):				
1980	35.8	30.8	41.4	38.9
1985	36.9	30.5	35.7	43.0
(3) below R4000 pa (1985 prices) (%):				
1975	27.3	22.8	14.4	na
1980	19.1	15.8	21.3	22.7
1985	20.0	19.3	23.2	26.1
(4) above R12,000 pa (1985 prices) (%):				
1975	11.1	9.7	14.7	na
1980	15.4	14.0	9.3	10.2
1985	25.1	19.3	25.1	15.9
Employment (% of labour force):				
1980	60.6	62.7	53.5	53.8
1985	48.9	49.5	49.8	45.7

PTA   — Pretoria (sample from Mamelodi and Atteridgeville)
WR/ER — West and East Rand (sample from Daveyton, Dobsonville, Kagiso, Katlehong and Tembisa)
JHBG   — Johannesburg (sample from Soweto)
VAAL — Vaal triangle (sample from Sebokeng, Evaton, and Sharpeville)

Source: Bureau of Market Research, University of South Africa (UNISA), 'Income and expenditure patterns of urban multiple households in Pretoria/the West and East Rands/ Johannesburg/Vaal Triangle, 1980/1985', *Research Reports* Nos 94.1, 94.3, 94.4 and 94.7 (Pretoria, 1981) and 130.2, 130.8, 130.9 and 130.13 (Pretoria, 1986).

Appendix 2: Selected Economic Indicators, Black Households in the PWV (Other Sources)

	JHBG	PTA
Estimated proportion of households with income:		
(1) below Household Subsistence Level (%):		
1978	49	43
1980	55	49
(2) below Household Effective Level (%):		
1978	80	87
1980	79	82
(3) below R4,000 pa (1985 prices) (%):		
1980	69	69
(4) above R12,000 pa (1985 prices) (%):		
1980	0?	0?

JHBG — Johannesburg, data from Soweto;
PTA — Pretoria, data for Mamelodi and Atteridgeville.

The above are all preliminary estimates calculated on the basis of data from Markinor (as republished in various editions of the South African Institute of Race Relations' annual *Race Relations Survey*, 1978-82), and HSLs defined by the Institute for Planning Research, University of Port Elizabeth, *Fact Papers* (1978-82).

Keenan provides the following data for Soweto townships:

(1) Growth of average real per capita incomes, 1982-85 (%):
Moroka	—	not available
Phiri	—	25
White City	—	17

(2) Proportion of households with incomes below the Household Effective Level (%):
Rockville	1978	29
	1980	37
Moroka	1978	25
	1981	34
	1985	48
Phiri	1985	52
White City	1985	62

Moroka and Rockville are better-off townships; White City is very poor.

Source: J. Keenan and M. Sarakinsky, 'Black poverty in South Africa', *South African Labour Bulletin* (1987); P. N. Pillay, 'Poverty in the PWV area: a survey of research', conference paper No. 18 of the *2nd Carnegie Inquiry into Poverty and Development in Southern Africa* (Cape Town, April 1984).

4. The Flight of the Herschelites: Ethnic Nationalism and Land Dispossession

WILLIAM COBBETT & BRIAN NAKEDI

Most of the chapters in this volume and, indeed, in many others, concentrate their attention on the crucial struggles occurring in the urban areas of South Africa. This emphasis is as correct as it is understandable, for it is in the urban areas that the real power of South Africa is to be found — both in terms of state power, and in terms of the various forces aligned against the apartheid state.

While the urban areas will undoubtedly provide the terrain over which the eventual future of South Africa is to be fought, it is nonetheless important to redress the balance, and focus a spotlight on the less obvious and much less dramatic struggles that occur in the rural areas.

This seems to be necessary for a number of reasons. Firstly, for many of the oppressed classes, it is in the rural areas that their confrontations with the apartheid state, and its predecessors, have been waged. Yet these very real battles have been fought without the knowledge or attention of the majority of the population. They have therefore been waged with very little possibility of solidarity action, with no television crews in attendance, documented only in the experience of the protagonists. They are, indeed, the 'hidden struggles' of South Africa. Rather than taking a dramatic form, they more often occur as wars of slow attrition over a protracted period. The stakes, however, can be very high indeed.

Secondly, a focus on the rural areas is vital precisely because of the relative paucity of research that has been conducted in these regions. And, finally, the results of these struggles, which have been fought over generations, will have a vital bearing on the future complexion of any liberated South Africa, especially insofar as the distribution of land and population is concerned.

To give an example of the above points, it is only necessary to consider the single most important policy of the state's social engineering, the brutal exercise in forced removals. For decades the state had been controlling the movement and settlement of black people through its influx control and pass law policies. However, in the past three decades, the scale of the exercise assumed dramatically different proportions, with in excess of three and a half million people being forcibly uprooted and moved.

They were moved from places where they had always been, to other places they had never seen. Their houses were bulldozed; they were physically attacked when they resisted; they were dumped and they were forgotten. The only early attempt at a systematic recording of this massive human misery was made by a lone priest, Cosmas Desmond, who travelled the country while trying, at the same time, to awaken people to the tragedy being enacted.[1]

It was not until the late Seventies and early Eighties that a significant attempt was made to create a picture of the policy on a national scale. The work of the Surplus Peoples Project has done much to redress the balance, yet the whole area of forced removals, land dispossession and other rural struggles remains badly under-researched.[2]

History is not only recorded by trained historians roaming the countryside: besides making their own history, many people document it as well. The writing of this chapter owes little to the research skills of the two authors. Rather, this is the story of the people of Herschel — our task has merely been to attempt to put it all together.

The struggle of the group of Sotho from the district of Herschel is a familiar one in South Africa. A life of collective economic and social activity was disrupted by the intrusion of state-engineered ethnic politics — the politics of patronage and privilege.

When the Herschelites would not conform to the new structures of power that had been imposed, they were harassed out of the area. The bantustan 'leader' appointed to look after their interests saw them, temporarily, as a useful lever in the pursuit of greater importance and power — when they no longer served that purpose they were discarded. Along with a collection of broken promises, they had acquired a new political vision.

HERSCHEL

Herschel district is situated on the south western border of Lesotho, and was originally designated as part of the Ciskei bantustan. However, in a chessboard move often employed in bantustan politics, it was transferred to the Transkei in 1975 in exchange for land between East London and Queenstown.[3] This transfer was contrary to the wishes of its population (predominantly Hlubi with Xhosa and Sotho minorities) who had indicated in a referendum in October 1971 that they had no desire to be ruled by the Matanzima regime.[4]

The Transkei was the first bantustan to adopt nominal 'independence' from the central government in October, 1976. The feelings of some of the Herschelites on this issue were so strong that Chief Malefane and his Sotho followers chose to leave the area, forming part of a larger group of some 15,000 refugees. They were lured by the illusory promise of better prospects in Sebe's Ciskei,[5] where Malefane later died 'in exile'.

There were further problems following 'independence'. In the adjacent Maluti district, in which another Sotho minority resided, there was resistance to the domination of the Xhosa, leading to weak secessionist moves that were harshly dealt with. As Murray points out, this was all part of the policy of 'ethnic nationalism', a key plank in the state's strategy of divide and rule.[6] These rumblings of discontent took place against a wider picture of bantustan and central government intrigues over the distribution of land and leaders in South Africa at the time. In the late Seventies the Van Der Walt Commission was considering a variety of proposals for the consolidation of the ten bantustans.

The QwaQwa bantustan, adjacent to Lesotho's north-western border, is the smallest and most densely populated of the ten apartheid creations. Situated in mountainous terrain and distant from any sizeable urban economic centres, its population influx in the Seventies was staggering. Its population density of 54 persons per square kilometre in 1970 had risen to 622 persons in 1980, and has subsequently continued to increase.

The extremely high population density was one of the reasons which led the Chief Minister of QwaQwa, Mopeli, to offer to buy Herschel from the Transkei in 1979. A more interesting and sinister reason, however, was the desire to enlarge QwaQwa as a prelude to its mooted unification with Lesotho.[7] This strategy — of damming 'surplus' people on the border of a neighbouring state before offering them the land in exchange for the 'problem' — was also being seriously considered by South Africa in connection with the Kangwane bantustan and adjacent Swaziland. Neither of these hare-brained schemes was to bear any fruit.

There were further murmurings of QwaQwa's desire to buy Herschel in 1982. The proposal also included a land swap: QwaQwa would obtain Maluti, in exchange for which the Transkei would receive Griqualand East. Matanzima retorted by saying that the existence of Sotho-speaking people in these areas did not give them sole claim over the land above other groups resident there. 'Transkei's constitution', he added, 'accommodated people of various language groups and cultures and each was free to maintain his culture and language without interference.'[8]

For his part, after failing to increase dramatically the size of his fiefdom, Mopeli took to articulating the grievances of Sotho minorities in other bantustans. The rest of this chapter looks at the treatment of a group of Sotho in Herschel, and assesses their recent history in the light of Matanzima's claims of plural equality, and Mopeli's efforts on behalf of the Sotho 'diaspora'.

MEMORIES OF LIFE IN HERSCHEL

Details of the Sotho's life in Herschel 'before the troubles' reveal a community living as a collective identity, both economic and social. However, the past is at times characterised in an all too idyllic fashion, flattened out into a seemingly timeless recollection of happy and industrious events, untroubled by intrusion from South Africa's struggles or, indeed, the cash economy. Nonetheless, these possibly idealistic memories are what the people live on, and as such have their own reality. As one man reminisced:

> Herschel was Trust Land which was governed by six chiefs: two of the chiefs were Sotho speaking and four were Xhosa speaking.[9] However, these chiefs were under the white commissioner.
>
> Each male, immediately after he got married, was given a stand of 75 square metres and land for cultivation of about 4-7 morgen. This land was given without paying a cent. It was our land. We were only paying general and poll taxes. A married man would pay R3 per annum and a single man R2 per annum.
>
> After getting his stand for a house, one would build a house for his family made up of stones. Roofing was done by grass. On land for cultivation, we would cultivate mealies, corn, wheat, beans and pumpkins etc. The cultivating was done by the men and the women. They would be assisted by others to harvest weeding [sic]. There was no irrigation system because the rainfall was high, causing continuous floods. After each harvesting each family head had to organise African beer, bread and soft porridge, so that other community members could

come and help by taking the crops home. The crops were conveyed by means of cattle.

Starting from every April to the end of August each man had to go to the *kgotla* (common place) and start braiding the grass, which would be used for roofing and containers for the crops. The roofing grass would be left at the *kgotla*, and anybody who would need the roofing grass would go there to obtain it for their own use. During these working times, boys were always present so they could get training.

And we would actually not sell our crops unless if one would like to buy blankets or salt. Then we would sell mealies to the Boer shop owners, cattles [*sic*] we would sell to the community members and sometimes to the Boers. We were not selling for profit, but in order to meet our necessities of life.

Men and boys would look after the livestock and some were living in the forest permanently having small houses for the sole purpose of looking after the livestock. We would sell the wool to the Boers.

We were living communally in the true sense of the word. I am saying this because no one could starve, having cattles or not, or whether they were involved in the land cultivation or not. If my neighbour did not have anything, it was my responsibility to see that he gets milk and food every day. During slaughtering I had to share the meat with my neighbour. After having slaughtered a cattle one had to invite all boys of the village to come and eat the internal organs of it, and men would be invited to come and eat the head. Women would also come and eat intestines.

If somebody did not have land for cultivation and I had [land], he would bring his cattle to help me cultivate my land or bring some seeds to cultivate with me. Now after he had contributed in that form we were shar[ing] equally after harvesting. If a member of the community did not have cattle or sheep other men who were rich in livestock would lend them 3-5 cattle and a number of sheep. This would serve a dual purpose — cultivation and milk production. Where any of the cattle or sheep were to reproduce the borrowers could retain the sucklings. The borrower could return the original sheep or cattle after many years when he was established.

There was no one who was suffering. There was no poverty. We believed in the principle of sharing. Each one helped one. There was no exploitation of man by man.

Women would remove weeds from the cultivated land, decorate their houses with traditional paintings, and cutting grass to make brooms, carpets, baskets and so on. In essence women were the carriers and childbearers and had little say in decision making.[10]

While children did undergo a modicum of formal schooling, the priority lay in preparing them for an agricultural future. The local schools did not go above Standard Four, anyway, and involved a daily walk of some ten kilometres.

We had little interest in formal education because the natural resources were here in abundance, hence we could not see the importance of formal education in our daily lives. Basic arithmetic and writing skills were required for counting our cattle and sheep. Our people believe and still believe in attending initiation schools. During adolescence the boys would attend initiation schools where circumcision and other training, on manhood, marriage and family care, would be conducted.

Justice, too, was an all-male affair.

The chief would call a gathering (*pitso*) of all the men in the village to come to the kraal and listen to the proceedings of the case. Eight men plus the chief would constitute the justice bench. Imprisonment was not applied, but the accused would merely be fined. In the case of theft, the complainant would be compensated. In my opinion the justice system was fair. It was not only done but was seen to be done. Only on rare occasions the court had to sit as the people basically lived in peace and harmony, and they did not see the need to indulge in criminal practices.

While the passing of time, and the harsh conditions in which these people find themselves today, may have served to improve and idealise these recollections somewhat, it is nonetheless clear that much was to change when the reality of Transkeian 'independence' intervened in the form of an aggressive and covetous ethnic nationalism.

TROUBLES BEGIN

An estimated 28,000 Sotho were living in Herschel. While it is not clear what formal titles the Basotho had to their land, it is possible to argue that they occupied it with rights of perpetual succession. However, with the granting of Transkeian 'independence' in 1976, it became clear that the ruling bureaucracy would promote the interests of the Xhosa. In 1975 Matanzima himself had made this much clear, returning from an overseas trip in which he claimed to have sought help for those who 'had sucked Sexhosa from the breast'. Certainly, any group that had snubbed his 'country' in a referendum could expect little help from him or his supporters.

The Sotho in Herschel had written in 1975 to the Minister of Cooperation and Development, M.C. Botha, complaining that the transfer of Herschel to the Transkei had been made without any consultation. Having no response from central government, 'T.K. Mopeli influenced us to be under QwaQwa and we agreed, but the condition being that we must remain in Herschel and Maluti respectively.'[11]

Before he fled the area, Chief Malefane led a delegation of Sotho from Herschel to meet with Matanzima on 7 September 1976. There were two whites in their delegation, who were there at the invitation of the QwaQwa authorities. Their plea not to be incorporated into an 'independent' Transkei met with little response.

> George Matanzima was repeatedly interfering when we were talking, and Malefane told him that if he was going to continue interrupting when he (Malefane) is on stage then he would stage a walkout together with his delegation like Verwoerd did at the United Nations. We ultimately staged a walkout because of him (George). George was interrogating us as if we were under house arrest, and that was irritating.[12]

With the granting of 'independence' to Transkei in October, 1976, 'we made a strong plea to the South African Government through the honourable Chief Minister T.K. Mopeli that the Basothos at Herschel, together with their land, are of no intention to share the arranged independence with Chief Matanzima.'[13]

David Tseki was visited by two captains of the Transkeian police, to 'talk to me that I must leave politics and forget about the land struggle we were waging in Herschel.' He also claims that the officers offered him a large sum of money. He was also invited 'as a VIP' to the Transkeian 'independence' celebrations, but declined the offer.

The official Transkeian response came in March 1977, when 15 members of the Herschel Sotho were detained under the new 'state' security legislation, some being held for up to six months in solitary confinement. After their release on 19 October their leaders fled to QwaQwa, and David Tseki was appointed their new leader in Herschel.

On 14 August 1978 Tseki's house was raided by Transkeian security police, who confiscated his personal documents. Following this, he was advised by a friendly local magistrate, and later by a couple of policemen, to leave Herschel immediately. A few weeks later, on 29 September, he was stopped at a roadblock. He was allowed to go home, but was told to report to the police station later that day.

I realised there was trouble like the magistrate told me and as a result I did not go back to Herschel but I went to Aliwal North and after three days my wife joined me there and then I went to QwaQwa; she returned to Herschel. She was [put] under house arrest for three months.

The Transkeian police, however, continued to harass the Sotho in Herschel. In January 1979, seventeen persons were detained: after their release, ten of them were redetained in December of that year. David Tseki's flight was therefore followed by a few hundred Sotho from Herschel, who went to Zastron in July and August, 1980.

In November 1980, the Sotho in Herschel submitted a memorandum to Mopeli, which contained their final decision 'of immediately leaving Herschel'. In this document, they detailed the grievances they felt over the issue of their treatment since 'independence'. 'We are no longer prepared to continue living under the present shameful bias and unjust Transkeian government. We are therefore appealing to the RSA to give us refuge.' The following were cited as examples of their persecution:

(i)   Our cattle are simply pounced upon before our very own eyes, sold and slaughtered by the Xhosa people without fear of arrest.
(ii)   Our houses and household furniture are being confiscated before our very eyes.
(iii) Our farm implements are being wrenched from our hands, thus preventing us from ploughing.
(iv)   Our ploughing fields are given to Xhosas thus depriving us of our only source of income.
(v)   Our businesses are closed down and later literally given to Xhosas . . . without receiving any compensation, let alone given any reasons or causes of such brutal actions.
(vi)   Our people and their leaders are daily harassed, tracked down and thrown into prisons without cause. Their main sin being Sotho people.
(vii) We are heavily taxed, despite the fact that work opportunities are only given to Xhosa-speaking people. To add more fuel to the fire we are expected in fact compelled to pay the following heavy taxes:

TAX (male and female)   — R20
LOCAL TAX   — R10
BOOK OF LIFE   — R2.50
PASSPORT   — R1.00

What confidence could we longer have in such a government? All these evils we ascribe to one factor, namely that we are not regarded as belonging to the Transkei. We therefore wish to be allowed to leave Transkei so that we will become a people working for the honour and glory of God, in a country that we can call our own because that which belonged to us has been given to the Xhosa people.[14]

The memorandum was acknowledged by Mopeli, who 'forwarded it to the Hon. Commissioner General of the South Sotho National Unit so that he may in turn send it to the Hon. Minister of Cooperation and Development'.[15] This was followed by a telex from Mopeli to Matanzima in Transkei, albeit some six months later, stating that 'the government of QwaQwa is very much concerned about the treatment of the South Sotho people in Herschel and appeals to you for their protection'.[16]

In the interim, however, Mopeli and members of his cabinet had held a meeting in Cape Town with a high-ranking South African delegation led by Koornhof, Minister of Cooperation and Development. Mopeli argued that the situation in Herschel was critical: 'The case is such serious [sic] that in the near future we might be confronted with a refugee crisis. More than 100,000 people are determined to leave Herschel immediately.' [17]

The discussion turns to high farce when 'The Hon. the Minister' muses, 'I wonder as to whether Foreign Affairs cannot offer help by the application of their influence with regard to this matter.' A Mr Bastiaanse of Foreign Affairs replies, 'We have already got Ambassador du Plooy's opinion with regard to this matter. He has shown that in terms of both the Transkei and South African legislature that S. Sothos in the Herschel area [are] citizens of Transkei and that we have no *locus standi* in this matter. This can be further viewed as interruption in the interior affairs of Transkei.'[18]

Mopeli, after complaining of a lack of land, was forced by Koornhof to concede that land near Harrismith, that was to be made available in late 1982, could be used for the resettlement of the Herschel people. The promise of land in QwaQwa, at a place called Riversdraai, was conveyed to the refugees in Zastron by Mr Pansegrouw, the Commissioner General of the South Sotho National Unit. This, at least, was the perception of the refugees.

After a meeting between Matanzima, members of his cabinet and a South African delegation, the Transkeian government issued a *Memorandum of Agreement*, which set out the conditions under which the refugees in Zastron could return to Herschel:

(1) that they apply for Identity Documents
(2) that they pay their arear [*sic*] taxes, for which a reasonable time will be given
(3) that they undertake to show full allegiance to the chiefs duly appointed over them.[19]

STRUGGLE BY CORRESPONDENCE

The Sotho refugees had, however, given up all their aspirations to ever live in Herschel again. Instead, they wrote to Mopeli stating that 'should a solution be arrived at that we must finally be re-settled elsewhere in the Republic we must immediately be placed directly under the QwaQwa government. We must be given land that should be added to QwaQwa equal to size and sufficient to settle [the] 28,000. This has been our cry since 1976.'[20]

A week later, a new approach was attempted, in which the refugees challenged the state to implement their own policy. 'We appeal to you Sir, our honourable Chief Minister to implore on our behalf the Central Government to bring the National Policy of Separate Development to its logical conclusion. Is the Central Government not purposefully ignoring our rightful request that our Honourable Chief Minister should lose face with the South Sotho people in Herschel?' [21]

It is hard to know what to make of this plea for the effective implementation of apartheid. At face value it would appear to be the plea of an ignorant and conservative chief wanting to further his sectional interest. Another reading, however, would indicate a high degree of political understanding, that of a leader forced to accept the reality of apartheid and thus attempting to play the game in Pretoria and Mopeli's own terms.

Certainly, it was clear that a new approach was necessary, especially in the wake of the visit of the Commissioner General to Zastron the previous week. It is alleged that on this visit he made a statement to the effect that 'I cannot help all you baboons on this and that side of the mountain.'

Through you Sir, we request the Commissioner General to give us this office which will be prepared to attend to the pleas of the so-called baboons. One may also ask himself: Which other baboons are at this side of the mountain? Does this statement refer to us all South Sotho people?
We appeal to you Sir to restrain the Central Government from forcing us to go back to Herschel. We are not prepared to go to Herschel, we would rather die than go back.

In a subsequent letter, showing signs of increasing frustration at the continuing harassment of Sotho in Herschel, another appeal was made to Mopeli, 'Your Excellency, we implore you, we pray you, release your people from the brutal snares of Transkeian tyranny.' [22]

Many of the refugees were moved to QwaQwa in 1981, where their numbers grew to some 800 by November of that year. Some were housed in the Phuthaditjaba Guest House, but most were accommodated in tents. David Tseki and the other members of the Basotho-Ba-Herschel (Sotho of Herschel) committee continued to operate from QwaQwa and from Zastron, where they could be closer to events in Herschel.

According to the (one-way) correspondence, cattle continued to be confiscated from Sotho, and their houses were also being demolished. Additionally, it was alleged the Transkeian authorities were actually refusing to acknowledge the Sotho in any way, and were even refusing to accept their tax payments. As proof of this, statements by six people who had been obstructed in this way were sent to the QwaQwa government.

What was increasingly concerning the affected Sotho was the lack of effort by their own 'government'. In June 1982, after much deference to 'your busy time', Mopeli was reminded of a collection of unanswered correspondence. Again, Mopeli was appealed to in quasi-biblical terms: 'We appeal to you sir, for the sake of peace, for the sake of humanity for the sake of generosity, let our people go!'

There were signs, however, that the refugees were beginning to see their struggle in a wider context, rather than simply identifying Xhosa nationalism as the sole culprit.

We have been brutally deprived of our land, shall the Central Government continue to perpetrate this brutal action by helping the Transkeian Government in their persistent harassment of our people. Why are we forced to say, there is no sincerity in the policy of the Central Government? Why are we forced to use the following slogan and practically too, against the Transkeian Government, 'Resistance to Tyranny is the Truest Obedience to God'.[23]

Although the Sotho refugees had given up hope of returning to the land of their forefathers, a letter was nonetheless sent to Matanzima reminding him of their historic claim to the land. 'We Have Monuments in Herschel which is proof that Herschel is the land of the Basotho. Even if I may leave the land of Herschel together with my people, Herschel will still remain the land of the Basotho for eternity.' [24]

The refugees continued with their correspondence and pleas to the QwaQwa authorities. In particular, they were concerned at the lack of action taken by their 'own government' in fulfilling promises that had been made to them. In December of 1982, they wrote to Mopeli stating that,

We, the South Sotho people of Herschel, who have since remained in QwaQwa as refugees, no longer regard ourselves as refugees but loyal and legal citizens of the QwaQwa National State. The Commissioner has . . . promised us that we would be given land at the end of 1982. This promise was made by him at Zastron in August 1981. This promise has since not been fulfilled.[25]

It was the fervent hope of these refugees that they be given land to continue their livelihood as farmers, and to be left alone thereafter. It would appear that the QwaQwa authorities, however, while making certain promises on the one hand, contemplated no such future for these people. In a memorandum drawn up by the QwaQwa Minister of Internal Affairs, some nine months earlier, the private position of the QwaQwa cabinet was clearly at variance with their public pronouncements of support. 'The Cabinet of QwaQwa strongly feels that workable efforts to resettle these people at Botshabelo (Onverwacht) receive the highest priority. If this problem is not resolved in a friendly manner then this government's reputation will lie in tatters.'[26]

Botshabelo township is situated some 55 kilometres from Bloemfontein, and over three hundred kilometres away from QwaQwa itself. It is the largest 'resettlement camp' — or more properly, dumping ground — in the country. More importantly, it is zoned exclusively for township development, and makes no provision for agricultural activities.[27]

In September 1983, Mopeli himself addressed the Herschel people resident in QwaQwa. A number of further promises were made at this meeting, *inter alia* that the refugees would be housed in QwaQwa for 2 to 3 years, and the houses would be provided on a rent-free basis; that these houses would suffice until land for their resettlement at Riversdraai (near Harrismith) became available; and that the Department of Cooperation and Development would assist in the feeding of the refugees.

Less than two years later, however, it seems that the conditions were arbitrarily changed by the QwaQwa authorities. The Herschel refugees were told to pay a monthly rent of R31.26 for their 'match box' houses, or alternatively purchase them for R5892.95 each.

In July 1985, eviction orders were served on those still refusing to pay rent. Some of the refugees, not believing that they were ever going to see 'the promised land', had started paying rent. This division in the community was clearly seen by the authorities as a way of finally 'discharging' the QwaQwa government's duty to its nominal citizens.

The issue even led to a remarkably rare occurrence, a letter from Mopeli to Tseki. 'I wish to say . . . that even if you [have] whipped up your emotions and distorted facts, what remains the main issue *is that you are to pay monthly rentals for the houses you are living in. That is the issue.* The rest of what you are saying is nonsense.'[28]

A number of meetings had been held with Mopeli in an attempt to resolve the issue. The 100 families that continued to refuse to pay rent, however, were soon to find themselves in court. 'In court Mopeli was told by the Chief Magistrate that it was not possible for us to be evicted nor to pay rent as according to the terms which were agreed on our arrival in QwaQwa. Both parties were advised to make an out of court settlement as the judgement by the court would not be in Mopeli's favour.'[29]

THE SELL-OUT

Faced with this humiliation, Mopeli re-opened the option that he had always kept hidden from the refugees — resettlement at Botshabelo. 'During our discussion with him about Botshabelo, we said that we could only agree to be moved to Botshabelo on condition that we were going to get our own piece of land as we were promised by Pretoria so that we could cultivate and graze our livestock.'[30]

None of the Herschelites had seen Botshabelo — only Mopeli knew the reality of conditions in what was, by now, South Africa's second largest township. Mopeli went to see his superiors in Pretoria, hoping that they would rid him of his 'problem'.

The result was a telex to Mopeli from the Director General of the ironically named Department of Development Aid. Sixty stands were to be provided for the refugees in Botshabelo, and tents were to be provided for a limited period as the Herschelites were expected, like most Botshabelo residents, to construct their own dwellings. Food was to be provided for the first three days — after that the refugees would be on their own. They imagined that, armed with their extensive farming knowledge, they would soon be growing their own crops and tending their livestock. Accordingly, the refugees were moved to their final destination in June 1986, nearly a decade after Transkeian 'independence'.

> We agreed to move to Botshabelo thinking that we were going to get the promised land so that our families whom we left behind in Herschel could join us there. Only to find when we arrived in Botshabelo things were not as we expected them to be. Then we realised that their promises were blatant lies.

In a final act of revenge, Mopeli had ordered that the Herschel families be separated and scattered throughout the huge township. It was a long way from the promised land.

> People were very hostile towards us as we were given stands which were in actual fact allocated to other people. Owners approached us with the relevant documents to prove their ownership of the stands by law. This chaos was part of the Pretoria and QwaQwa governments' tactic to destroy us, break our morale with the hope that we would go back to Herschel.

The refugees moved, without permission, to Section M of the township, where they are still to be found today — a forlorn collection of tents, surrounded by miles of empty land on which they are not allowed to farm. They are fed by Operation Hunger. Somehow, their resolve to return to their former lifestyle is as strong as ever. 'The remaining 28,000 people whom we left behind are still waiting for the promised land also. We are looking forward to reunite in the promised land.'

Most of the people have left families and livestock behind in Herschel, waiting for the day of deliverance. The Herschelites have lost much — but in so doing, they seem to have gained a new appreciation of the reality of politics in South Africa. As David Tseki says:

> First and foremost I would like to point out that Mopeli has misled us. He sold us out and he is very unreliable. In short he is a liar and not to be trusted because he is part and parcel of the system. I want to point out that throughout the political discourse with Mopeli my political horizons widened with the political irregularities.

The Sotho from Herschel in Botshabelo now have a particularly clear idea what the proposed incorporation of Botshabelo into QwaQwa will mean for the inhabitants. Mopeli's position on the issue is also clear. Faced with the widespread rejection of the plan by the people of Botshabelo, he is relying on the backing of the armed might of Pretoria to confirm his authority in the area. A recent newspaper report quoted him as saying that 'incorporation will go ahead before the end of this year, regardless of the views of the residents'.[31] Hundreds of youths have recently been detained for opposing incorporation. For David Tseki,

> The incorporation is nothing less than furthering the aims of Apartheid because the homelands are still the cornerstone of the system. This is one of the tactics and strategies which [are] employed by the ruling minority block to divide us.
>
> Take, for example, the Transkei and Ciskei, there the Xhosa tribe has been divided and today there is a feud which is in fact endless. They are fighting over power which is not there but it is in the hands of the South African regime.
>
> My people and I having realised what Mopeli has done to us [as] a homeland leader we are not prepared to be under his rule when we should get the land which we were promised and actually [are] still fighting for it. That point must be made very clearly to him and the whole world. I won't forget Mopeli when he said his government won't disappoint us but will fulfill all the promises he had made to the Herschel people. I repeat! Mopeli is a liar!!
>
> I want to state it in no uncertain terms and with utter dismay that I am totally against incorporation of Botshabelo into QwaQwa. I am looking forward to see a new South Africa which will be non-racial, unitary and have [a] one man one vote system. Our demands are as enshrined in the Freedom Charter.

CONCLUSION

The dispossession of this group of Sotho residents in Herschel must be seen in a wider context. Their story is the story of countless other communities who have been deprived of their access to land, not only in the recent period referred to here, but going back into the last century. South Africa, as it is today, is predicated on the enormous and widespread theft of land, more often than not wrested from its owners in a violent manner.

The Herschel case contains some important pointers to help us understand the nature of oppression in South Africa. It is significant, for example, that the real culprit of the piece, the white minority government, somehow manages to hide itself in the wings. The struggle over land and power is seen to be a *tribal* struggle — Pretoria is happy to play the role of benign mediator between the warring factions.

In such manner are many struggles played out in South Africa today — the bantustan bureaucracies, in exchange for the power of privilege and patronage, successfully mediate and diffuse the struggles away from the central state, on whose behalf they act. More importantly, in struggling over issues created by the policy of ethnic nationalism, communities are forever struggling over gains that — while maybe important in the short term — are not addressing the question of central state power. This is precisely the role of the bantustans, and their bureaucracies. They are earning their keep in the eyes of their paymasters in Pretoria. There are, however, important contradictions in the policy, which tend to act against the apartheid state and its functionaries.

Take the Herschel people as a case in point. It is clear from reading the voluminous correspondence that their overwhelming priority was to regain access to their means of production, land, and to return to their peasant status. It is equally clear that if Mopeli had provided them with this basic wish, he would have engendered a great deal of support for himself and his bantustan. The contradiction facing Mopeli, and the other bantustan leaders, is that they do not have power over real resources, nor were they meant to have it. The patronage which they are able to dispense does not amount to state power — without central state intervention they cannot create employment, but merely reallocate a few jobs; there is no land for them to redistribute, and so no farms for the Herschelites. Mopeli is not in power to impress his 'subjects', he is there to repress them.

In so failing, the bantustan system turns conservative and pliant people into voices of opposition. In their tents in Botshabelo, the Herschelites have undergone a process of proletarianisation and marginalisation — they are now workers without jobs, peasants without land. They are part of the half million people dumped on Bloemfontein's periphery, imprisoned by poverty, their only escape provided by the very intermittent value of their labour on the 'free market'. Their politics now echo the language of the townships. They now speak with a new language — the language of a future united and democratic South Africa. Once again, they seek their promised land.

NOTES

1. Desmond's activities led to his banning and house arrest. His films on the topic, notably *The Dumping Ground*, were banned. His seminal book on the early removals is *The Discarded People* (Harmondsworth: Penguin, 1971), which was subsequently banned in South Africa.
2. See L. Platzky and C. Walker, *The Surplus People* (Johannesburg: Ravan Press, 1985); G. Mare, *African Population Relocation in South Africa* (Johannesburg: SAIRR, 1980); J. Yawitch, *Betterment: The Myth of Homeland Agriculture* (Johannesburg: SAIRR, 1981); and B. Freund, 'Forced resettlement and the political economy of South Africa' in the *Review of African Political Economy*, No. 29, 1984. There is a welcome growth of historical research; see, for example, B. Bozzoli (ed.), *Town and Countryside in the Transvaal* (Johannesburg: Ravan Press, 1983); and W. Beinart, P. Delius and S. Trapido (eds), *Putting a Plough to the Ground* (Johannesburg: Ravan Press, 1986).
3. *Survey of Race Relations in South Africa, 1975* (Johannesburg: SAIRR, 1976), p.117.
4. C. Murray, 'Defining the unit of study: notes on the Orange Free State', paper presented at a conference on the Interactions of History and Anthropology in Southern Africa, Manchester University, September 1984, p.2; see also, *Survey of Race Relations in South Africa* (Johannesburg: SAIRR), 1971 (p.121) and 1972 (p.180).
5. See Murray, *op. cit.*, p.3.
6. *Ibid.*
7. *Rand Daily Mail*, 29 Sept. 1979.
8. *The Citizen*, 16 July 1982.
9. Trust land refers to land set aside for African settlement in terms of the Land Act of 1913, as amended 1936. It was this Act which entrenched the racial division of land in South Africa, and which has provided the cornerstone of the bantustan system.
10. Interview with David Tseki, Botshabelo, April 1987.
11. Interview with David Tseki, February, 1987.
12. Interview with David Tseki, Botshabelo, February 1987.
13. Memorandum by David Tseki, Zastron, 29 Feb. 1982.
14. *South Sotho: Herschel Memorandum*, dated 19 Nov. 1980, Phuthaditjaba Guest House (QwaQwa).

15. Letter from Mopeli to Tseki, dated 19 Nov. 1980.

16. Telex dated 13 April 1981.

17. 'Minutes of the discussions held in Cape Town on Tuesday 17 February 1981 with members of the QwaQwa Cabinet'. The minutes appear to be a rather poor translation from Afrikaans. Mopeli's figure of 100,000 refugees is a wild exaggeration of the situation, and leads one to conclude that he was attempting to use the refugees as a ploy for more land.

18. Minutes, *op. cit.*

19. *Memorandum of Agreement*, Umtata, 10 Aug. 1981.

20. Letter from Tseki to Mopeli, 9 July 1981.

21. Letter to Mopeli, dated 17 Aug. 1981.

22. Letter dated 2 Nov. 1981.

23. Letter dated 17 June 1982

24. Letter from Zastron, dated 29 Aug. 1982.

25. Letter to Mopeli, dated 12 Dec. 1982.

26. Memorandum signed by the Minister of Internal Affairs, dated 19 March 1982. (My translation from the Afrikaans. W.C.)

27. On Botshabelo, see W. Cobbett, 'A test case for planned urbanisation' in *Work In Progress (WIP)* No. 42, 1986; and W. Cobbett, 'Behind the "curtain" at Botshabelo: redefining the urban labour market in South Africa' in *Review of African Political Economy*, No. 40, 1987.

28. Letter from Mopeli to Tseki, dated 25 Nov. 1985 (translated from Sotho; emphasis in the original).

29. Interview with Tseki, April 1987.

30. Interview with Tseki, April 1987.

31. *The Star*, 20 July 1987.

5. The United Democratic Front and Township Revolt

MARK SWILLING

INTRODUCTION

Recent years have witnessed the revival of organised mass opposition to apartheid. Fighting in the townships, labour unrest, classroom revolts, rent strikes, consumer boycotts, worker stay-aways and guerrilla warfare — all these have become increasingly familiar features of South Africa's political landscape since 1976. From the time of the launch of the United Democratic Front (UDF) in 1983, however, radical black opposition has assumed an increasingly organised form, thereby enhancing its power and effectiveness.

It will be argued in this chapter that, since the inception of the UDF, black resistance in South Africa has become increasingly effective because of the UDF's capacity to provide a national political and ideological centre. However, it will also be argued that the contemporary history of township revolt was not due to strategies formulated and implemented by the UDF's national leadership. Instead, with the exception of the crucially important election boycotts of 1984, the driving force of black resistance that has effectively immobilised the coercive and reformist actions of the state has emanated from below, as communities responded to their abysmal urban living conditions.

The result was the development and expansion of local struggles and organisations throughout the country. As these local struggles spread and coalesced, the UDF played a critical role in articulating common national demands for the dismantling of the apartheid state. Thus the black communities have been drawn into a movement predicated on the notion that the transfer of political power to the representatives of the majority is a precondition for the realisation of basic economic demands such as decent shelter, cheap transport, proper health care, adequate education, the right to occupy land and the right to a decent and steady income.

The formation of the UDF was the outcome of a range of political responses and struggles in black townships as the contradictions of South Africa's dual structure of racial oppression and class exploitation generated new tensions, stresses and conflicts for the urban communities. The burgeoning black trade union movement that began in Durban in 1973 started flexing its muscles after its legalisation in 1979. Throughout the country black workers struggled to force employers to recognise unions as legitimate representatives of the working class.[1]

Having established themselves in the workplaces by the late 1970s, these unions shunned distinctions between economic and political issues and stridently challenged state policies.[2] Some of the more important workplace struggles included the 1979 Ford strikes in Port Elizabeth, food worker strikes in Cape Town in 1980, general strikes in the Eastern Cape auto factories in 1980-81, the emergence of militant general unionism in East London during the early 1980s, and the East Rand general strikes of 1982-3. These militant struggles frequently connected with community campaigns and in so doing contributed to the development of an oppositional political environment that helped prepare for the establishment of community organisations outside the workplace.

Beginning with the Eastern Cape and Soweto in 1979 and spreading throughout the country, local organisations mushroomed in the African, coloured and Indian areas. They built up a mass base by campaigning around such matters as housing, rents, bus fares, education and other urban services. In Port Elizabeth the Port Elizabeth Black Civic Organisation (PEBCO) was formed in 1979 as a coordinating body for the emerging neighbourhood residents' associations that were articulating housing grievances.[3] In 1980 a widespread schools boycott broke out in Cape Town that resulted in coordinated action around education demands between students under the leadership of the Committee of 81, teachers organised into Teachers Action Committees and parents represented by various area-based Parents Committees.[4] This boycott spread to the rest of the country, and was to last until 1981 in the Eastern Cape.

During 1981-2, mass-based community and factory struggles broke out in the Transvaal. These included the Anti-South African Indian Council's campaign against government-created representative institutions in the Indian areas, bus boycotts in the small rural towns, anti-Republic Day campaigns, general strikes over wages and working conditions in the industrial centres of the Witwatersrand, protests against rent increases and inadequate housing on the Rand[5] and an increasing number of ANC-initiated military attacks. Finally, during 1982 and 1983, new community organisations emerged in Natal, initially to oppose bus fare increases, but later to resist rent hikes in state-owned housing estates.[6] In East London a bus boycott that began in mid-1983 lasted nearly two years and ended when commuters succeeded in altering their transport conditions.[7]

These struggles, and many similar smaller-scale ones, steadily consolidated a political culture that articulated the principles of non-collaborationism with government institutions, non-racialism, democracy and mass-based direct action aimed at transforming urban living conditions and challenging white minority rule.

FORMATION AND ORGANISATION OF THE UDF

In January 1983 the Reverend Allan Boesak, speaking at the final conference of the Anti-South African Indian Council Campaign in Johannesburg, made a call for the formation of a front to oppose the government's new constitutional proposals designed to seat representatives of the coloured and Indian minorities in two additional houses of parliament. This *raison d'être* was later expanded to include opposition to new influx control laws and local government structures for Africans — the so-called 'Koornhof Bills', in particular the Black Local Authorities Act of 1982 which provided for the establishment of autonomous municipal institutions in the African townships.

A series of regional conferences subsequently took place in Natal, Transvaal and the Cape to work out the organisational basis and ideological position of the Front. Finally, a national launch was convened in Cape Town on 20 August 1983. The approximately 600 organisations that eventually affiliated to the UDF included trade unions, youth organisations, student movements, women's groups, religious groups, civic associations, political parties and a range of support and professional organisations.

The UDF was conceived of as a front, a federation to which different groups could affiliate and a body which could link different social interests who shared common short-term objectives. It has a national executive and regional executives for Natal, Transvaal, Western Cape, Eastern Cape, Border, Northern Cape, Northern Transvaal and Orange Free State. Affiliates, according to the constitution, have equal voting powers on the regional and national councils which elect officials despite substantial differences in size.

By early 1984 the UDF's affiliates were classified as follows:

Region	Student	Youth	Trade unions	Women	Civic	Religious	Political	Others
TVL	12	16	8	8	30	11	9	16
Natal	8	15	5	3	28	4	11	7
W. Cape	23	271*	2	20	27	4	9	4
E. Cape	3	13	3	2	2	2	4	4
OFS	1	1	0	0	0	0	0	0

* 235 of these youth organisations were affiliates of Inter-Church Youth.

(*Source*: Statistics from list of UDF affiliates compiled by the UDF and submitted as exhibit D7 in *State v. Mawalal Ramgobin and 15 others*.)

This list of affiliates, although officially compiled by the UDF, is misleading. Since early 1984, literally hundreds of community organisations allied to the UDF have sprung up around the country. For example, although only two OFS affiliates are listed, there are currently six major community/educational organisations operating in Bloemfontein alone and about ten more have sprung up in several small northern OFS towns during 1984-86. The same applies to many small Eastern Transvaal, Eastern Cape and Western Cape towns.[8]

Furthermore, the table gives a misleading picture of the organisational strength of the UDF in various regions. For example, whereas only 33 affiliates are recorded for the Eastern Cape, the UDF is strongest in this region and relatively weak in the Western Cape and Natal. The strength of the Eastern Cape organisations has to do with the relatively small, contained size of the communities, the existence of a single language group, the particularly depressed economic conditions, a strong tradition of political resistance, the absence of a viable state-supported 'moderate' group, and the existence of a particularly skilful and energetic group of contemporary leaders such as Mkhuseli Jack (Port Elizabeth), Weza Made (Uitenhage), Gugile Nkwinti (Port Alfred), Mafa Goci (East London) and the late Matthew Goniwe from Cradock.

The table also gives a misleading impression of the UDF's trade union support. Although the major trade union federations have not formally affiliated, they have developed strong working relationships with the UDF over the years. For example, the Federation of South African Trade Unions (FOSATU) and the Council of Unions of South Africa (CUSA) collaborated with UDF affiliates during the Transvaal regional stay-away in November 1984, which was supported by over one million people who stayed away from work and school in protest against army occupation of the townships, poor educational conditions and declining living standards.[9] During 1986, the Congress of South African Trade Unions (COSATU) worked closely with the UDF to coordinate nation-wide stay-aways on May Day and 16 June[10] and, in early October, these organisations committed themselves to a joint campaign of 'National United Action' against the State of Emergency.

A common combination of organisations in each community is a civic, youth congress, students' organisation (a branch of the Congress of South African Students (COSAS) until its banning in 1985), women's organisation and, in the metropolitan areas, a trade union local that acts more independently. There is no doubt that although church and youth groups predominate on the UDF's list of affiliates, it is the civics, youth congresses and student organisations respectively that are the UDF's most important bases. Although the leadership of these local organisations varies from region to region, a common pattern is that civics tend to be led by older residents, workers, professionals and clergymen regarded by the community as capable and respected leaders.

Contrary to a common view, the civic leaders are rarely traders and business people, the Soweto Civic Association being an atypical example. The youth congresses are often led by fairly well-educated unemployed youths or young employed skilled workers who count as their constituency those young township dwellers who have been excluded from the job market by the recession and from school by age-limit restrictions.[11] The student organisations are led by school-going political activists and the women's groups are frequently led by young and middle-aged women who have graduated from either trade union movements or educational organisations.

In addition, there are also a range of *ad hoc* and constituency-based committees established to handle specific campaigns or represent particular groups with special grievances. The most well-known organisations of the *ad hoc* variety include the Consumer Boycott Committees and burial committees. Examples of groups represented by constituency committees include squatters, communities threatened with forced removals, commuters opposed to their transport conditions, hostel dwellers, traders, detainees, unemployed groups, professionals (e.g. journalists, clergymen) and the various Crisis Committees which deal with issues ranging from educational problems to housing grievances and crime.

The complex patchwork of local community organisations, which has become the organisational foundation of the UDF, developed out of local urban struggles that took place before and after the formation of the Front. Initially, these struggles involved minor conflicts between communities and local authorities over issues such as transport, housing, rent and service charges. However, the combined impact of the inevitable coercive response and official refusal to make concessions transformed the local urban struggles into campaigns with a national political focus. However, what is significant is that because these local organisations were rooted in struggles over urban problems that affected the daily lives of most members of the communities, they were able to bring their mass base into the political campaigns.

A brief survey of some examples will help substantiate the above argument: PEBCO, formed in 1979 to coordinate protests against rent increases; Soweto Civic Association, formed in 1979 to oppose the community councils and housing conditions; the Joint Rent Action Committee, formed in 1982-3 to oppose rent increases in the Durban townships; the Cape Housing Action Committee, formed in 1981 to coordinate housing struggles in Cape Town; the East Rand People's Organisation, formed in 1982 to articulate squatter demands for housing; the Cradock Residents Association, formed in 1983 to oppose rent increases; the Committee of 10, formed in 1983 to represent commuters boycotting the bus service in East London; the Vaal Civic Association, formed in 1984 to oppose the Councils and rent increases; the Langa Coordinating Committee, formed in 1985 to represent squatters threatened with removal; the Tembisa Working Committee, formed in 1986 to demand better housing conditions; and the Duncan Village Residents Organisation, formed in 1985 to oppose their forced removal and to demand better housing.

These and numerous other examples provide more than enough evidence to support the view that local organisations emerged out of struggles around local urban problems. They also constituted the basic components of a movement with national political demands that were expressed programmatically by the UDF.

The strength and organisational coherence of the UDF's local affiliates varies from region to region. By mid-1986 (i.e. prior to the 1986 State of Emergency), the Eastern Cape local organisations were by far the strongest in the country due to the skill and energy of the leaders, the level of support the organisations enjoyed, and the extent to which the communities had been drawn into the various structures of the UDF's local affiliates. In the Western Cape, on the other hand, the local affiliates are relatively weak, especially in the African communities.

During 1985-6 the leadership of the Western Cape African organisations split along class lines, resulting in open violent confrontation between Ngxobongwana, the corrupt slumlord 'Mayor' of Crossroads and chairperson of the Western Cape Civic, and youth congress activists. The result was the destruction of the squatter settlement of Crossroads and the defeat of the youth congress activists after security forces exploited the division by actively supporting Ngxobongwana's faction. In 'coloured' areas, the grassroots residents associations that grew out of the student-parent cooperative structures, established during the 1980 schools boycott, split along ideological lines between UDF affiliates and those supportive of a Trotskyite position associated with the Unity Movement.

Deep divisions in Natal's African areas have plagued UDF community organisations in this region, preventing them from consolidating the grassroots organisational gains made during the 1982-3 period of agitation and mobilisation around transport and housing issues. Instead, Zulu nationalism has been cultivated and exploited by Gatsha Buthelezi's Inkatha movement, with the aim of building a reactionary alternative to mainstream national democratic and trade union organisations. Inkatha's local leadership, rooted in powerful petty bourgeois political networks, have not hesitated to use violence in an attempt to eliminate UDF affiliates from Natal's African townships.

The Transvaal is too large and complex to allow for generalisations. Nevertheless, the UDF's local affiliates in this region are much stronger than in Natal or Cape Town, while not as coherent or effective as those in the Eastern Cape. In recent years sophisticated local organisations, mobilising around urban issues, have emerged in the Pretoria-Witwatersrand-Vereeniging (PWV) region. By the end of 1986, these organisations were particularly strong and well organised in most areas surrounding Johannesburg/Pretoria (e.g. Soweto, Tembisa, Mamelodi and parts of Lenasia), and in many small towns in the Eastern Transvaal (e.g. Warmbaths, Witbank and Nelspruit).

However, in other areas, UDF affiliates enjoyed considerable legitimacy despite relatively weak and incoherent organisational structures at grassroots level (e.g. some Vaal and East Rand townships). In general, Transvaal organisations have not been faced with paralysing ideological divisions as in the Western Cape or an aggressive reactionary alternative like Inkatha in Natal. The massive size, steady deterioration and bankruptcy of the PWV's black townships have combined to facilitate the building of fairly strong local organisations committed to articulating community demands.

There are also important regional variations in the relationship between regional executives and local affiliates. As far as the Eastern Cape and Border regional executives are concerned, based in Port Elizabeth and East London respectively, they have had very weak links with organisations outside these centres. In both areas, the strength of the UDF has been located at the local level. The same does not apply to the Western Cape. Relatively weak local organisations coupled to ideological division have increased the importance of the Western Cape regional executive as an ideological and organisational centre.

In Natal, the impact of Inkatha repression in African areas has enhanced the importance of the relatively protected Indian activists who have organised successful local organisations affiliated to the Durban Housing Action Committee. This helps explain why the NIC leadership plays such an important role in UDF politics at a regional level in Natal.

The combination of extensive repression (which was to affect the Transvaal executive particularly badly during 1984-6) and the demographic concentration of the region (with twenty-nine major townships in the PWV alone) made it impossible for the Transvaal leadership to consolidate strong linkages between local and regional structures. It is not uncommon for local organisations to have had absolutely no contact with regional leaders. Instead of the regional executive acting as the regional coordinators of oppositional activities in the Transvaal, local grassroots leaders emerged to take responsibility for particular areas, e.g. Pretoria and environs to the north, East Rand (stretching from Germiston to Heidelberg), Soweto, Vaal/N.OFS and Eastern Transvaal (including the Lowveld).

What sort of people lead the UDF? The men and women who have served as its patrons, spokespeople and office-holders span four generations of black political protest. There are the veterans of the mass campaigns of the 1950s, old ex-ANC stalwarts like Archie Gumede from Natal, Oscar Mpetha from Cape Town, Henry Fazzie and Edgar Ngoyi from Port Elizabeth, and some of the Federation of South African Women leaders like Albertina Sisulu and Helen Joseph from Johannesburg, and Frances Baard from Pretoria. Then there are the survivors of the first Umkhonto we Sizwe guerrilla offensive of 1961-65. The present national chairperson, Curnick Ndhlovu, is one such survivor, and the ex-chairperson of the Border regional executive, Steve Tshwete, who was recently forced into exile, is another. A surprising number of less well-known members of this generation of political activists who have served lengthy prison sentences are very active in many Eastern Cape community organisations, e.g. Mike Nzotoi and Anthony Malgas of Port Elizabeth and Joe Mati of East London.

A proportion of the UDF leadership comes from Indian Congress politics, particularly those responsible for reviving the Natal Indian Congress in 1971. Mewa Ramgobin and George Sewpersadh from Natal are two of the best-known of such figures.

Probably the most important and politically sophisticated leaders in the UDF graduated from the ranks of the Black Consciousness movement of the early and mid-1970s. These include Mkhuseli Jack from Port Elizabeth, and Curtis Nkondo, Terror Lekota, Popo Molefe and Aubrey Mokoena — all from Johannesburg. It is impossible to calculate how many current UDF activists were politicised by the Black Consciousness movement of the 1970s. Throughout the country in the youth congresses, civics and trade unions, there are such people working diligently to organise the workplaces and communities. It is significant that many have served prison terms during which time they came into contact with prominent political leaders who persuaded them to drop the exclusivist black nationalism of Black Consciousness and adopt the non-racial class analysis framework of the 'Charterist' tradition — i.e. the tradition espoused by the ANC and UDF.

Finally, there are political activists whose first political experiences derived from the construction of community, youth, trade union and student organisations during the later 1970s and early 1980s. These people became increasingly important during 1985-6, after the security forces had detained the better-known seasoned activists, when they found themselves responsible for ensuring the continuation of organisations under extremely difficult conditions. These people span a number of generations and are most evident in the street and area committees that have emerged since 1985. Less articulate ordinary working class people tend to be more at home in these decentralised bodies than in the high-profile mass meetings that have traditionally been meeting points for black political movements.

The heterodox social and class composition of the UDF leadership belies attempts to explain its ideological position using simplistic class categories. In particular, some writers make unsubstantiated claims about its 'petty bourgeois leadership'.[12] Unfortunately, the meaning of these terms is never defined. One implication is that the UDF is dominated by people with bourgeois class origins and therefore cannot be expected to adopt a proletarian ideology. Leaving aside for the moment the questionable assumption that ideological affiliation is reducible to class origins, these writers have misrepresented the class origins of the UDF leadership.

Although the UDF is undoubtedly multi-class, a high proportion of the UDF's leadership are (or have come) from poor working class backgrounds. The Eastern Cape regional executive is a good example. The president,

Edgar Ngoyi, is a house painter by profession. After being politically active in the ANC in the 1950s he was charged and sentenced to 17 years on Robben Island. Henry Fazzie, vice-president, was a full-time trade unionist in the 1940s and 50s. He was also charged in the early 1960s and sentenced to 20 years on the Island. Stone Sizani, publicity secretary, is a skilled worker in a chemical factory and previously held a job as an organiser for the (then) African Food and Canning Workers' Union (AFCWU). Michael Dube, recording secretary, is a factory worker at Nova Board. Only Derek Swartz, general secretary, and the late Matthew Goniwe, regional organiser, are not workers. Swartz is a teacher and Goniwe was a headmaster in Cradock.

The Western Cape regional executive has a slightly different profile. The president, who used to be a petrol pump attendant, was subsequently imprisoned for his political activities and has remained unemployed after his release. The vice-president started his adult life as a mine worker in the Transvaal. He then worked in Cape Town on a migrant labour contract where he became an organiser for the South African Congress of Trade Unions (SACTU) during the 1950s. He was later imprisoned for his political activities and has remained unemployed since his release due to police harassment. The second vice president was a clothing worker but is now unemployed, again due to police harassment. The remaining nine members of the executive are teachers, lecturers and students — four of whom have working class origins while the rest come from middle class backgrounds.[13]

Using a sample of 62 UDF leaders from six regional executives (Transvaal, Natal, W. Cape, Border, E. Cape and N. Transvaal) about which reliable biographical information exists, it is possible to show that 33 are currently in economic positions that can be defined as working class, while the rest are teachers/lecturers (16), doctors/nurses/social workers (4), lawyers (5), priests (2), technicians (2) and students (2). Significantly, there is not one business person in this sample. Instead, this profile reflects the existence of a working class and intellectual/professional leadership.[14] This contrasts with the leadership profiles of other black political organisations, such as AZAPO and Inkatha, which have relatively few working class leaders and, especially in the case of Inkatha, a substantial number of business people in leading positions.

It is also arguable that the level of repression national and local-level leaders have had to suffer has made it extremely difficult, if not impossible, for them to find the space to become petty accumulators. (Dr Motlana of the Soweto Civic Association is the obvious exception. However, like his contemporary Mike Beea of the Alexandra Civic Association, he has been increasingly marginalised by more radical elements in the Civic, Youth and Student Congresses, who do all the organisational work.)

All the UDF leaders cited in the above sample have been politically active for at least 10 years (in the case of the ex-Black Consciousness activists) and others for 30 years in the case of the ex-ANC members. Nearly all have experienced apartheid's prisons as detainees or political prisoners. Some of the ANC/SACTU stalwarts have already served 10-20 year sentences, with the ex-Black Consciousness activists having served shorter terms. Those who have not served prison terms have invariably spent substantial periods of time in detention.

Significantly, the men and women who lead the UDF have come to hold these positions as a result of their activities in political, trade union and local organisations. Using the sample of 62 leaders cited above, and taking into account the fact that individual leaders have had experience in more than one type of organisation prior to their election to regional office, it is possible to show the following: 20 were active in civic associations, 16 in political organisations (including the ANC and Indian Congress), 14 in trade unions, 10 in youth organisations, 8 in student movements, 5 in white organisations and 3 in women's groups. Forty-two leaders have come from the ranks of the civic, trade union and youth organisations, these being the most active in the poor working class communities.

Reflecting the heterogeneity of its class composition, the UDF's ideological make-up is equally complex. The major affiliates subscribe to the national democratic programme of the Freedom Charter (adopted by the ANC in 1955). The basic ingredients of this programme involve firstly a commitment to the dismantling of white minority rule and the establishment of a non-racial unitary democratic state based on the fundamental principles of the rule of law, constitutional equality, freedom of association and other democratic liberties. Secondly, this programme involves the dismantling of the white capitalist power structures through a combination of nationalisation, land redistribution and welfarism.[15]

UDF ideologues have been careful to demonstrate that although the Freedom Charter is basically anti-capitalist, in the sense that if implemented it will dislodge the basic foundations of *South African* capitalism, this does not make it a socialist document. Instead, their depiction of the Freedom Charter, and hence the 'national democratic struggle', as 'anti-capitalist' reflects a concern to present the ideology of the UDF in a way that mirrors its multi-class character.[16] At the same time, however, UDF publications and speakers maintain that the extent to which the South African revolution culminates in a socialist order will depend to a large extent on whether the working class manages to establish its hegemony within the Front, and in so doing to guide the struggle towards attaining socialist goals.[17]

Common adherence to the national democratic programme and multi-class strategies by UDF affiliates, however, does not mean that differences of emphasis and interpretation are absent. Some UDF leaders — particularly those close to the trade union movement — openly depict the anti-apartheid struggle in terms of a 'history of class struggles' of 'the boer struggle against the workers'.[18] This emphasis, which is common in the Eastern Cape — although by no means absent in other regions — was graphically reflected in March 1986 when a prominent Eastern Cape youth congress leader greeted a crowd of 60,000 people in Uitenhage in the name of the most prominent international and South African communists, starting with Karl Marx and Lenin and ending with Joe Slovo and Moses Mabhida. This socialist position is also frequently coupled to sophisticated criticisms of 'petty bourgeois nationalist' regimes in Africa and the practices of similar elements in the South African liberation movement.[19]

When it comes to strategy, socialists in the UDF have emphasised the linkages between oppression in the communities and exploitation in production.[20] Talking at the 1987 NUM congress, UDF publicity secretary Murphy Morobe said:

We know how it is for people to go to work in the morning and find their shack demolished when they come back home. To such people it is completely artificial to build a Chinese wall between trade unions and community organisations. . . . Therefore who would deny the patent symbiotic relationship between the rent boycott and struggle for high wages?

In similar vein, a rent boycott pamphlet issued by civic activists in Soweto in late 1986 under the slogan 'AN EVICTION TO ONE IS AN EVICTION TO ALL', demanded 'that because of low wages, unemployment, retrenchment, rent be reduced to an affordable amount'. The pamphlet ended by calling for a boycott of all 'shops, garages, cinemas, dry cleaners, funeral parlours, etc.' owned by the councillors. In Alexandra a similar pamphlet was issued in late 1986:

We produce the goods, but we get low wages. And when we want to buy, things are very expensive. Because the bosses have added big profit. We even are the ones who build houses, but they are expensive. Our little money is taken away by *rent* and *inflation*, which are other names for **PROFIT**. WHO GETS THE PROFIT? GOLDSTEIN, SCHACHAT, THE LANDLORD STEVE BURGER.

WORKERS, WE CANT ESCAPE WITHOUT BOYCOTT. THE SYSTEM IS PROFITS, HIGH RENT, SLUMS, OPPRESSION BY SOLDIERS, DONKEY WORK FOR THE BOSSES. BE UNITED, WORKERS, RESIDENTS OF ALEXANDRA. HOLD THE BOYCOTT. DONT PAY RENT. [Emphases in original]

A discussion paper entitled 'Organising for people's power' that was distributed in various Transvaal townships provided an explicit class analysis of the relationship between workplace and community:

The growth of the labour movement and the emergence of worker leaders not only in trade union struggles but in relation to student and civic battles as well, highlighted the fact that our struggle is not only against the government but against the bosses who own and control the key sources of wealth and development. Their vested interests stand directly in the way of the needs and aspirations of the working class. . . . For example, most people cannot afford to pay rent. The rents themselves are not that high however. They are only crippling because people are paid poverty wages. The fight for lower rents must go hand in hand with the struggle for a living wage.

The rhetoric of the imams and clergymen involved in the UDF is more conservative than that of many of the radical working class leaders. They refer to divinely ordained human rights and liberal conceptions of individual liberty. Some of the Indian Congress leaders take their Ghandian philosophical heritage very seriously. However, for socialists within the UDF, this marriage of proletarian and liberal/religious political ideologies is a reflection of the objective reality of racial oppression and class exploitation which has made it necessary for all oppressed classes to unite against the common enemy of white rule. This 'popular democratic struggle', they argue, 'is a fight of both workers and non-workers against racism and the anti-democratic and militaristic nature of the apartheid state'.[21]

In this they find themselves in conflict with some trade unionists and the Azanian Peoples Organisation (AZAPO).[22] Whereas the former object to class alliances on the grounds that workers invariably find themselves sub-ordinated to 'petty bourgeois' interests, the latter has adopted a virulent black Marxist-Leninism of the North American variety that depicts the black working class as a revolutionary vanguard capable of fighting 'racial capitalism' untainted by the 'populist' 'petty bourgeois' influences of non-workers, particularly if they are white.

The organisational foundation of the movement the UDF has emerged to represent is rooted most firmly in local communities throughout the country. Beyond its local affiliates, the UDF's regional and national executives have provided a set of national leaders, symbols, spokespeople and ideas that have provided discrete local organisations with a national identity. The UDF as such, i.e. its regional and national structures, was important largely at a political and ideological level because local struggles have been presented by UDF leaders as component parts of a national liberation movement.

To quote Graeme Bloch, a member of the Western Cape regional executive:

> At the very least, leadership is responsible for thorough and ongoing political assessment at a national level and for outlining a range of options and responses that may be fed back into the various affiliates. This does not grow spontaneously in a simple one-way fashion from the day-to-day concerns of affiliates, and at its ideal serves to enhance and give direction to their ongoing campaigns.[23]

As an extra-state organisation operating under authoritarian conditions, the UDF has enjoyed a remarkable degree of direct and indirect control over various means of mass communication. The various 'community newspapers' have played an indispensable role in cultivating the growing consciousness of a shared national political identity. These newspapers include: *Grassroots* in Capetown, *Speak* in Johannesburg, *Ilize LaseRhini* in Grahamstown, *Ukusa* in Durban, *The Eye* in Pretoria, *SASPU National* published by the South African Students Press Union in Johannesburg, *Isizwe*, a popular theoretical journal published more recently by the UDF, and a UDF newsletter called *Update.*

In addition, the UDF has been able to benefit from sympathetic journalists located in the mainstream commercial newspapers and since 1985, from the 'alternative' weekly, *The Weekly Mail.* The liberal universities have also played an important role with progressive SRCs providing media and speaking forums to support key UDF campaigns. Then, of course, there are the numerous cultural groups, writers, film groups, musicians, publishers, support organisations, churches, educational organisations and academic groups which have, in one way or another, committed themselves to propagating an anti-Apartheid discourse that reinforces the overall ideological framework of the UDF.

In short, although the UDF's organisational power is reducible to the capacities of its affiliates, its regional and national structures have a political and ideological autonomy that has had substantial influence on political relations in local communities, and on South African and international perceptions of township leadership. It is, therefore, both the sum of its parts — and an autonomous national political force.

PERIODISATION OF UDF POLITICS

The UDF is a front, not a centrally coordinated party. This makes it impossible to ascribe the wide range of mass protests since 1983 to initiatives originating from within the front. Nevertheless, it is possible to periodise the general orientation of the activities of the UDF and its affiliates into four phases.[24]

As has already been pointed out, the first phase of the UDF's activities began when it was formed to organise nationwide opposition to the new Constitution and the 'Koornhof Bills'. The central thrust of this campaign was to use the inadequacy of these forms of political representation to demand substantive political rights. The subsequent successful election boycott dealt a severe blow to the state's reformist initiatives. More importantly, the success of the boycott tactic established the UDF as a viable extra-parliamentary alternative. The UDF slogan that expressed this objective was 'Apartheid Divides, UDF Unites'.

The significance of this phase was that the UDF was operating primarily on state-determined terrain and hence its politics can be described as reactive. The objective, therefore, was not to pose alternatives to apartheid or seriously establish organisational structures designed to sustain a long-term struggle for social transformation. Rather, the UDF was keen to counter the divisive tactics of state reforms by calling for the maximum unity of the oppressed people and urging them to reject apartheid simply by refusing to vote. The concern to build this consensus was reflected, for example, in the decision not to make the Freedom Charter the formal statement of principles of the UDF because at that stage, the UDF still wanted to draw in non-Charterist groups like Black Consciousness and the major trade union federations.

The reactive phase of UDF politics ended with the Million Signature Campaign, which aimed at collecting a million signatures for a petition against apartheid. Although the objective of the campaign was to challenge the legitimacy of the apartheid state at an ideological level, it did, for the first time, provide township activists with a vehicle for some solid door-to-door organising. For example, in a number of Eastern Cape towns, the organisational infrastructure for what later became strong community organisations was laid during this period of grassroots organising. However, in some areas in the Transvaal, particularly in Soweto, activists refused to collect signatures, believing the campaign to be a weak and futile form of protest politics that could achieve very little. In the event, the campaign failed to get a million signatures.

The second phase of UDF politics began after the tri-cameral parliament elections in August 1984. Soon after they were over, struggles initiated by local community organisations began to centre around more basic issues affecting everyday township life. The result was a series of bus boycotts, rent boycotts, squatter revolts, housing movements, labour strikes, school protests and communal stay aways. The depth and geographic extent of these actions coalesced into an urban uprising that took place largely beyond the organisational controls of the UDF's national and regional leadership and culminated in the declaration of a State of Emergency in July 1985.

This shift, from national anti-constitutional campaigns to local community struggles, was not due to changes in national UDF policy. On the contrary, the shift was the product of the activities of local community organisations and activists mobilised around concrete urban and daily life issues. Some of these organisations had been active since 1979, such as PEBCO and the Soweto Civic, while others were only formed in 1984-5, for example, the Vaal Civic Association and many of the youth congresses. These local organisations exploited the contradiction between the state's attempts to improve urban living conditions and the fiscal bankruptcy and political illegitimacy of black local government.[25] They managed to ride a wave of anger and protest that transformed political relations in the communities so rapidly that the UDF's local, regional and national leaders found themselves unable to build organisational structures to keep pace with these levels of mobilisation and politicisation.

The deepening recession and the illegitimacy of state reforms were the underlying causes of this urban uprising. The recession — which began to set in during the first quarter of 1982 — not only undermined real wage levels, but also limited the state's capacity to subsidise transport and bread prices, finance housing construction and the provision of urban services, and upgrade educational and health facilities. The illegitimacy of state reforms and, in particular, the failure of the new Black Local Authorities to attract support from the African communities meant that economic grievances were rapidly politicised and the struggles, that resulted articulated both economic (i.e. collective consumption) and political demands, namely the need to reconstitute the structure of political power as a precondition for resolving the crisis of urban living.

There were other decisive moments during the uprising. Firstly, the Vaal uprising, which took place in September 1984, was sparked off by the rent increase announced by the Lekoa Town Council. The uprising led to the death of at least 31 people and the beginning of a rent boycott in the region which has continued into 1987. Secondly, the nationwide schools boycott: this began in late 1983 in Cradock where students protested the dismissal of Matthew Goniwe — a local headmaster and UDF leader (subsequently assassinated in 1985). The boycott then spread to Pretoria in early 1984 and to the rest of the country by the end of the year. The demands of the schools movement included recognition of elected Student Representative Councils, an end to sexual harassment of female students and corporal punishment, release of detained students, and upgrading of educational facilities.

Thirdly, the mass worker stay-away in the Transvaal in November 1984 marked the beginning of strong working relationships between community organisations, student movements and the trade unions. The stay-away was called to protest against the army's occupation of the townships and the students' educational demands, and was suppported by 800,000 workers and 400,000 students. This was followed by the equally successful, but organisationally more complex, stay-aways in Port Elizabeth-Uitenhage in March 1985 in support of the demand for a reduction in the petrol price and in protest against the security force action that resulted in the death of at least 43 people in Langa on 21 March — the anniversary of the Sharpeville Massacre.[26] It was the Langa massacre that triggered the Eastern Cape's participation in the countrywide revolts.

These mass actions successfully mobilised unprecedented numbers of people. They had new features which signalled a turning point in the recent history of black protest: they managed to mobilise all sectors of the township population including both youth and older residents; they involved coordinated action between trade unions and political organisations; they were called in support of demands that challenged the coercive urban and educational policies of the apartheid state; and they gave rise to ungovernable areas as state authority collapsed in many townships in the wake of the resignation of mayors and councillors who had been 'elected' onto the new Black Local Authorities.

Recognising the UDF's failure to cope with this level of mass mobilisation, an internal discussion document circulated by the UDF's Transvaal Education Forum in May 1985 noted 'that we have been unable to respond effectively to the spontaneous waves of militancy around the country'.[27] The UDF's 1985 theme, 'From Protest to Challenge. Mobilisation to Organisation', was part of the UDF leadership's attempt to find ways of transforming 'mass mobilisation' into coherent 'mass organisation'. To achieve this, UDF documents and speakers began emphasising the need to create strong organisational structures on the local, regional and national levels built according to more traditional party-type methods: accountability, direct representation, ideological cohesion, national rather than localised campaigns, disciplined legal rather than illegal forms of struggle.

The state's coercive response to the rising levels of mobilisation, during the last few months of 1984 and early 1985, prevented the UDF leadership from consolidating the Front's structures. After the army occupied the townships in late 1984, community struggles became increasingly militarist as large groups of youths began engaging the security forces in running street battles that claimed hundreds of lives.[28] The militant voluntarism of the youths eclipsed the organisational concerns of the activists, making it even more difficult for the latter to establish durable long-term structures. The first few months of 1985 were the most intense period of what amounted to urban civil warfare, leading eventually to the declaration of a State of Emergency in July 1985, as the state was forced to admit that it had lost control of many townships. This marks the beginning of the third phase of UDF politics.

This phase was marked on the one hand by an attempt by the state to crush the organisations that were at the core of the national uprising, and on the other hand by the development of ungovernable areas. Ungovernability referred primarily to those situations where the organs of civil government had either collapsed, or had effectively been rendered inoperable by mass and/or violent opposition. The State of Emergency was part of the state's attempt to buttress the powers and extend the utilisation of the security forces in the townships. The responsibility for re-establishing civil government in the townships fell largely on the shoulders of over-extended police forces and relatively inexperienced military personnel.

In the end, the State of Emergency failed to restore civil government, largely because the permanent presence of the security forces in the townships fuelled, rather than quelled, resistance. The militant youth, organised into quasi-military action squads, were able to use crude guerilla tactics to harass the security forces sufficiently, thereby preventing them from being more proactive, forcing them to merely defend themselves and detain the prominent community leaders. It is also clear, in the light of the later 1986-87 Emergency, that the state was not committing itself to a full-frontal coercive assault against opposition groups (a policy that was probably due to its belief that Western support was still a possibility).

During this period the activists found themselves sandwiched between the militarism of the youths and the terror tactics of the security forces. Whereas the youths were criticising them for being too moderate, the security forces were hunting them down and detaining them. It was this unenviable position that forced grassroots activists to organise new durable decentralised organisational structures, strong enough to withstand the effects of repression and bring the militant youths under control. The result was the establishment of what many activists refer to as the 'alternative organs of people's power'.

The process of creating these 'organs of people's power' began in earnest towards the end of 1985 and marks the beginning of the fourth — and probably the most important — phase of UDF politics. The structures of 'people's power' involve sophisticated forms of organisation based on street and area committees. Each street elects a street committee, which in turn elects representatives to an area committee. The larger the township, the greater the number of area committees. These structures have developed most effectively in the Eastern Cape and parts of the Transvaal. They have, however, spread to some small Western Cape and Natal townships.

Significantly, street and area committees have helped activists bring the militant youths under control, by dividing youth squads into smaller more disciplined units attachable to a street or area committee and they have proved reasonably effective in countering repression. Tight local-level organisation has helped to lessen the damaging effect which detention, disappearance or death of leaders might otherwise have had. Obviously they are not invulnerable. There is evidence that many Eastern Cape street committees ceased to operate towards the end of 1986, as security forces began detaining the entire membership.

One dimension of the attempt to establish organs of 'people's power' was the consumer boycott movement in the Eastern Cape. Consumer boycotts began as early as March 1985 and proved most successful when they were called in support of local community grievances. These demands included rent reductions, improved housing, installation of proper services, the deracialisation of trading facilities, withdrawal of troops and the establishment of non-racial municipalities. At one time fifteen East Cape towns were affected by the boycott. High levels of unity and solidarity, sustained over long periods of time (in some cases six months), helped consolidate and strengthen community organisations.

The success of the Eastern Cape consumer boycott movement helped it spread to other regions. However, unlike in the Eastern Cape, the initiative in other regions came from UDF regional leaders who attempted to call consumer boycotts without the necessary organisational infrastructure and in support of general political demands, rather than specifically local demands. Additional problems included profiteering by township business people, and the difficulties involved in organising the huge Natal and Transvaal townships. The result was a much more erratic response in the Transvaal, Western Cape and Natal.

Although local activists organised the most successful consumer boycotts around basic community grievances, the regional and national UDF leadership tended to present the objectives as, firstly, the unification of all sectors of the community around a common set of short and long-term demands; and secondly, the need to put sufficient pressure on the white middle class shopkeepers to support these demands and, in so doing, detach their support from the white state.[29] Accordingly, the local Chambers of Commerce, reflecting the anxiety of near-bankrupt retailers, were the first to capitulate, in some cases actually negotiating the withdrawal of troops from the townships, as well as promising to desegregate central business district facilities and undertake other reforms.

The consumer boycott worked best where organisation was most highly developed. In the small towns like Port Alfred or Cradock a quite remarkable consensus existed within the community with a virtually total participation, few reports of intimidation, and a united leadership exercising a high degree of control and discipline. In Cradock, for example, at the behest of the leadership, youthful activists refrained from trying to kill the discredited community councillors. In Port Elizabeth, boycott organisers managed to ensure that township business people did not raise their prices, and in Uitenhage organisers decided not to boycott shops owned by Cheeky Watson, a well-known white supporter of the black political organisations.

Regional differences in the effectiveness of the boycotts reflected the varying quality of UDF organisation and influence in 1985. In Natal, for example, the often bloody antipathy which exists between the UDF and Inkatha has seriously weakened UDF organisation in the black townships.[30] However, where trade unions initiated consumer boycotts in Natal, the campaign was relatively successful because the factories provided important spaces for organisation to take place, protected from Inkatha intimidation. However, even the trade union-initiated consumer boycotts had eventually to be called off after Inkatha business people threatened violent retaliation.

In the Transvaal, Pretoria and the East Rand were better organised than Soweto. But it is in the Eastern Cape communities, where the UDF seems most deeply entrenched, through its various affiliates, and where street and area committees were strongly developed, that the consumer boycott was most effective.

Notwithstanding the deaths, disappearances and detentions which have decimated the leadership of the UDF since its inception, the roots of the movement for national liberation that it represents began to penetrate certain communities too profoundly for its influence to be eradicated coercively. And with this democratic entrenchment in many working class communities, the UDF is likely to generate an increasingly radical conception of a liberated society. The concept of 'people's power', for example, is more than a mobilising slogan. The new forms of organisation which have developed during the revolt in the townships are in themselves rudimentary organs of self-government. The collapse of state authority and the legitimacy of the UDF-affiliated community organisations has enabled these organisations to take responsibility for administering a number of township services.

Evidence that political consciousness in the townships has become increasingly combative emerged during 1986 with the spread of the rent boycott to 54 townships countrywide, involving about 500,000 households and costing the state at least R40 million per month. Significantly, most of the townships hit by rent boycotts are in the Transvaal because, since 1985, these communities have been rapidly organised — in some cases, such as Soweto, on a street committee basis.

The rent boycotts are a response to both economic and political grievances. Economic grievances are directly related to the level and quality of urban subsistence: declining real wages as inflation increases the costs of basic foodstuffs and transport by 20 percent; overcrowding, with a national average of 12 people per household; massive housing shortages (conservative estimates are of the order of 600,000 housing units); rising rent and service charges (sometimes by 100 percent), and a growing number of unemployed people as the unemployment rate moves above 40 percent. Political grievances are directly linked to the state's failure to give blacks substantive political rights in general, and the persistent inadequacy and illegitimacy of the Black Local Authorities in particular.

A UDF information pamphlet issued in August 1986 starts by pointing out that rent is not being paid because 'people are simply unable to afford it', and proceeds to link the boycott to political demands:

> The [rent] boycott is also part of an attempt to make all the structures of apartheid unworkable. The black local authorities are structures designed to make apartheid work — to make people participate in their own domination by a white minority government. The rent boycott weakens these structures and demonstrates to the government that there can be no taxation without representation and that the people will accept nothing less than majority rule.

In most cases the rent boycott began in response to a sudden change in the relationship between the communities and the state: the shooting of 30 people in Mamelodi, the declaration of the 1986 State of Emergency in Port Elizabeth, the forced removal of people in Uitenhage and the failure of a local official to keep his promise to meet the community in Parys. The cumulative effect of all the rent boycotts, however, is that they have united largely working class communities around a strategy which has the potential to sustain itself for a considerable length of time. Once people do not pay rent for two or three months, the chances of them resuming their payments are low because the state expects them to pay their arrears as well. The rent boycotts are a good indication of the extent to which the black majority are prepared to cease supporting the state system in a very practical way.

More importantly, however, unlike the consumer boycotts which aimed at pressurising the state via the efforts of middle class white commercial interests, the rent boycott challenges the state directly. It undermines the fiscal foundations of township administration and has received the full support of both trade union and community organisations. One result of this unity is that trade unions succeeded in preventing employers from agreeing to a State Security Council recommendation that rents be deducted from pay packets through stop-orders, although the state is seemingly bent on resurrecting the plan.

It is unlikely that the 1986-7 State of Emergency will 'normalise' local government and 'restore law and order' in the townships as long as the rent boycott persists. Nor is it likely the rent boycott will end before the State of Emergency has been lifted. In short, through the rent boycott, the communities are directly confronting the state over a sustained period of time.

THE UDF AND BLACK POLITICS

A recent article by Alex Callinicos dismisses the UDF as a 'populist' organisation whose local affiliates are weak and small, limited by a failure to make connections between oppression in the community and exploitation in the workplace, reluctant to identify class distinctions, and dominated by an intellectual petty bourgeois leadership that subscribes to a reformist ideology.[31]

There are very few black communities in South Africa where no UDF affiliate exists. From the small rural and urban villages in the Northern Transvaal, to the metropolitan agglomerations of the Witwatersrand, to the towns and metropolises of the Cape, there are UDF affiliates. The strength of the UDF derives primarily from the popularity and organisational capacity of its affiliates, even though these differ considerably in size and effectiveness. The national executive, in and of itself, does not constitute a significant organisational force, mainly because most of the leadership has spent much of the last three years in detention, or in hiding. Some regional executives are more active because they interact more intimately with the local community organisations. The UDF's primary organising activities are appropriately rooted in South Africa's oppressed and exploited communities.

This does not mean that national initiatives are non-existent. It has already been mentioned that the UDF played a crucial role in national campaigns against the new Constitution and the Black Local Authorities. Other national campaigns included boycotts of international sports teams, opposition to the State of Emergency and the so-called 'Le Grange Bills' in early 1986 (i.e. amendments to the Internal Security Act and Public Safety Act to provide for additional powers for the security forces) and more recently the National United Action campaign which involves joint action with the Congress of South African Trade Unions and the National Education Crisis Committee.

Although the UDF's support is best judged in terms of its organisational practices and structures, some recent surveys into black political attitudes also suggest that the UDF and the organisations, personalities and political traditions it is identified with are the most widely supported in the African townships.[32] The HSRC survey points out that 'Mandela definitely enjoys greater support than any other black leader' and that organisations like the ANC and other related extra-parliamentary groups enjoy about three times more support than pro-government black leaders and organisations.

The results of two surveys[33] into support among urban blacks for various political groups are listed in the table below:

Political group	HSRC survey	Schlemmer survey
ANC/Mandela	20.0%	27.0%
UDF	19.8%	11.0%
AZAPO	19.6%	5.0%
Inkatha/Buthelezi	18.9%	14.0%
Other/none	55.0%	43.0%

If it is assumed that ANC supporters are also UDF supporters by virtue of the fact that both organisations subscribe to the Freedom Charter, and that the only major difference between them is the ANC's commitment to armed struggle, then it becomes apparent that support amongst urban Africans for the ANC/UDF political movement far outstrips support for AZAPO or Inkatha. The fact that both these surveys were done in 1984 means they do not reflect how the UDF's support base has expanded since then. The UDF had only been in existence for less than a year at that stage and since 1984 nation-wide township rebellion has been oriented around UDF affiliates.

It is also interesting to note why UDF supporters said they supported the UDF. The HSRC identified the following reasons:[34]

Reason for supporting the UDF	Percentage
Fights for democracy	35.6
Solves our problems	17.1
Represents all groups	12.7
Makes people aware of their rights	8.6
Helps people fight for their rights	5.8
Will help blacks	5.8
Does nothing wrong	2.4
Will bring peace to South Africa	2.4
Unites blacks	1.4
Represents students	0.7
Other reasons	6.2
No reason	1.4
Total	100.1

In short, the overwhelming majority of respondents who said they supported the UDF did so because in one way or another they see the UDF as an organisation that will help black people achieve political rights and resolve their social problems. This conforms pretty closely to how the UDF's national leaders have attempted, against all odds, to present the aim of the Front.

If we take into account the mass campaigns, organisational networks and (less reliable) attitudinal survey data discussed above, it is difficult to see how Callinicos can conclude that the UDF is not supported by a sound organisational base. Although no doubt this base is regionally uneven, he is incorrect to make judgements about the UDF purely on the basis of an assessment of its Western Cape structures as they were in 1983.

There are enough examples of struggles and campaigns conducted under the auspices of UDF affiliates to confirm that the connection between exploitation in the workplace and oppression in the community has not been ignored. The most outstanding examples are the numerous transport struggles in East London, Durban, Cape Town, Port Elizabeth, Kirkwood and Soweto. Struggles over transport revolve primarily around working class commuters, because they feel most acutely the relationship between oppression in outlying townships and exploitation in their city-based workplaces located between 15 and 200 kilometres from home.[35]

The same connection has been made in the rent boycotts as has already been discussed above. Although civic leaders quoted in the press refer to rent boycotts largely in terms of a struggle against apartheid local government, the pamphlets distributed and speeches made by the youth and working class activists on the ground constantly make the link between economic exploitation and the abysmal, deeply resented living conditions in the townships.

Connections of this kind, forged during painful violent struggles, gradually became the foundations for united action between trade unions, community organisations and student movements — action which culminated in the dramatic nationwide stayaways of 1986.[36]

As far as the capacity to make distinctions between different class interests is concerned, evidence from two sources can be used to refute the claim that within the UDF this is done to a limited extent. Firstly, consumer boycotts have been used extensively since 1983 to mobilise community pressure against township businessmen who supported, or were involved in, the Councils. In pamphlets, speeches and interviews, activists repeatedly depicted the councillors and businessmen in class terms as petty accumulators (in addition to being 'puppets' of the white government).

Secondly, the education manuals and booklets distributed by the various educational support groups allied to the UDF never fail to identify in *class* terms the various components of the 'oppressed people'. For example, a booklet compiled by the Cape Town-based Education Resource and Information Centre, called *Forward with Knowledge*, has a chapter called 'Workers and other classes', which explains in some detail the complex relationship between workers on the one hand and capitalist, unemployed, peasant, petty bourgeois and professional classes on the other. The booklet concludes with a chapter on 'Principles, strategies and tactics' where it is stated: 'Our first principle is based on the struggle to end all forms of exploitation, in particular the exploitation of workers by bosses. From this comes our first basic principle: THE WORKERS ARE THE LEADING CLASS IN OUR STRUGGLE' (emphasis in original).

Finally, the UDF is presented as a multi-class organisation dominated by a petty bourgeois leadership.[37] The empirical inaccuracy of this view has already been demonstrated. At local, regional and national level the class character of the UDF is such that it cannot be defined as the property of any one class. Instead, as the critics admit, the UDF is widely supported by a range of classes. However, this paper has attempted to show that as levels of conflict between the oppressed communities and the state have escalated outside the workplace, the UDF's local affiliates have become progressively more entrenched in the poor working class communities — a pattern reflected in the class composition of the UDF leadership.

During 1986 this led to a radicalisation of its ideology and democratisation of its structures, as working class people asserted their right to control their organisations both in and outside the workplaces. This is why the state, after the 1986 Emergency was declared in June, decided to launch a full frontal assault to head off this radicalising movement. Not surprisingly, the state has pursued this objective more systematically and ruthlessly in the Eastern Cape than in any other region.

In the final analysis, two organisational forms have come to complement one another within the broad parameters of the UDF. Firstly, the processes associated with the development of the local community organisations are similar to those that urban sociologists have understood as 'urban social movements'.[38] The new urban sociology literature has understood the genesis of these movements in terms of contradictions in the urban political economy, and the way these manifest themselves outside the workplace. The movements tend to represent multi-class constituencies with common demands that challenge the logic and values of the interests that dominate the design, organisation and control of the cities. Secondly, South Africa's urban social movements are also the constituent parts of a national liberation movement with objectives that envisage the complete dismantling of the present white minority regime.

The dual urban social and national liberatory function of the UDF and its affiliates is a necessary condition for the transformation of the cities, a process that must inevitably involve the transfer of political power to the majority. Like the relationship between collective bargaining unionism and political unionism in the workplace,[39] local urban social movements have become inextricably tied to the national liberation movement because of the dual structure of racial oppression and class exploitation that remains the cornerstone of the South African social formation. Equally, just as the formation of COSATU can be understood as the fusion of political and collective bargaining unionism, so too can the UDF be understood in terms of the distinct but complementary functions of urban social and national liberation movements.

As far as lessons for the future are concerned, two issues will become important when the space for open legal organisation is regained. Firstly, to what extent will a 'front' structure be appropriate in the future? Although a structure of this kind has proven to be appropriate in most authoritarian societies, the two outstanding features about the democratic movement are the strength of the trade unions and the resilience of the local-level community organisations. Depending on the terrain of struggle that will arise in the future, a structure may be necessary which is founded more coherently on the democratic structures of these community and workplace organisations.

Secondly, how can an organisational infrastructure be developed capable of coping with the rapid radicalisation and politicisation of the masses that inevitably occur during periods of rebellion? A critical problem faced by political activists since the uprising began in 1984 was how to hold back political mobilisation, in order to build up organisations to guide and direct the oppositional movements. A combination of repression and inadequate organisational resources prevented them from resolving this problem. In the end, the communities — particularly the youth — moved too quickly to take on the full might of the state unprotected by strong national organisation, despite the street committee system.

CONCLUSION

The UDF has been shaped by pressures and processes largely beyond its control, as the dynamics of black resistance have shifted from reactive politics to the attempt to establish proactive organs of democracy in the communities, schools and factories. Whereas the former involved reactive strategies to contest the legitimacy of state reforms on terrain determined largely by the state, the latter has evolved as the reforms have, to all intents and purposes, failed.

Today the mass-based community organisations can play a crucial role in shaping the political terrain, in a way they have never been able to in the past. Despite the UDF's severely weakened national organisational structures, due to the impact of successive repressive assaults, its affiliates and leaders will nevertheless remain crucial representatives of South Africa's black majority in the future.

When considering the future of South African black politics, it would be a mistake to accept in part or in full the state's propaganda that has attempted to depict the UDF as a minority group located on the radical left wing fringe. Nor is it the unproblematic vehicle for a reformist petty bourgeoisie bent on capturing state power to use against big white capital and the black working class. It is not a pressure group, nor is it a political party. It is essentially what its architects had always intended it to be: a front representative of a very broad spectrum of oppressed class interests. Beneath this formal level of public appearances, however, is a highly complex network of local organisations that have mounted campaigns and struggles which have begun to generate an increasingly radical conception of a liberated society, and the road that should be adopted to achieve this goal.

No matter how far South Africa's rulers go to crush the organisational capacities of the UDF and its affiliates, the ideas, aspirations and struggles that have made it what it is will continue to inspire present and future generations to continue the struggle for political and economic justice. We may be in for a prolonged period of extremely harsh repression that might succeed in annihilating the organisational structures built up over the past few years, but the state is clearly making a fatal mistake by thinking this will facilitate the success of a reform programme that excludes the demands, interests and ideologies of constituencies represented by the UDF and its allies.

NOTES

Parts of this article are based on a paper co-authored by Tom Lodge and myself that was published in French in *Les Temps Modernes*. I am also grateful to Jeremy Seekings and my honours students for their criticisms and ideas. The conclusions reached in this paper, however, are my own.

1. R. and L. Lambert, 'State reform and working class resistance', *South African Review 1* (Johannesburg: Ravan Press, 1983).
2. E. Webster, 'Social movement unionism in South Africa', in P. Frankel, N. Pines, and M. Swilling (eds.), *State, Resistance and Change in South Africa* (London: Croom Helm, 1987).
3. See C. Cooper and L. Ensor, *PEBCO: A Black Mass Movement* (Johannesburg: Institute of Race Relations, 1980); M. Evans, 'The emergence and decline of a community organisation: an assessment of PEBCO', *SALB*, Vol.6, Nos 2 and 3, 1980.
4. See F. Molteno, 'Students take control: the 1980 boycott of coloured education in the Cape Peninsula', paper presented to the Sixteenth Annual Congress of the Association for Sociology in Southern Africa, University of Cape Town, 1-4 July 1985; M. Swilling, 'The 1980 Cape Town schools boycott', unpublished research paper, Department of Political Studies, University of the Witwatersrand, 1981.
5. See J. Keenan, 'Migrants awake: the 1980 Johannesburg Municipality strike', *SALB*, Vol. 6, No.7, May 1981; M. Swilling, 'The politics of working class struggles in Germiston, 1979-1980', paper presented to History Workshop Conference, University of the Witwatersrand, February 1984; J. Seekings, 'Political mobilisation in the black townships of the Transvaal', in P. Frankel, *et. al., op. cit.*; and the various articles in *SALB*, Vol.7, No.8, 1982.
6. J. Reintges, 'An analysis of the opposition politics of JORAC', Annual Conference of the Association of Sociology of Southern Africa, Durban, July 1986.
7. M. Swilling, ' "The buses smell of blood": the 1983 East London bus boycott', *SALB*, Vol.9, No.5, 1984.
8. 'Affiliation' is not used in this paper to refer to the formal procedure that a local organisation should go through to affiliate to the Front. Instead, the word is used to

refer to relations of cooperation, ideological identification and mutual support that exist between hundreds of organisations and the Front, without these organisations having gone through the formal affiliation procedure. The fact that formal procedure is extremely difficult under semi-clandestine conditions has not diminished the extent to which local organisations identify themselves as 'UDF affiliates'.

9. Labour Monitoring Group, 'Report: the Transvaal regional stayaway', *SALB*, Vol. 10, No. 6, 1985.

10. See Labour Monitoring Group, 'May Day stayaway 1986', *SALB*, Vol.11, No.6; Labour Monitoring Group, 'June 16th stayaway', *SALB*, Vol.11, No.7, 1986.

11. T. Lodge and M. Swilling, 'The year of the Amabutho', *Africa Report*, March-April 1986.

12. See A. Callinicos, 'Marxism and revolution in South Africa', *International Socialism*, 31, 1986; N. Alexander, *Sow the Wind* (Johannesburg: Skotaville, 1985); S. Friedman, 'The real lessons from that May Day stayaway', *Weekly Mail*, 9-15 May 1986.

13. 'Sowing confusion', *New Era*, Vol.1, No.1, March-April 1986, pp.37-8.

14. I am grateful to Tom Lodge for providing me with some of this biographical information.

15. See P. Hudson, 'The Freedom Charter and socialist strategy in South Africa', *Politikon*, Vol.13, No.1, June 1986; M. Swilling, 'Living in the interregnum: crisis, reform and the socialist alternative in South Africa', *Third World Quarterly*, April 1987.

16. See R. Suttner, *The Freedom Charter — The People's Charter in the Nineteen-Eighties*, 26th T.B. Davies Memorial Lecture, University of Cape Town, 1984.

17. S. Njikelana, 'The unions and the Front: a response to David Lewis', *SALB*, Vol.9, No.7, June 1984.

18. Thozamile Gqweta, president of the South African Allied Workers Union (SAAWU), speaking at a UDF meeting in Natal, 18 July 1984, p.61 of transcript of meeting proceedings, exhibit M44 in *State* v. *Mawala Ramgobin and 15 Others*.

19. The conflict between nationalist and socialist positions in the UDF cannot be reduced to differences between protagonists of the 'internal colonialist' and 'racial capitalist' theses. The parochialism of white student politics is responsible for this simplification.

20. See pamphlet appended to article by Labour Monitoring Group, 'Report: the Transvaal regional stayaway', *op. cit.*; interview with Cape Youth Congress activist quoted in 'Building working class power — the role of the youth', *Inqaba ya Basebenzi*, Nos 20/21, September 1986; interview with Moses Mayekiso in *Socialist Worker Review*, 80, October 1985; interview with Tumahole Youth Congress activist in *Financial Mail* and various articles in *Isizwe*, 1, 2, March 1986.

21. 'Why we cannot participate in an election referendum related to Botha's constitutional proposals', internal discussion paper circulated within the Transvaal Anti-President's Council movement.

22. The Azanian People's Organisation (AZAPO) is the main bearer of the Black Consciousness ideological tradition previously represented by the South African Students Organisation (SASO) and the Black Peoples Convention, both banned in October 1977. Founded in 1978, in the course of the next two years it incorporated class analysis into its political discourse. It now occupies a position which, in rhetorical terms at least, is to the left of the UDF in terms of its socialist and anti-imperialist sentiment. AZAPO is conspicuously reported in the English language press, largely because many black journalists are sympathisers. AZAPO, however, is not a mass movement and though it claims a following distributed in nearly a hundred branches, its membership seems to be largely middle class and concentrated in Durban and Johannesburg. It has not played a significant role in the popular uprisings since September 1984 (except possibly in Sharpeville, near Vereeniging, and in some northern Transvaal towns).

23. G. Bloch, 'The UDF — "A national political initiative"', *Work in Progress*, No. 41, April 1986, p.27. This was written in reply to R. de Villiers, 'UDF: front or political party?', *Work In Progress*, No. 40, February 1986. Whereas De Villiers (a member of a UDF affiliate in Natal) argues that the Front is not and should not be more than simply the sum of its parts, Bloch replies that although it is still valid to retain the Front-type structure, conditions of struggle have 'all required a response that was new, flexible, dynamic and organised. It was not the UDF that extended the boundaries of political activity, although it gave impetus and shape to this. Rather, pressure from the dominated classes drove the UDF forward.'

24. By periodising the activities of a movement and the organisation which represented this movement, I am not suggesting that these phases were consciously organised or that they represent totally separate forms of political action. Instead, it is possible to identify the existence of dominant dynamics at different moments in time; dynamics which exist alongside others in ways which are always locally and regionally uneven. Nevertheless, generalisations can still be made about the national impetus of black opposition during different periods.

25. For a detailed explanation and account of these processes, see Seekings, *op. cit.*

26. See Labour Monitoring Group, 'Report: the Transvaal regional stayaway', *op. cit.*; Labour Monitoring Group, 'Report: the March stayaways in Port Elizabeth and Uitenhage', *SALB*, Vol.11, No.1, September 1985; M. Swilling, 'Stayaways, urban protest and the state', in South African Research Services, *South African Review 3* (Johannesburg: Ravan Press, 1986).

27. *From Protest to Challenge. Mobilisation to Organisation,* Johannesburg, mimeo, 1985, p.6.

28. Lodge and Swilling, *op. cit.*.

29. R. White, 'A tide has risen. A breach has occurred: towards an assessment of the strategic value of the consumer boycotts', *SALB*, Vol.11, No. 5, April-May 1986.

30. A. Sitas, 'Inanda, August 1985: "Where wealth and power and blood reign worshipped gods"', *SALB*, Vol.11, No.4, 1986.

31. Callinicos, *op. cit.*, pp.6-7.

32. See surveys conducted by the Human Science Research Council (HSRC) compiled by C.P. de Kock, N. Rhoodie, and M.P. Couper, 'Black views on socio-political change in South Africa', in J. Van Vuuren, *et al.* (eds.), *South Africa: A Plural Society in Transition* (Durban: Butterworths, 1985); and L. Schlemmer, *Black Workers' Attitudes to Disinvestment* (Durban: University of Natal, 1984).

33. De Kock, *et al., op. cit.*, p.356.

34. *Ibid.*, p.353.

35. J. McCarthy and M. Swilling, 'Transport and political resistance: bus boycotts in 1983', *South African Review 2* (Johannesburg: Ravan Press, 1984).

36. Labour Monitoring Group, 'May Day stayaway 1986', *op. cit.*, and 'June 16th stayaway', *op. cit.*.

37. See Callinicos, *op. cit.*; Alexander, *op. cit.*, and Friedman, *op. cit.*

38. See S. Lowe, *Urban Social Movements. The City after Castells* (Basingstoke: Macmillan, 1986) and P. Dunleavy, *Urban Political Analysis. The Politics of Collective Consumption* (London: Macmillan, 1980).

39. See the contribution by Lambert and Webster, elsewhere in this volume.

6. Kwandebele:
The Struggle Against 'Independence'

TRANSVAAL RURAL ACTION COMMITTEE

INTRODUCTION

'Independence is being uprooted, eradicated with all its roots and being thrown into the deep ocean'. With these words the speaker of the Kwandebele Legislative Assembly announced the dramatic turnabout by the homeland parliament, which some months earlier had supported independence, and acknowledged the extent of popular feeling against independence for the homeland.

This was the outcome of a popular uprising — the 'three month war' — against Pretoria-style independence, which had begun with a mass meeting at the Royal Kraal on 12 May 1986, and which had ended with the above statement on 12 August.

During those three months, a popular alliance emerged consisting of the Kwandebele royal family, the youthful 'comrades', the homeland's civil service, local white farmers, and the population at large. It took on the Kwandebele government, with its Mbokodo vigilante group, as well as the might of the police and the South African Defence Force (SADF). In the process over 100 people died, Mbokodo was decimated, the entire civil service went on strike, most of the shops in the area were burned and well over 300 people were detained under emergency regulations. During the strugggle, the population became politicised and was able to take power into its own hands.

The Kwandebele war began as a spontaneous reaction to the brutality and violence of Mbokodo. The vigilantes had Chief Minister Skosana as their president, while the vice-president, and real force behind Mbokodo, was former Minister of the Interior, Piet Ntuli, who was later to die in a car bomb explosion. Mbokodo was the spark which set Kwandebele alight, but the fire soon developed its own momentum — the fight against Mbokodo was transformed into a battle against independence, involving thousands of people in boycotts, demonstrations, stay-aways and strikes.

Most significantly, the royal family was constantly able to consult the comrades and the civil service. This allowed decisions on the beginning or ending of boycotts and strikes to be taken in a disciplined manner, thus strengthening their impact. The continual pressure this group exerted on the authorities to release detainees also succeeded. In what seemed like an amnesty, most of the Kwandebele detainees were released as independence was abandoned. This facilitated the high school pupils' return to school and the end of the boycott which had begun three months earlier.

What follows is the history of the people's struggle against Kwandebele independence and Mbokodo.

HISTORY

The Ndebele are a small grouping of people who were scattered throughout the Transvaal during the 19th century, some of whom settled in the area around Roos Senekal in the eastern Transvaal. In the 1920s a group settled on a farm near Groblersdal under the protection of a local Sotho chief. In the mid-1970s, when the government belatedly realised that no territorial provision had been made for the Ndebele ethnic group, Kwandebele — the last of the ten homelands — was established on a piece of land arbitrarily carved out of the central Transvaal. The land lacks any historical or ethnic justification as the original 'homeland' of the Ndebeles.

In the 1950s and 1960s the structures of territorial separation and the homeland system were forged by the Nationalist government. During these years the Ndebele people in the central Transvaal remained subject to the Sotho territorial authorities that were established and that were later to form part of the present day Lebowa. As the momentum for the creation of separate homelands for each of South Africa's ethnic groups gathered pace during the 1970s, groups of Ndebele people began to urge Pretoria to grant them recognition — state officials were only too happy to oblige. In 1974 the Ndundza tribal authority was elevated to regional authority status, and in 1977 a South Ndebele territorial authority was established. In 1980 a legislative assembly for the territorial authority was created, with Kwandebele being granted self-governing status in 1981.

CONDITIONS IN KWANDEBELE

Since its beginnings, with 25,000 people on about 55,000 hectares of land, Kwandebele has grown dramatically. It now comprises some 300,000 ha. of land with an estimated population of 465,000. (This excludes the 120,000 in Moutse.) Most of these people have moved in over the past ten years, the majority of them seeking a place to settle as a result of one or other form of forced removal. Consequently, the population consists primarily of evicted farm workers, non-Tswanas fleeing persecution in the newly 'independent' Bophuthatswana, and people forced to leave urban areas because of the housing shortage or the pass laws. During the 1970s they flocked into the sprawling shanty villages that grew up on the stony Transvaal *veld.*

Living conditions are appalling. Most areas are without a proper infrastructure or facilities. Water is scarce and has to be brought in by water tanker, at vast expense. There are virtually no job opportunities. Kwandebele, in short, is typical of any South African resettlement camp, its only advantage being space to build, and its relative proximity to urban areas. Nevertheless its expanding commuter population finds itself travelling between 3-6 hours to get from home to work in the urban areas. Others have become weekly migrants in order to avoid the travelling time, working in such places as Pretoria, the East Rand and Johannesburg. There are few other places in South Africa that are so depressing and dreary as the endless shanty-covered hills that constitute Kwandebele. The daily struggle for survival in this stony, dry and inhospitable land is exhausting and disspiriting — life is a never-ending round of work and travel, interrupted by a few hours sleep.

THE IMPACT OF KWANDEBELE'S RULERS

Kwandebele's rulers were quick to jump on the independence bandwagon. In 1981, the year in which the territory was granted self-governing status, Mr S. S. Skosana, Chief Minister of Kwandebele, denied that there was any intention of opting for independence. In May, however, the first meeting was held between the South African government and Kwandebele to discuss such a move. After this meeting it was said that Kwandebele would opt for independence once it had its own capital, industrial infrastructure and more land — suggestions pointed to 1984 as the likely year.

In a subsequent interview, Skosana was quick to admit that he did not understand the consequences of opting for independence. He stated that he did not blame his people if they did not know what independence was about: 'How can my people know what independence is all about when I don't even know myself. But we're learning.' Skosana's crude attitude to one of South Africa's thorniest political problems was exemplified in his statement that '. . . maybe I am stupid, but independence for me became a logical step when I accepted a territorial authority. It's either you agree or you don't. There is no middle ground and people who don't agree with this system should be with Mandela or Sobukwe.'

The 1984 target date for independence was put back in May of that year when Piet Koornhof, then Minister of Cooperation and Development, said that the granting of independence to Kwandebele was expected to take a 'considerable time', since Kwandebele would only get independence once it could run its affairs smoothly.

From the outset Kwandebele's rulers were hopelessly ill-equipped to deal with this situation of human misery and poverty. In 1981, for example, they excluded pensions and disability grants from the budget. This left the aged, disabled and destitute without any state support. The following year, R4.3 million — more than half the amount budgeted for social services, education and agriculture — was spent on an impulsive purchase of construction equipment.

Skosana, with a standard four education, was one of the most highly educated members of the cabinet. His family and close colleagues are about the only people to have really benefitted from the establishment of Kwandebele. Not only do they control the state apparatus, but they use this access to dispense favours — most often in the form of business or taxi licences. A 1982 newspaper report dealing with this aspect of Kwandebele spoke of a 'cabal of businessmen politicians whose tight hold over business life keeps competition to a minimum'. It is said that most of the businessmen in Kwandebele are related to one or other cabinet member. Cabinet minister Ntuli hotly denied this, as well as an allegation that cabinet ministers used their position to secure trading licences for themselves. He said that at least two cabinet members had got their trading licences *before* they became members of the cabinet. Ntuli, at the time of the interview, had a supermarket and a restaurant and was awaiting approval of his liquor licence application — he was also in charge of the ministry that had to approve his application for the licence.

The antics of Skosana and his colleagues may elicit smiles. However, there is little that is humurous about Kwandebele — over the years its rulers have moulded a society characterised by fear and repression; a society that has been described as 'closed' because of its reluctance to allow access to any outsiders (except, of course, officials of the South African government). In 1981, for example, officials of the South African Council of Churches, the South African Institute of Race Relations and the Black Sash were detained and questioned for up to ten hours whilst on their way to secure permits to be in the area. Journalists have also found it difficult to report on events in Kwandebele because of the insistence on permits which are extremely difficult to obtain. Any attempts by outsiders to create even small-scale self-help projects, feeding schemes or educational facilities have been closely monitored and, in some cases, prevented from continuing. At one stage even Operation Hunger had its activities curtailed.[1] Skosana's authoritarian and undemocratic rule does not affect outsiders only. Life for the ordinary residents of Kwandebele is characterised by a climate of fear and suspicion generated by the tight control exerted by its rulers over the population at large.

In November 1984 Kwandebele's one and only election was held. Until then all 46 members of the legislative assembly were nominated. Women were barred from voting: Skosana explained that women had first to be taught how to vote by their husbands, and not by strangers. 'It's better done at home than in public places'. The Kwandebele population's perception of their rulers as a firmly entrenched group of nominated people helped explain their lack of interest in the homeland elections.

All of these factors, together with Kwandebele's economic unviability and the increasingly overt brutality of those who sought to preserve the Kwandebele *status quo*, were fundamental reasons for the widespread and militant resistance to independence.

This growing resistance reached a climax between May and August 1986. In particular the proposed incorporation of Ekangala, the actual incorporation of Moutse on 1 January 1986, and the official establishment and recognition of the Mbokodo vigilante group, were flashpoints around which opposition to Skosana's regime mobilised and consolidated.

THE INCORPORATION OF MOUTSE AND EKANGALA — COLONIALISM SOUTH AFRICAN STYLE

Moutse and Ekangala were the first two areas to challenge the notion of a Kwandebele homeland. Their bitter struggles against incorporation paved the way for the more generalised Kwandebele revolt that followed. In particular the militant opposition of the Moutse residents to Kwandebele rule in early 1986 created a political climate of opposition and unrest that was taken forward by the Kwandebele population itself later in the year.

Ekangala

Ekangala is situated about 100 km from Johannesburg and the East Rand townships and is about 20 km outside Bronkhorstspruit. It is a 'model' township built by the East Rand Administration Board (Erab) on behalf of the central government as part of a policy of creating decentralised growth points through 'orderly urbanisation'. East Rand residents moved into the new township from 1983. Their decision to live in Ekangala was a result of the desperate housing shortage on the East Rand caused by the government's policy of no longer building houses in urban areas.

Ekangala's new residents soon found that life there was prohibitively expensive. Rent was between R100 and R200 a month compared with an average of R30 in the East Rand townships. An additional burden was transport costs of about R5 for a single journey to work, with commuters spending up to eight hours a day travelling. To deal with these and other problems, the community formed the Ekangala Action Committee (EAC) which negotiated with the authorities and succeeded in solving a number of problems related to transport and electricity costs.

On 9 February 1985, Gerrit Viljoen, then Minister of Co-operation and Development, announced that Ekangala would be incorporated into Kwandebele — this was immediately rejected by the township residents, who said they were moved under false pretences as there had been no mention of Ekangala being incorporated into Kwandebele when they moved. They insisted that they were South Africans and did not want to lose their citizenship or their Section 10 rights.

The Action Committee made the community's views clear to the South African authorities. The latter refused to discuss the issue with the EAC, but soon afterwards appointed a committee which allowed for representation of Kwandebele's government. A petition signed by most of the community also received no response. The next step, a peaceful march by residents on 23 March, was broken up by police who fired teargas. A schoolboy was shot dead.

Since then the Action Committee has not been given permission to hold open air meetings (there are no halls in the township that can be used by the community) and during 1985 a reign of terror was inflicted on the Action Committee and its followers by Kwandebele loyalists. The Committee drew up a memorandum on the issue and submitted it to the central government which only replied many months later. This memorandum, like the petition, was signed by over a thousand householders in the township. In it the community clearly outlined the reasons for rejecting Kwandebele.

2.3   We are location people . . . used to location law where each man is equal according to his property. There is a Mr Mahlangu at Ekangala who acts as a chief. He has set up a tribal 'court'. This 'court' fines people and gives sentences of corporal punishment. We are not a tribe and we do not accept the system of being fined, asked for money and controlled by chiefs. This is the homeland system . . . which we as location people long ago left behind.

2.4   We have seen that there are many problems in the homelands. People are mistreated or expelled because they are of the wrong ethnic group. For example, many of the people who now live in Kwandebele went there because they were expelled from Bophuthatswana as non-Tswanas. We think that non-Ndebeles would have problems with pensions, jobs and houses under Kwandebele. These difficulties would force the non-Ndebeles to leave one by one. Already representatives of the Kwandebele government are telling us to leave Ekangala.

2.4.1 We fear that this discrimination would not apply to non-Ndebeles only, but to everyone who does not support the homeland system. Many Ndebeles support the Action Committee's aims because they have found it difficult to get business licences. It seems that the only people to get trading licences are Ndebeles who have connections with the Cabinet.

2.5   We have already seen the violent and lawless way in which the Kwandebele people act. Instead of discussing things with people, they take the law into their own hands and assault us. Ever since the incorporation issue came up we have been assaulted by Kwandebele government supporters. If they behave like this while Ekangala is still under the Erab [East Rand Administration Board] we fear that they will be much more violent when Ekangala is incorporated into Kwandebele, or Kwandebele becomes independent.

The above sentiments were based on the bitter experience of many Ekangala residents. F. K. Mahlangu, a Kwandebele cabinet minister, and many other prominent Ndebele residents of the township had participated in these attacks, the first of which took place at the end of March 1985 and was directed against supporters of the Action Committee. Mrs Betty Bembe, for example, was pulled out of her house in the middle of the night by armed men wearing balaclavas. She and her daughter were beaten and she was told that if she did not want to be part of Kwandebele, she should leave. The same night Enoch Dumakude was also attacked. He was assaulted at his home by a group of men including F. K. Mahlangu, then put in the boot of a car and taken into the *veld* where the beating continued. During the assault he was told that 'Ekangala is a place for Ndebeles, and not a place for dogs from the East Rand'. Mr Dumakude subsequently fled Ekangala when the same men started to search for him again.

Peter Kose, the chairman of the Action Committee, was singled out for sustained and brutal harassment. On 30 March his house was attacked and all the windows and doors broken. His daughter was expelled from school, as were the children of the secretary of the Action Committee. A while later Mr Kose was forced into a car belonging to a Mr Peter Sibiya, who then tried to take him to the home of Mahlangu. Kose managed to escape. On 16 June he was again abducted and severely beaten by a group of vigilantes. Attempts by residents to get the police to intervene came to nothing. When Peter Kose tried to make a statement to the police they initially refused to accept it — his statement was only taken after legal intervention.

On Saturday 27 July Mr Kose was again assaulted by the same people. There are statements from numerous eye witnesses who saw him being beaten up. He was swung around by his feet so that his head knocked on the ground. When he was unconscious he was put in the boot of a car and taken to Mr F. K. Mahlangu's house where he was again beaten and tortured. Eventually the police intervened. They fetched Kose from Mr Mahlangu's house and put him in a police cell where he remained for a substantial period without medical treatment. His assailants were not arrested. Instead, the police accepted charges of assault laid by the assailants against *him*. After legal intervention the charges were dropped.

The memorandum quoted above was one response to the situation. For others it was easier just to leave Ekangala. And so, in the latter part of 1985, families began to trickle away, reflecting a belief that the situation could only get worse. Finally, the Action Committee and its supporters took a decision to leave Ekangala and to move back en masse to the East Rand.

Moutse

Moutse was incorporated into Kwandebele on 31 December 1985, in defiance of the feelings of the residents of Moutse. For years previously, the mainly Pedi speaking population of Moutse, estimated to be 120,000 strong and living on 66,000 hectares of land in the central Transvaal, had voiced their opposition to the incorporation. The reasons they gave included fear of losing their South African citizenship; fears of the consequences of being subject to alien and violent rule by Skosana and his vigilantes; and fears of being forced to accept Ndebele as a medium of instruction in Moutse's schools.

The Moutse residents also voiced a concern that their property rights would not be respected in Kwandebele (much of Moutse is tribally or privately owned), and that businessmen in the area would, as non-Ndebeles, lose their licences and access to government loans. The Bantoane tribe also feared that money from selling mineral rights would now go to Skosana instead of to the tribe. The Moutse residents also echoed the fears of the Ekangala people about ethnic discrimination and loss of access to pensions and work contracts.

In 1980 Moutse was excised from Lebowa and brought under central government administration, in preparation for incorporation into Kwandebele. However, this plan was effectively delayed by the resistance of the Moutse community. Skosana seems to have consistently demanded Moutse — with its well-developed infrastructure, its hospital and its many businesses — as a prize for the taking of independence.

The government initially negotiated directly with the Moutse representatives. Their adamant refusal to consider incorporation, however, caused the government to change its strategy. From about 1983 it insisted that the issue be resolved through discussions with the governments of Kwandebele and Lebowa, thereby excluding the recognised representatives of the community. Finally in 1985, it would seem that the South African government managed to persuade Chief Minister Cedric Phatudi of Lebowa to cede Moutse to Kwandebele in exchange for the Zebediela orange estates, a new railway line, some land at Mokerong, and the Saliesloot and Immerpan resettlement camps which had been established for residents of Moutse who refused to live in Kwandebele.

In late 1985 the Moutse community was informed of the decision to incorporate — presented as a *fait accompli*. Their response was one of intense anger, and they began to protest and resist. Teachers, for example, refused to accept transfers to the Kwandebele Department of Education and Culture, while a youth organisation was formed with the explicit aim of fighting the incorporation.

Despite this resistance from the Moutse community, as well as massive international protest, the South African government went ahead with the proclamation. Towards the end of December there were rumours that Ndebeles would attack the community immediately after incorporation. Ndebele vigilantes had already attacked villagers from Kgobokoane, which borders Kwandebele. These fears were reported by Chief Mathebe, the head of the Moutse regional authority, to the South African police at Dennilton on 31 December 1985. A Major Malan was initially reluctant to help, but finally agreed to do so.

However, when the attack did come, in the early hours of the following morning, there was no immediate police intervention. From about 4 a.m. Ndebele vigilantes, with white crosses painted on their foreheads and armed with pangas, sjamboks and knobkieries, invaded the Moutse villages of Moteti and Kgobokoane. They looted houses, attacking the occupants, stole money, and abducted as many men as they could find. These hapless residents, many of whom were already seriously wounded, were loaded onto trucks and taken to the community hall in Siyabuswa, where they were held captive, beaten, tortured and humiliated for up to 36 hours before being released. At least one man is known to have died before reaching home, while others were maimed for life. During this entire period, none of the 380 men from Moutse received food or water.

Inside the Siyabuswa Hall the prisoners were made to strip, and then beaten with sjamboks and kieries. They were forced to shout slogans such as 'Mbokodo' and were taunted with the fact that Kwandebele now controlled Moutse. They were also forced to do physical exercises until they were exhausted. During this ordeal soapy water was thrown onto the floor of the hall. The men were forced to stand in this slippery liquid and were then beaten. One of the victims described how they were eventually sitting in a pool of bloodstained water. Many of the victims have identified senior members of the Kwandebele government as being present during their torture, including Skosana, the Chief Minister, and Piet Ntuli, then Minister of the Interior, who also participated in the beatings. Charges of assault were subsequently laid at Dennilton Police Station against Skosana, Ntuli and two other cabinet ministers, with no result.

The New Year's Day abductions failed to cow the Moutse residents or lessen their determination to oppose incorporation. From 1 January Moutse was in a state of turmoil. On the one hand many residents have passively resisted having anything to do with Kwandebele, whether paying tax at the administration office or renewing a business licence. On the other hand there have been numerous incidents of unrest, often directed at the security forces who are seen to be maintaining Kwandebele's control over Moutse. The upheaval that incorporation brought to Moutse was, in many ways, the forerunner of the revolt that swept Kwandebele.

MBOKODO — STATE-ORGANISED TERROR

Mbokodo[2] was formally launched early in 1986 and generated a widespread hatred and fear of the Kwandebele ruling group. It is a widely known fact that about half of the Kwandebele cabinet were members of Mbokodo which, from its inception, brutally suppressed dissent of any kind. The public launch, with a free feast for over 400 men, was a clear attempt to buy support. It can be argued that Mbokodo was to be projected as a cultural organisation, similar to Buthelezi's Inkatha in Natal. Skosana portrayed it as a peace-keeping force with membership open to people who wanted to 'help look after the Kwandebele territory'. He also insisted that Mbokodo was not 'political'. 'They just keep the peace.'

In addition to having Skosana as its president and Ntuli as vice-president, Mbokodo's executive council of 25 members included the MP for Siyabuswa, the minister of Citizen Liaison and Information, the speaker of the Kwandebele Legislative Assembly and a variety of well-known businessmen, taxi owners and government members.

The powers given to Mbokodo at its launch were defined as: protecting the interests of the community; dealing with people who enforce boycotts in Kwandebele; looking into problems affecting family life; and dealing with any trouble maker after his arrest. (Skosana said Mbokodo would 'fetch such a person from the police and hit him'.)

Skosana said that the organisation was being launched officially because there had recently been false accusations against Mbokodo. 'People claiming to be its members were harassing the community. We started this homeland with only R16.40 in our coffers and only 240 Ndebeles and one school to our credit. We are now able to count our money in millions. I cycled all over getting our people together. Now that we have built expensive schools, people want to burn them. Mbokodo will deal with such people'.

Mbokodo's launch and the definition of its powers merely served to confirm a *de facto* situation. It is not clear how long Mbokodo has operated as an organisation, but as early as 1984 there were reported vigilante attacks on Kwandebele residents, while the attacks on Ekangala residents started early in 1985. Skosana himself says that Mbokodo was established in 1976: 'The cultural society was formed when there were riots and schools were burned.'

The core grouping of prominent MPs, businessmen and taxi-owners within Mbokodo had access to resources such as vehicles, halls and schools where they kept and tortured prisoners. They were armed with a variety of weapons, including firearms. Ntuli figured prominently in reports of attacks and was widely believed be the real power behind Mbokodo. In particular he seems to have coordinated the attacks on Moutse residents, and was known for his virulent racist statements about Sotho people. For the rest, Mbokodo's members seemed to be mainly businessmen who paid allegiance to its leaders in order to obtain business licences and patronage. There were also those who were press-ganged into joining Mbokodo as its cannon fodder. Many were high school pupils recruited by the local Mbokodo kingpin. Such an invitation was not to be taken lightly, for those who refused faced becoming victims. Such was the experience of Henry M, a matric scholar at a Kwandebele high school. In a statement made after he had fled Kwandebele he said:

> I left my school because I was beaten for refusing to join Mbokodo. This group started in December to fight the Pedis in Moutse. The president of Mbokodo is Mr Ntuli. . . . He said the South African government has given us this place (Moutse) and we can't leave it to the Pedis living there. They must come to the office in Kwandebele and register under Kwandebele and say they belong to us. The first time they came to me was in December and I refused to join. They go to all the boys in their homes at night and say they must be prepared to go and fight the Pedis. They give them knobkieries and sjamboks. I refused because I do not want to fight. . . . Many of the boys did go and fight and some have been killed. I know of eight who were killed in December . . . near Dennilton.
>
> Many people join Mbokodo because they are afraid of being beaten up. The older ones have joined to help their nation and also because they have businesses and want to protect them, but many have left and have gone to live in Johannesburg and other places because they are afraid of being beaten up.
>
> I heard that the Mbokodo often go to Moutse to fight. They ask all the Mbokodo to come to one place and the trucks will take them. . . . It is surprising that they only go out at night. It is not published in the papers, or on the radio, it is secret, but we hear about it. . . . On February 14th 1986 they came to me again and asked me to join and when I refused they beat me with sjamboks, all over my back, my arms and my legs. The next morning I packed my things and left Siyabuswa. I was admitted to Baragwanath hospital overnight. My body is still full of wounds and scars from the lashes.

Sjamboks and knobkieries were the most common weapons carried by the Mbokodo and were wielded to lethal effect. The numbers of those who were abducted and beaten up by the Mbokodo is unknown, as is the number of those who died as a result of their assault.

On 12 August 1986, the day that independence was officially rejected, Mbokodo was outlawed. It is now a punishable 'insult' to call someone an Mbokodo. Many of the key Mbokodo members have been killed in the past few months, while others have fled. At the time of the rejection of independence some were said to be hiding in a camp at Verena. A call has since gone out for Mbokodo members to re-integrate themselves into the community — for those whose atrocities are well known, however, returning to face the wrath of their victims may be a very unpleasant prospect.

Schools and Mbokodo

During its short life, Mbokodo paid particular attention to 'disciplining' scholars — scholars and youth, in turn, were in the forefront of the struggle against Mbokodo. The first public indication of Mbokodo's attitude to those scholars it regarded as 'trouble makers' came in December 1985 after a group of Mamelodi[3] youths on a Christmas Day picnic in Kwandebele were attacked and held prisoner by Mbokodo. The children had allegedly broken a taxi's window — they claimed to have paid the taxi driver R50 for the damage. Three of the youths were then arrested by the police, but later released to continue their picnic. At about 7 p.m., as the picnickers were preparing to leave, a large group of men arrived and took them to a place where they were assaulted from 8 p.m. until 3 a.m. During the assaults they were accused of being COSAS[4] members who wanted the homeland scholars to revolt and boycott.

This incident created considerable tension between Mamelodi youth and Kwandebele taxi drivers operating in the area, with taxis being stoned. This tension was settled within the Mamelodi community, but Minister Ntuli's comment on the incident was highly revealing. He told a *Star* reporter that he couldn't understand why taxi-drivers were being assaulted by children, 'because the children were not assaulted by them (the taxi drivers) but *by members of our vigilante group*'. He added that trouble had started in early December when he had received word that Mamelodi youths would attack the homeland on 18 and 19 December because the Kwandebele students were at school and writing exams. From then on he had ordered his men to start manning roadblocks and patrolling villages. 'The men on patrol received information about four kombis whose occupants allegedly harassed people in our villages. They were traced and trapped at Vlaklaagte No.1. The occupants were then taken to Kwaggafontein where they were assaulted.'

Although the Kwandebele scholars did not initially participate in school boycotts, there are nevertheless indications that students in some schools did begin to come together to discuss their problems and to talk about the possibilities of forming SRCs, despite the risks this involved. On 28 February 1986 the principal of Mmashadi High School in Siyabuswa called in the police and Mbokodo to 'discipline' students who had allegedly held a meeting the previous day. At the morning assembly the principal said that he did not appreciate such meetings being held behind his back and that should the students wish he would be prepared to allow them to form an SRC.

The assembly was dismissed and the students then gathered to discuss the formation of an SRC before moving back to their classes. In the meantime the principal had gone to call the police and Mbokodo. A few minutes later, about five police Casspirs and numerous government vehicles containing Mbokodo men arrived. The police fired teargas and sjambokked the fleeing pupils. Five teachers and five students were arrested by the police and immediately handed over to Mbokodo. In the meantime the children who had run into the village were caught and sjambokked. They were put into Casspirs and taken back to school, many of them bleeding. Lessons were forcibly resumed in the presence of the police and Mbokodo — the injured pupils not being allowed to receive any medical treatment. The arrested teachers and pupils were taken to the community hall, where they were assaulted and tortured with assegais. They were then put in tiny cells adjoining the hall where they were again stabbed with assegais. They were denied access to toilets. The Mbokodo allegedly told these prisoners that 'because you are north Sotho, you will be taken [from here] by your next of kin as corpses'. The teachers were released after two days, but the fate of the five students is unknown.

In mid-April a boycott began at Benginhlanhla High School in Siyabuswa to protest that only matric students received free books. Shortly after the boycott started Mbokodo vigilantes came to the school. The pupils fled, but some were caught at roadblocks set up in the village. For the next two days they were kept prisoner at Siyabuswa community hall and in Kwaggafontein where they were assaulted with sjamboks, given shocks with cattle prodders and forced to endure Mbokodo's water torture. Three of the ten students taken prisoner were later treated in hospital. In addition, a man who helped them in their attempts to evade arrest was severely beaten on the soles of his feet. Similarly a middle aged woman accused of helping the students was forced to strip, doused with water and slapped.

During April, members of the Kwandebele royal family were continually confronted by residents expressing their opposition to Mbokodo and independence. It was decided that the chiefs and headmen should ascertain the feeling of the people. Many headmen, however, were too scared to call meetings, while others who did so were harassed by Mbokodo.

This is the context of the events of 18 April at Mandlethu High School in Vlaklaagte No.1. It was customary for students at the school to study there at night so that they could share the limited textbooks. From 1986 Mbokodo members stopped this practice and beat up any students found in the school grounds after dark. They also prevented female students from wearing their (compulsory) school track suits, stating that girls must not wear trousers. Another grievance was that students were forced to join Mbokodo. Lastly, there was a general complaint that parents who came home late from work were being beaten by Mbokodo. On Friday 18 April the students went to see the local chief, Samuel Mahlangu, to ask his help in solving their problems with Mbokodo.

There the students requested that two Mbokodo leaders, Mr Skosana the Vlaklaagte MP, and Mr Ngoma, a shopkeeper, be present. The students' grievances were then put to the chief and Mbokodo members. MP Skosana said he would discuss the grievances with other Mbokodo people and reply in a week's time. During that week, some scholars who had joined Mbokodo told the students that they would not get a reply and that Mbokodo was waiting to see what they would do. Students also heard that Mbokodo were looking for so-called ringleaders. On Monday 28th, the day the answer was expected, Mbokodo members told their fellow students that the only reply they would get would be violent.

Later the same day pupils heard that Mbokodo was definitely coming and decided to leave. Before they could do so vans with armed Mbokodo men surrounded the school. As students tried to run out they were beaten. At that stage the police arrived and dispersed the crowd with teargas and rubber bullets. They also freed about 30 people who had been taken prisoner by Mbokodo and were locked in an induna's shack near the school. By now the entire village was in turmoil with parents trying to find and protect their children from the rampant Mbokodo. The police eventually intervened, telling Mbokodo to leave. That night the Mbokodo continued the rampage in Vlaklaagte. They looted houses and assaulted residents, some of whom fled the area permanently.

Mbokodo's Murder of Jacob Skosana

The same day, Jacob Skosana, a Vlaklaagte resident, was told that his daughter, a primary school student, had been arrested by Mbokodo. He rushed to look for her, while voicing his antagonism to Mbokodo. Later that day he was abducted by Mbokodo members who forced their way into his home, beat him up, and dragged him out. His wife was allegedly raped during the abduction. He was put into a car known to belong to Mr Mthimunywe, a local businessman, and driven off in the direction of Kwaggafontein. At the same time, a Mandlethu student leader and relative of the Chief Minister was also abducted by Mbokodo, beaten and taken to Kwaggafontein. There he was put in a hall with many other wounded and beaten students. From 5.30 to 8.30 p.m. he saw many more students brought in. His story continues:

> They then took me out to the toilet. Mr Jacob Skosana was there. He was badly beaten. He had no shirt and I could see the marks on him. He could hardly move or speak. They were continuing to beat him. I was told to take off my clothes and I was then beaten all over my body with kieries and sjamboks. After they beat me they took me back to the hall. I was bleeding all over my body and I also had head injuries. . . . [Later] I was . . . taken by Mr Mthimunye to another room with David Nkosi, a student. I was handcuffed. We were left in that room. By then it was about 11.30 p.m. During that period I heard the Mbokodo people saying that Jacob Skosana should be killed because he was on the side of the students. I then heard a noise like a gunshot. I didn't know who was shot because I was locked in.

Apparently Mr Skosana's body was taken to his home in the early hours of the following morning and dumped on the stoep. The Mbokodo men then lit a fire at the gate and kept watch to prevent anyone from moving the body indoors.

The murder of Jacob Skosana so outraged the local community that the public outcry led to the arrest of about 20 Mbokodo members on murder charges. The most prominent were immediately let out on bail and apparently not charged. There were later unconfirmed rumours that the case file went missing from the police offices. Jacob Skosana's funeral was eventually set for 13 May, after the police had refused to release the body for almost three weeks. Skosana's murder and the brutal treatment of the Mandlethu scholars contributed to rising popular pressure for action against Mbokodo.

Mbokodo Prison Camps

Despite the arrests and limited charges that followed this murder, Mbokodo continued to act as a law unto itself. In particular, the establishment of prison camps was an indication of Mbokodo's sense of its own power. During the early days of the Kwandebele revolt, many youths went missing, and, it was rumoured, they were being held prisoner in these camps.

These fears were found to have substance after Johannes Ramahlale escaped from one of the camps and informed the police. He told how he had been abducted by a group of men led by a prominent businessmen. He was put in the boot of a car with four other youths and taken to the camp near the Ballbank police station. With his feet tied together, he was assaulted and ducked in a dam of dirty water. He also said that some of the others who were tortured had their stomachs trampled and were forced to stand barefoot on burning coals. There were fifty-four prisoners in the camp, most of them having received no food or water for six days. Following Johannes's testimony and the publicity which followed, the police stormed the camp and freed the prisoners. During an interview on 30 May Skosana denied Mbokodo involvement, 'This was not Mbokodo, just people. Mbokodo has been suspended for three weeks. It is still suspended.'

RESISTANCE TO MBOKODO AND INDEPENDENCE INTENSIFIES: THE WAR BEGINS

A week after Jacob Skosana's murder the issue of independence was raised again — the bombshell was dropped by P. W. Botha on 7 May when, following a meeting between representatives of the South African and Kwandebele governments, he announced in parliament that Kwandebele would take independence on 11 December 1986. This news was an instant spark to existing tensions. The Kwandebele royal family — opponents of both independence and Mbokodo — were urged to take action. Accordingly, a meeting of all the chiefs in the area was scheduled at the royal kraal for 12 May, to try and decide how to deal with Mbokodo. The entire cabinet was invited, but only two members arrived — travelling in Casspirs. Villagers from all over Kwandebele poured into the royal kraal as the gathering swelled to an estimated 20,000 people.

The meeting demanded that Mbokodo be disbanded; that there should be no independence; and that the Kwandebele Legislative Assembly and cabinet should resign because they had agreed to independence on the basis of false claims that they had a mandate from the people. In response to these demands the Deputy Chief Minister is reported to have stated that Mbokodo had been suspended three weeks previously. He said that there would be a meeting to re-discuss the independence issue and that the legislative assembly would consider resignation. A report-back meeting was set for two days later, and residents dispersed with high hopes.

The following day was that of Jacob Skosana's funeral. Restrictions were imposed on the funeral by the local magistrate stipulating, *inter alia*, that a maximum of 50 people could attend the funeral, and that it must occur on a weekday. The restrictions were ignored as thousands of residents from Vlaklaagte village, including all the schoolchildren, attended the funeral. Predictably, the police arrived at the funeral. They gave warning that it was considered to be an illegal gathering and ordered the mourners to disperse. The police and army then fired teargas, rubber bullets and birdshot. Scores of people were arrested and many were injured. Sara Mthimunye, a 19-year from Tweefontein, was killed when she fell under a bus whose passengers nau been teargassed. The crowd then went on the rampage, setting fire to shops allegedly owned by members of parliament and Mbokodo. Buses were hijacked to transport the mourners home. That night police roadblocks were set up all over the villages and Mbokodo began to retaliate.

In the morning a spontaneous stay-away occurred. Bus drivers, instead of driving their passengers to Pretoria, turned around and began to make their way to the royal kraal at Ndundza, where thousands had gathered. However, what none of the Ndundza-bound people knew was that the permission sought by Prince James Mahlangu for the meeting had been refused by the magistrate.

As the 25-30,000 strong crowd gathered, the police and the security forces moved in. Teargas was fired into and around the royal kraal from a helicopter, and into the buses. In one case a bus driver jumped out of his vehicle when a teargas cannister exploded near his face, leaving the bus to career wildly down the road leading from the royal kraal. In another incident a 10-year-old boy who jumped out of a moving bus to avoid teargas was run over and killed. The royal kraal was a scene of pandemonium and chaos. As the large security force contingent opened fire with teargas, rubber bullets, birdshot and buckshot, many people were trampled and injured. Many of the older people collapsed as they were overcome with teargas. A 35-year-old man died after being shot in the mouth and a young man was found some time later lying dead in the street.

Allegations by journalists that they had seen the police laughing whilst firing teargas at people, and that the security forces had generally behaved in a provocative and irresponsible manner, were denied by the head of the Kwandebele police who refused to comment on events at the royal kraal. He had earlier refused to speak to the press and referred all enquiries to SAP headquarters in Pretoria. Pretoria in turn said that Kwandebele was outside its jurisdiction.

Following the disrupted meeting, widespread confrontations developed between residents (mainly youths), Mbokodo and the security forces. That evening at Tweefontein E, five youths were reported to have been shot dead by a local Mbokodo shopkeeper named Ngoma when a group of youths attacked his shop. The names of those killed were reported to be James Mashiloane from Phumula, David Kudube from Manaleng, Grace Sidane from Kwezobuhle, Samuel Kabinde from Vlaklaagte No.2 and John Koma from Kwaggafontein A. Jacob Skosana from Manaleng was injured and admitted to Kalafong hospital. David Radebe, a 26-year-old man, was also said to have been killed by Mbokodo members on 14 May.

These confrontations continued on a daily basis until August, when the decision to take independence was finally abandoned. In the South African media, and particularly under State of Emergency conditions, the events in Kwandebele during this period were portrayed as a series of random acts of brutal violence without purpose or logic. In the daily unrest reports issued by the Bureau for Information, Kwandebele figured prominently as an area where necklacings, lootings and stonings by 'groups of youth' instilled fear into the population at large. This perception, however, in no way characterises the complexity of both the events and the political forces participating in the 'anti-independence war'.

The Role of Youth and the Scholars

As has happened in so many areas of South Africa in recent years, the Kwandebele youth took upon themselves the role of defenders of the people. Hundreds of youths had left their homes to avoid Mbokodo capture, and taken to the *veld* where they operated in groups to defend their area. It is they who took on the full might of both Mbokodo and the security forces, with many dying or being detained in the process.

A striking aspect of the role of the youth in the war was their capacity to sustain close relationships with both local villagers and the Kwandebele royal family. In this sense, the government characterisation of the youth as wild and undisciplined bands terrorising the local population does not reflect reality. In various areas youth even began to use tribal authority offices with the agreement of the headmen. Consultation with parents also took place, as was demonstrated by the schools boycott.

From mid-May all students in Kwandebele, including primary school students, went on boycott. This was with the consent of their parents who, in some instances, went to the schools to tell the teachers that their children would not be coming to school until the people's demands had been met. At the request of the youth, the three demands of the 12 May meeting were expanded to include a call for the withdrawal of troops from the area, and for detained children to be released.

Stay-aways and the Role of the Civil Service

During the first week of June there was a call for a stay-away. No Kwandebele workers went to work for two days and there were no buses for commuters into Pretoria and other areas. Kwandebele's 2,000-odd civil servants also responded, so enraging Minister Ntuli that he ordered them to fill in forms giving reasons for their absence. He also told them to re-apply for their jobs, warning that those who did not give 'acceptable' reasons would be fired. It is unclear to what extent this threat was carried out.

The participation by the civil service in the stay-away substantially broadened both the base and the strength of those opposing Kwandebele independence, and raised the possibility of paralysing the entire administrative apparatus. On 15 July the entire civil service again went on strike — this time for an indefinite period, in response to an anonymous pamphlet calling on all outsiders working for the Kwandebele government to return home until the people's demands had been met.

For two weeks the Kwandebele administration was totally crippled, the judiciary did not function, pensioners could not be paid and even the school teachers were out on strike. This posed an unusual dilemma in South Africa's education crisis, for scholars felt that primary school children should go back to school, and it was the teachers' absence, rather than that of their pupils, that prolonged the boycott. The demands put forward by the civil service during the strike were in keeping with the popular demands put forward at the royal kraal.

The stand taken by the civil service was a highly unusual one. In most homeland areas the civil service is a conservative group whose members will stand by the state because they are dependent on it, not only for their salaries, but for access to resources such as trading licences. In this respect the action taken by the Kwandebele civil servants was unprecedented. In part their willingness to take direct action seems to be related to the fact that the majority of them had been seconded from outside Kwandebele. As non-Ndebeles they also seem to have fallen victim to Mbokodo taunts and attack.

The White Farmers

It is interesting that during the war white farmers resident on the edges of Kwandebele opposed the Skosana regime. Part of the reason for this was a long-standing relationship of cooperation with the Kwandebele royal family who opposed independence and Mbokodo. But the farmers' opposition to Skosana was also born of self-interest. They saw that as long as Mbokodo existed, and independence was being promoted, there would never be peace in Kwandebele. This threatened the stability of the entire area, adversely affecting their access to labour. The Elands River Farmers Association in particular took a stand against Mbokodo and independence. They made representations to both the South African government and the security forces in an effort to ensure that popular demands would be won and peace would return.

The Royal Family

The Kwandebele royal family played a critical role in the resistance. As has been seen, from April they were hearing grievances relating to Mbokodo, and set in motion a process of consultation with the local population. It was also they who called mass meetings throughout the conflict. Members of the royal family, and Prince James Mahlangu in particular, played a key role in facilitating the success of opposition. There are no records of meetings or discussions, but it is clear that the royal family was the only group with access to all of the different forces involved in the struggle. They met with the comrades, had contact with the civil service and long-standing relationships with the white farmers, and possessed the authority to meet and make representations to senior South African government and security force members.

The loose and broad alliance described above succeeded in putting inexorable pressure on the Kwandebele government. The response of this government showed both a lack of understanding of the issues involved, and as a reliance on repression that could not be sustained, especially once Mbokodo had been forced so far onto the defensive that some of its members were attempting to defect to the comrades.

The relationship between Mbokodo and the security forces also changed as the war proceeded. Instead of being in the forefront of attacks against the comrades, Mbokodo members were reported to be travelling with the security forces and pointing out comrades from the safety of Hippo armoured cars, rather than taking action themselves. One notable exception to this, however, was the massacre that took place at Tweefontein on 12 June, the day the State of Emergency was declared. Mbokodo, under the leadership of Piet Ntuli, viciously attacked and massacred villagers who had killed one of Ntuli's guards. Ntuli himself shot the victims and at least six people died. The security forces were said to have been present at the time the massacre happened. Thomas Mnyakeni, who witnessed the incident, was himself shot and subsequently disappeared. He was last seen being driven off in a government ambulance. Since then his family has believed him to be in detention but have not seen him. However, when all the other detainees from his village were released in mid-August, Thomas was not amongst them. All efforts to find him have proved futile.

By mid-July it was clear that Mbokodo was now completely on the defensive. With many of its members dead or in hiding it was a broken force. The Kwandebele government also seems to have been in disarray. Press statements ceased to be issued, and rumours circulated to the effect that S. S. Skosana had taken to his bed.

THE RESPONSE OF THE SOUTH AFRICAN SECURITY FORCES
AND THE SOUTH AFRICAN GOVERNMENT

The official South African response saw Kwandebele as just another unrest area, with the Bureau for Information including items on unrest in Kwandebele in its daily press briefings. In July the Bureau released a statement on Kwandebele which contained no indication that the depth and the breadth of opposition to independence was understood. The Bureau for Information attributed the strife to 'tension between the government of the region and royalty'. It added that the chiefs and headmen were dissatisfied with the proposed constitution. The Bureau also blamed the situation on 'radicals'. It said 'large groups of comrades from the Witwatersrand have been operating in the area'. The Kwandebele Commissioner General likewise attributed the situation to 'purely domestic power struggles'.

From 12 June hundreds of people, mainly youths, were detained and others were charged with public violence, arson, looting, etc. On 26 June, in the face of escalating violence, the authorities took stronger action. They issued a set of Emergency regulations for Kwandebele which were amongst the most stringent anywhere in South Africa. The reasons for detention were clearly extremely arbitrary. The cases cited below are just three of many such instances. In one case, a jilted husband went with eight young men to bring his wife back home. On arrival at her house the men discovered that she was not there and made her parents accompany them instead. When the estranged wife arrived home and discovered that her parents were gone she went to the 'soldiers' and took them to her husband's home. Her parents were released and the eight young men were then detained under emergency regulations for over two months and accused of wanting to necklace the two old people. They were never charged.

In the second incident two young men from Bundu Inn were hitching home after a soccer match. They were given a lift on the back of a bakkie. The bakkie drove off at speed and raced through the village. The youths became scared and as the bakkie reached the outskirts of the village they jumped out. One of the youths fell badly and was knocked unconscious. As the other youth was trying to revive him, the bakkie returned and the driver offered to take the unconscious youth to hospital. His friend refused, but the driver insisted and loaded the unconscious boy onto the bakkie and drove off.

Enquiries for him at Philadelphia hospital proved fruitless. The friend then went home where he was told that the driver of the bakkie had taken the wounded youth to the soldiers and that he was now being kept in detention at Dennilton police station. This youth was detained for over two months. In the third incident a group of people from Tweefontein were on their way to an *iqhude* — an Ndebele rite of passage — when they were stopped at a roadblock and detained. They too were kept for over two months.

These detentions become in themselves a source of tension. The youths who were still boycotting classes by mid-July promised that they would return to school should their imprisoned colleagues be released. The royal family and the white farmers seem to have taken this issue up with both the police and the Commissioner General. Yet, until the end of July there was no indication that the detainees would be released at all.

There were, however, developments on another front. By now the police seem to have realised that Mbokodo's excesses had to be stopped. Towards the end of July there were at last indications of police willingness to take action against Piet Ntuli. Shortly before his death Ntuli was arrested and was said to be facing charges of car theft (about 50 stolen cars are said to have been found at his home). In addition he was found in possession of an arms cache.[5] The willingness to arrest Ntuli was quite clearly a recognition of the need for a scapegoat. In this sense his arrest was a political strategy that may well have had as its aim the need to salvage independence. If enough crimes could be laid at Ntuli's door, Skosana would regain enough credibility to proceed with independence.

Ntuli's Death

On 29 July Piet Ntuli — widely regarded as the force behind Mbokodo — was killed by a car bomb. His death was taken as a sign of impending victory for the forces opposed to independence. The news led to widespread rejoicing throughout Kwandebele. Feasts were held, and people danced in the streets shouting '*Mahlungu amahle*', meaning 'good bad-tidings'.

In Kwandebele it is widely believed that Ntuli was killed, as one journalist put it, by 'agents of Pretoria'. Evidence given for this by residents includes information that in the two weeks preceding his death, senior government officials had indicated to key figures that Ntuli would shortly be removed. Ntuli was heard shouting at Pretoria officials that since he wasn't the official head of Mbokodo, he should not carry the blame for its actions. Residents also claimed that only the 'system' could have had access to the sophisticated technology used to make the bomb which killed Ntuli. In late August the ANC claimed responsibility for his death.

In the weeks following Ntuli's death, word from both Pretoria and Siyabuswa was that independence was definitely going ahead. With Ntuli, now the scapegoat for all the problems, out of the way, the road seemed to be open for those functionaries whose hands were not so directly tainted with blood.

Ntuli's death was fundamentally important. The horror of the way he died made many pro-independence MPs and Mbokodo members reconsider their stand. His death also strengthened the resolve of all the anti-independence forces to continue their struggle. The release of most detainees in early

August strengthened this feeling. For whatever reason, the authorities were seen to have conceded an important demand of the Kwandebele people.

INDEPENDENCE IS CANCELLED — THE 12 AUGUST VICTORY

Pressure was put on the Kwandebele cabinet to call a meeting of the legislative assembly. With Skosana now on his sick-bed, F. K. Mtshweni, a known Mbokodo member, was acting Chief Minister. There are indications that the cabinet tried to postpone this meeting. In the first week of August the chiefs met with the government and pressurised the legislative assembly to meet. August 12 was finally set as the date. The agenda, however, omitted the independence issue and included only discussion of unrest and Mbokodo.

The legislative assembly met in a packed converted school in an electric atmosphere — Kwandebele's people had come to see independence buried. During a discussion on unrest, Prince James Mahlangu raised the issue of independence. An unsuccesful attempt was made to block the discussion, and a motion was introduced rejecting independence. Speaker after speaker supported it. Eventually an anguished Skosana cried out that everyone had turned against him. He then sat forward, head in hands, until at last the Speaker, Solly Mahlangu, announced that the consensus was clear — independence was no more and Mbokodo was outlawed. At the end of the parliamentary session there was universal rejoicing throughout Kwandebele. A great people's victory had been won.

The Aftermath

The decision by the Kwandebele Legislative Assembly to reject independence was unprecedented in South African history. It seemed to signal a defeat to the bantustan system that had implications for any other homeland leader considering independence. It was an ironic decision — reached within the homeland parliament itself and supported by the normally conservative chiefs. Yet it must be recognised that this victory was won through the strength of the Kwandebele people.

In the wake of the rejection of independence, the political situation in Kwandebele has been extremely fluid. On the one hand there was a dramatic downturn in unrest incidents and, once all detainees had been released, the children returned to school. On the other hand, it has become clear that there is still likely to be a long and drawn out struggle over the direction Kwandebele will take.

In the weeks immediately following the rejection of independence, F. K. Mahlangu, and F. Mtshweni, two former Mbokodo members and Skosana supporters, took control of the administration. In a press statement they said they accepted the rejection of independence, but added that the construction of the new capital would go ahead. At the same time rumours circulated that Skosana and his group were planning to challenge the legislative assembly decision, on the grounds that no formal vote had been taken before independence was cancelled.

At the same time, Prince James Mahlangu and the royal family waited in the wings to take power. Yet, the legislative assembly meeting required to propose a vote of no confidence in the existing cabinet has not materialised. Nor has the rumour that a Kwandebele election would be called. In early September there were indications of a renewed SADF presence in Kwandebele, as well as rumours that Skosana *et al.* were planning independence at some time in the future.

Finally, the Moutse issue is again causing increased tension. Immediately after the rejection of independence, Moutse organisations waited expectantly for an announcement from Prince James and his supporters that the incorporation would be cancelled should they take control. However, no such announcement has been forthcoming. On the contrary, Makhosana Klaas Mahlangu, an influential member of the anti-independence camp, and the only MP to have resigned his parliamentary seat in protest at the Moutse incorporation, changed his tune. In a press statement he said his opposition to incorporation stemmed from the fact that it had happened under Skosana's administration. Under a new administration he felt the incorporation would not be a problem. The Moutse Civic Association responded that the residents of Moutse did not wish to be in any homeland. They also said they felt the majority of Kwandebele MPs had rejected independence out of a fear of popular anger, and pointed out that the cancellation of independence had not addressed the fundamental problems of poverty and unemployment in Kwandebele, nor led to a reassessment of the bantustan policy as a whole.

Within three months of the anti-independence victory, Kwandebele's fragile peace was threatened. Prince James Mahlangu and his brother Andries were detained under State of Emergency regulations on 10 November 1986, and tribal records were confiscated by police. The following day six people were detained, including prominent anti-independence activists. These detentions have been widely interpreted as meaning that plans for a renewed attempt at independence are under way. It may be assumed that the task will be easier with the royal family out of the way. Any attempt to go for independence will be contrary to the clearly stated will of the majority of Kwandebele's people. The chances of renewed conflict and violence in the near future therefore seem to be high. The Kwandebele war is not over. Moutse may well become a flashpoint again. The independence victory may turn out to have been the first step in a protracted struggle against the homeland structure itself. But one thing is clear. The struggle of the people of Kwandebele has been a critical turning point in the capacity of the bantustan system to sustain itself.

Postscript — 'Independence' on the Agenda Again?

Following the detention of the royal family on 10 November the civil service again struck in protest. The death of S. S. Skosana of sugar diabetes on 17 November added to the tension. The detainees were then released, and were thus able to attend the legislative assembly to elect the new chief minister.

The pro-independence forces scored a notable victory in electing George Mahlangu, a close confidante of the late Piet Ntuli. This coup finally dashed any possibility of the royal family taking control of a non-independent Kwandebele. Speaking to the press after his election, the chief minister refused to make any comment on the vital issue of independence. This approach again fuelled speculation that it was merely a matter of time before independence was once again a reality.

In early 1987 an attempt was made to downgrade the status of the Ndunza tribal authority, and aspersions were cast on the legitimacy of the Ndunza's claims to royal status. At the same time, the Manala tribe was brought into the pro-independence camp, and attempts were made to enhance its status in Ndebele politics. The crackdown on the Kwandebele royal family, and the pattern of harassment and detention, reflected broader processes within the homeland. The youth were, once again, a particular focus of attention, as Mobokodo activity re-emerged.

At the opening of the legislative assembly on 10 April the Deputy Minister of Education and Development Aid, Gerrit Viljoen, said that the government was giving 'constant attention' to the transfer of more legislative powers to Kwandebele. At around the same time, and in direct contradiction to assurances given to residents in 1986, Ekangala was finally incorporated into Kwandebele.

On 6 May, as the whites voted for more repression, the Kwandebele government again opted for 'independence', to be made retrospective to 11 December 1986 — the original date. F. K. Mahlangu, Minister of Citizen Liaison and Information, who in August 1986 had said that the cancellation of independence was a result of its rejection by the people of Kwandebele, was now quoted as saying that the decision to opt for independence was a time of rejoicing for the people of the country. A number of known opponents of independence were purged from the assembly before the vote was taken.

Within 24 hours of the announcement, reports were coming in of the destruction of government property, and all schools in Kwandebele were reported to be affected by a boycott. Offices at the new 'capital', KwaMhlanga, were burned, while known opponents of independence were also attacked in a series of raids, fire-bombings and assaults. These events were accompanied by a massive increase in security force presence and actions in the area.

On 16 May, the Kwandebele Commissioner of Police is reported to have said that the violence in the area was related to criminal actions, and was not connected with the independence decision. The leader of the opposition in Kwandebele, Cornelius Mahlangu, was dramatically arrested as he left the British Consulate in Johannesburg, having just briefed Western diplomats on the situation in Kwandebele.

Whatever the Kwandebele authorities may choose to believe, it is clear that offering independence is like holding a lighted match to dry *veld*. It is clear now, as it was a year ago, that only a firm and unambiguous decision to drop the independence issue is going to restore a semblance of peace to the area.

NOTES

As most of the evidence presented in this chapter was taken directly from sworn statements and affidavits, there is a corresponding paucity of footnotes and references. [WC & RC]

1. Operation Hunger is a private charity, providing subsistence foodstuffs, clothing and other materials to hundreds of thousands of malnourished and often starving people, mostly located in the homelands.
2. Literally, 'millstone'.
3. One of the townships in the Pretoria area.

4. Congress of South African Students, which the South African government has outlawed.
5. It is important to note that whilst the police were reluctant to take action against Mbokodo, they do not seem to have supported and worked with it to the same extent as did the SADF.

7. Counter-Revolution as Reform: Struggle in the Bantustans

JEREMY KEENAN

INTRODUCTION

The last ten years or so, especially since 1977-8, are frequently referred to as the 'reform era' in South Africa. Harold Wolpe, in an analysis of this period, noted that 'the major burden of the analysis of the contemporary conjuncture in South Africa by the left in general, and the ANC in particular, has been to demonstrate that legislative and other policy changes introduced by the regime — for example, provision for the legal recognition of black trade unions, the abandonment of the legal reservation of certain jobs for whites only, the spread of Africans into white collar jobs, concessions to black businessmen, some constitutional adjustments and the bantustan policy — do not amount at all to *real* reforms of the system of apartheid.'[1]

Such an analysis is fundamentally correct. As this chapter will demonstrate, we are not witnessing the reform of the system of apartheid, but its *reformulation*. Indeed, it will be argued that the process referred to as 'reform' is, in reality, 'counter-revolution'. Nevertheless, as Wolpe has warned, 'while it is clearly politically important to expose the shallowness of the so-called reforms, the preoccupation solely with the question of whether or not the "reforms" amount to a substantial move towards the liberation of black people is insufficient'.[2]

Recognition must be given, as Wolpe has urged, to the fact that these reform policies have opened up new spaces of contestation. What needs to be investigated, he argues, is the extent to which these 'reforms' have transformed the political terrain, set up new bases of conflict and contradiction, and paved the way for possible new alignments.[3]

The political terrain of South Africa has been dramatically transformed, even since Wolpe raised these concerns. It would require a skilled analysis to do even partial justice to the nature of this very complex and rapidly shifting terrain in the space of a single chapter. This chapter is limited to one dimension only, namely the political struggles that have emerged in the Transvaal bantustan areas, with particular reference to Bophuthatswana.

By and large, the struggles taking place within these areas have been grossly neglected. For analysts outside the country this is understandable: for those inside there are fewer excuses. The net result is that, with a few exceptions, much of what is happening in these areas goes unrecorded. Yet more than 50 percent of the country's African population is constrained to the bantustans, under the most repressive conditions. Diplomatically, it is of course both understandable and necessary that the bantustans are not recognised.

136

But in South Africa they are a legal reality which, directly or indirectly, affects the lives of most of the 26 million or so Africans in South Africa.

Even though the economic functions of the bantustans have changed, and perhaps diminished in overall direct significance, from being primarily the reproducer of cheap labour power to their most recent function as the fundamental institutions for the containment and control of the country's absolute surplus population of Africans — the unemployed and the unemployable, the young and old, sick and disabled and the destitute — they have acquired an even greater political centrality in the apartheid state, particularly in its reformulated mode. An understanding of the nature of political struggles taking place within them is essential for the development of an adequate analysis of the contemporary conjuncture in South Africa.

During the past year or two most of the Transvaal bantustan areas, especially Bophuthatswana, Kwandebele and Lebowa, have witnessed a dramatic escalation of popular resistance to the structures of the apartheid state. This increased struggle has been characterised by widespread state violence, most notably the Winterveld shootings of March 1986, and by the turning of Kwandebele and much of Lebowa into 'no-go' areas.

This heightened resistance has also been marked by the Emergency, on the one hand, and by the proliferation of numerous local political organisations on the other, the most common of which have been the regional crisis committees, action committees, civic associations, women's organisations and youth organisations. The formation of most of these structures has been a defensive reaction to the intensification of state control and repression in these areas. This has, more often than not, involved the provocative presence of the South African Defence Force (SADF), police and/or state-backed vigilantes, as well as the state's more or less indiscriminate use of violence and terrorism to stifle legitimate demands of the people, and attempt to quell the emergence of a more responsible and representative local leadership.

There are two characteristics of these organisations which are significant. In most cases they originated as single-issue organisations, responding to such issues as rent increases, boycotts, state violence etc., and then widened out to take on the general 'defence' of the community, and its organisation on a wider political front.

The second, and more significant characteristic has been the role of the youth. The development of crisis committees, civic, women's and other associations has, in many cases, followed on from, or been precipitated by, the initial formation of youth organisations. Not only have youth organisations assisted in the establishment of other structures, but in most areas they have played a leading role in trying to link local organisational structures into wider regional and national structures.

There are many reasons why the youth have played such an important part in the upsurge of resistance in the bantustans: two warrant comment. The first is that the increase in state violence and consequent disruption of education in the 'urban' areas has led to many youth moving to the bantustans, albeit temporarily, to attend schools in those areas, or to escape state violence in the townships. The second reason is the process of 'reform' as counter-revolution, which has been accompanied by increased repression in the bantustan areas, and a dramatic increase in unemployment in these areas, both of which have affected the youth most severely.

The South African government's public explanation for this intensified and widespread popular resistance to the apartheid state within the bantustan areas identifies it as part of a concerted strategy, coordinated and directed externally by the African National Congress (ANC) and its 'communist(ic)' masters, and internally by its perceived 'surrogate' forces, notably the United Democratic Front (UDF), to make the country ungovernable and hence to overthrow the state.[4] All incidents and outbreaks of resistance and violence against the state are linked and elevated in this way to the conspiratorial design of a grand strategy — the 'revolutionary onslaught'.

This sort of explanation, and its xenophobic language, apart from satiating the prejudices of Reagan, Thatcher and the like, is designed primarily to obfuscate and deny the reality of this escalating popular resistance. The reality of these struggles is their pervasiveness, 'grass-rootedness' and legitimacy, and the representativeness and responsibility of their political organisations and leadership.

It is these qualities which pose such a threat to the state and which have provoked such a violent reaction. The maintenance of the 'reformulated' apartheid state depends on the denial and dismantling of any form of democratic and representative political organisation and leadership, for such structures are, by definition, the very antithesis of the apartheid state.

The greatest danger of misunderstanding the nature of this contemporary resistance in the bantustan areas lies in the tendency of 'writing history backwards'. Rather in the same way as the state has tried to explain the outbreak and escalation of the struggles as a concerted and coordinated ANC and UDF-directed strategy, so is there a danger of progressive forces themselves attributing too much centrality to the roles of national organisations such as the ANC or UDF in these struggles.

In some areas, as for example in some parts of northern Lebowa/Transvaal, resistance has indeed been inspired by UDF elements. In others, the current upsurge in popular resistance has emerged at a singularly localised level with those involved in the organisations having little or no knowledge of the UDF or other national organisations. Such organisations affiliated to the UDF only after they had emerged within their particular local sites of struggle, while there are still some areas where key local organisations have not formally affiliated to the UDF or any other national organisation.

In many of these areas the role of the national bodies in the emergence and organisation of resistance has been more in providing a coherent ideology than as an active and concrete structure. Nonetheless, it is the emergence of strong grassroot organisations from within the communities themselves that has become the real strength of the UDF.

The second crucial feature of the contemporary struggles in the bantustan areas is that in almost all cases they are a direct reaction to the state's 'reform' programme. This programme, far from stabilising the post-1976 situation in South Africa, has been instrumental in escalating resistance to the apartheid state and its appendages in the bantustans.

The following section of this chapter briefly explains and examines the nature of the state's strategy in the period since P.W. Botha came to power in 1979, a period generally referred to as the 'reform era'. In so doing it highlights four of the main corollaries to this strategy which, singly or in combination, have provoked much of the contemporary 'unrest' and popular resistance in the bantustan areas. These are:

1) the increased use of violence by the state in its attempts to 'stabilise' conditions for the implementation of its 'reform' programme and, in conjunction, the intensification of state violence, control and repression in the bantustans;
2) the burgeoning corruption of both the central and local bantustan authority structures;
3) the new forces of capital investment in the bantustans in both agriculture and industry, which have led to increased land dispossession and more intensive forms of oppression and exploitation;
4) the increasing poverty and unemployment in the bantustan areas.

While there is a clear overall pattern underlying the spread and escalation of popular resistance in the bantustans, the specific development and organisation of these struggles cannot simply be 'read off' from the national struggle. They cannot be fully explained without an appreciation of their local contexts.[5] Indeed, where national organisations have intervened directly in these struggles they have sometimes tended both to misunderstand and ignore the local specifics of the struggle and the needs of the people involved in it, sometimes, as in the case of Winterveld in Bophuthatswana, with detrimental results.

REFORM/COUNTER-REVOLUTION AND REPRESSION: TWO SIDES OF THE SAME COIN[6]

The Crisis of the 1970s: the Background to 'Reform'

During the 1960s the economy, and especially the manufacturing sector, experienced a period of almost frenetic growth fuelled largely by direct foreign investment and characterised by the increasing concentration and centralisation of production. The way for this 'boom' had been paved by the state in the 1950s and early 1960s by its smashing the organisations of widespread popular resistance and its implementation of a number of 'reforms' aimed at disciplining the black working class and making it more susceptible to the rigours and demands of a more industrialised and mechanised economy.

Although the rate of economic growth of the 1960s was not to last, the structural transformation of the economy to a more capital-intensive and monopolistic phase of accumulation continued at an accelerated pace. This more capital-intensive phase of production made new demands on the labour force. It required more skilled workers, a demand which could not be sufficiently met from within the ranks of the white working class.

As the 1970s advanced it became increasingly apparent that ideology, in the form of certain items of apartheid legislation in the workplace, such as the colour bar and job reservation, and also in education and training, were contributing to a skills shortage and consequently impeding economic growth. On the other hand the drive towards more capital-intensive production was also increasing structural unemployment.

The 1970s were also characterised by a general intensification of class struggle. This was signified on the one hand by an upsurge in worker militancy and the re-emergence and growth of independent and predominantly black trade unions, and on the other hand by a heightening of popular mass struggle, predominantly in the townships, against state policy and the organs of state administration. During the 1960s the numbers of black workers involved in strike action never exceeded 10,000 in any year. Yet 1973 saw 370 strikes involving 98,029 workers, a pattern which was extended throughout most sectors of the economy and most parts of the country during 1974 and 1975.

This upsurge in resistance to the apartheid state fuelled by a number of other contributory factors, notably the rise of the Black Consciousness Movement (BCM) during the first half of the 1970s and the success of the anti-colonial struggles, especially in the neighbouring Portuguese territories during 1973-4. The revolt of 1976-7 marked a deepening of the crisis and its manifestation on a broader front.

'Total Strategy': Reform or Counter-revolution?

The state's response to this crisis was to implement a number of policies under the umbrella of 'Total Strategy'. The aim of this strategy was to combat the perceived 'total onslaught' facing the country. It amounted to a counter-revolutionary programme aimed at removing the perceived causes of unrest, and thereby undermining the omnipresent 'agitators' supposedly responsible for the unrest by removing the issues around which they were mobilising. These issues were identified by the state as unemployment and inadequate housing and amenities in the townships. This strategy was structured around the attempted socio-economic upliftment of a section of the black population, while simultaneously crushing all opposition. The state has tried to sell this counter-revolutionary strategy to both black and white South Africans, and to the outside world, by calling it 'reform'.

Political 'Reform'

The political side of 'reform' has been secondary to the socio-economic side, and is arguably just as much of a failure. The major constitutional 'reform' has been the creation of the 'tri-cameral' parliament, a structure designed to exclude Africans from central political representation. Africans were, instead, to be granted extended local government rights, with their 'national' political rights remaining linked to the bantustans.

While the tri-cameral parliament has been rejected by the vast majority of the population, the township local government structures have been shattered by overwhelming opposition and have collapsed. This has resulted in the SADF invading and, in many instances, taking over the actual administration of the townships.

As has been already stressed, 'reform' or counter-revolution is predominantly repressive. This is a primary function of the bantustans and the military structures being installed at all levels of the country's administration and government.

The 'independence' given to some of the bantustans is linked to 'reform' by the state, it being argued that Africans can exercise *full* political rights within their own independent nation states/countries, in which 'real' economic and political 'development' is alleged to have occurred. South Africa has countered criticism of its bantustan policy by inviting the world to look at Bophuthatswana — the self-proclaimed showpiece of the bantustan system. Bophuthatswana is portrayed as being economically independent of South Africa and completely free of discrimination and apartheid — freedoms all 'guaranteed' by a Bill of Rights embodied in the Constitution.

The reality is somewhat different. The primary function of the bantustans, the fundamental bases of apartheid, is to contain and control the increasing absolute surplus population — the unemployed, unemployable, aged, etc. The legal status of 'self-government' and 'independence' of these regions serves to 'absolve' South Africa from all responsibility for social security, the actions of their police and political repression.

The internal political mechanisms whereby this control is maintained operate on a similar basis to those in the urban areas, namely through the incorporation of a collaborationist petty bourgeoisie consisting of business people, state functionaries, tribal and community authorities etc. One of the basic mechanisms of incorporation is the sanctioning by the ruling party of embezzlement, fraud and general corruption.[7]

The extent of this corruption in Bophuthatswana has led to its becoming insolvent and having to be bailed out by the central government, whose officials have taken over the Bophuthatswana Treasury and Department of Finance in a move described as a 'stabilisation policy similar to that of the IMF'.[8]

Bophuthatswana's self-acclaimed Bill of Rights is now as bankrupt as its Treasury. Bophuthatswana's internal security legislation overrides the Bill of Rights. Police harassment, torture, detention without trial, denial of access to the courts and due legal process, forced removals, ethnic discrimination, theft of freehold land, denial of freedom of association for trade unions and the banning of political opposition are now everyday occurrences.[9]

A 'Creeping Military Coup' [10]

The repressive basis of 'reform' is embodied in the very philosophy on which the South African government's 'reform' strategy is predicated. The origins and underlying philosophy of the government's concept of 'Total Strategy' can be traced directly to the thought of the French military strategist, General Beaufre, whose writings are now set works in South Africa's military academies.[11]

As Sarakinsky points out, 'according to Beaufre, political action should only take place after the situation has been closely analysed . . . action, in the form of reforms, should be implemented in such a way that they *undermine the enemy* '.[12]

This advice helps explain the proliferation of government commissions of enquiry in the post-1977 period into almost every facet of South African society, such as the Riekert and Wiehahn Commissions referred to, which themselves came out of the Cilliers Commission into the causes of the 1976 Soweto uprising.

Reforms in state structures and apparatuses have been made on the basis of the recommendations of these various commissions. In implementing 'reform' it is clear that the state has also drawn on the advice of Samuel Huntingdon, a conservative American political scientist who visited South Africa in 1981. In essence his strategy for implementing 'reform' was 'a combination of Fabian strategy and blitzkrieg tactics'.[13]

Huntingdon sees repression as an integral component of reform. He suggests that *effective repression may enhance the appeal of reform* to radicals by increasing the costs and risks of revolution, while at the same time reassuring critics that the government is able to maintain control.[14] While Beaufre's and Huntingdon's ideas underlie the broad strategy of the South African state, Huntingdon himself has been critical of the fact that 'reform' has lagged far behind repression, and raised expectations which remain unfulfilled.[15]

An important aspect of the 'reform era' of which most people, both within and without the country, are unaware, is that when referring to the South African state we are in fact dealing with a hierarchy of apparatuses which has become increasingly dominated by the military. The situation has been reached where every tier of government has parallel 'shadow military structures' in operation.[16] The basis of this 'shadow government' is the National Security Management System (NSMS) devised in 1979, the highest tier of which is the State Security Council (SSC) which parallels the Cabinet itself.

> This system, comprising mainly military and police officers, is an attempt to set in place structures of military command from municipal level up to and presumably responsible to, the State Security Council. The idea behind the system is the facilitation of a flexible military presence which can respond quickly at the community and grassroots level. Units of this bottom level are called the Mini Joint Management Councils. Their task is to collect intelligence on political activity in the community as well as preventing 'radical elements' who 'exploit' particular grievances. Thus their task is to report on conditions in the communities so that improvements can be made before 'radicals' can mobilise around them . . . in other words, the possibility [now] exists for the military to intervene in, or directly control, government at the local level, as well as at the national level.[17]

It is in this context that we can now talk of South Africa having undergone a 'creeping military coup' — we can further understand that 'reform' can be seen quite unambiguously as a counter-revolutionary strategy.

Bantustans as a Site of Repression and Control

The political function of the bantustans has an important economic component which is to try and demonstrate that the bantustans, especially the 'independent' ones, have viable economies which justify their legal status as 'national' entities. In its attempts to give some credibility to this myth, the South African government has further increased its subsidies and the 'attractions' of the bantustans to encourage the inflow of new forms and sources of capital under the ideology of free enterprise which, virtually unfettered by any legal constraints and regulations, has led to the intensification of oppression and exploitation.[18]

Control and Repression: Influx Control and Citizenship

The containment and control of an increasing proportion[19] of the African population in the bantustans is maintained partly through changes in influx control, though recent legislative changes make it difficult to assess accurately what is happening in this regard. Nevertheless, two points can be made. The first is that other legislation relating to approved housing, employment, squatting, slum clearance, etc. will effectively control the movement of blacks into 'white' urban areas. The second point is that the influx of blacks into these areas has been — and will increasingly be — affected by 'efflux' control from the bantustans, especially from the 'independent states'.

Prior to the abolition of the pass laws in 1986, and the introduction of the 'citizenship restoration' legislation, the predominant form of 'efflux' control in practice was through the granting, or rather the denial, of what are commonly but incorrectly referred to as work-seeker permits. Such permits no longer legally exist. The expression refers to the fact that residents of the 'non-independent' bantustans have had to pay a R1.00 fee to register as work-seekers in terms of the regulations governing tribal labour bureaux at tribal offices.

A person could not legally seek or accept employment, nor have his/her labour contract attested, without having registered at the labour bureau/ tribal office as a work-seeker. With 'independence', bantustans could charge what they liked for this privilege — often the asking price was between R30 and R40 and usually the permits were given only to people who were supportive of the tribal authority or local administration.

The 'bribe' and the exclusion of those who were perceived to be opposed to the tribal and/or bantustan authority, or who had been blacklisted by employers in South Africa, formed extremely effective forms of control over bantustan residents.

For citizens of the 'independent' bantustans the future is bleak. As 'foreigners', they can enter South Africa for fourteen days. If they find work it must be approved by the Minister of Manpower — approval will only be given, however, if there are no 'South Africans' available for the job. The contract must then be registered by an immigration official of the Department of Home Affairs, and then attested in the bantustan of residency. This means that it will become almost impossible for citizens of these bantustans to get legal employment in South Africa.

This is in line with the government's 'reform' initiatives, which are to 'export' as much of South Africa's unemployment as possible to the bantustans, especially the 'independent' units where its maintenance and control are nominally beyond Pretoria's responsibility, but not beyond its power.

Control and Repression: Security Legislation, State Violence and Intimidation

The bantustans, especially the 'independent' ones, have been delegated, or have introduced, 'security' powers which in many respects go even beyond those existing in South Africa itself. The extent of these powers makes the introduction of states of emergency unnecessary in these areas. Where there is a semblance of legal safeguards against the unbridled exercising of these draconian powers, as in the case of Bophuthatswana's 'Bill of Rights', recourse to such safeguards is overridden by security legislation, or simply prevented by intimidation.

The last year or two have been characterised by an increasing use of violence and intimidation by the state. The 'independent' bantustans have their own armies and police forces while the SADF and the SAP have effective free reign in the others. Where the state's forces are fettered by legal or other constraints, as is the case in some of the 'self-governing' bantustans, state-backed vigilantes are used to terrorise known and suspected opponents of the regime.

These forces maintain what can only be described as reigns of terror. They are usually permitted and encouraged to operate outside of, or granted effective immunity from, the law. The close working relationship between the security forces of the bantustans and South Africa, and their mutual disregard for the law, is well evidenced in the case of Bophuthatswana.

In early 1987 an employee of the South African Catholic Bishops Conference (SACBC) was abducted by a snatch squad of uniformed Bophuthatswana police while on a Pretoria street — in broad daylight and while in company. The Boputhatswana police were assisted in their action by the SAP. The victim was bundled into a police car and driven the 40 kilometres across the Bophuthatswana 'border' where he was detained and interrogated for two weeks, before being released without being charged.

The state's support of such actions can be further illustrated in the 1986 case of the Bophuthatswana colonel who ordered the police to open fire on a public gathering in Winterveld, resulting in the death of at least eleven people. He was promoted to Brigadier, even before the token and publicly-rejected commission of enquiry into the shootings had taken its evidence.

Intimidation, physical assaults and torture are now commonplace in the bantustans. In Bophuthatswana, for example, the police have been using terrorist methods for several years now, not just to suppress opposition to the regime, but also to deter people from trying to exercise their limited options in terms of the Constitution's Bill of Rights, notably their right to defend themselves in court.

Such action was demonstrated during the so-called 'squatter' trial of Bosplaas (Winterveld) residents, which lasted from May 1984 to October 1985. In August 1983 the Bophuthatswana government amended its Land Control Act in such a way as to provide it with the supposedly legal means of evicting the estimated 1,500,000 non-Tswana residents in Bophuthatswana from its territory. When the Bophuthatswana authorities realised that some of these people were prepared to defend themselves in court, the authorities adopted a number of tactics.

The prosecution repeatedly postponed the trial over a period of seventeen months while the security forces harassed, assaulted and even tortured both the accused and 'passers-by', with the object, as senior police officers stated, of 'teaching people a lesson about what happens to people who get lawyers and go to court'. People who tried to lay charges against the police were threatened with death. Some dockets were in fact opened, but never investigated. The result of this intimidation was that many innocent people fled the area, while others unwittingly paid admission of guilt fines.

The effect of police intimidation in Bophuthatswana was also well demonstrated in the events leading up to, and following, the 1985 schools boycott. At the end of 1984 pupils began to boycott schools in Pretoria's black townships. The boycott continued into 1985, but did not spread into the adjoining areas of Bophuthatswana until July/August 1985.

During the first half of 1985, but prior to the boycott spreading to Bophuthatswana schools, the Bophuthatswana police persistently harassed and assaulted school children, accusing them of being 'comrades' and supportive of the Pretoria schools boycott. The police action, clearly designed to intimidate the children from emulating their peers in Pretoria, was one of the main issues that actually led to the spread of the boycott to the Garankuwa and Mabopane schools in Bophuthatswana during the last two weeks in July.

The Bophuthatswana police reacted to this boycott by intensifying their assaults on pupils. The pupils responded by forming the Garankuwa Youth Organisation (GYO), the primary object of which was defensive. The parents, because of their own fear of the police, based largely on their experience of police brutality in the Winterveld area, failed to do much.

This brutality swelled the ranks of the GYO, giving it the appearance of a larger and more organised body. It was not until the end of January 1986, when the Metal and Allied Workers' Union (MAWU) and Archbishop Daniel brought legal action and consequent press publicity against the Bophuthatswana authorities, that the beatings and torture eased.

More recently, in 1987, a Pretoria lawyer has been trying to get a court order restraining the Bophuthatswana police from repeatedly detaining an alleged young female 'activist', against whom no charges have been laid, and submitting her to multiple rape before releasing her, only to repeat the detention and torture some weeks later.[20]

CORRUPTION

Corruption operates at three distinct but inter-related levels. The first is the large-scale embezzlement of public funds by the bantustan political leaders and their accomplices. Much of this money, involving millions of rands, finds its way into Swiss and other foreign bank accounts. This is the main reason for the current insolvency of Bophuthatswana. The effect of this level of corruption is to deplete the budgets of various government departments, most notably in the fields of social security, health, and public works, thus further impoverishing the bulk of the population resident in these areas.

The second level of corruption is associated with the necessity of gaining and maintaining the political support of various elements of the petty bourgeoisie, including both the 'traditional' tribal and community authorities, as well as the many levels that make up the hierarchy of the ruling political party.

A third level of corruption — which may be seen as an extension of the second — relates to the maintenance of local administrative control, which is usually in the hands of tribal or community authorities.[21] On the one hand the bantustan governments, which are dependent on the control maintained over the populace by the local tribal/community authorities, turn a blind eye to members of these authorities enriching themselves at the expense of the local population, it being recognised as a perk of the job.

On the other hand, the first two levels of corruption mean that insufficient funds are available for the necessary maintenance of this control in the form of tribal/community authority police, local party machinery, etc. Local authorities are therefore encouraged to contribute to their own funding. This is done by the illegal levying of numerous 'taxes', the institutionalisation of bribes for 'work-seeker' and other permits, the withholding (theft) of social security payments, etc.

Control, at the local level, has therefore become increasingly 'self-funded', thereby increasing resistance and opposition to the bantustan authorities. This resistance in turn requires an intensification of control and repression, usually in the form of larger contingents of police being drafted into the areas. These, in turn, often have to be funded or provisioned, at least in part, from local funds, which requires more levies, bribes and theft. Most bantustan areas are now characterised by the vicious spiral of increased poverty and resentment, requiring more repression on the part of the local authorities, which in turn requires greater extortion to fund it.

INDUSTRIAL AND AGRICULTURAL EXPLOITATION, OR 'DEVELOPMENT'

Part of the positive picture of 'reform' that has been painted by both the South African and bantustan governments, as well as by business interests, is that economic development — industrial and agricultural — has accelerated rapidly in the bantustans during the last few years, albeit from a pathetically low base. State-subsidised industrial decentralisation into these areas, apart from having been a massive drain on state revenue, has created relatively few jobs. Those jobs created are characterised by very low wages, poor health and safety conditions, prohibitions on trade union activity, and a host of illegal practices involving, *inter alia*, false pension and tax deductions, non-payment of overtime, sexual harassment, and the denial of access to doctors of choice.[22]

Over the past decade, while South African labour legislation has been relatively reformist, that in the bantustans has become increasingly repressive. This shift has been seen in the determination with which the four 'independent' bantustans (empowered to enact their own legislation) have moved to effectively prohibit the presence and activities of South African trade unions — a determination which has been predicated largely on mechanisms of control and repression.

Labour Legislation and Repression in Bophuthatswana — a Case Study[23]

Bophuthatswana has gone further than other bantustans in attempting to prohibit the presence and activities of trade unions, by passing its own much publicised Industrial Conciliation Act. This Act, passed in March 1984, was made retrospective to 1 July 1983, and is probably the most developed and comprehensive piece of 'legal' repression introduced by any bantustan in the field of labour matters.[24]

The Act was a direct response to the increasing presence and activity in Bophuthatswana of the emerging unions such as the National Union of Mineworkers (NUM), the Commercial, Catering and Allied Workers' Union of South Africa (CCAWUSA), and the South African Allied Workers Union (SAAWU).[25] The Bophuthatswana government was determined to stop these and any other 'South African' unions from organising in its territory, and to prevent any other forms of organisation through which workers could attempt to challenge the exploitative and oppressive conditions under which they generally worked.

Prior to the passing of the 1984 Act, the industrial conciliation machinery available to Africans in Bophuthatswana was the Black Settlement of Disputes Act of 1953, which allowed for nothing more than an in-house committee system of consultative status. Basic conditions of employment were still mostly covered by the antiquated Shops and Offices Act of 1964, and the Factories, Machinery and Building Works Act of 1941, both of which had been repealed in South Africa and replaced by the more enlightened Basic Conditions of Employment Act of 1983.

One reason why Bophuthatswana did not repeal these two Acts is because the Shops and Offices Act provided exemptions to the hotel industry which have allowed Sun City and Sun International's other hotels in Bophuthatswana to engage in labour practices which would have been outlawed in South Africa itself.[26]

In short, workers had little or no protection from exploitative and unfair labour practices other than the common law. The attitude of the Bophuthatswana authorities and most employers to anything that smacked of trade unionism was evidenced on several occasions when workers, provoked by appalling working conditions, engaged in strike action. On most of these occasions the Bophuthatswana authorities had no hesitation in using their police to break the strike and harass, intimidate and even torture known and suspected ringleaders, sympathisers and trade unionists.

, A good example of this attitude was given by the managing director of Sun City, Mr Peter Wagner, following the dismissal of a number of employees in 1983. Some of the dismissed, none of whom were members of a trade union, formed a committee called 'Delegation 21', which brought their grievances to the hotel management, and to President Mangope himself.

On the instructions of Mangope the six 'ringleaders' were dismissed. When interviewed about these dismissals nearly two years later, Mr Wagner stated that 'we were getting infiltrated by agitators from South African trade union organisers. . . . I can prove that every single member of the "21" was a member, and the government also (can prove), was a member of a South African union — and that is why the six got fired. But the average guy doesn't know that.'[27]

Bophuthatswana's 1984 Industrial Conciliation Act was presented by its Minister of Labour, Rowan Cronje — who had previously held the same post in Ian Smith's minority Rhodesian government. The Bophuthatswana legislation is remarkably similar to that drawn up by Cronje to stifle trade unionist activity in Rhodesia under the illegal Smith regime.

The Act provides for the existence of both registered and unregistered unions, but ensures that they will be strictly controlled.[28] Registration, as Haysom and Whiteside noted, should be viewed in the light of the registrar's wide discretion to register or deregister a union, depending on whether the union is a 'responsible' body 'reasonably capable of taking part in the negotiation of matters of mutual interest between employer and employee'.[29]

There is no definition of 'reasonable' and the fate of trade unions is entirely in the hands of the registrar. Futhermore, registration will be refused where another union exists to represent the same interest ('or part thereof').[30] The definition of an unregistered trade union is so wide that any body representing workers may be legally defined as an unregistered trade union. As Cooper commented, 'Besides bodies purporting to be unions, the definition includes the association of persons claiming "to represent the interests of or act on behalf of workers or any group of workers, whether employed or unemployed". Thus even a workers' committee would be considered to be an unregistered union and fall under the Act's provisions.'[31]

One of the main conditions of the Act designed to prohibit the activities of South African based unions in Boputhatswana is that the 'head office of their controlling bodies must be situated in Bophuthatswana, and that no person may be employed or appointed as an office bearer or official unless "he is ordinarily employed and ordinarily performs his work" in Bophuthatswana'.[32] The implications of this for unions active in Bophuthatswana were that they either moved their head offfices to Bophuthatswana, or withdrew. The desired result was that South African unions were effectively outlawed.

Bophuthatswana has also made it extremely difficult for South African unions to organise commuters living in Bophuthatswana but working in South Africa. Although the Act does not expressly prohibit trade unions from holding union meetings in Bophuthatswana after work, Rowan Cronje initially indicated that he would prohibit such gatherings.[33]

The Bophuthatswana authorities presumably felt that they could ban such meetings in terms of the Internal Security Act — meetings of more than 20 people requiring permission from the local magistrate. As Cooper noted, attempts by the authorities prior to the time of her writing in 1984 to block such meetings had, for the most part, been unsuccessful because they had been challenged under Bophuthatswana's Bill of Rights. In the last two years, however, Bophuthatswana has shown an increasing disregard for both its Bill of Rights and the rule of law, with meetings frequently being prohibited or broken up, often violently, by the authorities.

The Act is a complete contradiction of the existing Constitution and the Bill of Rights. Section 1 of para. 1 of Chapter 1 of the Constitution Bill states that Bophuthatswana 'accepts the principle of democracy, and an economy based on private and commercial ownership and free enterprise.'[34] But its concern for free enterprise extends only as far as employers.

There are other notable features of the Act. One is that it attempts to create a conciliation process that is industry-based, and that will — as far as possible — exclude the emergence of plant-level bargaining, as has developed in South Africa. Minimal industry-wide working conditions are set up through a system of industry boards and voluntary and statutory councils on which workers' interests are scarcely represented. But, as Cooper reported, 'Although this system does not prevent unions from approaching individual employers to negotiate conditions better than the minimums set, this, according to Cronje, is unacceptable and will be opposed.'[35]

The most significant feature of the Act, however, is that it virtually precludes legal strikes. 'Strikes are totally prohibited in "essential services" and during the currency of any agreement or determination which deals with the issue under dispute.' If the industrial board or council or conciliation board fail to settle a dispute, they may refer it to the industrial tribunal. But, 'If the Minister believes that referring a dispute to the tribunal will lead to a change or an addition to an existing agreement, he may decide not to refer it.'[36]

The final obstacle to the near impossible — a legal strike — is that the President may, if he deems it 'necessary or in the public interest', decide that a determination shall become binding — thus effectively prohibiting the holding of a legal strike.

In general terms, industrial relations legislation in Bophuthatswana is not very different from that pertaining in the other bantustans. Bophuthatswana is worth singling out, however, because it is portrayed by the South African government, and some of its friends in Europe — most notably certain members of the Conservative Party in Britain, and members of the ruling Christian Democrats (CDU) and the more extreme right wing Christian Social Union (CSU) in West Germany — as a 'country' free from apartheid and discrimination, whose citizens are protected by a Bill of Rights and which has introduced its own labour legislation, which has made 'provision' for the existence of trade unions.

But, as has been demonstrated, the reality of this legislation is that it effectively prohibits the presence of 'South African' unions, and any form of worker organisation genuinely representative of workers' interests. The legislation also effectively prohibits legal strikes and denies workers any say in the determination of minimal working conditions. There is no minimum wage legislation, nor does the much-heralded industrial tribunal have any jurisdiction in determining unfair labour practices. In addition, Bophuthatswana's implementation of its own Workmen's Compensation and Unemployment Insurance fund has had the effect of denying workers adequate social security.

This legal system, reinforced by Bophuthatswana's security legislation and its complete disregard and contempt for its own Bill of Rights and the due process of law, has provided those capitalists wishing to invest in Bophuthatswana with a cheap, readily available and oppressed labour force.

Such labour conditions, coupled with the massive state-subsidised incentives, have attracted capital investment, not just from within South Africa, but also from countries such as Taiwan, Israel, West Germany and England. Foreign and South African companies are encouraged to invest freely in Bophuthatswana — as such, 'foreign' companies may operate freely, but not 'foreign' trade unions.

'Free enterprise' in Bophuthatswana is nothing more than the freedom to exploit. The number of companies that have been established or relocated in Bophuthatswana from South Africa, simply to get unions 'off their backs', is considerable. This investment in the bantustans has enabled South Africa to present statistics which show these territories as having relatively successful economies, at least in terms of increasing capital investment and consequent job creation.

This investment into the bantustans can, of course, be shown to have relocated or created some jobs in these areas. The reality is that most of these jobs are, in fact, merely relocated from other (unionised) parts of South Africa, and thus serve to undercut unionisation not only in the bantustans, but in South Africa as a whole. The 'morality' of this job creation includes:

- Workers, unprotected by any minimum wage legislation, are paid exceedingly low wages.
- Overtime may be unpaid or, as in the case of Sun City, may be paid with time off in lieu of wages.
- Workers have little or no recourse to any legal protection against unfair labour practices.
- Sexual abuse of workers is rife. In the industrial centres of Babelegi, Garankuwa and Mogase, for example, women — who far outnumber men in the workforce — frequently have to submit to sexual abuse, not merely to get (and keep) jobs, but also to obtain their wages.
- There is little, if any, legislation covering health and safety conditions. Moreover, workers in practice have little or no recourse to workmen's compensation or to legal action for damages resulting from unsafe or unhealthy working conditions, or negligence on the part of the employers. Workers claim that in one British-owned factory in Bophuthatswana which manufactures asbestos products, workers who are discovered going to doctors of their own choice — rather than the 'company doctor' — are dismissed. These claims have been corroborated by doctors in the region.
- Police harassment and intimidation of workers is commonplace. 1986 in Bophuthatswana began with a brutal campaign by the police (under President Mangope's direct authority) against members of South African trade unions living in Bophuthatswana and commuting to work. After being beaten, detained and tortured, these workers were finally released after the legal intervention of the Roman Catholic Archbishop of Pretoria, Archbishop Daniel, officials of the Metal and Allied Workers' Union (MAWU), and their Johannesburg-based lawyers. President Mangope, in his capacity as Minister of Justice and Police, was found to have been in contempt of court.
- Many employers, believing that workers are too intimidated to bring action against them, engage in numerous practices relating to excessive working hours, pension and other deductions, physical assault, and other forms of punishment and victimisation that are unlawful, even within the bantustans.

The situation in the agricultural sector is even worse. In 1977 the Promotion of Economic Development of Bantu Homelands Act of 1968 was amended in such a way as to remove all restrictions on the flow of capital into agricultural projects in the bantustans. The scale of the resultant penetration of capital into the bantustans has been enormous, with tens of millions of rands invested since 1977.

There are several reasons for this transition in bantustan agriculture in the mid- and late 1970s. Firstly, by the beginning of the decade, capital had little or no interest in the preservation of a subsistence base in the bantustans as, by that time, the bantustans no longer functioned primarily to provide South African capitalism with a supply of cheap labour power. Moreover, the overall degradation and underdevelopment of the bantustans' agricultural base was such that — in contrast to the fifties and early sixties — there were few political and landed class interests to oppose this land appropriation.

Secondly, the bantustans offered many attractions to the rapidly modernising and increasingly monopolistic forms of commercial agriculture and agribusiness that were emerging during the seventies. Among these were low or even non-existent ground rents, a highly exploitable, cheap and relatively compliant labour force, captured markets and many forms of subsidy which effectively transferred the risk of production to the government or, more usually, onto the local population of the bantustan regions themselves.

In addition, there has been the added political intervention of the South African government's need to portray the bantustans as having their own viable economies. Related to this, and under the ideology of the 'free enterprise/market' system, the last few years have seen a succession of moves designed to pave the way for takeovers by private/commercial interests of all land in the bantustans capable of commercial cash crop production.

The net result of this attempt to 'privatise' land in the bantustans will be the final displacement of what is still a relatively significant proportion of the African population which still ekes out a modicum of subsistence from the land, and a further escalation of the chronic effects of poverty already pertaining in most bantustan areas.

The so-called 'development' of bantustan agriculture over the last decade has already resulted in tens of thousands of peasants and tribal subsistence producers having been dispossessed of their land, or of access to 'tribal' land. This 'development', destroying as it has many communities' last hold over the means of production, has had an enormous impact on the politicisation and conscientisation of dozens of communities throughout the bantustans, not only because of their proletarianisation, but because few of these agricultural projects have been introduced without threats, intimidation, deception, and resort to the types of exploitative (and usually illegal) labour practices already outlined.

In many parts of the bantustans the introduction of these 'agricultural development' projects, with their consequent land dispossession and labour practices, has been the focal point in the outbreaks of unrest and growing popular resistance against the apartheid state and its appendages in the bantustans. Indeed, the situation was reached in 1986 where many such projects required the armed protection of the SADF. We can legitimately talk not only of a 'creeping military coup', but also of the increasing militarisation of agricultural production.

POVERTY

Both relative and absolute poverty in the bantustans have increased dramatically over the past few years. Reasons for this include the overall decline in average black incomes, both individual and household, since 1976, as a result of reasons already mentioned here, *inter alia*, the state's labour policies and the intensification of the relocation of unemployment to the bantustans; the restriction of access to employment opportunities; the lack, and low remuneration of jobs in the bantustans; extreme forms of labour abuse and exploitation in these areas; the collapse of social security and health services; the dispossession of land and the consequent decline in agricultural subsistence income; and the various forms of corruption and extortion.

While there is a clear awareness of both the causes of bantustan poverty and the reasons for the system of control and repression, this same awareness is acting as a hindrance in the development of political organisation. In the Winterveld area, for example, many workers employed in the Bophuthatswana factories at Garankuwa and Babelegi, and even across the 'border' in Rosslyn and elsewhere, seemingly isolate themselves from the several worker and community organisations emerging in the area for fear that involvement will lead to their dismissal and the consequent exposure of their families, not only to hardship but also to the risk of death.

Although any generalisation is dangerous in that it disregards the specific local circumstances and experiences which are crucial in influencing people's perceptions and actions, there is evidence to suggest that the development of political organisation and overt resistance is most muted in those areas such as Winterveld, where survival is most precarious, and where there has been a relatively long tradition and experience of poverty, social cleavage and repression.

CONCLUSION

Historically, the primary function of the 'native reserves/bantustans' was economic — to reproduce a cheap supply of labour power. Over the last generation the *political* functions of the bantustans, which now act as the primary mechanisms for the control of the majority of the country's African population and as major ideological props to both 'separate development' and 'reform', have become increasingly more significant.

The economies of the bantustans now mainly serve to provide more substantive ideological flesh to their greater political centrality. This is best seen in the case of Bophuthatswana, where the major justification for its 'independence', and its subsequent attempts to gain international recognition, is its alleged economic independence from South Africa.

It is now being argued by supporters of the bantustan system that the insolvency of Bophuthatswana, with a total annual budget of about R1 bn, is immaterial in that South Africa can and will provide the necessary financial support to prevent a total economic collapse. This argument is correct, as is currently evidenced by South Africa's 'bailing out' of Bophuthatswana. But this sort of argument misses the real point, which is that the economic crises of these areas are precipitating and intensifying their own, and the wider, political crises.

There is an active realignment of class forces and interests now taking place which is generating a more unified and widely class-based opposition to the current regime and the fundamental structure of the apartheid state.

It would be premature to predict the ultimate form and direction that these class forces may take. But the new alliances and alignments between disparate and formerly opposed class interests indicate that the political implications of the current widespread resistance in the bantustans for the wider national struggle should be neither ignored nor underestimated.

NOTES

1. H. Wolpe, 'Strategic issues in the struggle for national liberation in South Africa', unpublished paper, 1983.

2. *Ibid.*, p.1.

3. *Ibid.*, p.2.

4. This sort of explanation is not limited to events in the bantustans. Rather, it is used by the state in an attempt to obscure the reality of all acts of resistance.

5. Analysts of the South African political economy must avoid simplistic national generalisations, and pay more attention to 'regional specificity'.

6. Most of this section is derived from the introduction to the forthcoming book by J. Keenan and M. Sarakinsky, *'Reform' and Sanctions Against South Africa: The 'Immorality' Question*, to be published by Zed Press.

7. See J. Keenan, 'Pandora's box: the private accounts of a bantustan local authority' in *South African Review 3* (Johannesburg: Ravan Press, 1986); also 'Bophuthatswana's corruption cover-up' in *Work in Progress*, No.43, 1986.

8. Personal communication, Department of Foreign Affairs, Pretoria, July 1986.

9. For details see J. Keenan, M. Sarakinsky and J. Yawitch, *Violations of Human Rights in Bophuthatswana* (London: CIIR, forthcoming).

10. This section is derived from an unpublished Honours dissertation by I. H. Sarakinsky, 'Historical and contemporary theories of the South African state and strategies for national liberation', University of the Witwatersrand, 1987. I am grateful to Mike and Ivor Sarakinsky for allowing me to draw on their work.

11. P. Frankel, *Pretoria's Praetorians* (Cambridge: Cambridge University Press, 1984).

12. I. H. Sarakinsky, *op. cit.* (emphasis added).

13. From S. Huntingdon, 'Reform and stability in a modernizing multi-ethnic society', *Politikon*, Vol.8, No.2, Pretoria 1981, quoted in I. H. Sarakinsky, *op. cit.*

14. *Ibid.*

15. S. Huntingdon, 'Whatever has gone wrong with reform?', *Die Suid Afrikaan*, No.8, 1986, cited in I. H. Sarakinsky, *op. cit.*

16. I. H. Sarakinsky, *op. cit.*, p.86.

17. *Ibid.*

18. See W. Cobbett, 'Industrial decentralisation and exploitation: The case of Botshabelo' in *South African Labour Bulletin*, Vol.12, No.3, March/April 1987.

19. The absolute numbers of Africans living in the bantustans and the size of the African absolute surplus population, which is located predominantly and increasingly in the bantustans, have both increased in recent years.

20. A notable feature of police torture in Bophuthatswana has been sexual abuse, particularly necrophilia, rape and the infliction of pain to genitalia. The Minister of Police, Law and Order is His Excellency, Chief (Dr) Lucas Mangope, President of the Republic of Bophuthatswana.

21. A good example of how this works can be seen in J. Keenan, 'Pandora's box', *op. cit.*, pp.361-71.

22. See also W. Cobbett, *op. cit.*

23. This section is reproduced from J. Keenan and M. Sarakinsky, *op. cit.*

24. For a detailed analysis of this Act, see Carole Cooper, 'Bophuthatswana's Industrial Conciliation Act', *SALB*, Vol.9, No.5, 1984, pp.36-44.

25. *Ibid.*

26. Under an exemption provided by this Act, hotels are entitled to pay their workers time off in lieu of wages for overtime.

27. Peter Wagner, Managing Director of Sun City, transcript of interview, 11 December 1984.

28. Cooper, *op. cit.*

29. Section 37 of Act No. 8 of 1984.

30. N. Haysom and A. Whiteside, 'A separate development: Labour legislation in the homelands', *Industrial Law Journal*, Vol.5, Part 4, 1984, pp.259-60.

31. Cooper, *op. cit.*

32. *Ibid.*

33. *Ibid.*

34. Republic of Bophuthatswana Constitution Bill, 1977.
35. Cooper, *op. cit.*
36. *Ibid.*

8. From Bantu Education to People's Education

ERIC MOLOBI

INTRODUCTION

The problems of education facing black South Africans have a long history. Our people have never had a say in the planning, structuring and implementation of education. From colonial times, through to 1948 when the present Nationalist government assumed political power, there has always been resistance against oppressive schooling. As early as 1658, slaves at the Cape rejected the form of education offered to them. Later, many African chiefs spurned mission schools by withholding children. From the 1920s until the introduction of Bantu Education in the 1950s, students have always adopted strikes as a form of protest.

In 1953, when the government introduced Bantu Education, teachers immediately reacted against it. Many were dismissed as a result of their actions. In 1954, part of the Resist Apartheid Campaign launched by the African National Congress (ANC) was explicitly directed against Bantu Education. In 1955, the ANC's National Executive decided to launch an indefinite school boycott which would not commence until provision could be made for students who would be out of school. This was the beginning of the African Education Movement which attempted to organise education outside of state control. As a result of its oppositional stance, this Movement faced the wrath of the state through bannings and harassment.

In the 1960s, students in schools and colleges continued to protest vehemently against Bantu Education through strikes and demonstrations.

SOWETO 1976

In the 1970s, resistance to apartheid and Bantu Education reached a new climax culminating in the uprising of 1976. A number of factors blended together to create a climate of revolt. These included all the elements of an inferior education system, from the overcrowding of schools resulting in a teacher/student ratio of 100:1, to underqualified teachers using hopelessly inadequate and old facilities. The massive protests in Soweto in 1976 also took place against the backdrop of a depressed economy. The success of the liberation struggles in Mozambique and Angola were still new. The final cutting link in the chain of events that led to the 1976 revolt was the government's introduction of Afrikaans as a medium of instruction.

More than a thousand people were killed. On that fateful day of 16 June,

155

20,000 students marched peacefully into volleys of deadly police bullets. Even 14-year-olds lost their lives. In 1977, more than 14 organisations were banned, amongst them many student organisations. To the consternation of black parents and educationalists, the government-appointed Cillie Commission of Enquiry (1980) reported that Bantu Education was not the cause of the uprisings, but only a minor contributor to the revolt.[1] Nonetheless, the state was forced to withdraw Afrikaans as a medium of instruction.

The students demanded and formed Student Representative Councils (SRCs) and began to organise themselves again — and in the process established the link between their fate and that of workers. For students clearly saw Bantu Education as a system training them to become slaves. The Congress of South African Students (COSAS) became one of the biggest and most popular student organisations. Early in 1984, COSAS with the help of parents, began to confront the Department of Education (DET). They put forward a number of demands including:

- the recognition of SRCs;
- the recognition of popularly-drafted student constitutions;
- the cessation of corporal punishment;
- the scrapping of Bantu Education.

When the UDF was formed in 1983, COSAS became a founding member, thus helping to initiate one of the most important alliances of student and community organisations. When, in 1985, the government decided to ban COSAS, this was seen as a testimony to the power of student organisations and struggles.

THE PRESENT EDUCATIONAL CRISIS

In the midst of continuing rent boycotts in early 1985 the Vaal complex exploded into revolt.[2] Sustained resistance to governmental attempts to control the townships has continued ever since. The schooling situation was immediately affected, in the townships of Soweto, Atteridgeville, Mamelodi and beyond. This signalled a new phase in the education crisis, a phase without any precedent. The Soweto Parents Crisis Committee (SPCC) was formed in that year. Its constituent parts came to encompass, for the first time, students, ordinary parents, teachers and civic organisations. The demands of students were articulated and the SPCC attempted to hold talks with the State Education Department. The students' demands were forthright and clear:

- the release of detained students;
- the recognition of SRCs;
- the reconstruction of damaged schools;
- the provision of proper school facilities;
- the provision of free textbooks;
- the unbanning of COSAS;
- the reinstatement of dismissed teachers;
- the total scrapping of Bantu Education.

No fruitful results arose from putting forward the students' demands. Instead, the government responded by unleashing the forces of repression. In

July 1985 the regime declared a State of Emergency. New draconian measures were applied in the townships, affecting the running of the present school system. Heavily armed South African Defence Force (SADF) personnel stood at school entrances. Identity documents were issued to all students, down to the smallest child. Pupils without their new 'passes' were barred from leaving school premises outside prescribed hours. The brief of the military was simple: to detain any school child who was found outside school premises or who failed to produce a pass on entering school. There were even cases of armed soldiers who refused to leave classrooms, while teachers were manhandled by soldiers in front of their own students. During the period 1986-7, a number of teachers were expelled for 'being political'. Some teachers were also transferred, without any consultation and on short notice, to distant rural areas.

The schooling situation under these conditions has generally become chaotic. Since 1984, there have been numerous examples of pupils who have remained in one class without any hope of ever writing exams or passing to other classes. In the Cape, there are whole townships and areas where there is not even one school in operation. In response to schools being closed by the authorities, students have demanded that they be re-opened. Is it surprising that when students in this situation are repulsed by the SADF, they have angrily destroyed entire school buildings across an entire township, as in Duncan Village?

In the midst of this escalating crisis, the Department of Education and Training has refused to heed calls from the communities, teachers, parents, and students to talk to the National Educational Crisis Committee (NECC). Many parents, students and teachers want NECC to meet the DET. Within the NECC, our position has been crystal clear: namely that there are a few points that must be met before talks can take place. These are:

- a guarantee that we shall not be detained at any talks;
- a guarantee that our Executive members and student/teacher leaders will be released; and most importantly
- a guarantee that we shall be able to consult with the students, parents and teachers prior to and after any talks.

The DET has ignored these calls to talk and failed to discuss our necessary preconditions. In the meantime, 73 schools in various areas of the country have been closed indefinitely. The NECC, which is one of the most representative organisations articulating the aspirations of the students inside the country, has itself been subject to repression. Some of our Executive members are currently [1986] in detention and there is presently a vicious campaign of vilification and misinformation being waged against us. Late in 1986, one of the NECC's leading executive members, Mrs Joyce Mabhudafasi, was picked up and detained. Ironically, she had gone to one part of the country to find out whether the NECC could continue to hold talks with the DET even if not all of its demands were met.

This whole process has politicised and radicalised students and communities. The DET is caught up in a situation where it loses control of schools and is then forced to close them. Calls that these schools should be handed over to the communities have fallen on deaf ears. A situation of massive stalemate has emerged, which can only result in a traumatic experience for millions of our school children. The South African state machinery, caught up in a crisis exacerbated by an economy in a long-standing recession, has no other alternative but to press hard on everybody. Our analysis of the situation is that the State of Emergency is something we are going to live with for years to come, whether it is openly declared or not. This implies that the crisis in education, which cannot be divorced from the overall crisis of the apartheid regime, will continue for a long time as well.

We appreciate the concern and willingness of concerned persons outside South Africa to listen to an account of what actually happens inside South Africa. This confirms our belief that the thread that joins person to person, the thread that runs between communities and nations, is a reality that can and needs to be nurtured by those who care for human life and dignity.

SCHOOL AND UNIVERSITY

The NECC believes that universities cannot remain isolated from the communities they serve. In a situation where black schooling is in a shambles, our position is that universities — or at least progressive academics within them — should work with the communities beyond university walls. This means not working *for* but working *with* communities. Presently, these communities want Bantu Education scrapped and replaced with a non-racial democratic People's Education. The NECC, together with other trade union federations like COSATU, teachers' associations like the National Education Union of South Africa (NEUSA), the African Teachers' Association, the Western Cape Teachers' Union (WECTU), and others, are working together in formulating curricula for a new South Africa, especially on subjects such as History and English. Research units have been set up with certain faculties of sympathetic universities, and proper checks and participation have been assured to safeguard community interests. In this way, universities can begin to take a cue from affected communities without adopting the usual condescending attitudes that cloud universities' roles with the aura of being 'scientific'.

DEVELOPMENT OF ALTERNATIVE PROGRAMMES

Let me mention briefly that the education crisis in South Africa has presented a situation of unprecedented opportunism. Never in the history of our country has so much money been publicly pledged to help in the education crisis. There is simply a plethora of funders and new programmes. Some of these are fly-by-night operations, set up by con-men who rip off our people with exorbitant fees while pocketing money from overseas donors. The fashionable concept of 'alternative education' has become a misnomer, acting as a blank cheque to wealth and status. Even big business uses it in its own programmes, some of which are highly dubious in intent and operation.

We in the NECC counterpose to such notions the concept of 'People's Education'. Our position is that since education as we have known it has been used as a tool of oppression, People's Education will be an education that must help us to achieve people's power. People's Education is therefore decidedly political and partisan with regard to oppression and exploitation.

For us People's Education for people's power entails, in a nutshell, the following:

- the democratisation of education, involving a cross-section of the community in decisions on the content and quality of education;
- the negation of apartheid in education by making education relevant to the democratic struggles of the people;
- the achievement of a high level of education for everyone;
- the development of a critical mind that becomes aware of the world;
- the bridging of the gap that exists between theoretical knowledge and practical life; and
- the closing of the chasm between natural science and the humanities, between mental and manual labour, with emphasis on worker education and the importance of production.

In this regard, People's Education is fundamentally different from the vogue 'alternative education' programmes that shun the reality of the conflict in South Africa, and in some cases have a hidden agenda of the depoliticisation of education and the creation of an apolitical black middle class. In reality of course these hidden agendas and intentions have a blatant political purpose: the defence of the present situation. People's Education, by contrast, becomes an integral part of the struggle for a non-racial, democratic South Africa.

THE ROLE OF EXTERNAL BODIES

We look at various 'aid' packages that are aimed at black education in South Africa in the light of our concept of People's Education. How can external bodies help in promoting our objectives?[3] Here I wish to provide five general proposals that, no doubt, will need further discussion and amplification, but will provide general indications of our orientation to external help.

First, it is imperative for any organisation or individual intending to act in solidarity with our struggle to know that we in South Africa, due to conditions at the ground level, cannot just accept aid without knowing what the objectives of the giver are. What is the agenda of the funder? This must be known.

Second, the situation in South Africa is changing very rapidly. We are fast getting out of a situation where the old approach of funders setting up a Board consisting only of 'highly qualified' individuals and so-called 'public figures' is acceptable. The administration of projects and the setting of criteria for selecting students cannot be left in the hands of such individuals. Such a situation leads to a lack of accountability to the democratic processes the educational provision is meant to foster. One must ask: to whom is money being given? Are these persons or organisations accountable to democratic structures? Are the persons whose names are prominent on letterheads simply lending their blessing to the organisation, or are they actively engaged in ensuring its responsiveness and relevance to community needs? Who, for example, decides on the criteria for the distribution of funds? And do the selected criteria match the conditions of the day? Let me give one example of present problems in these areas. Some of the most highly publicised scholarship programmes have turned down applicants because they are said to be 'political'. In a situation which is already highly politicised, what does it mean to exclude those who have committed themselves to the people's struggle?

All of this flies in the face of the fact that many of these 'highly politicised' students, especially at the university level, are recognised to be among the hardest working and most needy students. We now know, for example, that some of the donor countries have selected people who are civil servants in the Bantustans. If the criterion of 'non-political' is used, are the students wrong if and when they question the political intentions of the aid, and also the ideological positions of those actually administering the programme? Here lies the crux of the matter.[4] The other criterion one often encounters is that of giving scholarships to so-called bright students at the high school level. How can one unilaterally apply such a criterion in a situation where the entire schooling process is abnormal and gripped by crisis? Do programmes that ignore such local conditions have any place in present-day South Africa?

Third, it is normal practice that outside aid comes with built-in intentions. For example, does the idea of airlifting thousands of students from South Africa and sending them to various countries fit in well with the overall needs and desires of the communities from which these students come, the organisations and the overall democratic struggle being waged in that country? How do those who have completed their overseas studies fit in once again with their home communities? Do they return back home and contribute, or have they been trained to be absorbed by big foreign multinationals and South African monopolies? The question at issue here is that some of these scholarship programmes apply elitist criteria which really are a reflection of the elitist education systems they have known and represent. I must be understood clearly here: I don't say we should scrap all these programmes. But I am saying that we must scrutinise what their intentions are, how they are applied, and what their end results are.

Fourth, why are scholarship programmes only available for students to study in the donor country and within South Africa? Why cannot a recipient choose his or her country as well as the university they will attend? Presently students are often shuttled off to unknown destinations, a process which leaves too much room for the intrusion of ill-informed if not dubious decisions by donors. There surely is no practice of democratic principles here.

Fifth, the content of other projects funded inside South Africa raises similar questions. What criteria apply in the project that is funded? Does the idea of pursuing overall political change in the country become an in-built principle? Do projects aspire to establish a fundamental change in the racist and oppressive educational system that prevails? Or do proposed programmes intend only to create islands of 'stable education' in the midst of everyday crisis, with the implicit design that today's elitist educational practices are only extended? It must be said that monumental schemes set up inside the country, ostensibly to engender elitist students, have crumbled. A case at issue here is Pace College in Soweto.[5]

CONSULTATION AND ACADEMIC FREEDOM

Within the broader democratic movement inside South Africa there exists what we we now regard as a firm principle, and that is consultation. Perpetual consultation of a formal and informal nature takes place at all times between organisations, and where possible, the communities. This occurs despite the fact that the State of Emergency was partly designed to bring this virtually sacred principle to an end. We would like to see this principle extended to those external agencies offering help and contributions of various types. I know for certain that a number of scholarship offers and projects inside the country have been planned as 'full packages' and then implementation starts with a range of variations. What is clear is that such schemes that ignore consultation are bound to run into serious problems in the near future. Just now there are many of such 'full packages' in areas like:

- the training of teachers;
- the training of pre-school tutors;
- the setting up of private schools involving massive amounts of money;
- vocational training, etc.;
- academic programmes of all stripes and hues.

The areas mentioned above are all areas where need does indeed exist. What is important to black South Africans involved in educational matters is how this need should be met.

I need to mention one important aspect which has once again become prominent in education, namely academic freedom, including the exchange of academics to and from South African universities. This matter is presently under intensive discussion within the broad democratic movement. But it needs to be noted here that we certainly shall not view this matter in isolation from the political struggles of our people. We cannot look at it in isolation from the international campaign of isolating South Africa culturally. The question of academic freedom therefore ceases to be the privileged domain of academics and universities alone. It already operates within a context of detentions of lecturers, teachers, students and parents. It assumes a connection with bannings of student leaders and organisations, the closing down of schools, the lack of facilities, inadequately trained teachers, the teaching of an inferior Bantu Education system, and the lack of democratic structures within the very universities where one finds the outcry for so-called 'academic freedom'. Should we fail to see this, we shall be strengthening a misconception of academic freedom. The idea that speaks of academic freedom as unrelated to broader social freedoms is thus questionable. Any type of a vague, nebulous and illusory freedom, which can only be enjoyed by academics and institutions of higher learning, and serves only to satisfy individuals who in many instances simply enjoy the public glamour of criticising apartheid from afar, is questionable. No doubt, the need for international exchange and sharing of science and knowledge is important. But it would be unacceptable to disconnect that need from the basic needs of freedom and human dignity. Academic freedom can therefore never take place in a vacuum.

In relation to conferences on South Africa that are organised abroad, is the leadership of our people in the liberation movement consulted? Who are these academics invited from South Africa? Are they part of the broad democratic movement engaging the enemy inside South Africa? What about those invited from the country where the conference is being organised? What has been *their* role and what are their views *vis-à-vis* our national democratic struggle and the struggles spearheaded by the liberation movement? How will these conferences affect the international campaign to isolate South Africa? These are relevant facts that basically affect academic freedom.

CONCLUSION

In conclusion, I would like to emphasise the fact that we have entered a new phase of popular struggle and counter-measures of heavy repression in South Africa. Many complex forces are at play. Progressive and democratic organisations are going through very difficult times. There are attempts to bolster reactionary structures, to counter the successes of organisations like the UDF, COSATU and the NECC. Some of the aid from other countries — particularly from the labour movement and from educationalists — has been ostensibly aimed at weakening apartheid organisations and structures. This is why it has become important for the South African recipients of such aid to find out its relationship to the foreign policy of the donor country. There are questions like: do we accept funds from the very same hand that feeds the forces of repression, from Latin America and Asia to other parts of Africa? Or do we regard such a source as 'dirty money'? In the light of similar considerations, representative organisations in South Africa feel bound to scrutinise the level of democratic control over foreign aid when it approaches our shores. Again, do we accept aid from sources that are simultaneously helping reactionary forces and projects within our country, thus undermining the democratic movement even as we attempt to consolidate the successes of our people? This is what makes the principles of consultation and accountability to democratic forces vital to the cause of black education.

NOTES

1. Commission chaired by Justice Cillie, *Report of the Commission of Enquiry into the Riots at Soweto and Elsewhere* (Pretoria: Government Printer, RP 55/1980).
2. See the chapter by Seekings in this volume for a description of these events.
3. It should be made clear here that the author's original remarks were directed at a meeting in London in September 1986 of a charitable body, the World University Service. Though this version of his talk has been adapted for our purposes, some of the proposals that follow should be read in the light of the author's original audience [WC & RC].
4. This, and other comments, are of relevance to those about to administer a new scheme of studentships for South Africans announced by the Thatcher government in 1986. When withdrawing from UNESCO, the British government promised that part of the £6 million subscription would be used to fund scholarships for foreign students. The South African scheme, to cost £1 million a year, will commence in October 1987. The government apparently believes that the political stability of post-independence Zimbabwe was partly achieved through the education of large numbers of Zimbabweans in British institutions. The South African scheme, it seems, is a planned rerun [WC & RC].
5. Pace College was an American scheme set up to find potential business leaders in the black community. Its educational philosophy, which was naïvely transposed from the US, rested on highly individualistic and capitalistic principles. The College was deeply resented by Soweto residents, both adults and school children, and was forced to close [WC & RC].

9. State Control, Student Politics and the Crisis in Black Universities

NKOSINATHI GWALA

INTRODUCTION

The crisis in South African black schools over the past decade has generally overshadowed the struggles taking place in black universities. My aim in this chapter will therefore be to discuss the nature of the black universities, thereby locating the struggles taking place there. It is my contention that these struggles cannot be properly understood unless situated within the internal structures and dynamics of these institutions.

Four main factors or issues necessitate a more thorough analysis of black universities in South Africa. The first is the continuing and deepening crisis in black education of which black universities are also a part. The second is the intensification of the international academic boycott and isolation of South African universities. The latter issue is raised particularly by Cobbett,[1] mainly posing the question of how white, particularly liberal universities should relate to black universities within the context of the academic boycott. Third, the important question of the transformation of university education in South Africa has been mainly debated, though inadequately, amongst the radical academics from the liberal universities, thereby ignoring and peripheralising the black universities. Fourth, there has been a tendency among academics from liberal white campuses to dismiss these institutions as 'bush colleges' and therefore institutions of apartheid. This attitude is dangerous particularly because, in spite of being creations of separate development, these universities account for a significant number of black university students[2] and are unlikely to disappear, even in a post-apartheid society.

This chapter opens with the historical evolution of black universities, followed by a close examination of their internal structures and functioning. These two factors are very important in understanding the shape taken by the struggles in these institutions. The next sections deal with the material conditions obtaining in South Africa in the 1970s and the 1980s as they affected the struggles within the black universities, and particularly the relationship between the class interests of the bantustan petty bourgeoisie and the homeland universities. The chapter is concluded by some remarks on the struggle for transforming university education in the country and the relationship between white universities and black universities.

HISTORICAL EVOLUTION OF BLACK UNIVERSITIES

Although black university education in South Africa dates back to 1916, with

163

the establishment of the South African Native College (later Fort Hare) at Alice in the Cape Province, the first black universities were established in 1960 and 1961.[3] The passing of the Extension of University Education Act effectively changed the status of Fort Hare, previously affiliated to Rhodes University, to being a tribal college for Xhosa students.[4] The reasons for the establishment of these institutions cannot be properly understood outside the context of the political restructuring taking place in the 1950s and 1960s in South Africa. Analysing the emergence of the apartheid state, although it will be brief here, is also vital in understanding the establishment of ethnic colleges for blacks. Although the coming into power of the Nationalist Party in 1948 is rightly associated with the beginning of apartheid in South Africa, this tends to give the impression that it was the election of the party *per se* which brought about apartheid. This view also obscures the role played by the changing nature of capital accumulation and the historical oppression of blacks in creating the necessary conditions for the rise of an apartheid state. It is to these issues that I will now turn to in order to situate apartheid, and consequently the establishment of ethnic university colleges.

The Second World War marked the beginnings of a long economic boom throughout the Western capitalist countries, which was particularly characterised by the consolidation of monopoly capitalism, and renewed drives to capture new markets beyond the national geographic borders of the advanced capitalist countries. South Africa, having historically evolved into a source of cheap labour power as a result of the oppression of blacks, became a major beneficiary of foreign investment. This new investment, coupled with the massive growth of imperially backed local mining industry prior to the War led to a rapid diversification of economic activity into manufacturing and consequently the 'reproduction within the South African industrial sector of the monopoly capitalist relations of production of the imperialist metropolises'.[5]

However, the opportunity provided by the growth of the manufacturing sector was primarily threatened by a growing and politicised urban African working class, and the mass mobilisation of the African population under the leadership of the ANC. The state, as the ultimate guarantor of the necessary conditions for capital accumulation, played a leading role in mediating the intensified class struggle in the 1950s. The determination of the state to remove the economic and political threat of the African working class provoked a series of measures in the 1950s culminating in the harassment and banning of African unionists and political organisations in the early 1960s. These measures were an attempt to find a permanent solution to the 'problem' of African resistance, and were to evolve into the bantustan system. The state's response to this potentially serious threat was to try to develop a system of social control which permanently located the urban proletariat in the rural areas in terms of family, cultural and political ties, while continuing to reproduce its economic dependence in urban wage labour. The apartheid system — with its policy of restructuring the original reserves into self-governing bantustans — provided the institutional framework through which such a policy could not only be implemented, but also rationalised.[6] These apartheid measures and the 'ethnicisation' of the African population were originally formulated in the Bantu Authorities Act of 1951 and refined through the Promotion of Bantu Self-Government Act of 1959. In terms of the latter Act eight African ethnic groups were recognised as 'national units', which were to be given self-government and ultimately 'independence'. The concretisation of these measures led to the complete political and social restructuring of South African society along racial and ethnic lines. Africans in particular were reclassified as temporary sojourners in the cities as long as they still provided labour, and were to exercise their political and economic rights within the bantustans, located in remote and rural areas of South Africa.

It was therefore within this context that separate black universities were established in 1960. This further explains the nature of staff composition and bureaucratic and ideological controls existing in these institutions up to this day. These universities were established, first, to legitimate and concretise the notion of separate racial and ethnic groups in South Africa. Second, at a political and ideological level, they were established not only to divide the oppressed but also to 'supplement the racist pedagogy that instills a sense of a God-given mission of domination to the Afrikaner youth with a more domesticating tribal-oriented pedagogy for the oppressed groups'.[7]

Although these institutions were to be located in the bantustans themselves, and apparently under the control of each ethnic group as politically constituted under a client petty bourgeoisie, the state was not prepared to let up on the total control over these institutions. As the Minister of Bantu Education said in 1957, 'Control of [black universities] by the government is needed as it was necessary to prevent undesirable ideological developments — such as had disturbed the non-white institutions not directly under the charge of the government'.[8] But perhaps the most revealing statement in understanding the subsequent internal politics of black universities was the one made by the same minister in supporting the transfer of Fort Hare from Rhodes to the Department of Bantu Education:

> Where one has to deal with under-developed peoples, where the state has planned a process of development for those peoples, and where a university can play a decisive role in the process and directions of that development, it must surely be clear to everyone that the State alone is competent to exercise the powers of guardianship in this field.[9]

Black university education, prior to its ethnicisation in 1959, was provided mainly by Fort Hare and, to a lesser extent, by the English-speaking universities i.e. Wits., Natal and Cape Town. The impact of the reorganisation of black university education had a tremendous impact on the racial composition of university students, and also created extensive constraints on the movement of black students. For instance, at Fort Hare in 1959 there were 100 'Indian' students and 70 'coloured' students, but by 1968 there were only African, and predominantly Xhosa-speaking students. The same 'racial purification' was taking place at the English-speaking universities, now barred from registering black students unless with ministerial approval. Although all black[10] students were severely affected by the new restructuring, African students were the hardest hit.[11] There was subsequently a significant drop of black student registrations at white universities between 1959 and 1967 as shown by the following table:

Black Students Registered in White Universities in Selected Years

Year	African	Coloured	Indian	Total
1956	227	270	470	967
1958	298	441	658	1,397
1959	300	541	815	1,656
1961	237	396	875	1,506
1967	137	303	731	1,171

Source: IRR *Survey of Race Relations*, 1957-1967.

It is also worth noting that before the retribalisation of university education, the number of black students — though a small fraction of the total number of students registered at white universities — was growing steadily. However, by the end of the 1960s the racial restructuring of universities was almost complete, and the exceptions were mainly the few ministerially-approved registrations of black students at white universities. The establishment of 'bush' colleges within the context of separate development under the state's 'competent guardianship' led to the emergence of peculiar types of institutions with their own unique internal dynamics, to which I now turn.

CLASSIFICATION OF BLACK UNIVERSITIES

There are three main types within the total of 19 universities in South Africa — 4 English-medium universities; 6 Afrikaans-medium universities; and 8 black universities. These institutions are not only different in terms of race and medium of instruction, but have quite distinct political and ideological outlooks. For instance, the English-speaking universities have a liberal political and ideological outlook, characterised by a contradictory location between the contending political forces on the one hand, and their pronounced ideals of academic freedom on the other. From within the contradictions of these institutions, there has emerged a radical scholarship that has significantly altered the nature of intellectual and political debates within the academic arena. The Afrikaans universities are distinctly conservative and openly racist and at the same time act as production sites of loyal servants of apartheid. The black universities are much more complex because they embrace within themselves reactionary administrations as well as highly-politicised and progressive student bodies. Black universities can be classified into three types: (a) 'autonomous'; (b) homeland; and (c) urban universities.

'Autonomous' Universities

The universities in the first category are those of Zululand (Ngoye) and the North (Turfloop). These universities were established in 1960, and have now been granted 'autonomy'. The inverted commas around 'autonomous' are used to capture the ambiguous position of these universities. This ambiguity lies in the fact that although they were originally established to cater for certain African ethnic groups — Ngoye for Zulus and Swazis, and Turfloop for Shanganes, Vendas, Tswanas, Pedis and Sothos — they are currently not formally incorporated into any of the existing bantustans. However, their 'autonomy' is not as it looks on paper, since they are located right in the heartland of existing bantustans, a location which seriously undermines their autonomy. In a nutshell, these universities are autonomous in so far as they have been given administrative powers, but seriously undermined by the type of control exercised by the *broederbond*-type academics and the external influence of the bantustan petty bourgeoisie controlling the territories within which they are located.

Homeland Universities

These universities are those of the 'independent' bantustans — the Universities of Transkei (UNITRA), Fort Hare, Venda and Bophuthatswana (UNIBO). With the exception of Fort Hare, this is a new breed of 'bush' colleges. Fort Hare is the oldest of all black universities and has been the latest to be incorporated under an independent bantustan. It was formally one of the autonomous universities until the end of 1986, when it was transferred to the Ciskei. The case of Fort Hare is a vivid example of the destruction caused by apartheid of university education in South Africa. It has moved from being a highly respected black campus to a 'bush college' in 1959, and now to the worst version of this species, i.e. a bantustan university. Subsequently, even its limited autonomy has been eroded and it has become an institution under the control of the capricious and repressive Sebe administration.[12] The other three homeland universities were originally satellite campuses or branches of the autonomous black universities.[13] The homeland universities are mainly characterised by their close control by the bantustan bureaucracies. Although when all of them were established they subscribed to non-racialism and academic freedom, subsequent developments have proved otherwise, as will be evident later.

Urban Universities

There are three urban universities for blacks: the Universities of Durban-Westville (UDW) for 'Indians'; Western Cape (UWC) for 'coloureds'; and Vista for urban Africans. Although it is rather anomalous to classify the latter with the first two institutions, since it is a mere urban version of the African 'bush colleges', it shares certain characteristics with them. Firstly, all of them are urban versions of 'bush' ethnic colleges. Secondly, they are meant for groups which are regarded as part of 'white South Africa', although in the case of urban Africans the right to permanent urban residence was only granted to some in the late 1970s. Nevertheless, these common characteristics should not conceal the fundamental differences between these institutions, each of which is dealt with separately below.

UWC was established in 1960 together with the other African universities to cater for the coloured population, and was placed under the control of the Department of Coloured Education. It has, however, subsequently become autonomous. Of all the black universities UWC has changed its character most significantly — so much so it is being dubbed in some circles South Africa's university of the future.[14] The appointment of a progressive Principal, coupled with the employment of critical scholars and a bigger intake of African students, has fundamentally changed the bush character of the university. Critics have further observed some interesting developments at UWC over the past three years. Positive relationships are developing between lecturers and students, conservative academics are 'on the retreat', and strong links are developing between the university and the wider community, particularly the oppressed masses.

UDW was established in 1961 for Indians as part of the ethnicisation of university education under apartheid. Although UDW still displays many of the characteristics of the other black universities in terms of political and bureaucratic control, there are interesting developments taking place there. The past two years have seen an intense three-way struggle between the state, the collaborative petty bourgeoisie within the Tricameral Parliament and (though in the background) progressive organisations and academics. This struggle has been over the key appointments within the university, such that staffing has become a hotly contested issue. The outcome of these battles may have a significant impact on the future of this institution. One cannot rule out, of course, the possibility of the Tricameral petty bourgeoisie striking a compromise with the state, thereby having more say over the affairs of the university. At the same time, a route similar to UWC cannot be ruled out. In spite of UDW being an autonomous institution, each contesting party would like to see administrators sympathetic to its own interests taking positions of power there.

Vista university was established to cater for urban Africans, and, according to the minister of [black] education, also to provide training for the anticipated rapid growth in the number of African matriculants and the country's need for trained manpower.[15] The establishment of Vista was a measure of the extent to which the state was still determined to pursue segregated education in spite of its declared 'reform' intentions. For instance, Vista was not allowed to register students other than Africans without written permission from the Minister. It also displayed many of the characteristics of the other black universities, as captured, for example, in the rejection by Wits. and other liberal campuses of the state invitation to sit on the Vista Council. As the Wits. Council spokesman wrote:

> This attitude was not adopted because the university did not favour the provision of additional facilities for blacks, but because existing universities were not granted permission to contribute towards the need which exists, and because Vista University will not have the same degree of autonomy and academic freedom of existing universities in urban areas. ... [Additionally] the University Council [of Wits.] does not wish to be officially associated with the establishment of a new segregated university of this kind.[16]

This position, though perhaps understandable, left Vista under the tight control of the state and academics from Afrikaans universities.

In spite of the foregoing differences amongst the black universities, not a single one of them has escaped ongoing disturbances since the emergence of radicalised student bodies in the late 1960s. They also have a lot in common in terms of their internal structures and functioning, which has partly earned them the sobriquet 'bush colleges'.

INTERNAL STRUCTURES AND POLITICS

The uniqueness of black universities lies primarily in their internal functioning and the nature of control exercised by the administrators in these institutions. Since the major defining characteristic of black universities is the intensity of control over both the educational process and student activity, I will specifically discuss two distinct aspects of control prevalent in these institutions. These are bureaucratic control and control over intellectual production.

Bureaucratic Control

This type of control refers to the authoritarian rule of the office bearers in the day-to-day administration of these institutions. Three loci of power are important in the black universities: the office of the Rector, the University Council and the Senate. The office of the Rector, or Principal, is much more powerful compared to its counterpart on the liberal campuses. The powers concentrated in this office become clearer when it comes to student discipline and control. For instance, the student disciplinary code at UNITRA provides, *inter alia*, that the Principal and the Vice-Principal and one or more members of Council and/or one parents' representative shall constitute the Disciplinary Committee. But, it continues: 'The Principal may, at his discretion, delegate his powers under these rules. . . . If the Principal receives information which indicates misconduct by a student, the Principal shall act as a disciplinary committee.'[17] This provision effectively leaves student discipline in the hands of the Principal, a powerful tool that has been used by the Rectors to expel politically active students in almost the same way in all black universities.

In spite of the powers of the Rectors, the highest decision-making body is the Council. A closer examination of the University Councils shows that they are dominated by Afrikaner academics and state-appointed members. For example, up until 1984 the 24-member Council of the University of Zululand consisted of 8 members appointed by the State President, and 2 each appointed by the KaNgwane and KwaZulu bantustans.

The Senate, which is the body responsible for the day-to-day academic administration of the universities, is an even more interesting body, showing where power really lies in these institutions. The Senate is constituted, by and large, by heads of departments and professors of the university. An analysis of some of the black universities shows that they are effectively controlled by graduates of the repressive and racist Afrikaans universities. The following table shows the places where the highest qualifications of heads of departments at selected campuses were obtained.

Qualifications of Heads of Departments, by Place of Qualification (%)					
University	UNISA	Afrikaans	English	Black	Other
Turfloop [1984]	16.6	53	3.03	16.6	10.6
Medunsa [1982]	—	70	20	—	10
Ngoye [1986]	19.5	47.8	4.3	4.3	21.7
UDW [1985]	8.6	29.3	24.1	5.1	32.7

Source: University Calendars for the years bracketed.

The strong predominance of Afrikaans-university trained academics is evident. Furthermore, 80 per cent of Afrikaans university graduates had never studied within any other environment. Other points are worth noting. The University of South Africa (UNISA), the correspondence university, is also Afrikaner-controlled in terms of educational content and reproduction of the dominant ideology through its famous 'study guides'. The black universities, as already shown above, are as good as extensions of Afrikaans universities in respect of their staff and administration. Therefore one can safely regard graduates of UNISA, Afrikaans and black universities as having gone through the same type of education and ideological training. The Afrikaans universities have been described as catering mainly for the production of the governing bureaucratic elite, and adhering to the conservative traditions of white racial domination, Calvinism, unrigorous neo-positivism and rote-learning, as opposed to critical debate.[18] The table also shows a strikingly low percentage of graduates from English-speaking universities teaching at black campuses. The narrow background of academics in black universities is further revealed by the training of heads of departments, both black and white. For instance at Turfloop, out of 13 African heads of departments in 1984, 9 were graduates of the same university, 3 graduates of UNISA and one unknown. At the University of Zululand in 1986, out of a total of 10 African heads of departments 6 were UNISA, 2 from the same black university, 1 overseas and 1 from the University of Cape Town. This pattern has serious implications for the calls that have been made to Africanise black universities — the best known being that of the Black Academic Staff Association at Turfloop in the mid-1970s. In present circumstances, however, Africanisation will mainly promote products of the very same style of learning and thinking.

The continued control of black universities is not untypical of similar processes in other spheres of apartheid. Although the state has given certain institutions 'serving' blacks (e.g. bantustans, community councils) over to the control of blacks, real control still resides with Pretoria. This has been most evident in the case of bantustan bureaucracies, where there are still a number of seconded officials occupying key administrative positions. While many of these officials are appointed under the guise of guiding these institutions through their initial stages of development, they actually end up being permanently controlled by such officials. For example, many bantustan government departments still have senior officials originally placed by Pretoria, and the various bantustan 'development' corporations are still under the control and direction of Afrikaner managers. This was closely related to the state's original fear that giving self-government to blacks could prove to be a gamble, particularly in the context of increasing black militancy in the 1950s under the leadership of the ANC. This concern was echoed time and again by successive government Ministers warning the collaborative petty bourgeoisie in the bantustans to be careful of being 'flattered by jackals'.[19]

Although the state might have planned to relinquish all positions of power in these apartheid institutions after a while, it could not arrest the historically inevitable process of the extended reproduction of an Afrikaner bureaucratic elite. A comment by Poulantzas is relevant here: 'the fact that primary reproduction of social classes depends on the class struggle also means that its concrete forms depend on the history of the social formation'.[20] Poulantzas also points out[21] that the specific form and tempo of the reproduction of the traditional petty bourgeoisie in France was largely dependent on its long-standing alliance with the bourgeoisie. Similarly, the extended reproduction of the Afrikaner petty bourgeoisie in the bantustans and black universities has been facilitated largely by the fact that it is part of the hegemonic faction within the state. This process becomes even more difficult to stop particularly because one feature of the bantustans is to create unprecedented sources of personal accumulation and upward mobility, not to mention the potential for corruption. The result has been a never-ending series of secondments and internal promotions, thus ensuring permanent control of institutions originally designed to be taken over by blacks. One only has to look at the township superintendents, administration boards, black Technikons and vocational schools to see the extent of Afrikaner control over 'black' institutions.

Tight control over these institutions by the kind of academics described above has resulted, amongst other things, in rigid and formal staff-student relationships and 'an almost exact reproduction of the teacher-pupil relationship in schools'.[22] It has also led to racial tensions between black and white staff members resulting in dormant and racially-divided staff associations. However, the effect of the hegemony of Afrikaner academics has been most devastating on the academic process itself.

Afrikaner Control and Intellectual Production

The attention that has been given to the problems of Bantu Education in black schools has tended to obscure the nature of education and intellectual production in black universities. As in all capitalist societies, education in South Africa is geared towards the reproduction of the dominant relations of exploitation and domination. Since apartheid is the major instrument of domination in South Africa, education also serves to reproduce apartheid relations of domination — concretely articulated by the existence of separate education systems for different 'racial' groups. However, most of the work published on black universities tends to focus more on the structural problems of these institutions and very little on the process of education itself.

Nkomo,[23] for example, announces his intention of analysing the educational process of Bantu Education in black universities, but disappointingly ends up not having tackled this vital question. What he does instead is show how these institutions have unintentionally produced radical student politics, thus undermining the *raison d'être* of Bantu Education. Although this is a legitimate area of analysis, the way he has tackled it tends to overlook the destructive effects of Bantu Education. For instance, Nkomo states that African student behaviour did not follow the intent of government policy makers because the Africans' reactions to Bantu Education were never taken into consideration. Specifically, two explanations for the contradictory outcomes on Bantu Education and the subsequent uprisings of recent years are suggested. The first is that Bantu Education has developed a culture of its own which is at odds with official intentions. The second is that forces external to in-class instruction have exerted as great an influence as the official curriculum.

It is particularly the reasons advanced by Nkomo to explain the contradictory outcomes of Bantu Education which, whilst true, confuse the political and academic effects of Bantu Education. Although it is the case that Bantu

Education has created its political opposite, we should not lose sight of the fact that it has also at the same time produced academics who border on 'intellectual sterility'. This can be illustrated by two factors. Firstly, the very same politically radicalised students have no critical and analytical academic skills, and instead they unproblematically reproduce the very same neo-positivist and ideologically-laden conceptions of reality. This becomes more evident in the area of social sciences.[24] Secondly, an overview of student struggles at black universities shows that they have largely been confined to 'external' issues of political repression in South Africa, and hardly any struggles around the syllabus. While students have mobilised around arbitrary student discipline at these places and around wider political issues, they have generally acquiesced to the content and style of what they are taught. In fact the struggle for people's education in South Africa has originated, and is still largely confined, within the schools and has not spilled over into the universities. I would therefore argue that, while the educational struggle in South Africa is essentially political, it is important to distinguish between its political and educational objectives. Whilst I fully agree with Nkomo that Bantu Education has failed in its politico-ideological intentions, it has been relatively successful educationally, by controlling and suppressing the intellectual and analytical abilities of black students. It therefore becomes important to understand the process of intellectual production in these bush colleges.[25]

The educational process in black, particularly African, universities is also affected by the geographical isolation of these institutions. All the homeland and autonomous universities, with the exception of a few branches, are located hundreds of kilometres away from the major urban centres of South Africa. The white universities, by contrast, are conveniently located in or near the major cities. This isolation leads mainly to two kinds of problems. First, it makes inter-campus interaction and sharing of ideas almost impossible. Both students and lecturers are out of touch with developments in other universities, which is so vital in an academic environment. Second, both students and lecturers are insulated from wider social phenomena that usually take place in the major urban centres. This isolation creates a sharp discontinuity between what is taking place in the classroom and the socio-political environment. The effect of this isolation manifests itself through lack of research even in the very areas surrounding these institutions. In fact more research on rural areas in South Africa is carried out by the white universities. This isolation is further compounded by the 'lack of funds' for members of staff to attend major conferences and workshops held in other universities.[26]

Attempts at breaking this academic isolation have also been frustrated by the fact that frequently outside speakers invited to these institutions have to be approved by the university authorities. Usually it is required that a guest speaker's background be submitted to the university authorities before permission is granted. As a result, well-known anti-apartheid activists only talk at white liberal institutions, while at black universities it is mostly pro-government officials or people comfortably 'neutral' to the authorities. This control of visiting speakers, and hence intellectual exposure of students, is best shown by the types of guest speakers invited to graduation ceremonies, who are either state functionaries, bantustan bureaucrats or representatives of big capital.

The tightest control over the educational process has been in the control over the syllabi, examinations and external examiners. Although the original black universities established in 1960 became independent from UNISA in 1969, most lecture material is still largely drawn from UNISA study guides. The syllabus is characterised by its unchanging nature, in spite of the rapid social changes in the country. Lectures, instead of being places for debate and critical exchange of ideas, are places for dictating notes summarised from some outdated or politically 'neutral' American textbooks. This approach results in students learning those notes like the Bible. The 'best' students are those who are able to reproduce the notes. What is ironic in these circumstances is that generally the students have become so addicted to these notes that lecturers who try to discard them and encourage students to do independent reading are accused of wanting to fail students.

Examinations are usually characterised by questions requiring regurgitation of lecture notes dictated in class rather than critical thinking. The control over examinations is such that even branches of these universities, hundreds of kilometres apart, are expected to set exactly the same questions. This immediately stifles lecturing styles and requires conformity to the 'standards' set by the heads of departments controlling the academic process in these institutions. The external examiners are usually appointed from Afrikaans universities who, as already pointed out, are well known for their ultra-conservative political and ideological outlook.

The design of curricula is another area through which control is exercised over the students' sources of knowledge and intellectual development. The curriculum excludes 'controversial' issues, particularly those relating to exploitation, apartheid and black resistance in South Africa. As is the case in schools, discussion of black political opposition is absent and actively discouraged, and instead there is glorification of Afrikaner prowess and white superiority. For example, at UNIBO, in 1985, a lecturer who taught a course on African nationalism in South Africa in the twentieth century was requested by the head of department not to mention the ANC in the course outline. At the same institution, most of the lecturers who were deported in 1986 were those who had developed good relations with students and had also encouraged a critical awareness amongst students.[27]

Another characteristic of the educational process in black universities is the lack of debate in the lecture room. This is, firstly, because of the repression of alternative ideas, so that what is learnt is what is given or prescribed by the lecturer. The second factor relates to the student composition of the homeland universities. In these universities there is a very big percentage of part-time students employed by the bantustan bureaucracies, who are not willing to be critical of the authorities who pay them.[28] Also, some of these students are aspirant bureaucrats of their bantustan governments.

However, all these problems in the educational process of black universities are due not only to the ideological orientation of the Afrikaner academics and their products, but also to by the sheer academic incompetence of many of the graduates of Afrikaner universities, where ideological indoctrination takes precedence over intellectual and academic rigour. Therefore education in black universities is essentially an extension of Bantu Education in the school system, a factor which has not only given 'bush colleges' their distinct character, but also has largely contributed to the growing politicisation of students.

STUDENT MILITANCY AND THE CRISIS IN BLACK UNIVERSITIES

The undemocratic nature of black universities is in many respects the mirror image of the repressive and undemocratic structures in the wider South African society. As a result, the struggles waged by students and the reaction of the authorities are both influenced by, and a replication of, the wider political struggles. In spite of the pseudo-independence given to some homelands, disruptions in the bantustans have been closely connected to political developments in South Africa. This section will therefore look at the growing politicisation of black university students as well as the reaction of the bantustan petty bourgeoisie to these developments.

The Radicalisation of Black Students

Although there have been some regional differences in the nature of the struggles at black universities, the pattern of student radicalisation has tended to take a national rather than a regional character. In order to capture the tempo and pattern of student radicalisation, it is important to trace it historically, whilst situating it within the wider political dynamics and, at the same time, understanding the issues being contested in the terrain of education. Although radical student politics can be traced as far back as the establishment of Fort Hare in 1916, the focus here will be the 1970s and 1980s, a period marked by increased student militancy.

However, it is important to look at the social composition of the student population in order to understand the nature of student politics in black universities. As in all capitalist societies, privilege and access to university education is determined by class. For example, as early as 1959 Kuper found that of the 75 African students registered at the University of Natal in Arts and allied disciplines, 59 per cent came from middle class, and mainly professional backgrounds, while 35 per cent came from distinctly working class families. In the same study, Kuper found that of the 63 African medical students, 63 per cent came from middle class backgrounds, and only 16 per cent came from working class families.[29] Although there is an inadequacy of comparable data, a study done by De Clerq in 1984 shows that there has been no significant change in the social composition of the black university student population. In her UNIBO sample, she found that 65 per cent of the students came from middle class families, and also came from the economically prosperous regions of Bophuthatswana. This figure, she notes, is hardly representative of Bophuthatswana's total population of which only 1.4 per cent held matriculation qualifications in the same year.[30] Given the middle class background of the majority of black students one would expect conservative student politics to emerge. On the contrary, increasing militancy has been manifested. The main reasons for this are:

- the acuteness of racial oppression in South Africa;
- the deepening political crisis;
- the intensification of struggles in the townships from which many of these students come;
- the tradition of resistance which is firmly entrenched in black universities; and
- the harsh and authoritarian methods of policing students in these institutions.

As indicated above, Fort Hare, particularly in the 1940s and 1950s, was a hotbed of political resistance by black students, mainly because it brought together students who shared similar life circumstances and experiences under apartheid.[31] However, student militancy was heavily controlled at Fort Hare after 1959 when it was transferred to the Department of Bantu Education. The 1960s were generally a quiet period in student political activity due to intensified repression in the whole country and the authoritarian measures introduced at Fort Hare and the newly established 'bush colleges'.[32] The ethnicisation of these universities was also used as a control mechanism because students expelled from one university could not be admitted to another university that did not cater for his/her ethnic group. Another contributory factor to the absence of political activity was lack of organisation due to the banning of progressive organisations that were an important political link with student politics.

The only student organisation that was actively challenging apartheid at the time was NUSAS, which was mainly operating on the English-speaking liberal campuses. The university authorities in black universities kept tight control over students in an attempt to keep them away from NUSAS. For instance, when UWC students elected an SRC in 1967 the Rector categorically stated that he did not want it to affiliate to NUSAS. In 1968, the Council of Turfloop also turned down an application by the SRC to join NUSAS. It was not until 1969 that black student organisation emerged in South African universities, with the formation of the South African Students Organisation (SASO). There were a number of reasons why SASO emerged in the late 1960s, immediately became radical and embraced Black Consciousness (BC) as its ideology. Firstly, as the following table shows, the number of black students between 1958 and 1970 had grown by more than 200 per cent:

Number of University Students, 1958 and 1970

Year	White	Indian	Coloured	African
1958	32,137	1,318	704	1,797
1970	73,204	3,470	1,883	4,578

Source: IRR, *Survey of Race Relations*, 1958, 1959, 1970.

The number of students in the black universities themselves had grown correspondingly between 1961 and 1970, as shown in the next table:

Number of Students at Black Universities, 1961 and 1970

Year	Ft.Hare	Ngoye	UWC	UDW	Turfloop	Total
1961	360	41	161	120	129	811
1970	610	591	936	1,654	810	4,601

Source: IRR *Survey of Race Relations*, 1958, 1959, 1970.

However, it was not the numbers *per se* which contributed to the radicalisation of black students, but the fact that universities brought together students with a common experience. This is, of course, one of the fundamental contradictions of apartheid, that by bringing together commonly oppressed people in schools, townships and factories, it created conditions and a political platform for the expression of a racially-based political consciousness. Also, the late 1960s coincided with the first generation of black university students who had been born under apartheid, post-1948. It was this factor which largely accounted for the emergence of BC as a major vehicle of black resistance in the late 1960s and early 1970s. Therefore for these students it was racial domination that constituted their immediate life experiences. The cumulative effects of repression and racism inevitably found their oppositional expression in BC.

The second factor that contributed to the radicalisation of black students in the late Sixties was the influence of the civil rights movement in the US, although this influence was contested by SASO.[33]

A third influence on student politics at this time was the student uprisings in Europe, US and Japan in the late 1960s. These uprisings gave students a claim on the leadership of progressive struggles. The emergence of SASO was a significant landmark in the history of black universities in that they were transformed from being pure institutions of Bantu Education into major sites of political struggle. For instance, SASO transformed SRCs from being dummy bodies into vibrant organisational vehicles for student protest.[34] The founding of SASO also ended the political isolation of black campuses and created national unity and direction in student politics. Over and above this, SASO also acted as a vehicle through which black students could connect to the wider political struggles. It was no surprise then that by 1972 SASO was represented on all black campuses and its membership estimated at about 6,000. It was also in 1972 that the power of student politics began to be felt throughout the country. This was felt notably through the boycotts in solidarity with the expulsion of Tiro, a prominent SASO leader, from Turfloop. These boycotts even extended to liberal campuses. In 1973, UWC was closed down four days before the official end of first semester, because of a disagreement between the students and the authorities over the SRC constitution. In response to the continuing crisis at UWC a mass rally was held at Athlone on 8 July 1973 which attracted an estimated 12,000 people.

The emergence of SASO and the ensuing struggles of the 1970s permanently changed the nature of student politics in black universities. These events led to the establishment of a political tradition of student militancy in black universities which has survived up to this day.

However, the student uprising of 1976, the climax of BC, ushered in new forces which were to have a significant impact on student politics and ideology in the 1980s. The 1976 uprisings gave birth to a new social force in South African politics — the youth. This new force was to change the character and tempo of township resistance and throw South Africa into a deeper political crisis. It was also this highly-politicised youth which was to shape the nature of student politics and organisation in the late seventies.

If there was one major achievement of BC, it was the mass psychological liberation of blacks from the mental bondage of apartheid. This liberation released a new political energy within the oppressed to advance the struggle for liberation further. However, BC in itself was unable to harness this political energy and translate it into sustained political resistance. Apart from the problems created by the banning of BC organisations in 1977, there were further structural and ideological problems within the movement itself. The principal contradiction within BC was its definition of the struggle in South Africa primarily in racial terms. Although BC defined 'black' in broader terms than the 'ethnic nationalisms' of the state, the definition nonetheless fell within the state's and liberal perception that the conflict in South Africa was largely between black and white. This created the problem of trying to eliminate racial domination through a racially constituted struggle.[35] BC could no longer contain this contradiction, particularly in the light of the emergence of the politics of non-racialism amongst the oppressed in the late 1970s. This non-racial movement was mainly led by the then emerging labour movement that was committed to building working class unity across the racial divide. Another development necessitating non-racialism was the release of many ANC activists who, having served their jail terms, immediately reconnected with popular struggles. It was this non-racial 'Congress-type' politics that consolidated itself in the formation of the United Democratic Front (UDF) in 1983 and effectively replaced BC as the ideology of the popular masses. These developments also brought the ANC back onto the centre stage of South Africa's popular politics.

These events were to result in a sharp ideological discontinuity between pre- and post-1976 student politics in South Africa. Concretely, this culminated in the Azanian Students Organisation (AZASO — founded by the BC oriented Azanian People's Organisation, AZAPO) splitting away from its mother body and committing itself to non-racialism. Perhaps the significance of all these events was that they changed the content and direction of educational struggles from a call for equal education to education for democracy, and currently to people's education — with the Freedom Charter as the primary ideologically mobilising document. Another significant difference between pre- and post-1976 struggles was the development of a non-racial student movement involving both black and progressive white students. The distance that had existed between SASO and NUSAS was changed to a working alliance between NUSAS and progressive black student organisations. This non-racial student movement has also been strengthened by the growth in numbers of black students on liberal campuses after 1976. Black students have also changed the nature of student politics on liberal campuses by taking township struggles into these institutions.[36]

It is difficult to identify the main thread running through struggles at black universities because these struggles have been less coherent than those in the schools. However, in spite of these difficulties there are common features that are worth noting. First, the radicalisation of black students has taken place around the broader political struggles in South Africa. In spite of the geographical isolation of these institutions, student politics have been closely connected to urban struggles. Second, since the 1980 school boycotts, the struggle for alternative education has been led and shaped by the pupils at schools. For instance, student boycotts in many black universities in 1980 were sympathy boycotts mainly endorsing pupil demands. Third, other struggles at black universities have been highly localised and isolated from each other. Fourth, there is yet to emerge a student programme of action directed at challenging the 'bush character' of these universities. In other words, there has been no coherent strategy aimed at transforming the black universities — as has happened in schools around the demand for peoples's education — in spite of the potential for such a development. Even the AZASO (now South African National Student Congress — SANSCO) campaign on the Education Charter hasn't really taken root in black universities. In spite of the growing politicisation and radicalisation of black students on these campuses, Afrikaner control and the dominant relations of intellectual production have remained intact, hence the growing intransigence of university authorities in handling student protests and demonstrations. Nevertheless, student militancy has created objective conditions, and laid the material basis, for a sustained challenge to the nature of 'bush' and university education as a whole, as shown by the frequent boycotts and periodic closures of these institutions.

Student Resistance and Homeland Politics

The conflicts in African universities can be described as involving three contestants: the students, Afrikaner academics and the bantustan petty bourgeoisie (although the state is always in the background of the events). Although all the African universities subscribe to academic freedom and claim that they are 'autonomous', reality tells a different story. Given the fact that the bantustans are controlled by a bureaucratic petty bourgeoisie that is dependent on the continued existence of apartheid structures, student politics have become an immediate threat to their class interests. Since student politics have been anti-apartheid as well as explicitly anti-bantustan, the bantustan petty bourgeoisie has had an interest in controlling the course of events in these institutions. Conflict and confrontation between bantustan authorities and university students dates back to the days of SASO. However, the conflict has been most dramatic in the 1980s with more homelands getting 'independence' and the bonus of a university.

Control by bantustan governments over their respective universities has been both direct and indirect. For instance, many of the African universities have their nominees in the Councils of these universities. Over and above these, student resistance has led to more direct control over the affairs of these institutions by bantustan authorities. For example, the Bophuthatswana Internal Security Act passed in December 1985 gave the government the power to bar students from any educational institution in the bantustan, including the university.[37] Both students and staff members can be banned, or, if 'non-Tswanas', they can also be deported. Also in Bophuthatswana, new members of staff have to obtain security clearance from the government before they can take up their posts.

These powers, which prevail almost equally in all the homeland universities, have been used to smash student resistance and to neutralise those members of staff promoting critical awareness amongst students. The homeland universities in particular have employed a number of young progressive academics from the liberal campuses, who went there with the belief that: 'by boycotting bush colleges, one is merely clearing the way for Broederbond-type academics and denying South Africa's black student population a better and progressive education'.[38] However, it was such academics who were particular victims of the deportations at UNITRA in 1984 and UNIBO in 1985. In this way, the bantustan authorities have been able to keep radical scholarship out of the campuses. With the incorporation of Fort Hare into the Ciskei this trend is likely to continue. As a result of these controls there has been reluctance by both staff and students to speak out on 'controversial' issues.

However, the confrontation between bantustan authorities and students has not taken place only in 'independent' homelands. One of the most bloody confrontations has taken place between Chief Buthelezi and his Inkatha followers, and students at the University of Zululand. The conflict between Buthelezi and students at this university has been going on since 1976, when students staged a demonstration against the award of an honorary doctorate to Buthelezi. This demonstration, which was a setback to Buthelezi who had hoped to establish his legitimacy amongst the students, laid the basis for bitter struggles and turned into an annual confrontation when Buthelezi was appointed Chancellor of the university in 1977. Since then the graduation ceremony at Ngoye has become an Inkatha mini-rally as well as a scene of violent clashes between students and Inkatha warriors. For example, at the 1980 graduation ceremony the President of the SRC was sjambokked in full academic attire because of his opposition to the free access to campus given to fully-armed Buthelezi warriors.

This confrontation at Ngoye has been due largely to student opposition to bantustan leaders and Buthelezi's ambitions to get the university under the control of the KwaZulu government. Although Buthelezi seemingly has lost the battle for the incorporation of the university under KwaZulu — because he doesn't want to take independence, and the university is legally autonomous — he hasn't given up the battle to control it. One sortie, after student demonstrations against him, was to threaten to bar all student teachers from practising in KwaZulu schools unless they apologised to him.

The build-up of the clashes between Buthelezi and students led to the bloody clashes on 29 October 1983 between Inkatha followers and students, which left four students and one outsider dead. Buthelezi's response to these events is very informative in terms of understanding the KwaZulu bantustan and its attitude towards opposition. Instead of apprehending those responsible and calling for restraint on the part of his followers — which would have been consistent with Inkatha's professed 'non-violence' — Buthelezi retorted that:

> Our youth are the sons and daughters of a warrior nation, and they had gone to the University to commemorate one of the greatest warriors in Zulu history, and the simple facts of the matter are that this violence so carefully plotted . . . produced the inevitable counter-violence.[39]

Buthelezi's preparedness to smash opposition at the campus and his unwillingness to lose control over the events at the university was further illustrated by events immediately after the 1983 massacre. Despite staff members having overwhelmingly voted for his removal as Chancellor, the University Council expressed full confidence in Buthelezi's Chancellorship. Buthelezi himself responded to the call for his resignation by threatening to withdraw as patron of the university foundation, and had earlier warned that:

> I would rather die than cast my Chancellor's robes aside and stand naked before a small group of jeering hoodlums . . . .[If] the current state of affairs continues much longer at the university, the people themselves will root out the evil-doers, whoever they may be. Were the campus to be closed to Inkatha its fences would be trampled down. If attacks were mounted from it . . . the people of KwaZulu would if necessary take it apart brick by brick with their bare hands and scatter its staff and students.[40]

Although the administrations of 'bush colleges' should not be simply taken as stooges of the bantustan petty bourgeoisie, their autonomy is only recognised in so far as they are not in conflict with the interests of the bantustan petty bourgeoisie and the Afrikaner academics. The easy access that university authorities allow to bantustan politicians is also facilitated by the fact that the interests of the Afrikaner academics and the bantustan petty bourgeoisie converge around the maintenance of bantustans and the smashing of progressive opposition to these structures.

CONCLUSION

The struggles taking place in black universities should be regarded as posing the question of university education under apartheid more sharply, not only for black universities but also for South African universities in general. The advancement of the struggle for transforming university education does not lie in the boycotting of black universities by academics from liberal campuses — a tendency that has been prevalent within the South African left. There are a number of problems with such an attitude. Firstly, this attitude tends to absolve the liberal universities as institutions of apartheid themselves. The fact that they are constituted as ethnic institutions firmly locates them within the broader politico-ideological apparatuses of apartheid — an issue yet to be confronted by progressive academics. Secondly, such an elitist attitude by liberal campuses presupposes that all is well within these institutions, and they should be looked upon as models of post-apartheid universities, when in fact they are a far cry from this. The liberal universities are still dominated by a liberal bourgeois ideology with big capital having a controlling interest in them. Thirdly, an elitist attitude towards black universities tends to collapse the administrative apparatus and the student population into one homogeneous institution, i.e. 'the bush college'. As the analysis above has shown, there is a big difference between, on the one hand, the Broederbond-type bureaucrats and, on the other hand, the highly politicised student population. What we should rather be talking about is how progressive academics can support the student struggles in black universities, and ways and means of linking up with the small group of progressive academics in these institutions. Elements of a future strategy should revolve around the isolation of the conservative bureaucrats and strengthening oppositional forces in these institutions. The struggles in black universities, and the intensifying academic boycott of South Africa, present a challenge and an opportunity for the left to take up the questions of academic freedom and the transformation of university education seriously. A 'holier-than-thou' attitude can only be counter-productive and divisive, in an otherwise undivided struggle for liberation in South Africa.

NOTES

1. W. Cobbett, 'The tactics of academic boycott', *Work in Progress,* No. 45, November/December 1986.
2. In 1983, out of an estimated total of 184,448 university students in South Africa, about 30,000 (16 per cent) were studying at black universities. Institute of Race Relations (IRR), *Survey of Race Relations* (Johannesburg: IRR, 1983).
3. In terms of the Extension of University Education Act of 1959, the university colleges of Zululand, North and Western Cape were established in 1960, and Durban-Westville in the following year.

4. M.M. Balintulo, 'The black universities in South Africa' in J. Rex (ed.), *Apartheid and Social Research* (Paris: Unesco Press, 1981) and IRR, *Survey of Race Relations* (Johannesburg: IRR, 1960).

5. R. Davies, *Capital, State and White Labour in South Africa 1900-1960* (Sussex: Harvester Press, 1979), p.335.

6. D. Innes, *Anglo: Anglo American and the Rise of Modern South Africa* (Johannesburg: Ravan Press, 1984), p.172.

7. Balintulo *op. cit.*, p.148.

8. Balintulo *op. cit.*, p.149.

9. *Ibid.*

10. Used in this chapter to mean 'Indian', 'coloured' and African. Elsewhere 'black' refers exclusively to 'African'. [W.C. & R.C.]

11. For instance in 1960, 190 African students applied for ministerial approval to attend English-speaking universities and only 4 were granted permission (IRR, *Survey of Race Relations*, 1960). Furthermore Wits. University which had 73 African students in 1958 — which was the highest number of African students attending a white university — only had 5 in 1970.

12. For most of 1986, Fort Hare was occupied by the Ciskeian police, two of its most prominent academics were in detention and a significant number of students did not write examinations.

13. UNITRA was a satellite campus of Fort Hare at Umtata, and UNIBO and Venda were branches of the University of the North (Turfloop).

14. Association for Sociology in Southern Africa (ASSA), *Report on the Proceedings of the Association for Sociology in Southern Africa Conference on the Teaching of Social Sciences in Black Universities Held at the University of Zululand* (Umlazi: University of Zululand), 30 May 1986.

15. IRR, *Survey of Race Relations* (Johannesburg: IRR, 1984).

16. *Ibid.*, p.380.

17. UNITRA Calendar, 1985.

18. M. Townsend, 'Open, repressive or black education', *Zululand Geographer*, Vol. 5, No. 2, September 1986 and ASSA Report, 1986.

19. L. Kuper, *An African Bourgeoisie: Race, Class and Politics in South Africa* (New Haven: Yale University Press, 1965).

20. N. Poulantzas, *Classes in Contemporary Capitalism* (London: Verso Books, 1974), p.300.

21. *Loc. cit.*

22. ASSA Report, p.3.

23. C. Nkomo, 'Contradictions of Bantu education', *Harvard Educational Review*, Vol. 51, No. 1, February 1981.

24. See ASSA Report for details on this issue.

25. This comment should not be interpreted as meaning that these problems are exclusively found in black universities. There are traces of these in English-speaking universities and more of them in Afrikaans universities.

26. ASSA Report.

27. R. Morrell *et al.*, 'Deportations, detentions and disturbance: notes towards a contemporary history of the Universities of Bophuthatswana and Transkei', paper presented to the Association for Sociology in Southern Africa, July 1986.

28. The extent to which bantustan leaders are sensitive to criticism is best illustrated by the KwaZulu case where teachers and sponsored students are expected to sign a pledge which in part reads that 'I solemnly declare that I will never in word or in deed vilify, denigrate or speak in contempt of KwaZulu Chief Minister Mangosuthu Buthelezi, members of his Cabinet or the KwaZulu government' (*Weekly Mail*, 16-22 January 1987).

29. L. Kuper, *op. cit.*

30. Cited in Morrell *et al.*, *op. cit.*

31. Fort Hare in the 1940s and 1950s was, for instance, the home of the ANC Youth League, from amongst whom was later to emerge the current top leadership of the ANC.

32. For instance, the Ministers of Bantu, Indian and Coloured Education were each given wide powers over student activities, enrolment and overall administration of black universities. They were to approve, *inter alia*, the appointment of the Rectors and heads of departments and other categories of staff members. They could also authorise the expulsion of students. In 1967, the Minister of Bantu Education reported in parliament that at Fort Hare 30 students had not gained admission: 16 of them were refused admission on 'academic' grounds; 14 because, according to the Minister, 'their presence was deemed not to be in the best interests of the college . . . [and] it was [also] not deemed to be in the interests of the college to reveal the reasons'. IRR, *Survey of Race Relations* (Johannesburg: IRR, 1967), p.290.

33. See Nkomo, *op. cit.*, p.134.

34. Tight control over student activities on black campuses had led to the boycott of SRC elections at Fort Hare and Western Cape in the 1960s. But after the founding of SASO there was renewed interest in the SRCs, as they became the major link with other campuses. For instance at SASO's formation there were SRCs only at Turfloop, Ngoye and the Natal Medical School, but by 1973 not a single black campus was without a student-backed SRC.

35. B. Nzimande and P. Zulu, 'From civil rights to socialism: a profile of the South African youth', mimeographed paper, University of Natal, 1986.

36. For example, at Wits. in 1981, black students already comprised about 10 per cent of the student body while in 1985 they were 13.2 per cent of the total student body. IRR, *Survey of Race Relations* (Johannesburg: IRR, 1981, 1985).

37. R. Morell *et al.*, *op. cit.*

38. *Ibid.*, p.5.

39. Chief Buthelezi's speech in the KwaZulu Legislative Assembly in 1983 as reported in A. Middleton, *Commission of Enquiry into the Violence which Occurred on 29 October 1983 at the University of Zululand* (Ulundi: KwaZulu Government, 1985), Vol. 2.

40. *Daily News*, 8 August 1984, and 7 February 1984.

10. School Student Movements and State Education Policy: 1972–87

JONATHAN HYSLOP

INTRODUCTION

Youth has, at many decisive historical junctures, shown a greater eagerness to mount the barricades than its elders. Yet there can be few parallels for the dominating role that young people have played in the political conflict in South Africa over the last decade. In 1976-7 a school student uprising, mustering mass support, helped to block forever the State's road to the construction of apartheid along the lines of Verwoerd's blueprint. In 1980-1 renewed student action demonstrated the inadequacy of the piecemeal changes the state had made in education and other areas of social policy during the intervening period.

These events increased the pressure on the regime to develop its restructuring 'Reform' programme and to apply this programme in the educational sphere. But it was in the 1984-87 period that the revolt of the students had its greatest impact. Student protest provided the detonator for an explosion of worker and community struggle which confronted the dominant classes with their greatest challenge yet. 'Reform' policy, in education and every other sphere, was obstructed and threatened with permanent defeat by this mass movement. Students and youth formed the shock troops of the outbreak, mounting pickets, organising mass actions and engaging in street battles with the army and the police.

It is the contention of this chapter that an understanding of the role of school students in the South African struggle cannot be abstracted from an analysis of state education policy in this period. Too often, journalistic or political commentators provide far too simple an explanation of student militancy. 'Bantu Education', the argument goes, was designed to keep blacks in an inferior social position, at the level of manual labour. It was therefore inevitable, it is asserted, that students would rebel. There are two problems with this simplistic interpretation. The first is that Bantu Education, introduced in 1955, operated successfully for more than two decades before students rose up. Any analysis has thus to explain why rebellion against it broke out at specific points in time in specific ways. If the system was able to extract acquiescence from students for over twenty years, then the causes of revolt clearly relate to a specific socio-political conjuncture, rather than being self-evident. The second problem with the explanation is that the fiercest student struggles have arisen precisely as the state has moved away from Verwoerd's classic 'Bantu Education' ideology. Contemporary state education policy, with its technocratic and urban orientation, contradicts virtually every point in Verwoerd's conception of black education as focussed in the homelands.

'Bantu Education' seen as some ahistorical entity, founded in 1955 and remaining the same ever after, cannot be adduced as a satisfactory explanation of student revolt. To understand the role of student grievances in bringing about revolt we must analyse changes within the education system, drawing on the concepts of *class* and *social reproduction*. How the state attempted to regulate the reproduction of the labour force, how the dominated classes responded to these changes, and how the state and capital in turn reacted to these popular responses: it is by looking at these *historical* questions that the student movement can be understood.

ORIGINS OF EDUCATIONAL CRISIS: RESTRUCTURING AND RADICALISATION 1972-76

By the late 1960s, the Vorster government's stern imposition of the Verwoerdian apartheid model on South Africa was causing major problems for industrial capital. Intent on maximising the proportion of the black population resident in the 'homelands' and limiting the urban black labour force to migrants, the state's policies were hindering management's attempts to recruit adequate numbers of black semi-skilled operatives, skilled workers and clerical employees. In the field of education and training industry's problem lay in the state's prohibition of urban black technical training and its attempt to prevent the growth of urban black secondary education; its refusal to allow private capital to sponsor urban educational projects; and its concentration of black tertiary education facilities in the rural areas.

During the economic boom of the Sixties, big capital had not seriously contested these policies. But with the beginnings of slump at the end of the decade, the minds of both Anglophone and newly risen Afrikaner industrial capitalists were wonderfully concentrated on the problems facing them in regard to the reorganisation of their labour force. Pressure was brought to bear on the state, with some results. From the early Seventies, the government somewhat eased policies that were annoying industry such as statutory discrimination in skilled employment, and restrictions on the numbers of blacks in urban industry. In line with this 'verligte' turn of the Vorster government, education policy was restructured.

In 1972 the state changed its budgetary policy in relation to urban schooling, making far more money available for urban black schools than before. Private capital was encouraged to make donations to this sector. Programmes for the technical training of black youth in urban areas were initiated.[1] These changes in policy were seen by the government as mere pragmatic adjustments, within the overall vision of total apartheid. Nevertheless this half-turn was to have dramatic social consequences.

In the next few years, drastically higher numbers of urban youth passed into the school system, and more especially into its secondary component. Between 1970 and 1975, the numbers of secondary school students rose from 122,489 to 318,568.[2] Thus the segment of the school-going population most likely to be politicised was drastically increased. Structurally, this created an explosive situation. Rapid educational expansion is likely to generate political unrest if, as was the case in the early 70s, there is not an equal expansion of job opportunities.[3] Unemployed high school drop-outs multiplied. At the same time more blacks were being employed in clerical and technical jobs.

The rewards for succeeding in the educational lottery were becoming more attractive, just as the penalties for failure were becoming harsher. This created a volatile compound amongst students of high ambition, frustration and economic fear. Another destabilising consequence of such expansion is the strain which it imposes on educational institutions.[4] In many parts of the country, the expanded resources available to the schools seem not to have matched the student intake. More importantly, the state decided to restructure the black school system from a 13 year to a 12 year curriculum. This was imposed through sending the last two years of primary school into the first year of secondary school at the beginning of the fateful year of 1976, causing tremendous numerical pressure on secondary schools.

The expansion brought into the school a new generation — which Bundy, drawing on Mannheim, calls a sociological generation: a group with its own generational consciousness.[5] As Lunn has shown, at a cultural level the period saw the growth of a distinctively urban youth culture, as the sub-culture of the 'cats' — relatively educated, totally urbanised, sympathetic to statements of black political identity — began to differentiate out from the previously dominant, rather lumpen, sub-culture of the *mapantsula*.[6] From the early 70s, historical process was rapidly reshaping the consciousness of this generation.

The political calm of the 60s ended with the emergence in 1969 of the university-based South African Students Organisation (SASO), the spearhead of a new political current — Black Consciousness (BC). BC stressed the need for blacks to reject liberal white tutelage, the assertion of a black cultural identity, psychological liberation from notions of inferiority, and the unity of all blacks including 'coloureds' and 'Indians'. BC was weak in the organisational sphere. From 1972, its school student arm, the South African Students Movement (SASM) was active in the schools, but failed to develop really strong structures.

However, the ideological content of BC had a pervasive influence on urban youth, feeding into the frustration and deprivation they experienced and providing an alternative. It was thus vital in providing a new political awareness amongst students.[7] This awareness was sharpened by the rapid overall deterioration in the regime's internal and external position: the rise of worker militancy and the mass strikes of 1973; the defeat of Portuguese colonialism in Mozambique and Angola; the SADF's failed intervention in Angola; the rise of military struggle in Namibia and Zimbabwe. All of these increased the sense that the regime was isolated and could be challenged.

The generation that was to produce the student movement of the 70s and 80s had two further features which Bundy has identified as contributing to their militancy.[8] Demographically, the age distribution within the black population was changing, producing an overwhelming preponderance of young people: the 1980 census found that a majority were under 21.[9] This, I would suggest, provided part of the basis for a shift of the balance of power within the urban black family, in which parents became increasingly unable to command the obedience of their children. Secondly, Bundy points out, the sudden expansion of education systems provided a high number of first generation secondary students. There were thus more students with working class roots than would be the case in a more stable pattern of stratification, and thus more social links between proletariat and aspirant petty bourgeoisie.[10]

By 1976 the political conjuncture, the structural reorganisation of education, and changes within the political culture of urban black youth combined to give rise to a critical situation. The spark to set off an explosion came with the education department's insistence on the use of Afrikaans as a medium of instruction. This policy was an attempt by conservative elements in the Bantu Education Department (BED) to reassert Afrikaner cultural priorities against what they saw as the liberalising tendencies of *verligte* politicians. Despite opposition from bantustan leaders and school boards, BED officials in the Southern Transvaal intensified the enforcement of this principle during 1976.[11]

1976-77: THE FIRST CYCLE OF STUDENT STRUGGLES

By late 1974 and into 1975, there were indications of a new militancy among school students. In the Eastern Cape SASM was active. In 1975 at least two strikes occurred over educational grievances, one involving the occupation of a school. In Soweto there was a confrontation between students and security police. During the first months of 1975 tension over the issue in Soweto had risen, and in April the first school came out on strike. The strike then spread fitfully through another eight or so Soweto secondary and higher primary schools. On 13 June SASM then convened a delegate meeting at Naledi High School which established the Soweto Students Representative Council (SSRC). The SSRC called a demonstration for 16 June.[12]

The shootings of students by police outside Orlando West Junior High School on 16 June 1976 led immediately to widespread student uprisings, with attacks by students on property and institutions identified with the state, and a harsh police response which left many dead. Riots spread quickly through the Rand and to Pretoria. The closure of state schools by the Minister, and the dropping of the Afrikaans decision, failed to check the spread of the upheaval.[13] On 11 August conflict broke out in the schools of the African townships of Cape Town. Before the end of August, and in striking confirmation of BC's black unity line, students in the Cape Town coloured townships were drawn in, participating in militant demonstrations in central Cape Town. This was followed by a stay-away on 16 and 17 September. Within four months there were incidents in 160 different communities.[14]

The SSRC took the lead in organising broader resistance in Soweto. During the following months, they called four stay-aways. The first on 4 August was 60 percent successful. The second on 23 to 25 August drew about 70 percent support, but was marred by fighting between students and migrant workers opposing the boycott. However, these tensions were overcome politically, and a third stay-away on 13-15 April enjoyed broad support. Although a final attempt to call a stay-away in November failed, a boycott of Christmas festivities called by the SSRC was substantially effective.[15]

The SSRC carried their campaigns over to an attack on the puppet Urban Bantu Council, which they in effect destroyed by forcing the resignation of councillors.[16] The protests or boycotts continued sporadically until late 1977, especially in smaller towns.[17] But by the end of that year they were fizzling out, because of the repression which had killed hundreds of students and pushed thousands into exile, because of the late 1977 state clampdown on BC organisation, and because of simple political exhaustion.

Much of the written debate on the events of 1976 centres on the role and inspiration of the SSRC. Some have argued that it was narrowly elitist in its aims, being mainly concerned with pupils' grievances rather than broader political issues, and that it was unable to give effective leadership.[18] Others have seen it as a 'student government' challenging for political control of the townships.[19]

Without exaggerating its role — certainly the SSRC was not in any position to pose as an alternative state — the balance of evidence seems to support the latter position. The ideology of the SSRC was a rather inchoate mixture of BC and other influences. But it did effectively terminate normal state regulation and control over Soweto for a time; it did mobilise broad working class action; and it did take on political issues such as the local government system. Moreover it provided a political model for students elsewhere in the country who set up their own representative structures.[20]

Another controversy surrounds the role of the ANC: whether, through its underground structures or through the SSRC, it was the true inspiration of the revolt.[21] This seems on the whole implausible. While the changed situation in the former Portuguese colonies allowed the ANC to begin re-establishing its political networks inside South Africa, this process had certainly not proceeded to the point where it would have been able to lead a revolt.

An antipathy to BC ideology should not lead one to try and negate the fact of its influence on the generation of 1976.[22] Although the ANC made some propaganda and organisational intervention in 1976-77, it was in the aftermath of the rising that it really began to link up with the new political generation. Students who had faced police guns with empty hands were attracted by the ANC's policy of armed struggle. Those fleeing into exile found the ANC the only exile grouping with a strong organisation which could incorporate them. About 4,000 students joined the ANC for guerrilla training. In time some of them filtered back into the country, re-establishing more firmly the prestige and organisation of the ANC amongst the youth.[23]

1977-79: STATE AND STUDENTS REGROUP

In the period following the beginning of the uprising, the state was in considerable disarray. In part this was because of the unexpected nature and intensity of the movement. In part it was because the National Party was mired in the power struggle between the conservative proponents of traditional apartheid led by Connie Mulder, and the technocratic alliance of Afrikaner business and military chiefs around P.W. Botha. The result was that stop-gap measures softening some existing policies were pursued, without really decisive change.

In the educational sphere this took the form of abandoning the policy of Afrikaans as a compulsory teaching language, introducing compulsory education in certain areas, and developing teacher upgrading programmes. In addition, the Bantu Education Department was given the less offensive title of Department of Education and Training (DET).[24] Racial integration of private sector training of employees.[26] This drifting policy was clearly inadequate to meet the crisis.

In the aftermath of the banning of Black Consciousness movements in 1977, school students began to look for other forms of political expression. A considerable debate ensued on the type of political orientation to adopt, marked by the emergence of a strong current orientated to the political tradition represented by the ANC. This resulted in the emergence in 1979 of the Congress of South African Students (COSAS), a school student organisation which explicitly took a position founded on the Freedom Charter.[27] Those who continued to identify with the BC tradition found their political expression in the Azanian Students Movement (AZASM) and a considerable rivalry between AZASM and COSAS emerged.[28]

1980-81: THE SECOND CYCLE OF STUDENT STRUGGLES

In February 1980, school boycotts broke out in coloured schools in the Western Cape. The issues which sparked these boycotts were student objections to SADF national servicemen teaching in schools, the demand for free and compulsory education, and a call for the re-admission of barred pupils. The boycotts spread to coloured and Indian schools elsewhere in the country, especially on the Rand, and subsequently to DET schools.[29]

The Western Cape boycotts were notable for their high level of politicisation: student propaganda attacked the class basis of the education system and its role in reproducing cheap labour. This content may have reflected the influence in the region of a number of small left wing groups deriving from the defunct Unity Movement. In addition it reflected the rising influence of the trade union movement: during the boycott the students participated in a meat boycott in solidarity with striking meat workers.[30]

The politicisation also took the form of a contestation of the role of the school. Students organised alternative curricula and 'awareness programmes', and challenged teachers' authority.[31] The boycotts did force the state to considerably improve infrastructure in coloured schools, but by their end, boycotts were plagued by fragmentation and declining student interest.[32]

The boycotts in DET schools were widespread and hard fought: 77 African schools were closed by the DET in this period.[33] A particular centre of militancy was the Eastern Cape. Initial demands centred on educational deficiencies, but as students mobilised they also began to demand withdrawal of police from their areas, and to reject compulsory homeland citizenship. Violent clashes with police in July led to the collapse of the schooling system in the region for the rest of the year.[34] The boycott ended gradually in the early months of 1981.[35]

The implications were clear: piecemeal policy changes could not satisfy students or overcome the general education crisis. And students were increasingly politicised. It was in this context that the state addressed itself to the task of formulating a policy of restructuring in education which could form part of an overall counter-revolutionary strategy.

DE LANGE: REFORM STRATEGY IN EDUCATION

Once the power struggle in the National Party (NP) had been resolved, there was a sharp change of the state's political direction. The Botha leadership launched a series of attempts to restructure South African society along lines that would on the one hand cater to the needs of industrial capital and on the other hand provide a coherent counter-revolutionary strategy. Industry needed to employ more blacks at semi-skilled, skilled, clerical and managerial levels,[36] and this would necessitate accepting the existence of, and thus providing for, a permanent black urban population. The state had to defuse the revolutionary possibilities of the student and worker movements. Reform strategy sought to address both these needs.

The first phase of reform, implemented at the end of the 1970s and into the very early 1980s, was largely concerned with restructuring at the economic and labour market levels. Following the Riekert and Wiehahn reports, urban residence and employment rights were extended to sections of blacks, and black trade unionism legalised. At the same time, extensive state encouragement was given to the establishment of a black business class.[37] The political aim was to fragment black opposition through stratification: the state intended that conflicts would develop between urban blacks with residence rights and migrants who lacked such rights; between those included in industrial bargaining and those excluded; and between an emergent petty-bourgeoisie and the working class.

Furthermore, at an economic level, this new order would enable social reorganisation to meet the new labour requirements which the evolving monopoly structure of industry with its demands for technical/supervisory staff and semi-skilled machine operatives needed.[38] The weakness of this programme, however, was that it did not address the political grievances of blacks and therefore could not win their acquiescence.

A second phase of reform therefore evolved during the 80s which involved a combination of attempts at political incorporation of sectors of the dominated population with a measure of deracialisation of social institutions and the privatisation of welfare provision. Coloured and Indian people were to be incorporated through the tricameral parliament, Africans through strengthened local councils linked to the substantial financial resources of Regional Services Councils (RSCs) and through participation on a rather nebulous National Council which would discuss constitutional issues. (The hidden bottom line was that the white state would keep control of military/ police and fiscal functions.) There would no longer be a rigid opposition to integration of social facilities in private sector services and business. Conflict over welfare services would be reduced; the state would be absolved of responsibility in this regard by privatising such services to the maximum extent possible and by delegating their control to the RSCs. [39]

Something of both phases of reform strategy entered into its major expression in the field of education. This was the report prepared by a Human Sciences Research Council enquiry under the leadership of the influential academic, and later Broederbond leader, Professor J.P. de Lange. De Lange's report was overwhelmingly technocratic, stressing the need for education to be linked to economic development. It also embraced a partial de-racialisation of education. De Lange wanted equal quality of education for all ethnic groups. A more class-stratified schooling system was proposed. Primary schooling should be free and compulsory, while at secondary level there should be a vocational stream, subsidised by industry, and an academic stream subsidised by parental fee-paying.

These proposals clearly implied that each level of schooling would feed into the labour market, primary schools generating unskilled and semi-skilled workers, the vocational stream technicians and artisans, and the academic stream clerical and managerial workers. Private schools should be encouraged and racial integration in them allowed. The tertiary sector could also be integrated and should have a greater technical component. De Lange also advocated a single education ministry to replace the ethnically divided ministry, a move which, I would argue, was aimed to restore the political credibility of the education system.[40] De Lange's aims thus dovetailed with Botha's Total Strategy — importantly, the strategy was aimed to intensify class differentials while reducing racial ones. (This also related to whites: fee-paying and privatisation would obviously adversely affect the schooling of white working class children.)

The type of strategy elaborated by De Lange has formed the essential basis of state policy through the early 1980s. State spending on black education increased massively in this period. The DET budget (which does not include spending in the homelands) rose from R143 million in 1978/9 to R709 million in 1984/5,[41] although its low starting point meant that racial inequality remained profound (*per capita* spending ratios between white and black pupils in 1984 were of the order of 7 to 1, although this was a sharp change from the situation in 1970, when it stood at 18 to 1).[42]

Total enrolment of black pupils also rose spectacularly: African secondary school pupils increased in numbers from under 600,000 in 1980 to over a million in 1984.[43] An extensive school building programme was in operation with 12 new buildings a day being put up in African schools by 1984.[44] By late 1982 a number of black schools were being converted into technical and commercial schools; the Department was assisting schools to offer technical courses; and a string of technikons (technical colleges) were being created for blacks.[45] These changes did not occur in urban areas only, but were also put into effect within the bantustans. Bophuthatswana, for example, set up 15 new technical institutions between 1977-82, and increasingly geared its secondary education system to the needs of adjoining urban industrial areas.[46] The state also gave massive tax breaks to employers to encourage in-service training.[47]

In addition, private schools obtained subsidies,[48] while remaining statutory racial restrictions on entrance to them and to universities were allowed to lapse. For the state this was to prove a fatal combination of measures. While on the one hand this drastically increased the proportion of the school population most likely to be politically mobilised — secondary students — it failed to introduce policies which would be likely to mollify them politically.

The South African left has shown a peculiar inability to come to grips with the meaning of this restructuring. Many analyses of such moves portray them as cosmetic, not real. This position is exemplified by a comment in a publication put out by white radical students: 'apartheid education is forced to change . . . but not really'.[49] It seems to me extraordinary to assert that such a massive restructuring of education is not a social reality. The problem seems to arise because of a fear that any admission that reform is 'real' would be an endorsement of it.

This is a fundamental misconception: it embodies the mistake of thinking that reform can only be 'real' if it is an improvement or liberalisation of social conditions. Reform however is precisely a 'real' authoritarian restructuring. The way people live, the way the labour force is reproduced is being changed, but in the direction of greater state control and regulation. The power of the dominant classes is being preserved by reform but in a different manner, and in a way that gives somewhat more emphasis to class division and less to race. The point is surely not to deny the 'reality' of this process, but to analyse its implications. Failure to do so disarms opponents of the state: by simply engaging in blanket dismissals of state policy the need to counter specific state initiatives is ignored.

The De Lange strategy thus forms a central component of overall state reform strategy. Recent years have seen an attempt by leading groups in the state to implement this type of strategy in order to attain the restructuring of social reproduction, and on that basis, the counter-revolutionary political goals of the Botha leadership. But the attempt has not achieved success because of the impact of mass opposition by school students. As we shall see, they have succeeded in denying any legitimacy to the State's educational initiatives. Despite a substantial expenditure of resources, the State has been unable to buy support in the educational sphere.

However, a secondary form of opposition has also hampered the ability of the State to implement the full De Lange agenda. This has been the hostility to it of sections of the National Party. During the period when the cabinet was considering De Lange's report, the NP was undergoing the breakaway of the Conservative Party, which grouped together those who resented Botha's departures from the policies of the Verwoerd and Vorster eras. Moreover, many sympathised with the CP's views though they remained in the NP. Consequently the move by the NP toward becoming a fully technocratic, capitalist party was interrupted, as it tried desperately to keep on board those of its supporters who identified with the party's traditional right wing populism. In education the result was that the government rejected some of De Lange's proposals in order to placate its right wing.

When the government published its White Paper on education in November 1983, while much of De Lange was adopted as state policy (equal spending on all ethnic groups as an aim, expansion of technical orientation, privatisation) much was also refused. Christian National Education ideology was emphasised (in contrast to De Lange's technicism); segregation was stressed; a single education ministry was rejected in favour of various 'group' ministries.[50] While some of this was pure grandstanding for the benefit of right wingers, it also reflected real ambiguities within the cabinet. The consequence was that De Lange's strategy was carried out less thoroughly and effectively than it might have been.

During this period COSAS was endeavouring to strengthen its organisation, although it was far from being a mass movement. Some of its activity centred on propagating the theme that there was a need for student-worker unity.[51] In 1983 a campaign was conducted against age limits in the schools.[52] However the organisation's activities remained relatively localised and small-scale. Much the same could be said of AZASM, although it seems to have been less ideologically coherent and organised. In the course of 1983 the two student movements received a boost from their participation in the two new legal political fronts. COSAS became the school student wing of the United

Democratic Front (UDF). AZASM, on the other hand, was drawn into the uneasy alliance of socialists and black nationalists who constituted the National Forum (NF).

THE THIRD CYCLE BEGINS: EARLY 1984

At the beginning of 1984, a renewed series of boycotts began. Initially around limited, educational issues, these were eventually to mesh with wider political grievances. Out of this combination, youth would assume a dominating role in the massive social conflict that was to ensue. The initial issue at stake was the marking of the 1983 matriculation (school leaving/university entrance examination). A number of studies have established that the administration of this examination was poor and corrupt, and that it was virtually useless as a measure of black students' academic potential; moreover in the period between 1980 and 1983 pass rates had dropped sharply, leading to suspicions that the authorities were manipulating the results to limit the numbers of high school graduates.[53]

Matric was a particular grievance for students in Atteridgeville, Pretoria, who found unmarked scripts from the previous year in their school — after the marks had been published! COSAS took up the matric question and also promoted student demands around school conditions: they called for an end to corporal punishment and to sexual harassment of pupils by teachers, and opposed the age limits in force in the schools.[54]

COSAS also promoted the idea of 'democratic Student Representative Councils', as a way of increasing student power and organisation.[55] The initial epicentres of the boycotts were Atteridgeville and the small town of Cradock in the Eastern Cape. In Cradock, a popular local headmaster, Matthew Goniwe, was transferred from his post to the nearby town of Graaff-Reinet. Students at Cradock went on a boycott, and Goniwe was detained; but then Graaff-Reinet students joined the boycott.[56] Released later, Goniwe was subsequently assassinated, probably because of his role as a UDF leader.

The boycotts of early 1984 spread through the Eastern Cape and sporadically affected areas of the Rand and elsewhere.[57] In an attempt to placate students, the DET offered to establish a form of student representation including teachers, principals and official school committee members, but this proposal was rejected by pupils as not meeting their demands.[58] From then on the DET took a more confrontational position: between May and 23 July schools on the Rand and in Cradock and Pretoria were closed by official order.[59]

It is commonly suggested that the school student movements of 1984 were somehow more political or radical than those of the previous two waves of student struggle.[60] This seems a somewhat teleological view of the question. While student movements did become increasingly concerned with questions of national politics as 1984 proceeded, their initial mobilising issues were very much education-related; and previous movements had raised political and social issues. A clearer difference was that the students of 1984, especially through COSAS, had a real national organisation that could make calls to action evoking a national response.

During 1984 COSAS was able to generalise student demands from one area of the country to another. Its leadership had a clear strategy of using 'short-term' demands on education as a basis for mobilising students and then using the level of organisation thus achieved as a platform for action on national political issues.[61] In that year there was a substantial increase in the number of COSAS branches; in a certain sense COSAS had thus moved from being an activist group to a mass movement.[62] The extent of its organisation should not be exaggerated however: it was a mass movement in the sense that thousands of students responded to its calls, but that did not necessarily mean that more than a limited leadership fraction were actually organised into structures with regular and disciplined activity.

Another initiative of student militants in this period was to have an important impact on the national political scene. This was the building up of 'youth congresses', organising mainly unemployed young blacks in South Africa's townships. Between 1983 and 1984 student activists took the initiative in founding such organisations.[63] Many were initiated by COSAS and affiliated to the UDF; some others inclined to the NF.[64] By organising these disaffected and often somewhat lumpen youths into a political structure, the school students helped unleash an enormously powerful reservoir of radicalism.

AUGUST 1984 — DECEMBER 1985: 'LIBERATION BEFORE EDUCATION!'

The transformation of the school boycotts into the spearhead of a national political crisis did not occur until the second half of 1984. In the period August 1984 to December 1985 youth became the foot soldiers of a battle for control of the township streets. But, I shall also suggest, their movements took on forms which threatened to shipwreck the entire movement of popular resistance.

In late August 1984, the state held elections for the new coloured and Indian houses of the tricameral parliament. Rejecting these as dummy institutions, both COSAS and NF student organisations set up school boycotts as part of a wider boycott of the elections.[65] Some 800,000 students, mainly in coloured schools, participated in the boycott of the election for the coloured chamber on 22 August, and smaller numbers in the boycott of the Indian election the subsequent week.[66] There was also support in African schools for the boycott; the level of support in DET schools may have been of the order of 30,000 to 75,000 students.[67] NF organisations played a prominent part in the boycott in some areas and felt aggrieved that this role was not acknowledged by the media, which tended to concentrate on the UDF.[68] However, after this time, the NF had a decreasing share of the initiative within the student movement.

The election boycotts still did not spell the outbreak of uncontrollable crisis, however. The support for the boycotts in DET schools was limited, and those that participated, mainly on the East Rand and in the Eastern Cape, mostly returned to school.[69] Nor did the boycotts in coloured and Indian schools persist. It was the riots and police killings that took place in the 'Vaal Triangle' industrial area's townships at the beginning of September and the subsequent deployment of the SADF in this area that transformed school boycotts into a leading sector in a national political struggle.

In response to these momentous events, over 200,000 students in the Vaal

Triangle went on boycott.[70] The movement now began to pick up momentum nationally: the number of boycotting schools in the Eastern Cape rose from 10 at the beginning of September to 58 in late October: the number on the East Rand from 13 in early September to 56 in early October: and the 87 schools in the Vaal Triangle which struck in September remained closed.[71]

This crisis placed considerable pressure on the leaderships of community, trade union and political organisations to find ways of expressing solidarity with the students. A successful stay-away by workers in the East Rand township of KwaThema on 22 October in support of school students 'demands' provided a model for such action.[72] In the aftermath of this meeting, a planning committee was established in Johannesburg, embracing COSAS, community organisations and major trade unions, including the FOSATU trade unions which had previously been cautious of involvement in overt political campaigns.[73]

It was agreed by this planning group to call a Southern Transvaal stay-away which would support student demands for SRCs and an end to age limits, but would also raise wider economic demands (an end to rent and bus-fare increases) and call for the withdrawal of the army from the townships.[74] When the stay-away took place on 5 to 6 November 1984, both schooling and industry throughout the Southern Transvaal ground to a halt.[75] About 400,000 students from over 300 schools participated, and anything between 300,000 and 800,000 workers.[76] These developments heralded a qualitatively new level of resistance to state policy, and a rapid politicisation of youth on a mass scale. Moreover, the united action between students and workers on an organised basis was a major step forward for the student movement.

However, the youth and student movement was to experience difficulty in consolidating this alliance. This quickly became apparent in the Eastern Cape. In Port Elizabeth, a move to organise a stay-away in early 1985 rapidly produced conflict between the better organised union groupings (FOSATU and the General Workers Union) on the one hand, and political and youth movements on the other. Community organisation in Port Elizabeth was dominated by the youth congresses: militant and increasingly engaged in physical confrontation with security forces, but lacking the tradition of democratic organisation of the unions.

When difficulties over the planned stay-away arose, youths tried to solve the problem by threatening unionists. The outcome was that the stay-away was called in March without union support. Youths were able to make it work in the African townships by force, but a great deal of tension was generated. There was antagonism between students and unionists, and also the danger of resentment between Africans and the coloured community (where the unions had influence but youth organisation was limited), which had not supported the stay-away.[77] A tendency toward triumphalism on the part of the student organisations inhibited them from learning lessons from this experience. The lesson, that youth and students could not build effective alliances by imposing on workers, should have been apparent from the more successful experience of neighbouring Uitenhage: there more broadly based community organisation, which was not youth-dominated, produced an effective stay-away on 22 March, supported by all sectors.[78]

Through the remainder of 1985 waves of student boycott action washed across the country, affecting the majority of its African high schools[79] and many of its primary schools. Geographically, however, the movement was clearly centred in certain regions. Most of the conflict took place in the cities and small towns of the Eastern Cape, the Rand and the Vaal Triangle, and the small and medium-sized urban centres of the Southern Transvaal and the Northern Free State. Apart from some limited, if violent, student outbreaks in the Durban/Pietermaritzburg area, Natal was relatively quiet, as was much of rural South Africa and the towns of the central Cape, Northern and Eastern Transvaal and Southern Orange Free State.[80]

In the middle of the year the state made a determined attempt to break the student movement. July saw the imposition of a State of Emergency in regions of the Eastern Cape, Southern Transvaal and Northern Free State,[81] followed by detentions of large numbers of COSAS members[82] and in August, the banning of COSAS.[83] While these actions limited the effective coordination of the student movement, it had by now become too powerful to be stopped by decapitation, and the measures taken achieved only limited and temporary reductions in student action.

The Emergency also precipitated the outbreak of student revolt in the Western Cape, which had been politically quiet except for the demonstrations around the coloured elections. Within a week of the proclamation of the Emergency (which did not initially affect the Cape Town area) boycotts had started in the coloured schools controlled by the Department of Education and Culture, and shortly thereafter students in Cape Town DET schools joined in. There followed three months of street fighting between students and police, mass rallies, consumer boycotts and harsh repression. The students created a strong coordinating body, the Western Cape Student Action Committee (WECSAC), which led their campaign.

The DET tried to undermine the student movement by closing the schools in early September, but the students responded with a mass reoccupation of schools on the 17th of that month. Following the notorious Thornton Road shootings, in which police hidden on a truck ambushed and shot youths, killing three, the student movement reached a peak of rebellion. This was only partially contained by the imposition of a State of Emergency in the Western Cape on 26 October.[84]

During 1985 it became clear that the student movement had shifted its focus from educational demands as such to broadly political ones. Amongst short-term demands, the calls for the withdrawal of troops from the townships and the release of detainees became prominent. At a wider level, it was apparent that immediate and educational demands were now seen by large numbers of students as mobilising issues which were just a facet of a wider struggle to overturn the existing social order.

A political culture emerged which was centred on expressions of allegiance to the ANC and its political strategies. Songs of praise to Mandela, Tambo and Umkhonto we Sizwe, the ubiquitous invocation of the phraseology of the Freedom Charter, study groups which pored over underground ANC and SACP publications, the use of mock guerrilla uniforms and toy guns at funerals and demonstrations: all of these formed part of a now dominant political culture amongst youth which reflected the hegemony of ANC politics and ideology. An arresting element of this culture was the chanting of 'Viva!' at meetings, reflecting the transmission by ANC fighters of their training experience in Lusophone countries.

The strength of this ANC-orientated political culture was manifested in the way in which in this period it penetrated sectors of youth amongst which ANC influence had previously been weak. Notably it became a strong feature of student movements in the Western Cape, which had previously been dominated by the heritages of the Unity Movement, the Pan African Congress (PAC), and Black Consciousness.[85]

The activity of students in 1985 was marked by a ferocious willingness to confront the police, and also to attack those such as black councillors who were regarded as collaborators. To give one an idea of the scope of such militancy, let us look at just one twenty-four hour period in the Cape in mid-August. Within that time, youths in Worcester attacked a police vehicle with a petrol bomb and set alight municipal workshops, eventually being dispersed with birdshot; in Queenstown a crowd of 1,000 attacked the home of a councillor, and were dispersed by police fire; in East London five houses and two beerhalls were set alight; and in Port Elizabeth a similar number of buildings were burnt.[86] Clashes with police were frequent, as youths attempted to barricade streets[87] and the police dispersed student meetings[88] or marches.[89]

Youth and student militants enforced the boycotts by mounting pickets at school gates or bus stops: any young person carrying school books was liable to incur their wrath.[90] This militancy held up to an astonishing extent in the latter half of 1985, despite frequent searches of schools by the SADF[91] and measures which included the arrest of the entire student body at some schools.[92]

The student movement generated a militancy which presented a solid wall of rejection to state attempts, during the 1985-6 period, to supplement repression with incorporative tactics using the De Lange strategy. Although expenditure on black education remained well below that on white, DET expenditure was being boosted up sharply: R1,148 million was projected for the 1986-7 financial year.[93] By early 1986 the DET could claim that 188 new schools and 9,000 new classrooms in existing schools had been built, or were in construction since 1982.[94] 1985-6 saw the government identifying equality of educational expenditure between racial groups as an active policy goal, with a ten year period (1986-96) being projected for its attainment.[95]

Many De Lange priorities were also put into practice more energetically: state support for private schools, expanded technical and vocational education, teacher upgrading programmes, and, increasingly, desegregation of private schools and tertiary education.[96] Moreover a new structure was elaborated by government to coordinate educational restructuring: the Ministry of National Education.[97] While the existing separate ethnic education ministries were retained, National Education took on the role of coordinating educational spending policy and developing uniform administrative policies. These moves did not entirely represent a simple application of De Lange's recommendations. National Party ideological devotion to the concept of 'own' ethnic educational administrations meant that De Lange's proposal for a single ministry was still unacceptable.[98]

All of these state initiatives in the educational field failed to make any impact on the students. 'Bantu Education' — as the students continued to describe the DET — had lost any shred of legitimacy amongst the students, and there was overwhelming suspicion of its endeavours. The money thrown at the education system by the state could not buy any credibility amongst the students. Students were extremely aware of the limitations of the changes that had occurred: that white schooling was still far better funded; that black teachers remained inadequately trained; that the new administrative structure stopped well short of a single education system.

But, even if these issues had been better dealt with by the state, it is doubtful that students would have been mollified. By now, educational problems, for a vast mass of students, were just one aspect of their experience as part of an oppressed people. They looked towards a radical transformation of the society, not just for better school conditions. No conceivable state moves in the field of education could by now have contained student militancy. Thus, within the process whereby popular movements in South Africa were checking the regime's reform strategy, the student movement played a central part. Not only did it provide much of the foot soldiery of the popular movement: it also prevented the educational component of reform strategy from working. The government was unable to consolidate any degree of support through its restructuring in this field. This was a major political achievement of the student movement.

During the year it became apparent, however, that there were features of the student and youth movements which were not only organisationally counter-productive but also extremely divisive, threatening to do irreparable damage to the whole popular movement. The most important of these was the rise of an outlook which Colin Bundy has described as 'immediatism'.[99] In the turmoil of the struggle, many students came to believe that the state was collapsing and that a revolutionary victory was not far away.

This totally unrealistic perception (which national leaders often did too little to counter) led inevitably to adventurist and ultra-left political actions. Immediatism amongst students was best expressed in the slogan 'Liberation Now, Education Later'.[100] Assuming that revolution was imminent, some students began to view any return to school as a 'betrayal': boycotts became a principle rather than a tactic. By the end of the year, students were making calls for 1986 to be 'The Year of No Schooling'.[101]

This approach posed two major dangers for the student movement. Firstly it became very difficult to organise students who were not in school; student structures weakened and the discipline of the movement broke down.[102] Secondly, given that the state was *not* collapsing, there would inevitably be a demand from sections of working class youth for the educational opportunities which would enable them to get jobs. The immediatist perspective, by denying this reality, created the possibility of conflict between activists and those wishing to return to school. In Soweto in September, fighting was already occurring between those who had returned to school and activists.[103]

Another problem area was the relationship of the students with other sections of the community. Although student speakers often invoked 'the leading role of the working class', their treatment of workers suggested that in practice they often saw the leading role as being their own. Youth and students enforced consumer boycotts and stay-aways, sometimes arbitrarily called and badly advertised, by using physical force against alleged boycott breakers.[104] Bus drivers, for example, were attacked and sometimes stabbed.[105] Often little attempt was made by young people to explain the aims of a boycott and persuade people to participate.[106] As Zwelakhe Sisulu argues, these problems were generally worst where organisation was weakest.[107]

The consequence was in many cases a growing rift between students and the older generation. A related difficulty lay in the relations between students and teachers. Students often regarded teachers as working for 'the system' and thus subjected them to humiliating treatment or even violent attacks.[108] The consequent alienation between students and teachers was not overcome by the rapid growth of the National Education Union of South Africa (NEUSA) amongst teachers in 1985,[109] as it organised mainly young radicalised teachers, while the majority of older, more cautious teachers continued to adhere to the conservative African Teachers' Association of South Africa (ATASA).

Within the schools, adequate links between students and parents were often lacking. Many parents, despairing of the future of urban schooling, started sending their children to private schools, even at the cost of great economic sacrifice,[110] or sending them to attend schools in quiet rural areas. Thus student militancy began to fragment the unity of oppressed communities, rather than to consolidate it.

The organisational weaknesses of the students had another dangerous consequence. Lack of leadership (especially after the COSAS banning) and of formal structures, and weak or non-existent political education, laid the student movement open to exploitation by lumpen elements, and prey to a tendency to lash out blindly and violently at anyone who incurred suspicion. This trend towards politically destructive violence took a number of forms. One was a series of attacks, some fatal, on people held responsible for the deaths of students. Where a student was killed in shebeen brawl or criminal attack, the victim's friends would attack the house of the suspected perpetrators, burn it and sometimes kill the alleged culprit. In Soweto alone at least ten houses were burnt and six people killed in such incidents between August 1984 and April 1985. In many such cases the guilt of those attacked was open to question and the effect was to terrorise much of the community rather than to impose an alternative system of justice.[111]

A second form of this lumpen violence was the way in which school conflicts in the Durban area in August seem to have provided an opportunity for divisive conflict between sections of the oppressed. While it is unclear exactly what transpired in Durban's Inanda area, with the Left blaming Inkatha for the incidents and the Right the radical organisations, it remains an indisputable fact that the riots began when a march called by boycotting students attacked an Indian-owned shop. It seems that the march was joined by a lumpen element who carried out the racial attacks. The student movement cannot be held responsible, but the incident does illustrate the dangers which were present in an excessively amorphous movement of township youth.[112]

A third form of this lumpen politics was the violent feud that erupted between the student supporters of the UDF and the NF. Violent clashes took place between the factions throughout the year.[113] The difficulty of handling the youth seemed to make national leaders reluctant to reprove the excesses of their young followers; and some local level student leaders were clearly not exactly disapproving of the elimination of opponents.[114] In some quarters an atmosphere was created in which the distinction between having the 'wrong line' and being a 'police agent' was blurred. By late 1985 there were serious dangers that the student movement would degenerate through the spread of various types of fratricidal violence.

A final challenge facing the student movement was that of geographical isolation. By the end of 1985 urban black education had totally collapsed: out of 25,584 DET matric class students in 'white areas', only 10,523 wrote the final exam and less than half passed.[115] But in the bantustans which were, with the exception of Ciskei, largely unaffected by the student movement, normal growth in the numbers of students sitting exams took place.[116] Thus a tendency was developing for a sharp division to grow up between urban and rural youth. The danger was that if this continued across time it could harden into entrenched urban/rural social and political divisions.

The student and youth movements thus, despite their achievements, posed dangers to the future of the battle against apartheid. Could these dangers be averted? The answer was to come with a remarkable development in 1985-6: the rise of the National Education Crisis Committee (NECC) and its strategy of 'People's Education'. It was this turn of events which saved the student movement from devouring itself and gave it a renewed role in the political conflict.

OCTOBER 1985 — JANUARY 1987: 'PEOPLE'S EDUCATION FOR PEOPLE'S POWER'?

Although attempts were made in 1985 to construct a national parents coordinating committee which would attempt to mediate the crisis[117], this attained little credibility. However, there were also other attempts by parents, students and teachers to bridge the divisions which were opening up. The Western Cape was particularly advanced in this regard. In the coloured areas, a network of Parent-Teacher-Student Associations (PTSAs) was established which was largely responsible for creating a greater degree of student-community solidarity than was experienced elsewhere in the country.[118] In addition a mass based local teachers' organisation, the Western Cape Teachers' Union (WECTU) was formed to draw teachers into political action.[119] But local, piecemeal actions were clearly not going to overcome the national crisis facing the education struggle.

The beginnings of a national response emerged in Soweto in late 1986. In October the Soweto Civic Association convened a mass meeting of parents. Out of this meeting the Soweto Parents Crisis Committee (SPCC) was formed, with a brief to negotiate with the DET on the immediate central issues of the students' demand for end of year exams to be postponed and the withdrawal of troops from the townships.[120] SPCC leaders enunciated a strategy involving three key tasks: involving parents in students' problems; providing leadership structures for students; and overcoming the breakdown of communications between students and teachers.[121] They thus identified the main lines of fracture in the community and set about trying to create a healing process.

The establishment of the SPCC itself provided the channel for parent activity; as parents became aware of the danger that the students would prepare a Year of No Schooling, they rallied to the committee.[122] The SPCC also appreciated the need to draw in the bulk of teachers, who were in

ATASA, despite its previously poor political record: as Eric Molobi later commented, 'We can never throw willing allies into the hands of the enemy.'[123] Through the participation of two ATASA luminaries (H.H. Dlamlenze and R.L. Peteni) on SPCC, the alliance was consolidated.[124] One immediate fruit of this alliance was that headmasters in Soweto frustrated the government's plans to push ahead with the November exams by refusing to administer them.[125]

The creation of the SPCC immediately improved student-community relations in Soweto by providing a channel of communication. But clearly this was not enough. Firstly, the initiative needed to be generalised to a national level if its impact was to be a strong one: accordingly, the SPCC called a National Education Crisis Conference for the end of December. But, secondly, a greater problem was that students needed to be provided with a coherent alternative to the suicidal 'Liberation before Education' line. The SPCC realised that there was only one source from which students might accept direction on this issue: accordingly, at Christmas 1985 an SPCC delegation visited Harare for discussions with the ANC.[126]

The conference, representing a wide range of organisations involved in the education struggle, convened at the University of the Witwatersrand on 28 and 29 December 1985.[127] At the conference it was made clear that the ANC did not support the idea of an indefinite boycott until liberation. A new perspective was offered instead: 'People's Education for People's Power'. What was advocated under this rubric was a struggle over the nature and direction of the education system, rather than a withdrawal from it: those in the education struggle should try to impose their priorities on the state schools rather than opt out of them.

At the same time, this approach would be an integral part of the creation of structures of popular organisation, a component of an overall struggle to break the existing social order. This organisational goal would be pursued by setting up crisis committees around the country, which would create a network of PTSAs: the PTSAs would constitute an alternative educational authority, challenging state control of education. This strategy was approved by the conference. It was decided that there would be a return to school: the state would meanwhile be given three months to respond to a set of educational and political demands (the latter including legalisation of COSAS, ending of the emergency, and release of detainees). A new national body was set up to give leadership to the education struggle: the National Education Crisis Committee (NECC).[128]

These decisions were followed through with considerable energy and success. Mass meetings of parents, teachers and pupils were organised around the country drawing large crowds [129] (one in Port Elizabeth attracted 30,000).[130] This was in itself an important success in rebuilding community-student relations, and in the aftermath the NECC was able to make progress with creating PTSAs.[131] The mass meetings supported the NECC proposal that students should return to school on 28 January, rather than the official opening date of the 8th.[132] The return was a considerable vindication of the NECC. While few students in urban schools were back by the 8th, the bulk of students did return toward the end of the month.[133] The NECC thus succeeded to some extent in breaking the grip of 'immediatism' and the idea that the boycott was a principle. Another important achievement was that ATASA withdrew from state education bodies on which it sat, and began to support political calls to action.[134]

At the end of March, the NECC sought to consolidate the progress made by holding a conference in Durban. The event began dramatically; delegates were attacked by vigilantes (probably members of Buthelezi's Inkatha Movement); however the delegates not only drove off their assailants, but killed two of them into the bargain.[135] Despite dissatisfaction with the State's response to their demands, the delegates decided on a continuation of the return to school.[136] This was surely a wise decision: a renewed national boycott would certainly have had the same fragmenting effect as had the experiences of the previous year.

In an important keynote speech by Zwelakhe Sisulu, the People's Education strategy was forcefully restated: the need to unite all sectors of the community; challenging of state control over education and the transformation of schools into zones controlled by the popular movement; the integral connection of these processes to a wider challenge to state power.[137] The emphasis was on giving practical effect to the idea of People's Education. There was also an initiative to revive COSAS, with plans for mass action on the question of its banning to take place on 16 June .[138]

This account should not create the impression that it was a simple matter for the NECC to implement its policies. Youth activists had been steeped in 'immediatist' politics over a long period, and they were unlikely to change their attitudes easily, especially as the NECC could not deliver any quick and easy victories. There was some resistance to the return to school, even from student delegates at the conferences.[139] Moreover, given the lack of a national student organisation after the COSAS banning, the NECC had difficulty establishing local level communication with students.[140] There was also a lack of appreciation amongst some students and radical teachers of the need for a broad alliance of teachers: some students continued to humiliate their teachers,[141] while some activists opposed ATASA's participation in NECC,[142] which did not contribute to bolstering the NECC's approach.

Given the tensions and suspicions which thus abounded and also the continued presence of troops in the townships, it was not surprising that the return to school began to disintegrate in parts of the country. By March there were boycotts in a number of areas, particularly in the Southern Transvaal[143] and in the Durban region.[144] There was also a distinct spreading of student boycott activity into the Northern and Eastern Transvaal;[145] although rural areas remained far quieter than urban ones as a whole, some pockets of militant activism developed. Thus while the NECC's return to school held nationally, it was crumbling in some key areas. Moreover the unsettled conditions meant that in many areas where students were in school, they were not actually pursuing their studies,[146] which made even alternative education programmes difficult to organise.

A less decisive, but nevertheless important problem which the NECC could not solve was that of relations between UDF and NF student groups. NF student and other groups attended the first NECC conference but withdrew from it before the end.[147] When the second NECC conference was held, the NF held its national conference at the same time, also in Durban, and made independent calls for mass action on dates different to those put forward at the NECC.[148] There was a measure of responsibility on both sides for this situation.

The NECC was overwhelmingly UDF-orientated in its policies and composition, and this clearly made it a difficult environment for the NF to operate in. Some activists subjected creative educational work being done by non-UDF organisations to vicious criticisms, as if they had a monopoly on 'Peoples' Education'. But the NF's decision to withdraw from NECC suggests a failure to recognise the extent to which the NECC had obtained a grip over the mass movement on education. Whatever the merits or otherwise of the NF's critique of the NECC, most of the forces they thought that they were addressing were in fact with the NECC and its UDF allies. The belief that the NF could 'go around' this mass movement was thus naïve. The failure to create a fully united education movement, for which sectarianism on both sides was to blame, had some sad consequences; feuding between UDF and NF youth groups continued;[149] while in the Western Cape WECSAC disintegrated due to sectarian conflicts.[150]

At this stage of the conflict there was a degree of uncertainty as to how the drama would unfold. The state was itself giving double messages as to how it would respond to the mass movements' demands. This reflected a debate which was raging within the National Party leadership as to what was the right combination of restructuring and repression needed to bring the situation under control. It seems that the security establishment insisted that 'order' had to be restored before 'reform' could continue; while others favoured a combination of force with practical changes in policy which could generate some support for the regime.

During the early part of the year the NECC was able to negotiate with Deputy Minister Sam De Beer, a leading light in the conciliatory faction, and a number of government leaders dropped hints that a degree of change in education policy was possible.[151] However, around April, the hard-liners seem to have won the battle in the cabinet. Negotiations were refused, NECC officials began to be arrested, and a course was set by the state for the proclamation of the State of Emergency, which came in June.[152]

Meanwhile in the 'homelands', the degree of flexibility shown by De Beer was not manifested by their local 'governments'. The homeland education departments refused to talk to NECC.[153] In addition, they increasingly unleashed vigilante gangs on students. The most spectacular examples of this were in Kwandebele where students who had played a leading role in opposing the creation of an 'independent' homeland were attacked by 'Mbokotho',[154] and in Natal, where Inkatha supporters cracked down on the youth. The consequence was that the NECC was unable to establish any structures within the 'homelands'.[155]

The declaration of the second, national, State of Emergency in June 1986 put paid to the last vestiges of restraint in the state's handling of the education crisis. Detentions of NECC leaders were carried out on a wide scale. The schools, which were on holiday at the time, had their re-opening delayed until mid-July. It was announced that all students would have to re-register and would be issued with identification, and that other new security measures would be introduced at the schools.[156] This led to renewed boycott activity, centred on the Rand and in the Eastern Cape. Distinct patterns of a regional kind emerged: in the Eastern Cape many students refused to register;[157] on the Rand they generally did return to school, but refused to participate in normal schooling.[158] Many of those who returned to school burnt their new ID cards.[159] Clashes between students and police broke out once again.[160] By October there was considerable boycott activity amongst re-registered students.[161]

The State stuck to its hard line: the over 300,000 students who refused to register were excluded from school.[162] The DET closed some 73 schools at which boycotts were endemic, the majority of them in the Eastern Cape.[163] Despite this situation, the NECC had succeeded in convincing the majority of students to organise themselves within the schools rather than move back to indefinite boycotts. They encouraged students to write their end of year exams, and rejected the actions of groups of youths who attacked examinees.[164]

In the prevailing situation the issue of 'People's Education' became crucial. It was through the promise of a struggle to impose an alternative education system that students had been persuaded to return to school. The idea of People's Education had been exactly what the student movement required to respond to the circumstances of 1985. By emphasising that the school system could be an arena of struggle it had re-orientated students away from a self-destructive cycle of continual boycotts. By placing the question of what kind of education system was desired by the mass of the population on the table, it opened the way for creative political initiatives in the education field. But the idea suffered from considerable confusion in its implementation. Partly, this was because of a lack of clarity in the definition of 'People's Education' on the part of its proponents.

Definitions of People's Education oscillated between what I would call a 'practical perspective' and an 'ultimatist perspective'. The practical perspective recognised that it was impossible for the NECC to provide an educational service for millions of students outside of the DET structures: People's Education was to be fought for inside the schools. This was a strategy which it was genuinely possible to implement. As Vusi Khanyile of NECC explained:

> . . . the state must continue financing education, providing and maintaining the necessary infrastructure. . . . What we reject is the authoritarian structure of the DET, the content of its curriculum and the teaching methods employed. We must be sure that we can formulate an alternative in all these areas.[165]

Alternatives had to be prepared 'that we can begin to introduce in schools where the DET's authority has collapsed.'[166]

The ultimatist perspective, on the other hand, put forward the promise of creating new People's Schools completely outside the structures of the DET.[167] This view sometimes put forward by popular leaders, and spontaneously taken up by sections of school students, was attractive in that it implied the creation of a wholly new schooling system untainted by 'Bantu Education'. But it was utterly unrealistic. The NECC was in no position to provide teachers, accommodation and educational materials for large numbers of school students. The rhetoric of the ultimatist perspective tended to create the unrealistic expectation that a new People's Education system could simply be set into place.

This uncertainty in the definition of People's Education contributed to the difficulties in establishing definite People's Education programmes. A secretariat was established in April to coordinate such programmes. Because it was important to give this body political credibility, it was felt that it should not consist of educationists in a narrow sense.[168] However the composition of the five members — one was a journalist and three were radical religious leaders and theologians, all of whom had a high political profile — was not guaranteed to provide either rapid results or expertise in the field of secondary education.[169] Unrealistic promises that People's Education would be implemented in July did not help matters.

It was not until the last quarter of the year that working groups were activated to prepare People's Education study materials. These were planned to be ready in January 1987: they would provide study material sufficient for two afternoons a week.[170] An area which was not yet addressed was how the programmes would be taught. While some NECC leaders recognised the potential key role of teachers in People's Education,[171] it was not clear how this would be established. While the NECC stressed participatory, non-authoritarian learning, the teaching profession was steeped in authoritarian practice. There was no indication how this was going to be changed.

Obviously the conditions under which the NECC was working were extremely difficult and dangerous, and its activities were remarkable considering the circumstances. Nevertheless, there was clearly a dangerous discrepancy between the large promises of the 'ultimatist perspective' and the modest reality of what it was possible for NECC to deliver. It was only because large numbers of students had grasped the realistic perspective which the NECC generally put forward, that they were not stampeded back to mass boycotts. They had understood that the People's Education battle would be a long one. Despite the difficult conditions, students in some parts of the country battled to continue with the construction of PTSAs.[172]

The final vindication of the NECC's line did not come until the beginning of the next school year, in January 1987. Despite various state measures which were introduced to ban People's Education activities,[173] students engaged in a disciplined return to school.[174] Although this may in part have been contributed to by state intimidation and battle-weariness, it seems that in the centres of student organisation it was a definite tactical decision based on a People's Education perspective. Students were opting to wage their battle within and from the school. Some have charged that the NECC has acted as a kind of bureaucratic imposition on students which represents middle-class interests, and restrains their natural militancy.[175] This argument is far from convincing.

The way that the student movement largely operated in 1985 had led to division of the oppressed communities and in fact weakened student organisation itself. It was essential to create unity between students and the wider community, and to give the students a practical political perspective. In the face of the most enormous obstacles, the NECC — through its line of People's Education — largely succeeded in doing that during 1986-7. This was an impressive and, indeed, a historic achievement.

NOTES

1. J. Hyslop, 'State education policy and the social reproduction of the urban African working class 1955-76: the case of the Southern Transvaal', *Journal of Southern African Studies*, forthcoming, 1987.

SCHOOL STUDENT MOVEMENTS AND STATE EDUCATION POLICY 205

2. C. Bundy, 'Schools and revolution', *New Society*, 10 January 1986, p.53.
3. See the remarks by Hermann Giliomee, *Cape Times*, 2 November 1985; C. Bundy, 'Street sociology and pavement politics: aspects of youth/student resistance in Cape Town, 1985', History Workshop paper, University of the Witwatersrand, 1987.
4. Bundy (1987), *op. cit.*, p.8.
5. *Ibid.*, pp.3-4.
6. H. Lunn, 'Antecedents of the music and popular culture of the African post-1976 generation', MA thesis, University of the Witwatersrand, 1986, pp.197-206.
7. J. Kane-Berman, *South Africa: The Method in the Madness* (London: Pluto, 1979), pp.103-4; T. Lodge, *Black Politics in South Africa Since 1945* (Johannesburg: Ravan, 1983), p.323.
8. Bundy (1987), *op. cit.*, pp.4-5, 12, 20.
9. *Idem*, p.12.
10. *Idem*, pp.31, 8.
11. Hyslop, *op. cit.*
12. J. Hyslop, 'Food, authority and politics: student riots in South African schools 1945-1976', *Africa Perspective*, forthcoming, 1987.
13. Lodge (1983), *op. cit.*, p.328.
14. Kane-Berman, *op. cit.*, pp.2-5.
15. Lodge (1987), *op. cit.*, pp.328-9; R. Levin, 'Black education, class struggle and the dynamics of change in South Africa', *Africa Perspective*, No.17, Spring 1980, pp.32-3.
16. Levin, *op. cit.*, pp.32-3; Kane-Berman, *op. cit.*, p.127.
17. Levin, *op. cit.*, pp.32-3.
18. J. Davies, 'Politics, schooling and resistance in South Africa', unpublished paper, 1986; B. Hirson, *Year of Fire, Year of Ash* (London: Zed Press, 1979); Lodge (1983), *op. cit.*, pp.330-6.
19. Kane-Berman, *op. cit.*
20. *Ibid.*, p.148.
21. See, *inter alia*, Hirson, *op. cit.*
22. Lodge (1983), *op. cit.*, p.333.
23. *Ibid.*, p.339.
24. L. Chisholm, 'From revolt to a search for alternatives', *Work in Progress*, No.42, May 1986, p.18.
25. P. Randall, *Little England on the Veld: The English Private School in South Africa* (Johannesburg: Ravan, 1982), pp.192-3.
26. A. Bird, 'Black adult night school movements on the Witwatersrand 1920-80', *Africa Perspective*, No.17, Spring 1980, p.83.
27. Davies, *op. cit.*, p.16; Chisholm (1986), *op. cit.*, p.15; M. Bot, *School Boycotts 1984: The Crisis in African Education* (Durban: Indicator Project, 1985), p.16.
28. Bot, *op. cit.*, p.17.
29. Chisholm, *op. cit.*, p.15; Bot, *op. cit.*, p.16.
30. F. Molteno, 'Reflections on resistance — aspects of the 1980 students boycott', in M. Lawrence (ed.), *Kenton-at-the-Stadt 1983 Conference Proceedings* (Mafikeng: University of Bophuthatswana, 1984), p.48.
31. *Ibid.*, pp.35-49.
32. *Idem.*
33. Bot, *op. cit.*, p.16.
34. B. Pottinger, 'The Eastern Cape boycotts: where crisis has become a way of life', *Frontline*, March 1981, pp.18-24.
35. Bot, *op. cit.*, p.16.
36. L. Chisholm and P. Christie, 'Restructuring in education', *South African Review 1* (Johannesburg: Ravan, 1983), pp.254-5.
37. R. Southall, 'African capitalism in contemporary South Africa', *Journal of Southern African Studies*, Vol.7, No.1, October 1980, pp.38-70.

38. Chisholm and Christie, *op. cit.*, pp.254-5.
39. W. Cobbett, D. Glaser, D. Hindson and M. Swilling, 'Regionalisation, federalism and the reconstruction of the South African state', *South African Labour Bulletin*, Vol.10, No.5, March-April 1985, pp.87-116.
40. See Chisholm and Christie, *op. cit.*
41. V. Brown, 'Our debt to DET?', *Sash*, Vol.27, No.4, February 1985, p.21.
42. Bundy (1986), *op. cit.*, p.53; M. Orkin, 'The black matric rate: points for discussion', unpublished paper, 1985.
43. Bundy (1986), *op. cit.*, p.53.
44. Brown, *op. cit.*, p.21.
45. Chisholm and Christie, *op. cit.*, p.259.
46. F. de Clerq, 'Some recent trends in Bophuthatswana: commuters and restructuring in education', *South African Review 2* (Johannesburg: Ravan, 1984(a)); F. de Clerq, 'Education and training in the homelands: a separate development? A case study of Bophuthatswana', *Africa Perspective*, No.24, 1984(b), pp.20-40.
47. De Clerq (1984b), *op. cit.*, p.27.
48. Chisholm and Christie, *op. cit.*, p.27.
49. *SASPU Focus*, Vol.3, No.2, November 1984.
50. K. Hartshorne, 'Can separate mean equal? A commentary on the White Paper on education', *Indicator*, January 1984.
51. Davies, *op. cit.*, pp.16, 28.
52. Chisholm (1986), *op. cit.*, pp.15-16; *The Star*, 29 August 1985.
53. J. Shindler, 'African matric results 1955 to 1983', *SAIRR Topical Briefing*, 1984; M. Orkin (1985), *op. cit.*
54. *SASPU Focus*, *op. cit.*
55. *The Star* 29 August 1985; Chisholm (1986), *op. cit.*, p.16; Bot, *op. cit.*, p.2.
56. 'Why a national day of protest', NUSAS Projects Committee leaflet, Johannesburg, 30 May 1984; *SASPU Focus*, *op. cit.*
57. SAIRR, *Race Relations Survey* (Johannesburg: SAIRR, 1985), pp.68-9, 671-2.
58. *SASPU Focus*, *op. cit.*; Bot, *op. cit.*, p.10.
59. *SASPU Focus*, *op. cit.*
60. Davies, *op. cit.*, p.9.
61. *SASPU Focus*, *op. cit.*
62. *Idem.*
63. Chisholm (1986), *op. cit.*, p.17; Davies, *op. cit.*, p.19; M. Swilling, 'Stayaways, urban protest and the state', *South African Review 3* (Johannesburg: Ravan, 1986), p.35.
64. Davies, *op. cit.*, p.21.
65. *SASPU Focus*, *op. cit.*; SAIRR, *op. cit.*, p.70.
66. SAIRR, *op. cit.*, p.70.
67. Compare Bot, *op. cit.*, p.1 and Indicator, 'A chronology of township unrest', *Indicator*, Vol.2, No.4, January 1985, p.7.
68. N. Alexander, 'After the August elections', in N. Alexander, *Sow the Wind: Contemporary Speeches* (Johannesburg: Skotaville Publishers, 1985), p.172.
69. Indicator (1985), *op. cit.*, p.7.
70. Bot, *op. cit.*, p.1.
71. Indicator (1985), *op. cit.*, p.7.
72. Labour Monitoring Group (LMG), 'Report: the November stay-away', *SALB*, Vol.10, No.6, May 1985, pp.74-100.
73. LMG, *op. cit.*, p.83; Swilling, *op. cit.*, pp.27-8.
74. *Idem.*
75. LMG, *op. cit.*, p.88.
76. Swilling (1986), *op. cit.*, p.23; LMG, *op. cit.*, p.88.
77. Swilling, *op. cit.*, pp.36-7.
78. *Ibid.*, pp.39-40.

79. SAIRR, *Race Relations Survey* (Johannesburg: SAIRR, 1986), p.389.
80. *Ibid.*, pp.388-95.
81. *Ibid.*, p.456.
82. *Ibid.*, pp.440-4.
83. *Ibid.*, pp.386-7.
84. Bundy (1987), *op. cit.*, pp.18-19.
85. Bundy (1987), *op. cit.*, p.30; Davies, *op. cit.*, p.24.
86. *The Star*, 14 August 1985.
87. *Eastern Province Herald*, 16 March 1985.
88. *The Star*, 17 September 1985.
89. *Rand Daily Mail*, 25 April 1985; *Sunday Mirror*, 12 May 1985.
90. *The Star*, 7 August 1985; *City Press*, 6 October 1985.
91. *The Star*, 14 August 1985.
92. *The Star*, 23 August 1985, records the arrest of 500 children at a Diepkloof school, while *The Sowetan*, 23 August 1985, points out that some of these were as young as seven. *The Star*, 13 September 1985 records the arrest of 746 students in White City Jabavu.
93. *The Sowetan*, 1 April 1986.
94. *Idem.*
95. *The Citizen*, 3 May 1985; M. Bot, 'The future of African education: two opposing strategies', *Indicator*, Vol.4, No.2, Spring 1986, p.48.
96. *The Citizen*, *op. cit.*, Bot, *op. cit.*, p.48; K. Hartshorne 'Back to basics', *Leadership*, Vol.5, No.5, 1986, pp.64-6.
97. SAIRR, *op. cit.*, p.363.
98. *The Citizen*, 3 December 1986.
99. Bundy (1986), *op. cit.*, p.29.
100. *The Star*, 7 December 1985.
101. *City Press*, 8 December 1985.
102. I. Obery, 'People's education: creating a democratic future', interview with Ihron Rensburg, *Work in Progress*, No.42, May 1986, p.8.
103. *The Star*, 17 September 1985.
104. Z. Sisulu, 'People's education for people's power', keynote address, 2nd NECC conference, *Transformation*, No.1, 1986, p.113.
105. *The Star*, 10 August 1985.
106. Sisulu, *op. cit.*, p.113.
107. *Idem.*
108. *The Star*, 18 September 1985.
109. Chisholm, *op. cit.*, p.14.
110. *The Star*, 16 October 1985.
111. *The Sowetan*, 3 June 1985; *The Star*, 5 August 1985.
112. SAIRR, *op. cit.*, pp.21-2, 391, 549-50. For a possibly related incident in the Transvaal see *The Star*, 14 August 1985.
113. SAIRR, *op. cit.*, pp.547-9.
114. In a particularly chilling later example, a Sowetan student leader, asked to comment on the killing of the uncle of an NF/AZAPO leader, stated that although his members had not carried out the action they were not responsible for 'the community's anger against AZAPO'. *The Star*, 21 January 1987.
115. K. Hartshorne, 'African matric results: the disintegration of urban education', *Indicator*, Vol.4, No.2, Spring 1986, pp.54-7.
116. *Idem.*
117. *Sunday Mirror*, 26 May 1985.
118. Bundy (1987), *op. cit.*, p.24.
119. Chisholm, *op. cit.*, p.15.
120. Bot, *op. cit.*, p.47.
121. Vusi Khanyile, quoted in *Sowetan*, 29 October 1985.

122. *The Star*, 7 December 1985.
123. J. Campbell, 'No end in sight to schools crisis', *Work in Progress*, No.45, November/December 1986, pp.15-17.
124. *The Sowetan*, 29 October 1985.
125. *City Press*, 17 Nov.1985; J. Muller, 'People's education', *South African Review 4* (Johannesburg: Ravan, 1987).
126. H. Zille, 'People's education: a lost opportunity', *Die Suid Afrikaan*, Spring/Summer 1987, pp.25-8.
127. *Report of National Consultative Conference on Crisis in Education* (Johannesburg: SPCC, 1986).
128. Muller, *op. cit.*; Zille, *op. cit.*; Obery, *op. cit.*; '*Report. . .*' (1986), *op. cit.*
129. *The Star*, 6 January 1986.
130. *Weekly Mail*, 27 March 1986.
131. Sisulu, *op. cit.*, p.109.
132. *The Star*, 6 January 1986.
133. *The Star*, 8 January 1986; Campbell, *op. cit.*, p.15.
134. Sisulu, *op. cit.*, p.109; Hartshorne, 'Back to basics' (1986), *op. cit.*
135. *The Star*, 31 March 1986.
136. *Idem.*
137. Sisulu, *op. cit.*
138. Obery, *op. cit.*, p.13; *Weekly Mail*, 4 April 1986.
139. *Weekly Mail*, 4 April 1986.
140. Obery, *op. cit.*, pp.9-10.
141. *Weekly Mail*, 27 March 1986.
142. Obery, *op. cit.*, p.10.
143. Campbell, *op. cit.*, pp.15-16.
144. Anonymous, 'Political conflict and civil unrest in African townships in Natal', *Reality*, September 1986, pp.7-12.
145. Private informants.
146. Hartshorne, 'Back to basics', *op. cit.*, p.67.
147. *The Star*, 30 December 1985.
148. *The Sowetan*, 1 April 1986.
149. *The Sowetan*, 8 April 1986, 5 May 1986.
150. *Weekly Mail*, 16 May 1986.
151. Bot, *op. cit.*, p.52.
152. Muller, *op. cit.*
153. *Weekly Mail*, 27 March 1986.
154. J.A. Yawitch, 'Kwandebele — a rural trojan horse', *Sash*, Vol.29, No.2, August 1986, pp.24-5.
155. Anonymous (1986), *op. cit.*
156. Obery, *op. cit.*, p.12; Bot, *op. cit.*, p.50; *The Star*, 3 July 1986; *The Sowetan*, 7 July 1986.
157. Bot, *op. cit.*, p.50.
158. Bot, *op. cit.*, p.50; *Sunday Star*, 24 Aug. 1986.
159. *City Press*, 20 July 1986; Campbell, *op. cit.*, p.16.
160. *The Star*, 25 Aug. 1986.
161. Campbell, *op. cit.*, p.16.
162. Campbell, *op. cit.*, p.16; *The Star*, 28 July 1986.
163. Muller, *op. cit.*
164. Campbell, *op. cit.*, p.16.
165. V. Khanyile, 'Speech to ASP conference in Pietermaritzburg', unpublished paper, 3 December 1986.
166. *Idem.*
167. Obery, *op. cit.*, p.13; Zille, *op. cit.*, p.28.
168. Obery, *op. cit.*, pp.8-9.

169. *Ibid.,* p.9.
170. Muller, *op. cit.*
171. Obery, *op. cit.,* p.11.
172. Campbell, *op. cit.,* p.18.
173. Muller, *op. cit.*
174. *The Star,* 7 January 1987.
175. *Weekly Mail,* 17 January 1986.

11. Class, Race and the Future of Socialism

J O H N   S A U L

INTRODUCTION

In June 1976 the students of Soweto forced South Africa onto the front pages of the world's newspapers. Subsequently there has been a certain ebb and flow to the resistance in that country, but such has been the growth and consolidation of the forces pressing for change that it is now virtually impossible to keep the issue off those front pages. In this momentous decade, one particularly significant advance has taken place on the trade union front. Of course, the spontaneous resurgence of an increasingly organised working class had already made itself felt several years prior to the 'Soweto uprising', in the dramatic Durban strikes of 1973-74. The launching, in late 1985, of a new trade union central, COSATU, representing over half a million workers, is merely the most recent milestone in this continuing forward thrust. Considerable gains have also occurred on the terrain of political struggle more broadly defined. Not only have South African students remained a potent political force, but a whole panoply of additional organisations have surfaced in the black townships and elsewhere (the numerous 'civic associations', for example). Moreover, such tendencies have begun to find nation-wide, above-ground expression — above all, in the UDF, which first emerged in 1983 to become an umbrella organisation for well over 500 diverse, more localised groupings and a crucial actor in a range of national campaigns. But perhaps the most dramatic development of all has been the revitalisation of the ANC of South Africa. Never entirely moribund after being driven underground and into exile in the early 1960s, the ANC was nonetheless fairly marginal to the events of 1976. Today, thousands more South Africans are identifying with the ANC at each turn of the wheel, and nervous would-be-brokers (from the business community and elsewhere) are beating a path to the Lusaka headquarters. In fact, the ANC has reestablished itself as far and away the single most important force within the South African resistance movement.

How should we evaluate these and other actors in South Africa's revolutionary drama? What role will each have to play — and in what combination with each other — in the ongoing struggle to overthrow the apartheid state? What is likely to be the import of their presence in post-apartheid society — in determining the future of socialism in South Africa, for example? This chapter will address itself to some of these questions, primarily focusing on the role of the ANC. To answer them is, of course, no easy task. Certainly we must avoid the kind of glib and wildly speculative scenario-mongering that too often passes for analysis in South Africanist circles. Some clearing of the theoretical ground will be necessary as well. Over the years the Congress movement has produced a widely used conceptual apparatus of its own, but it is one which can obscure as much as it illuminates. Even more misleading has been a recent tendency, on the South African left, to talk in terms of a fissure between 'populist' and 'workerist' currents within the resistance movement. These (and other) terms too readily lend themselves to the purposes of demagogy rather than analysis — and may also help blunt revolutionary practice.

THE TERRAIN OF STRUGGLE

Before taking a hard look at the resistance movement, we must carefully examine the terrain upon which it seeks to map its course.[1] Most general, but also perhaps most fundamental, is the unique manner in which the structure of racial oppression forged by colonial conquest has interacted with the structure of capitalist exploitation produced by the dramatic transformation of South Africa's economy in this century. There has been considerable debate about the precise form of this interaction, and we shall see that it has implications for any attempt to characterise the composition of the movement (national-cum-racial liberation? class struggle?) that must form up to oppose the system. Here it bears emphasising that for extended periods of time in South Africa racial hierarchisation and capitalist relations of production have been mutually reinforcing. Thus, capitalist development has more than once breathed fresh life into the racial hierarchy, shaping it to its ends around the turn of the century, for example, the better to guarantee supplies of cheap labour in the crucial mining sector. For many analysts the term 'racial capitalism' has seemed useful in elucidating the complex nature of such a system.

It need come as no surprise that this linkage between racial domination and capitalist exploitation is as potentially contradictory as it has been mutually reinforcing. Indeed, one important dimension of the various crises in South Africa has been, precisely, the surfacing of a real strain between these two aspects. Severe crises must generally be resolved in one of two ways: either by revolution from below or by 'formative' action on the part of the dominant classes, designed to renovate and consolidate their rule. In the 1940s the response to crisis was a marked intensification of racial oppression — the apartheid option — which capital came to live with quite comfortably after an initial period in which at least some of its 'fractions' were tempted by other directions. In the 1980s, in contrast, the stripping away of certain racist dimensions of the system — albeit formidably difficult to achieve — has begun to seem far more urgent a requirement to many in such circles.

In part it is formidably difficult to achieve because the racist project has taken on a distinct life of its own, rooted in the very 'materiality' of racism in the South African setting. For, as noted, racism and much of the concrete structure of racial oppression in South Africa stem from the global expansion of Western capitalism and from the fact of colonial conquest that historically privileged the white population. Moreover, quite specific class forces and class alliances within the white population — fractions of capital (some more than others), many members of the white working class, bureaucratic strata — have developed vested and eminently material interests in their privileged positions within the racial hierarchy *per se*. Finally, these processes have given substance to certain historically resonant ideologies (of racial superiority and 'Afrikaner nationalism', for example) and congealed political practices, in various state apparatuses and the National Party itself, which retain relative autonomy and have social impact.

Under such circumstances, it is not surprising that there is no one-to-one correspondence between some 'logic of capital' and specific state initiatives. Historically, for example, important fractions of capital have found policies like the job colour bar to be a fetter on their manipulation of labour, and in recent years there has been an even more broadly based unease within the camp of capital about the costs of apartheid. It is true that the economic crisis South Africa has been experiencing since the 1970s is not entirely self-inflicted. Given the country's extreme dependence on the world economy — as exporter of minerals, secondary manufactures and agricultural products, as importer of oil and a wide range of technology and machinery — it has also reflected the negative impact of global recession. Nonetheless, many of the most overtly racist dimensions of South Africa's 'racial capitalism' have begun to be seen as contributory elements of the crisis, constraining the size of the domestic market and the supply of black skilled and semi-skilled labour.

AN ORGANIC CRISIS

There has been a movement — 'reform' — on some of these economic fronts. Unfortunately for power holders in South Africa, however, these problems are not merely 'economic' in the narrow sense. What they face is an 'organic crisis', defined by a rising tide of mass resistance that has placed the entire racial capitalist system in jeopardy. Not that economic and political dimensions are easily disentangled here. Thus economic crisis — the rising level of black unemployment, spiralling inflation — has fed black resistance, which has in turn fuelled the economic instability that has begun to make South Africa appear a 'bad risk' to bankers and industrialists and further mobilised the international sanctions lobby.

Ultimately, defence of the capitalist system is a political task, and here too many capitalists are increasingly uneasy with the apartheid solution. Its distinct disadvantage is that it etches the exploitative class relations characteristic of capitalism, quite literally, in black and white, for all to see. As Zac de Beer, a director of Anglo American, recently put it: 'We all understand how years of apartheid have caused many blacks to reject the economic as well as the political system. But we must simply get the facts across. We dare not allow the baby of free enterprise to be thrown out with the bath water of apartheid.' Such far-sighted capitalists can also theorise an alternative: a deracialised capitalism (paralleling the most stable elsewhere in the world) where class, not colour, is the crucial determinant in the social hierarchy and where the system's legitimacy is actually underpinned by 'bourgeois democratic' electoral procedures. Yet there is no consensus among capitalists as to how the transition to a democratically sanctioned capitalism might be realised. Nor is this merely a matter of the difficulty they might expect to experience in moving such an option through the white polity. Even the most canny of businessmen seem far from confident that the process of deracialising and democratising capitalism could be sufficiently fine-tuned as to tame, not feed, the revolutionary mobilisation currently taking place. Thus Anglo American chairman, Gavin Relly, for all his protestations against apartheid, has time and again rejected the notion of majority rule, of 'one person, one vote, in a united South Africa'. Capital's programmatic vacuum regarding the question of political power merely strengthens the apartheid state's ability to ram through its own 'solution' and to retain, *faute de mieux*, its central position as guarantor of capitalist hegemony.[2]

Of course, this proposed solution has not been notably successful, at times giving the appearance of a mere floundering about. But the central premise of current ruling-class practice has been asserted more clearly by the apartheid state than by the various direct representatives of capital. As the 1986 Emergency has shown even more starkly, this involves a refusal of any real give on political power and a willingness to use severe repression to make that refusal stick. Politicians do try to present such repression in a more benign light, suggesting, in the words of Constitutional Affairs Minister Chris Heunis, that 'I need a shield so that the reform process can go ahead; that's why I supported the Emergency'! But reform remains more a shell-game than anything else. The much-heralded removal of the pass laws has proven, on closer examination, to involve mainly new variations on the familiar theme of movement controls; the promised reinstatement of citizenship to those from whom it had earlier been stripped was found not to include the millions of residents of the already 'independent' bantustans. In the political sphere 'concessions' to Africans have boiled down merely to the proposed cooptation of some members of the African elite into a new, largely formal, central council and, at the local level, into new Regional Service Councils. Perhaps such initiatives can be seen as building-blocks for some confederal or consociational political settlement, to be introduced as a last-ditch effort to derail a more genuine democratisation; hence, too, the possible significance of the on-going 'KwaNatal *ndaba*', a set of negotiations between Chief Gatsha Buthelezi and his white counterparts in Natal which is seeking to hammer out some kind of multi-racial, intra-elite sharing of power. Yet the Nationalist government is still very far indeed from manifesting even this degree of tactical flexibility regarding fundamental questions.

'Divide and rule' has long been a staple of state strategy in South Africa, and the reinforcing of vertical divisions along ethnic lines has been one of the key objectives of the bantustans, for example. Even more attention is now paid to heightening the importance of *horizontal*, class divisions among blacks. The tricameral parliament, designed to reinforce racial stratification in the political arena, has been one example. In the African townships, however, community councils were supposed to give an urban African elite some equivalent of the semi-privileged status open to bantustan leaderships — a ploy, which, needless to say, has had the distinct tendency to blow up in the faces of apartheid planners, reinforcing rather than undermining the thrust of popular confrontation with the system. The same is likely to prove true of more recent variations on the theme.

At the same time it must be emphasised that these moves — as well as novel concessions made to African businessmen — do have some divisive impact. Certainly most Bantustan leaders have turned out to be gendarmes for the apartheid regime. In the urban areas, recent evidence suggests, the black vigilante movements which have emerged to counter radical mobilisation have taken their lead from privileged urban blacks (as well as from the South African Police), even when their actual 'foot-soldiers' have been more lumpen elements. The evident intention is to consolidate the new elites as junior partners in apartheid. Yet, in the absence of a strategy of 'bourgeois-democratic' cooptation, the limited nature of the concessions seems more likely to ensure that members of the elite who are prepared to cooperate will be confirmed as, at best, visible collaborators in outright repression.[3] Here lies the rub for the apartheid state — and, indeed, for capital, yoked as it still is to that state. For repression, divide-and-rule tactics and occasional concessions do little more than keep the lid on things, with varying degrees of success. They offer no real promise of undercutting economic and political contradictions or of preempting popular struggle. The resistance burns on, sanctions lobbies remain active and even relatively effective abroad, and business confidence, local and international, continues to sag. At the most, state repression has gained some ground in disorganising the resistance movement and in slowing the pace of change. It also tends to freeze potential tensions within the block of dominant classes, so that any business unease with the *status quo* finds primarily verbal, not practical, expression.

LINES OF FISSURE

As the resistance movement forces a transition to some kind of democratic resolution of South Africa's crisis, tensions and fissures within the dominant bloc will become more salient and determinative. Capital, now to a very considerable extent locked into the apartheid state, would then increasingly be freed to play another kind of game — in effect, freed by the popular movement to fight on new terrain for a bourgeois-democratic, rather than a revolutionary democratic-cum-socialist, denouement to the liberation struggle. Yet the fact that we are still some distance from the post-apartheid phase affects the nature of the resistance movement and poses a number of sharp dilemmas. Thus the need to bring considerably more pressure to bear against the state, in order to facilitate the transition to democracy, may have the effect of freezing into place potentially problematic alliances within the movement's own camp.

In the course of the transition, however, one can anticipate that divisions within the black population will become even more crucial than they are now, pulling apart those whose class interests sometimes appear to cohere around the common platform of opposition to racial oppression. The resistance movement in South Africa thus confronts a peculiar variant of the classic revolutionary dilemma much discussed by, among others, Marx and the pre-1917 Bolsheviks. How to overthrow the structures of racial oppression (a functional equivalent of the 'bourgeois democratic revolution') while positioning oneself favourably to win the struggle against capitalist exploitation (the proletarian revolution)? The dilemma is no mere abstraction. Certainly the more 'progressive' sections of capital (Zac de Beer, quoted above, is an example), as well as innumerable think-tanks around the world, have begun to reflect carefully about moulding a post-apartheid future, even if they appear paralysed by the political exigencies of the moment. This is one powerful reason why socialists within the resistance movement should be strengthening themselves to confront capital. Nor can they ignore the fact that the question of how the movement will deal with capital is already a focus of class struggle *within* its own ranks — and will be even more in the future.

It is often pointed out that urgent imperatives spring from the fact that, in the struggle against the apartheid state *per se*, the movement is ripe, the future is now. There is a strong temptation, therefore, to give special primacy to the struggle against racial oppression and to seek to be as inclusive as possible in expanding the movement's ranks — even to look for tactical advantages in drawing closer to the surface tensions within the dominant bloc. (This could mean, in particular, encouraging capital — considered, momentarily, as a potential quasi-ally — to be much bolder in pushing the pace of political transformation.) There is also a temptation to pitch the case for liberation to the lowest common denominator of anti-apartheid sentiment in Western countries — the better to win broad support there and hence to isolate the South African government. We shall see that such considerations are the stuff of current debate in and about the resistance movement. The theory and practice of balancing and synchronising the struggles against racial oppression and capitalism: this is the issue which lies close to the heart of the South African struggle.

THE ANC AND TERMS OF RESISTANCE

A detailed history of the reemergence of the resistance movement since the early 1970s would evidently be beyond the scope of this chapter. The five key components — the trade unions, the various initiatives of students and youth, the civic associations and other township-based organisations, the broad national above-ground coalitions (most notably the UDF), the resurgent ANC — would each require full-scale treatment, as a preliminary to a much needed assessment of how the movement as a whole seeks to deal with the complicated dual challenge identified in the previous section. Given the limitations of space, however, we will focus our attention primarily on the role within the movement, indeed very much at the centre of the movement, of the ANC. For it may well be that, whatever the range of other actors which are to be involved in the South African drama, it is the conceptualisations and practices developed by the ANC which will weigh most in defining any future that socialism may have in South Africa.

The stage was set for the ANC's resurgence, since 1976, by its achievements in the years of exile. The most important of these may have been the mere fact of managing to survive more or less intact — in sharp contrast to the Pan-Africanist Congress's pronounced tendency to self-destruct. But the ANC also firmed up a strong network of international contacts, not least from Eastern-bloc countries who were prepared to support it militarily. Then, as the situation heated up inside and as the ANC-in-exile gained somewhat easier access to South Africa with the victory of liberation movements in border countries, the ANC could dramatically underscore its presence on the scene by means of 'armed propaganda' (sabotage actions and the like). These, in turn, helped to revive the memory of the ANC's historical centrality in the resistance movement. Many older people with personal histories of ANC involvement began to resurface within the above-ground popular organisations of the late 1970s and early 1980s and many younger people found themselves pulled in the same direction. The establishment of an ANC underground designed for political as well as military purposes, and linking together inside and outside, began to give further coherence to the ANC presence — although, self-evidently, this is a more difficult variable to measure.

Equally important in raising its own profile has been the ANC's considerable skill in divining the public mood and then helping to give added resonance and concrete national programmatic expression to popular aspirations. Witness the role the ANC has played in the definition of such focuses and formulae as the anti-SAIC and anti-Republic Day campaigns, the Free Mandela initiative and the attack upon the tricameral parliament, the widely-publicised emphases upon, first, 'ungovernability' and then 'from ungovernability to people's power', and the successful attempt to bring the Freedom Charter back into prominence as a crucial touchstone of the movement's demands. Although the precise nature and extent of the ANC's interface with the UDF is difficult to determine, it has also been of obvious importance in giving visible, above-ground institutional form to the ANC's initiatives; the consultative role which the ANC has apparently played *vis-à-vis* the NECC provides another example. It would appear that, in many of these activities and campaigns, the ANC has been responding to assertions already bubbling up in the communities, at least as much as it has been stimulating popular energies. This is not necessarily a point of criticism. Indeed the organisation's principal task at the moment seems to be to move past the phase of armed propaganda and to develop greater political and military back-up and coordination for resistance based in the townships and bantustans. This has not proven to be an easy task, and the brute capacity of the state to bottle up the challenge (though not crush it outright) has not yet been deeply threatened.

The ANC's visible centrality in South Africa, and its growing presence in the international arena, have lent great importance to the problematic that it developed to comprehend and guide the transition. As is well known, the initial premise is a characterisation of the situation in South Africa as 'colonialism of a special type'. The ANC has sought through this formulation to give weight to the fact of racial oppression which, as we have seen, continues to be a cardinal feature of the South African social formation. For many within the Congress Alliance, moreover, the existence of colonialism of a special type necessarily entails a political strategy of 'two-stage revolution':

> The reality is that the chief content of the present phase of our revolution is the national liberation of black people. It is actually impossible for South Africa to advance to socialism before the national liberation of the black oppressed nation . . . . [To] proceed and say that the same nationalist struggle is also socialist in content is to make real confusion.[4]

From this perspective, the very use of the concept 'racial capitalism' is deemed to overstress class factors and to signal an insidious assault on the fundamental principles of both the ANC and the SACP. As Nyawuza has written in *The African Communist*:

> The real . . . aim of these new Marxists is to reject the *two-stage* theory of our revolution. To do this successfully, they have to question the validity of the thesis of 'colonialism of a special type' and then proceed to demolish the national-democratic stage thesis and question the role and genuineness of the non-proletarian forces in the struggle. They want to change the orientation and the language and all we stand for.[5]

A similar point has been made in a rather different way by one senior ANC spokesperson (Thabo Mbeki): 'The ANC is not a socialist party. It has never pretended to be one, it has never said it was, and it is not trying to be. It will not become one by decree or for the purpose of pleasing its "left" critics.'[6]

Of course, the ANC is also capable of adding a much sharper left-wing edge to its position, up to and including a strong warning against too comfortable a fall-back into the 'colonialism of a special type/two-stage revolution' model. Thus, even in the course of attacking the concept of racial capitalism, Pallo Jordan can acknowledge that 'much of the confusion among our friends in the international community is probably attributable to the imprecise terms our movement's discourse is usually couched in. Though we all employ the formulation, "colonialism of a special type", how many of us have bothered to define it?' In the same context (a review of books by Stephen Gelb and myself and by Sam Nolutshungu) he twins a critique of Gelb's and my 'speculation about the various class forces that constitute the ANC' with a rebuke to Nolutshungu for tending 'to treat the multi-class nature of the liberation movement as unproblematic'![7]

CLASS ANALYSIS

Clearly, such an ANC cadre is walking a tight-rope here, honouring the importance of the nationalist struggle without wishing to ignore the claims of class analysis and class struggle altogether. Take, too, the case of Joe Slovo, a leading cadre of both the ANC and the SACP, writing, like Nyawuza, in *The African Communist*. He uses strong language to criticise (*pace* Nyawuza) any rigid, two-stage model of the South African revolution: he argues that the 'dominant ingredient of later stages must have already begun to mature within the womb of the earlier stage' and that in South Africa there is indeed a certain simultaneity to the struggles 'for social as well as national emancipation'. Moreover, the 'most important' determinant of whether the revolutions will move toward the 'true liberation' which socialism represents is precisely the 'role played by the working class in the alliance of class forces during the first stage of the continuing revolutions'.[8] And what of Thabo Mbeki? It is worthy of note that, in the text quoted above, he immediately qualifies his stark statement that 'the ANC is not a socialist party', emphasising the 'notion of *both* an all-class common front *and* the determined mobilisation of the black proletariat and peasantry'. Indeed, 'the ANC is convinced that within the alliance of democratic forces that will bring about the outcome (i.e. "the defeat and overthrow of the present ruling class and the birth of a new democratic stage"), the black working class must play the leading role, not as an appendage of the petty bourgeoisie but as a conscious vanguard class, capable of advancing and defending its own democratic interests' (socialism?).[9]

Mbeki's attempt to complement the ANC's vocation as a multi-class, multi-racial, 'nationalist' movement against racial oppression with the centrality to the project of the working class is, of course, tension-ridden. But it is not necessarily contradictory. For Mbeki's twin emphases address the need to make sense of the lived simultaneity of the struggles against both racial oppression and capitalist exploitation. And this is a 'simultaneity' which shows no sign of soon disappearing. Thus, the first of these emphases — even in its one-sided 'colonialism of a special type/two-stage revolution' formulations — does take cognisance of the incredible energy which is to be found in the popular rejection of racial oppression in South Africa. It does not seem to be helpful to patronise this kind of consciousness, to dismiss it as being merely and simple-mindedly 'populist', as some left critics of the ANC are inclined to do. Elsewhere Stephen Gelb and I have suggested (following Laclau) that the term 'popular-democratic' captures better the positive thrust that expressions of nationalism, racial consciousness and democratic self-assertion are capable of having in South Africa.[10] Moreover, such popular-democratic assertions can be most effective in mounting the struggle against the anti-apartheid state.

Nor is such an alliance irrelevant to the ongoing effort to keep the struggle against capitalist exploitation on the agenda — both now and in the future, when a transition to socialism comes more concretely onto the agenda in a freshly democratic South Africa. But as Mbeki seems to be suggesting, à la (early) Laclau, much will depend on the role played by the working class in guaranteeing the proletarian-cum-socialist content of the process. We will return in due course to the question of how this proletarian presence is to be grounded and guaranteed. What can be affirmed here is that the establishment of a positive dialectic between 'popular democratic' and 'proletarian' moments is perfectly possible — and perhaps even essential to successful revolution in South Africa. It is on these grounds that one can agree with another point of Mbeki's, when he attacks 'the strange view that national consciousness and national liberation are the deadly enemies of class consciousness and class emancipation'. For the popular-democratic cast of the struggle in South Africa can actually help give a more broadly hegemonic thrust to working-class self-assertion, helping it to transcend economism for example; indeed, this may well have been the case with respect to the increased politicisation of the workers' movement in recent years. At the same time, it may be even more important to emphasise the other side of the coin: the ambiguities of popular-democratic assertions (including 'national consciousness and national liberation'), not least the dangers, so familiar elsewhere in Africa, of the petty bourgeoisie hijacking the struggle and advancing its own interests at the expense of those of the popular classes. It is, to repeat, proletarian assertions that can most effectively keep *socialism* on the agenda, can best demonstrate to all oppressed groups that socialist solutions are in their interest too. As one leading South African trade unionist, David Lewis, has put the point, 'socialism is not an ideology that divides the working class from other oppressed groups'. What is true, however, is that 'the working class leads the struggle'. Why? 'Because it is directly exploited by capitalism and because it is the working class that are capable of fighting the central force of capitalism, namely the rate of profit.'[11]

It is this kind of potentially creative tension which the better ANC formulations seems to exemplify. Of course, one might feel more confident if there were not quite so many texts from that movement that almost exclusively emphasise the popular-democratic side of the equation. At times these seem to be far more defined by the predominance of short-term tactical considerations than by the presence of any underlying revolutionary principles of the sort we have just been discussing. Not that there is a shortage of good reasons for some judicious 'opportunism'. Certainly many with the ANC would argue the wisdom of giving 'popular-democratic' themes most prominence as a possible means of encouraging divisions within the dominant bloc (making capital more rather than less likely to risk change — which it might gamble on then containing). As noted earlier, this can seem a wise course to follow in order to expand the range of international forces inclined to oppose 'apartheid pure and simple' or in order to keep 'on side' a wider range of social groups and classes within South Africa (the ANC's eminently cordial 1986 Lusaka meeting with representatives of the National African Federated Chambers of Commerce (NAFCOC) being, perhaps, a prime example of such a tactic). It is also true that the proletarian emphasis does not subside altogether in most ANC formulations. Yet sometimes it too can appear rather opportunistically invoked — in order to premise positive interactions with trade unions and the left, locally and internationally.

To some extent, then, the weights assigned to the 'popular-democratic' and 'proletarian' themes by various ANC statements and spokespersons will reflect differing hunches about the tactical 'mix' most appropriate to any given moment of the struggle. But another layer of complexity needs to be added here. For there is every reason to believe that the 'mixes' will also reflect differing *class lines* within the movement, will reflect — however much this may be muted in the short run by the importance of comradely solidarity and the deeply felt need to maintain a united front *vis-à-vis* the apartheid state — class struggle. Even the most minimal exposure to a range of ANC personnel will quickly demonstrate this fact, revealing a range of positions stretching from a quite narrowly premised 'petty bourgeois nationalism' to a clearly articulated social revolutionism.

A BOURGEOIS COALITION?

Needless to say, a class analysis of the ANC is no easy matter, although it is worth noting that one is implicit in some of the most articulate apologists for a process of carefully controlled change in the interests of continuing capitalist hegemony. Among this group there is even a certain smugness about the cooptability of the ANC to 'business' purposes. The reason (in the words of Adam and Moodley): 'Since the ANC ... to all intents and purposes represents an aspiring but hitherto excluded middle class . . . a historic compromise among big capital, small traders and bureaucrats would not flounder on class antagonisms.'[12] In parallel fashion Conor Cruse O'Brien apparently sees the ANC as eminently recruitable to his proposed 'multi-racial coalition'. 'Tambo himself is essentially a liberal,' O'Brien opines; 'he will get on well with Dr Slabbert.'[13] The shrewdest of capitalist actors in

South Africa are inclined to agree, Tony Bloom of the Premier Group recently professing himself 'desperately concerned that both Pretoria and Washington are making a historic and tragic mistake in refusing to negotiate with or recognise the ANC. Lasting stability will never be created without it.' Moreover, 'the ANC leadership may be very different in three years, when thousands more have died'! 'Only one man may be capable of achieving cohesion among blacks. People who have recently visited Nelson Mandela have come away deeply impressed with his moderation. Can he be South Africa's Charles de Gaulle? We simply have to take the chance.'[14]

This kind of analysis has to be taken seriously up to a point; even if rather grotesquely overstated, it does suggest that, if, as and when the transition to a post-apartheid society picks up steam, capital will be working overtime to seduce to 'moderation' those within the ANC who can be so seduced. However, Pretoria and Washington are probably right to be a little more sceptical about the ease with which the ANC could be coopted. It is highly unlikely that the ANC, already so deeply rooted inside the country, could fall completely out of step with the crystallising mood of the black townships. There 'popular-democratic' assertions are not easily distinguished from even more radical sentiments. As Patrick Laurence has written, 'South Africa's major extra-parliamentary opposition movements bristle with anti-capitalist sentiments. There is no doubt that there is a growing hostility towards capitalism among black youth. The reason is simple: capitalism is seen as the driving force behind apartheid.'[15] It is not surprising, therefore, that the ANC's Consultative Conference underscored more strongly than ever the centrality of the working class to the movement's endeavours. My own interviews with ANC personnel in Lusaka and elsewhere suggest a wide range of cadres who are fully alert to the need to wed the struggle for socialism to the cause for national liberation. They are confident that they can continue to strengthen this emphasis within the ANC, even that they can carry with them many whom Adam and Moodley might consider eminently available for cooptation to the 'neo-colonisers'. But they are aware that it is an ongoing challenge to do so — to balance the NAFCOC factor, as one of them put it — and that this will require effective political work, if not necessarily outright political confrontation, within the movement.

Our picture of the determinants of the ANC 'line', present and future, is further complicated by the fact that within the left of the ANC there is room for differing political projects. Evidently the most difficult question of all for all those who would advance a 'revolution within a revolution' from inside the ANC is precisely how (to revert to Mbeki's formulations) the working class can come to play its 'leading role' as a 'conscious vanguard class'. Some within the Congress movement have little problem in conceptualising the kind of interplay between 'national democratic' and 'proletarian' dimensions of the South African struggle that might be expected to strengthen the prospect of a socialist denouement. For this group, the guarantor that the revolution will in Joe Slovo's term be made 'on-going', and that the proletarian-cum-socialist card will ultimately be played, is the SACP. Slovo, though also writing in *The African Communist*, is much more forthright than Nyawuza in making this point:

> the ANC remains a mass nationalist movement . . . . It correctly welcomes within its ranks all liberation fighters, whatever their class affiliation, who support its revolutionary nationalism.

While its policy for the future, as set out in the Freedom Charter, is not inconsistent with an advance towards socialism, the ANC does not and should not demand a commitment to a socialist South Africa as a precondition for membership. [The SACP, on the other hand] is not a mass movement; it represents the aspirations of a single class — the proletariat. [In consequence] the party's mobilising propaganda will have a special content which the ANC's intervention should not and cannot have. There is not a daily problem facing the working people, whether in town or in countryside, which cannot be linked to the ravages of capitalism: and *it is only our party* which can present this connection in an undiluted way.[16]

Do such statements shed light on the one-sidedness of many ANC formulations of the revolutionary project? Certainly SACP-rooted intellectuals have had a significant impact on the codification of the movement's line. And if they started from the premises just articulated it would be easy to see why — acting in either good or bad faith — they might have an additional reason for helping to define the ANC's own vocation as exclusively popular-democratic. Of course, the party's stated position does raise intriguing questions as to how contradictory its leaders see the likely relationship between the ANC and the SACP in the post-apartheid rounds; unfortunately, this is something about which the latter's formulations have been less than clear. Many socialists will in any case be uneasy with this proposed division of revolutionary labour, in which yet another 'official' Communist Party defines itself as the (more or less exclusive) vanguard of the working class. Not that the SACP lacks an honourable and often heroic history of commitment and struggle. Indeed more than most such parties elsewhere, it has shown a capacity to keep pace with the evolution of popular aspirations in its own country and it may well continue to do so.[17] Yet it is also true that as regards many of the most questionable canons of Soviet-influenced orthodoxy, the SACP has not been one of the more open and independent of Communist parties. One searches in vain in the pages of *The African Communist*, the party's official publication, for more than predictable propositions on so important an issue (not least to workers) as Poland, for example. Moreover, the often savage tone adopted by many writers towards those on the left with whom they disagree does not augur very well for the SACP's commitment to a genuinely democratic climate in future.

WORKING-CLASS DYNAMISM

It is fortunate, therefore, that such misgivings — as well as the whole question of the prospects for a continuing radicalisation of the ANC — can be placed in a much broader and more promising context. After all, one of the most striking things about the South African working class is that it has not spent much time, in recent years, waiting upon some promised vanguard to 'mobilise' it. It has exhibited a dramatic dynamism, creating vibrant new institutions for itself, not least the recently minted Congress of South African Trade Unions (COSATU). It is precisely some of these unions that expressed their suspicion of movements and parties that might presume to speak for the working class without taking adequate account of that class's own voice! One thinks here of the 1981 speech by Joe Foster, FOSATU General Secretary, in which he contended that 'political movements are often controlled by the "petty bourgeoisie" who fear genuine worker-controlled trade unions. They strive to dissolve worker-controlled movements into a mass political movement dominated not by workers, but by the "petty bourgeoisie". According to them, the workers are only useful as a kind of battering ram they themselves seek to lead.'[18] Alec Erwin, national education officer of FOSATU (and now of COSATU), raised parallel concerns in a suggestive paper entitled 'The question of unity in the struggle'. Distinguishing between the 'politics of liberation' — ever 'in danger of cooptation' — and the more radical politics of 'transformation', he stressed the necessity for workers to begin 'building tomorrow today'.[19] The new COSATU has also been articulate about such long-term goals. General Secretary Jay Naidoo, in a statement shortly after COSATU's formation, gave the following account of a meeting he had recently had with the ANC in Zimbabwe:

> I told the ANC and SACTU delegations we did not want superficial changes or black bosses to replace white bosses, while the repressive machinery of state and capital remained intact. I expressed very clearly to them our commitment to see a society which was not only free of apartheid but also free of the exploitative, degrading and brutalising system under which black workers suffered. This meant a restructuring of society so that the wealth of the country would be shared among the people . . . . COSATU was looking at alternatives which would ensure that any society that emerged would accurately reflect the interests of the working class.[20]

There is some possibility of a *dialogue des sourds* in such exchanges, union voices like Foster's raising real and legitimate concerns yet themselves risking a caricature of the ANC's multi-layered complexity. Certainly, any simplistic charge of petty bourgeois populism ignores at its peril the fact that — as Dan O'Meara has put it:

> the ANC is indubitably the political grouping with the widest political base in South Africa and the strongest support amongst Black workers . . . . The political culture of Black workers over at least the last forty years has been largely moulded by 'the Congress tradition'. While this may be disturbing to the purist prescriptions of White Marxist intellectuals, this is the real and inescapable context within which working-class organisation takes place in South Africa.[21]

On the other hand, the shrill response by many, not only in SACP circles but also in the ANC, to contributions like Foster's and Erwin's is, if anything, even more disturbing. Too often this has involved a glib caricature of the latter's concerns as being 'economist' and 'workerist', rather than producing further reflection on the way in which such 'proletarian' preoccupations can be brought into ever more creative tension with the popular-democratic project.

The actual dynamic of the South African revolution — a radicalisation that cuts right across South African society, across presumed historical stages and across proposed organisational divisions of labour, as 'popular democratic' and 'proletarian' demands reinforce and push each other forward — is running well ahead of most of the formulations that attempt to codify and interpret it. In the present instance, too, political practice is running well ahead of pronouncement. Unfortunately there have been dismaying reports of intolerance within the resistance movement — UDF 'Charterists' set against 'workerists' set against advocates of 'black consciousness'. But it is the simultaneous promise of the present conjuncture in South Africa which is far more in evidence, most markedly in the very constitution of COSATU itself. Here 'workerist' unions (highly democratic shop-floor based unions, which have, however, also been linking themselves more actively to township-based political and economic actions in the past few years) and 'populist' (community-based, 'Charterist') unions have come together in an organisation of great importance.[22]

An even more significant straw in the wind, perhaps, was the meeting held in early 1986 between the ANC and COSATU, a meeting in which the South African Congress of Trade Unions (SACTU) also participated.[23] All parties 'recognised that the emergence of COSATU as the giant democratic and progressive trade union federation in our country is an historic event in the process of uniting our working class and will immeasurably strengthen the democratic movement as a whole.' Yet it was also 'recognised that the fundamental problem facing our country, the question of political power, cannot be resolved without the full participation of the ANC, which is regarded by the majority of the people of South Africa as the overall leader and genuine representative.' What of the future which these kinds of 'recognition' are likely to define? In the words of the official communiqué:

> They [the three delegations] agreed that the solution to the problems facing our country lies in the establishment of a system of majority rule in a united, democratic and non-racial South Africa. Further, that in the specific conditions of our country it is inconceivable that such a system can be separated from economic emancipation. Our people have been robbed of their land, deprived of their due share in the country's wealth, their skills have been suppressed and poverty and starvation have been their life experience. The correction of these centuries-old economic injustices lies at the core of our national aspirations. Accordingly they are united not only in their opposition to the entire apartheid system, but also in their common understanding that victory must embrace more than formal political democracy.[24]

This kind of linkage is important for the present; perhaps, for instance, it strengthens the possibility that, as part of the overall thrust against the apartheid state and the infrastructure of racial capitalism, the collective power of the black workers *at the point of production* will come to be wielded in an even more dramatic and crippling manner than it has been to date. The link is also promising for the future, although such an advance in the wedding of 'popular democracy' and socialist preoccupations still leaves big questions unanswered. To take merely one example, what does the ANC see as the role, *vis-à-vis* the working class, of its own SACTU? It seems unlikely that the ANC thinks it could unilaterally impose SACTU, now or at some time in the future, as a kind of transmission belt between the liberation-movement-cum-party in power and the working class. But just how ANC theorists plan that the possible autonomy of working-class organisation, and the focusing of working-class power, might be institutionalised remains unclear. So, too, does the long-term practice of those working-class organisations which are only now gingerly coming to terms with the fact of ANC hegemony but are also anxious to strengthen the proletarian side of the revolutionary equation — by both finding and institutionalising solutions of their own and, in all probability, contributing to the continuing radicalisation of the ANC. However difficult these questions may be, the door does seem open to experiment, to class struggle — premised on some greater awareness of the possibilities inherent in a positive simultaneity of popular-democratic and proletarian-cum-socialist assertions.

THE FREEDOM CHARTER

Positive simultaneity, creative tensions — certainly very little about the Southern African revolution is locked firmly into place. What, then, of the Freedom Charter — now more than ever the centrepiece of the ANC's presentation of itself — from which a number of recent writers have sought to divine programmatic indicators about the shape of post-apartheid South Africa?[25] The present chapter will not seek to add to that debate, much of which has been quite useful, but will conclude by suggesting the need to contextualise the Freedom Charter, too, in what has gone before.

The Freedom Charter is, first and foremost, a 'popular-democratic' document. It can be interpreted in an eminently petty bourgeois and reformist manner (and, indeed, has been, even by Nelson Mandela, albeit many years ago). Yet it also contains the seeds of a more radical possibility — in terms of land reform, in terms of popular ownership of the mines, banks and 'monopoly industry'. But, workers' control? Cooperativisation? The nature of planning? The extent of any short-term compromise with capital? On such crucial points the Freedom Charter is, in the main, merely 'not inconsistent with an advance towards socialism', in Slovo's phrase. As Slovo himself has stated, 'in practice, the question as to which road South Africa will begin to take on the morning after the liberation flag is raised over the Union Buildings will be decided by the actual correlation of class forces which have come to power.'[26] The 'actual correlation of class forces', but also the ways in which those who come to power move to deal with the concrete policy questions which confront them. For 'the morning after' will witness an unleashing of (legitimate) rising expectations on the part of the underclass who for so long have borne the burden of the exactions of racial capitalism. It may well be, given the complexities of the situation, that Slovo's hunch as to the need for a tempered pace of change in the immediate post-apartheid period is a good one: 'For some while after apartheid falls there will undoubtedly be a mixed economy, implying a role for levels of non-monopoly private enterprise represented not only by the small racially oppressed black business sector but also by managers and business people of goodwill who have or are prepared to shed racism.'[27] But to keep the long-term goal of socialist transformation alive, while trying both to propitiate capital *and* to outflank it on its own ground, is no easy task.

As the case of neighbouring Zimbabwe makes clear,[28] workers would be unwise to cede exclusive power over such delicate calculations to an unchecked political leadership. It is only too easy to be seduced, over time, into accepting the logic of capital as one's own — particularly in a South Africa whose economy is now so deeply integrated into the circuits of global capitalism.[29] Even with the best intentions, a leadership can prove unduly self-confident about the probity and the primacy of its own tactical calculations during the transition period, moving, in consequence, to choke off critical voices and to permit a collapse into authoritarianism. If nothing else, the experience of 'actually existing socialisms' in this century should have demonstrated how important it is that competing claims be openly reconciled and there be the widest possible range of forums for ventilating the most embarrassing questions about the precise pace and substance of socialist advance.

Perhaps it is here, in particular, that the weight of the organised working class (but also of organised women and other forces organised for progressive change) can help to draw out the best instincts of the Congress Alliance, diverting it from the twin authoritarian precedents, so ready to hand, of institutionalised petty bourgeois nationalism elsewhere in Africa and institutionalised 'Marxism-Leninism' elsewhere in the 'socialist bloc'. Hence the possibly broad significance of a resolution passed in July 1986 at the congress of the important COSATU affiliate, MAWU. Noting that 'true socialism' is 'fully democratic', the resolution goes on to state that 'the working class must have open and free debate on all issues, all ideas and all policies . . . . We must build a tradition of democracy and free debate for the future. Sectarianism can suppress free debate and can be a stumbling block in our efforts to build a democratic socialism.'[30]

Given the cruel exigencies of the present moment in South Africa, it is not surprising that sustained thinking about many of the concrete issues — economic, social and political — relevant to the next round in South Africa is not very far advanced, either within the ANC or in other sections of the resistance movement broadly defined. How much energy can actually be spared from the even more immediate and pressing task of 'smashing the apartheid *state*'? Yet a great deal of work must be done to think through the requirements in all the diverse spheres where specific decisions will be necessary. In the light of capital's own preparations for the next round, the more rapidly this task is advanced the better. As this is done, both now and in the future, all of the elements, ambiguities and tensions that we have identified will re-enter the picture, in ways that are not readily predictable. But the role of the ANC within the broader movement does, as we have tried to show, give room for guarded optimism about the future of socialism in South Africa — a future which, it need hardly be said, will have to be struggled for, not taken for granted.

NOTES

This chapter was presented at the conference on Popular Struggles in Africa organised by the *Review of African Political Economy* at Liverpool in September 1986. It was subsequently published in *New Left Review*, No. 160, November/December 1986, pp.3-22.

1. For a more detailed analysis of some of the points made in this section of the article, see John S. Saul and Stephen Gelb, *The Crisis in South Africa* (New York: Monthly Review Press, revised edition, 1986). In fact, throughout the chapter I have made use of formulations which also appear in my new introduction to this book.

2. The importance of this point bears emphasising. In Merle Lipton's *Capitalism and Apartheid* (Aldershot: Gower, 1985) she attempts to resurrect the liberal approach to South Africa by emphasising the contradictions between apartheid policies and capital's requirements and by stressing capital's ability to bend the state towards a reform agenda in recent years. In doing so, she merely consigns the question of political power — the crucial area where state and capital still unite in defence of racial capitalism — to a more or less residual category ('security', 'political apartheid'), seeking by such sleight of hand to save her hypothesis.

3. The failure of South African decision-makers to perceive the wisdom of such a course clearly exasperates some of capital's most outspoken protagonists within the academy. Thus Heribert Adam and Kogila Moodley, juxtaposing at every turn 'liberal modesty' and the benign model of a welfare capitalism against the bogeymen they conjure up to characterise the socialist alternative ('state-run utopia', the 'totalitarian temptation'), argue vigorously for 'deracialisation'. Perhaps the flavour of their argument can be seen most clearly in the case they make for the repeal of the Group Areas Act, necessary 'in order to allow market forces to play themselves out. Only this residential integration along

class lines can allow the emergence of a Black middle class that does not have to live in fear of being instantly expropriated by the masses of the less fortunate' (Adam and Moodley, *South Africa After Apartheid*, Berkeley: University of California Press, 1986, p.117). Along similar lines, Conor Cruise O'Brien has recently argued ('What can become of South Africa?', *The Atlantic*, March 1986) the wisdom of facilitating the emergence of a 'multi-racial bourgeois coalition'. Such a coalition, he noted, might not be 'wholly attractive', although 'it might, with luck, work quite well'. For it could help stave off the demands, in particular, 'of all the "outs" of black society, including the politicised unemployed'. Fortunate, then, that the 'new black South Africa, unlike other African countries, will have a large black middle class', a 'black bourgeoisie' ready to form a 'middle-class government', ready to 'find allies among the Whites', ready to facilitate a 'coalition of all those with something to lose, whatever the colour of their skin' (p.68).

4. Quoted from a particularly demagogic statement of the position by Mzala in 'The Freedom Charter and its relevance today' in an authoritative ANC publication, *Selected Writings on the Freedom Charter* (London, 1985). These formulations dovetail neatly with the orthodoxies of the international communist movement, in particular the necessity of a 'national-democratic' moment in many revolutionary struggles; indeed, one author — Nyawuza in 'New "Marxist" tendencies and the battle of ideas in South Africa', *African Communist*, No.105, 1985 — underscores this link quite clearly: 'The programme of the SACP, adopted in 1962, advances the thesis of "Colonialism of a Special Type" and the two-stage revolution. In 1969 the Morogoro Conference of the ANC adopted the *Strategy and Tactics* document, which took some of the Communist Party programme a stage further.'

5. Nyawuza, *op. cit.*, p.51.

6. T. Mbeki, 'The Fatton thesis: a rejoinder', *Canadian Journal of African Studies*, Vol.18, No.3, 1984, p.609.

7. Z.P.J. (Pallo Jordan), 'Black middle class — eleventh-hour counter-insurgency of acquiescence in continued domination', *Sechaba*, May 1983, p.24.

8. Sol Dubula (Joe Slovo), 'The two pillars of our struggle: reflections on the relationship between the ANC the SACP', *The African Communist*, No.87, 1981, pp.36-8. Significant, too, is Slovo's statement that 'the high level of capitalist development in South Africa has given birth to a distinctive form of class stratification, not only in the enemy camp but also among the black oppressed'. In consequence, 'as the national liberation struggle approaches its climax, we must expect a stronger urge from the non-working-class black forces to stop the revolution in its tracks and opt for a bourgeois solution'.

9. Mbeki, *op. cit.*, p.162.

10. An initial statement of this position can be found in the first edition of our book, *The Crisis in South Africa* (1981), and is included and further elaborated in the revised edition. The Laclau reference is to his *Politics and Ideology in Marxist Theory* (London: New Left Books, 1977), Chs. 3 & 4. This presents an argument far more useful, in my judgement, than the most recent developments of his theoretical project.

11. David Lewis, 'Recession and the working class', *South African Labour Bulletin*, April-May 1986, p. 47. See also Lewis's important article, 'Capital, the trade unions and national liberation struggle', *Monthly Review*, April 1986.

12. Adam and Moodley, *op. cit.*, p.257. Rather surprisingly, Adam and Moodley's slight and mischievous book has received a fulsome review in the *London Review of Books* ('Apartheid Apocalypse', 3 July 1986) from R.W. Johnson, who matches the authors' general complacency and sneering approach to the ANC. Johnson manages to predict both that 'South Africa's capitalism is unlikely to survive black majority rule unscathed' (because of 'pressure from below') *and* that such rule is likely to 'produce one of the continent's most conservative governments'!

13. O'Brien, *op. cit.*, p.68. Frederick van Zyl Slabbert was, at the time of O'Brien's writing, the leader of the opposition Progressive Federal Party and, like that party, has

been amongst those liberals most concerned about the possible perils of 'majority domination'.

14. A. H. Bloom, 'Can Mandela be South Africa's de Gaulle?' *New York Times*, 29 July 1986. A rather cruder version of such a scenario was given by President Reagan, elaborating on his fears about SACP control over the ANC: 'We know there are still sound people ... so, no, if you could do business with, and separate out and get the solid citizens of the ANC to come forward on their own, that's just fine' (quoted verbatim from a press conference transcript, *New York Times*, 13 August 1986).

15. P. Laurence, 'White capitalism and black rage', *The Weekly Mail* (Johannesburg), 13-19 September 1985.

16. Sol Dubula (Joe Slovo), *op.cit.*, p.35. Emphasis added.

17. The party seems to be having a certain measure of success in rooting itself inside South Africa. It is difficult to predict the precise long-term impact which the novel social forces and committed individuals mobilised in this process will have on the external wings of the SACP and ANC. See P. Laurence, 'Behind the red funeral flags', and H. Barrell, 'The view from abroad: conditions have never favoured the party more', both in *The Weekly Mail* (Johannesburg), 11-17 April 1986.

18. Joe Foster, as cited in Patrick Laurence, 'Superunion — born into defiance', *The Weekly Mail*, 6-12 December 1986. For a thoughtful critique of Foster's speech see Rob Davies and Dan O'Meara, 'The workers' struggle in South Africa — a comment', in *The Review of African Political Economy*, No. 30, 1984.

19. Alec Erwin, 'The question of unity in the struggle', *South African Labour Bulletin*, 11, 1, September 1985.

20. See the article entitled 'COSATU spells out its aims to the ANC', *The Star Weekly* (Johannesburg), 23 December 1985.

21. Dan O'Meara, 'Democratic trade unions and struggle against Apartheid', *Labour, Capital and Society* (Montreal), Vol.18, No.2, 1985, p. 418. O'Meara is reviewing, in sharply critical terms, a book by Dennis McShane, Martin Plaut and David Ward (*Power! Black Workers: Their Unions and the Struggle for Freedom in South Africa*, Nottingham: Spokesman, 1984) to which authors, judging from the context, the phrase 'White Marxist intellectuals' is meant primarily to refer.

22. This remains the case, however much the subsequent Emergency and intensification of state repression on the one hand and even certain difficulties internal to the union on the other may come to qualify the possibilities that COSATU represents. For further background see my 'South Africa: the crisis deepens', *Monthly Review*, Vol.37, No.11, April 1986.

23. SACTU was the key union central of the 1950s; it was closely linked to the ANC and the SACP and, although itself never formally banned, it has continued to operate alongside them from exile ever since. Of considerable symbolic significance, and of some current weight via its underground structures, its role has been greatly qualified by the emergence of the independent trade union movement inside South Africa. For a discussion of some of the problems and ambiguities in the sphere see 'Focus on labour', *Southern Africa Report* (Toronto), Vol.2, No.1, June 1986.

24. These quotations are drawn from 'Communiqué of the meeting between COSATU, SACTU and the ANC', 7 March 1986, reproduced in *South Africa Labour Bulletin*, Vol.11, No.5, April-May 1986.

25. See the wide range of contributions during 1986 in various issues of such progressive South African publications as *South Africa Labour Bulletin, Work in Progress* (Johannesburg) and *Transformation* (Durban).

26. Joe Slovo, 'Communist blueprint for South Africa', *Guardian Weekly*, 17 August 1986, p.9.

27. *Ibid.*

28. For a discussion of the dilemmas posed in Zimbabwe after liberation, some of which have implications for the situation in South Africa, see my 'Zimbabwe: the next round', *The Socialist Register 1980*, (London: Merlin Press, 1980).

29. Papers like those by Rob Davies ('Nationalisation, socialisation and the Freedom Charter') and Vishnu Padayachee ('The politics of international economic relations: South Africa and the International Monetary Fund — 1975 and beyond') presented at the University of York Conference on 'The Southern African Economy after Apartheid', September-October 1986, do begin to fill in our picture of the treacherous economic terrain, domestic and international, upon which any post-apartheid socialist project will have to be mounted.

30. Quoted in 'MAWU's first national congress', *South African Labour Bulletin*, Vol.11, No.7, August 1986.

Index